ALBERTA ART AND ARTISTS

ALBERTA ART AND ARTISTS

An Overview

PATRICIA AINSLIE MARY-BETH LAVIOLETTE

FIFTH HOUSE

COVER AND INTERIOR DESIGN BY BRIAN SMITH / ARTICULATE EYE

COVER IMAGES: CENTRE IMAGE: PETROGLYPH AT WRITING-ON-STONE, ALBERTA (PHOTOGRAPHY BY M. A. KLASSEN); CLOCKWISE FROM TOP LEFT: BISON EFFIGY (GLENBOW MUSEUM); HENRY GLYDE, *EXODUS* (ALBERTA FOUNDATION FOR THE ARTS); LAURA VICKERSON, *VELVET* (SHOWN AT HAGIA EIRENI, 5TH INTERNATIONAL ISTANBUL BIENNIAL); GORDON FERGUSON *RED HEAD* (UNIVERSITY OF LETHBRIDGE ART COLLECTION); ALEXANDER R. ROSS, *CHIEF CROWFOOT (ISAPO-MUXIKA)* (GLENBOW MUSEUM ARCHIVES, NA-29-1/PA-10-1); PATRICK DOUGLASS COX, *THE PIONEER'S DAUGHTER* (ALBERTA FOUNDATION FOR THE ARTS); DULCIE FOO FAT, *KANANASKIS AUTUMN: MOSS AND PINE NEEDLES* (WHYTE MUSEUM OF THE CANADIAN ROCKIES); NORMAN YATES, *LANDSCAPE FIFTY* (OXFORD DEVELOPMENTS, EDMONTON CENTRE); ROBERT GAGEN, *RAINSTORM, GREAT GLACIER, B.C.* (GLENBOW MUSEUM); ELLA HARTT, *LITTLE GIRL HOLDING RABBIT* (GLENBOW MUSEUM ARCHIVES, NC-39-296).

EDITED BY KIRSTEN CRAVEN
COPYEDITED BY TERRY MCINTYRE
PROOFREAD BY LESLEY REYNOLDS
SCANS BY KEITH SEABROOK / ABL IMAGING

THE TYPE IN THIS BOOK IS SET IN ADOBE GARAMOND PRO.

THE PUBLISHER GRATEFULLY ACKNOWLEDGES THE SUPPORT OF THE CANADA COUNCIL FOR THE ARTS AND THE DEPARTMENT OF CANADIAN HERITAGE. WE ACKNOWLEDGE THE FINANCIAL SUPPORT OF THE GOVERNMENT OF CANADA THROUGH THE BOOK PUBLISHING INDUSTRY DEVELOPMENT PROGRAM (BPIDP) FOR OUR PUBLISHING ACTIVITIES.

The Canada Council for the Arts since 1957 | Le Conseil des Arts du Canada depuis 1957

THE AUTHORS WOULD LIKE TO THANK THE ALBERTA FOUNDATION FOR THE ARTS FOR ITS SUPPORT.

Alberta Foundation for the Arts

EVERY EFFORT HAS BEEN MADE TO OBTAIN PERMISSION TO PRINT THE IMAGES IN THIS BOOK.
THE PUBLISHER WOULD BE PLEASED TO ADJUST CREDITS UPON REPRINTING.

PRINTED IN CHINA

07 08 09 10 11 / 5 4 3 2 1

FIRST PUBLISHED IN THE UNITED STATES IN 2007 BY

FITZHENRY & WHITESIDE
311 WASHINGTON STREET
BRIGHTON, MA 02135

LIBRARY AND ARCHIVES CANADA CATALOGUING IN PUBLICATION

AINSLIE, PATRICIA
ALBERTA ART AND ARTISTS : AN OVERVIEW / PATRICIA AINSLIE, MARY-BETH LAVIOLETTE

INCLUDES BIOGRAPHICAL REFERENCES AND INDEX.

ISBN 978-1-894856-61-4

1. ART, CANADIAN—ALBERTA—HISTORY. 2. ARTISTS—ALBERTA—HISTORY. I. LAVIOLETTE, MARY-BETH II. TITLE.
N6546.A4A28 2007 709.7123'09 C2006-905405-3

FIFTH HOUSE LTD.
A FITZHENRY & WHITESIDE COMPANY
1511, 1800-4 ST. SW
CALGARY, ALBERTA T2S 2S5
1-800-387-9776
WWW.FITZHENRY.CA

CONTENTS

PREFACE

Patricia Ainslie

In the spring of 2001, I approached Mary-Beth Laviolette, who was already writing an authoritative and in-depth book on contemporary art in Alberta, and suggested that together we write a comprehensive illustrated guide for the lay reader on the visual arts in Alberta from its early beginnings to the present. Enthusiastic about the idea, we each felt we were well-experienced to write such a book. Though our writing styles differ, both styles ended up being a good fit for the respective time periods we were writing about. In my case, my writing is more formal and suited to the two periods (historical, modern) that are now part of Alberta's art history. Mary-Beth, on the other hand, has a more casual journalistic style that is responsive to the fact that the contemporary period is both still in the making and also in a state of flux; it is a period of art history that has not yet run its full course. Also, to a greater degree than I could, Mary-Beth was able to take advantage of a much larger body of source materials (reviews, catalogue essays, and so on). This is due to the simple fact that many of the artists she features are still alive and practising, hence, the inclusion of quotes from the artists themselves and also from existing material about their art.

INTRODUCTION

Patricia Ainslie

Seeing Comes Before Words[1]

This book is intended as a guide to those newly interested in the arts of Alberta and will introduce the general reader to the visual arts of the province.[1] Each chapter provides a brief introduction to the topic, followed by a selection of images by only the most significant artists within the genre. To represent the breadth and diversity of our arts and also do justice to our rich history, we have included, except for a notable few, only one work by each artist. There may be controversy over the images we picked, but we have taken great care to select the strongest works most representative of an artist's career. In the case of artists who left Alberta, such as Roy Kiyooka and Roloff Beny, we included works that were made while they were here or were made closely related to the time they spent here—works which may not be the ones for which they became most famous. The captions provide some ideas about the artist's intent and give clues as to how to "read" and understand the work. Biographies found at the back of the book provide basic information about an artist's origins, training, and contribution. The bibliography will direct the reader to more in-depth sources.

By the very fact of its selective nature, this book cannot be complete, but the inclusion of many images is intended to provide a comprehensive visual record of the historical, modern, and contemporary art made here in Alberta. No book before has tried to cover the extensive scope that this one has. This is the first time such a broad survey has been undertaken, and we hope it will be useful to you. What you see in this book are reproductions. To gain a fuller understanding and build your experience of art, it is important to see the originals. Only then will you discover what the reproduction lacks. Each work of art is a unique experience; it has a physical presence and its own authenticity. Visit local public and commercial art galleries and museums and see the exhibits. Allow yourself to connect with the emotions provoked by the image from the lived experience of the artist. Every image embodies a way of seeing. The way we see things is affected by what we know and believe. What we see is in relationship to ourselves and is therefore intensely personal. The meaning we derive from art reflects our individuality and awareness and further involves assumptions about beauty, genius, civilization, and culture.

Alberta's art history is short, but its geography has had a profound impact on all who have come here. First Nations people had a deep connection to the land, while others were driven here with a sense of adventure and discovery, endured hardships, and marvelled at the profound beauty. Many with pioneer spirit embraced the challenge of frontier life. Some came with missionary zeal to build a place for art in this infant community. Always fierce individualists, Alberta artists did not form identifiable artistic groups, apart from the loose art associations found throughout the province. Because of this, national attention has been slow to recognize the vitality of the arts of Alberta. Yet exceptional work has been produced here, from the First Nations through to the early travellers and settlers to the surprising strength of the modernists and the internationally recognized contemporary artists.

European art began in Alberta with the itinerant artists of the 1840s, but was predated by the sacred and applied arts of the First Peoples of the Plains. For thousands of years, First Nations recorded their history on rock faces throughout the region. Rock art chronicles the religions and long histories of diverse groups, forming a lasting legacy.

Despite the difficulty of travel, the first European artists to venture west found inspiration in the land, and were in awe of its impressive beauty. Paul Kane was the first artist to make a comprehensive record of the West in his monumental quest for exotic subjects. After him, expedition artists who were talented amateurs captured topographical views in watercolour that are exceptional visual records. Unfortunately, few of these works survived, so those that remain are rare and unique.

This land is vast and various, a blend of the sinister and idyllic, the austere and luxuriant. Nineteenth-century artists, such as Paul Kane and James Alden, recorded what they saw, but their work was often infused with their emotional response to the impressive geography. By their interpretation, artists, particularly those working for Canadian Pacific Railway like Lucius O'Brien and Robert Gagen, strengthened our sense of national identity. But, coming from a nineteenth-century Romantic sensibility of exploration and expansion, their art also helped to accelerate European movement into Native lands.

Early travellers were curious about the original inhabitants, who seemed to have a mythic presence. Aboriginal people were seen as exotic, the "other," and were represented through a romantic lens. They were often thought of as a dying race. Nineteenth-century travellers, bred in the age of Romanticism, often equated "primitive" man with nature. They considered Aboriginal people as "noble savages," whose demise was inevitable. Even though some of the early images by itinerant artists are mainly documentary, they are not neutral; they are laden with Eurocentric nationalism. These include such works as Paul Kane's *Mah-Min or "The Feather"* (April 1848) and Edward Roper's *Rabbit Carrier, Blackfoot Chief* (ca. 1887). Aboriginal people were an impediment to nation building and their cultural disintegration was due to the concerted political and legislative efforts of the Canadian government.

In the late nineteenth century, a few notable amateur artists spent a few years in Alberta, including Richard Barrington Nevitt and Sara Mary Blake, who as an early settler unfortunately left few images extant. After the railway penetrated the Rockies in 1885, the first professional artists could travel here more easily and there were further images made by artists such as John Arthur Fraser, F. M. Bell Smith, and Lucius O'Brien. The artists earliest to set up shop in the newly emerging towns were the photographers. William Hanson Boorne was a pioneer, setting up his studio in Calgary in 1885, soon followed by Geraldine Moodie in Battleford, Saskatchewan, in 1895. Early photographers provided precise visual records but their selection of views, light, and atmosphere reflected their interest in the picturesque—not just the documentary.

Despite increasing settlement, the social and community infrastructure to support art was slow to develop as the West was still a struggling frontier. It was not until the early twentieth century that a firm base was established for art in the province. Banff had professional resident artists once photographer Byron Harmon settled there in 1903, followed in 1910 by wildlife artist Carl Rungius. The Group of Seven artists travelled west when A. Y. Jackson painted in the Yellowhead Pass in 1914 and returned with Lawren Harris in 1924, the same year that J. E. H. MacDonald began his annual trips to Lake O'Hara. The Group of Seven did not make a contribution to the developments here at this early stage. Edmonton had the first sustained centre for artists starting in 1924 at the Edmonton Museum of Arts, later to become the Edmonton Art Gallery. In a few decades during the twentieth century, work matured from the conservative art of early resident artists, a hangover from the nineteenth century, to the emotive painting of Maxwell Bates, Henry Glyde, and Marion Nicoll from the late 1920s to the 1950s.

It was not until the establishment of art classes at the Provincial Institute of Technology and Art in Calgary in 1927 that art came of age, took root, and spawned a community of professional artists in Alberta. Lars Haukaness laid the cornerstone for professional artists at the institute. He was followed by A. C. Leighton, who built a solid foundation, established the Alberta Society of Artists, and set up summer classes that led to the formation of the Banff School of Fine Arts. Henry Glyde left a lasting legacy through three decades of teaching in Calgary at the institute, in Banff, and in small communities, including Lethbridge and Vegreville. Then in 1946 he set up the first department of fine arts in the province at the University of Alberta in Edmonton. Many notable artists built upon this legacy as the University of Alberta in Edmonton took the lead in arts education by establishing a bachelor of fine arts degree in 1962.

The city of Calgary remained key to the development of art in the province. The institute had grown rapidly after the Second World War and was renamed the Alberta College of Art in 1960. Also during that year, the University of Alberta at Calgary was established with an art division run by Helen Stadelbauer. By 1967, the renamed University of Calgary had established a four-year bachelor of fine arts program.

Until the 1950s, art in Alberta remained primarily regional with landscape as an enduring theme. But over time, there was increasing diversity. Art was no longer limited to painting, drawing, and photography. Printmaking, sculpture, and ceramics became important means of artistic expression. Few artists had the means to create art full-time. Many, such as Ted Godwin and Roy Kiyooka, worked as teachers or in other professions. Maxwell Bates worked as an architect and John Snow worked for the Royal Bank.

Early European artists in Alberta did not adopt First Nations artistic traditions. Instead, they imposed a European tradition on the art developing here. For some European artists, First Nations became the subject of their work. Nicholas de Grandmaison completed hundreds of First Nation's portraits from the 1930s to the 1970s. Early First Nations artists Gerald Tailfeathers and Percy Two Gun adopted the European tradition. It was only with Alex Janvier in the 1960s that traditional First Nations heritage, imagery, and beliefs became fully incorporated into Alberta art. The definitive shift from modernism to postmodernism in the 1980s with an emphasis on pluralism, along with the weakened ethnocentrism of the art establishment, has resulted in Native artists developing a new relationship with mainstream art. Native activism in recent decades has brought questions of identity to the fore, leading Native artists to explore issues of self-definition and self-determination.

Modern art became an explosive, liberating force, channelling creative energy in new directions. Due to post-war prosperity during the 1950s, artists were increasingly inspired by international art. Experimentation became a driving force. Many artists travelled to Emma Lake in Saskatchewan to study with international artists. Some went to New York and London. Marion Nicoll, Stanford

Perrott, Maxwell Bates, Jack Taylor, and Katie Ohe all studied in New York, and Marion and Jim Nicoll, Maxwell Bates, Illingworth Kerr, Harry Kiyooka, Sybil Laubenthal, and Kenneth Sturdy studied in Europe. A few, such as Roy Kiyooka and Ron Spickett went to Mexico to study the rich artistic traditions there. Artists were inspired by the freedom to work expressively and intuitively away from the confines of representational art, and many embraced abstraction. Though for most this experimentation with abstraction was not sustained, the exploration of purely formal concerns did impact their future work. For Stanford Perrott and Illingworth Kerr, the foray into abstraction strengthened their formal, expressive approach to making art.

In the 1970s, Alberta art matured with the growth of educational institutions, the opening of new art galleries, the establishment of a ministry for culture (the now defunct Alberta Culture), and the lottery-funded Alberta Art Foundation (later included in the Alberta Foundation for the Arts). Alongside these institutions, print workshops, artist-run centres, and organizations like the Alberta Craft Council and the Works Festival (Edmonton) were created. The development of a more substantial infrastructure—coupled with support from the Canada Council and especially its new Art Bank—would spur an explosion of creative activity in the province, with few equals in the country.

And at the centre of it all were the artists, largely doing it at their own expense, pursuing, in many cases, more training and education and when the resources were available, accessing more opportunities to exhibit at home and abroad. It is from this critical mass that a much larger population of professionals emerged, ready to contribute to both Alberta's and Canada's artistic legacy. The last section in this book is dedicated to this diverse group. However, only a selection of some of its more notable participants can be showcased—those who, in general, have had active exhibition records inside and outside the province. It is worth noting that about a third of these individuals came as trained artists from somewhere else. For instance, there was Barbara Milne, Jeffrey Spalding, and Martha Henry from Ontario; Peter Hide, John Chalke, Allen Ball, Eric Cameron, and Graham Peacock from England; Lyndal Osborne from Australia; Cherie Moses and David Cantine from the United States; and Takao Tanabe from British Columbia.

Together these artists, with the native-born and resident population, faced an art world in the post-1970 period that was as complex, as divisive, and as multi-layered as anything ever seen before. In Canada and abroad, there were now as many movements and trends in art as there were strands of thread in a garment. Not only that, for an up-and-coming artist wishing to leave his or her mark, abstract art was no longer the only game in town. Modern art, one of the cultural achievements of the twentieth century (next to film and rock and roll), was under attack for being too preoccupied with aesthetics and, above all, too exclusionary of other kinds of content and voices. In this context, feminism and the forces of multiculturalism would leave an indelible stamp on recent art. Technology would also have a formidable impact, first in the form of video art and then second as other kinds of new media were quickly absorbed into contemporary art's expanding vocabulary. What primarily emerged from all this ferment by the end of the century was that there was no one way to make art. Very few certainties remained, including such time-honoured notions as originality and the male genius. Everything that art had been about since the Renaissance was up for grabs or—in the lingo of the time—deconstructed. If all of this chaos could be a little overwhelming for the individual artist, it was downright baffling and sometimes alienating to the non-art public, whose knowledge of art (and this includes the mainstream media), generally went no further than the late nineteenth century.

In Alberta, as in many other jurisdictions situated on the periphery of the established art world, there was both the blessing of being an artist able to observe and absorb from afar and the curse of being in a distant place. In some cases, artists were subject to the kind of colonial attitude that couldn't stop commenting on how isolated they must be making art in the western half of the continent. This was an attitude regretfully oblivious to the idea that working in another part of the world might bring its own fresh perspectives and not just a bunch of second-hand reflections on what was critically and curatorially "current" in art.

Yet, to live and work and still thrive with a sense of connection to the larger world of art (and art history) was and is a challenge, and many of the individuals in this book have risen to it with flying colours. Some, like Janet Cardiff, George Bures Miller, and David Hoffos, have grabbed international attention with their forays into technology and installation art. Chris Cran, Joane Cardinal-Schubert, Eric Cameron, John Hall, and Mary Scott have made national headlines while big national awards have gone to Ron Moppett, John Chalke, and others. And even if the trumpets have not always sounded from on high, there is the unmistakable buzz of a diverse set of energies at play in the 1970–2000 period. That activity continues unabated. With a roster of players emerging, submerging, and re-emerging, Alberta, too, can be said to have developed its own vigorous art scene that reaches out but also sustains a sense of itself and a confident otherness.

---

1. John Berger, *Ways of Seeing* (London: British Broadcasting Corporation, 1972) 7.

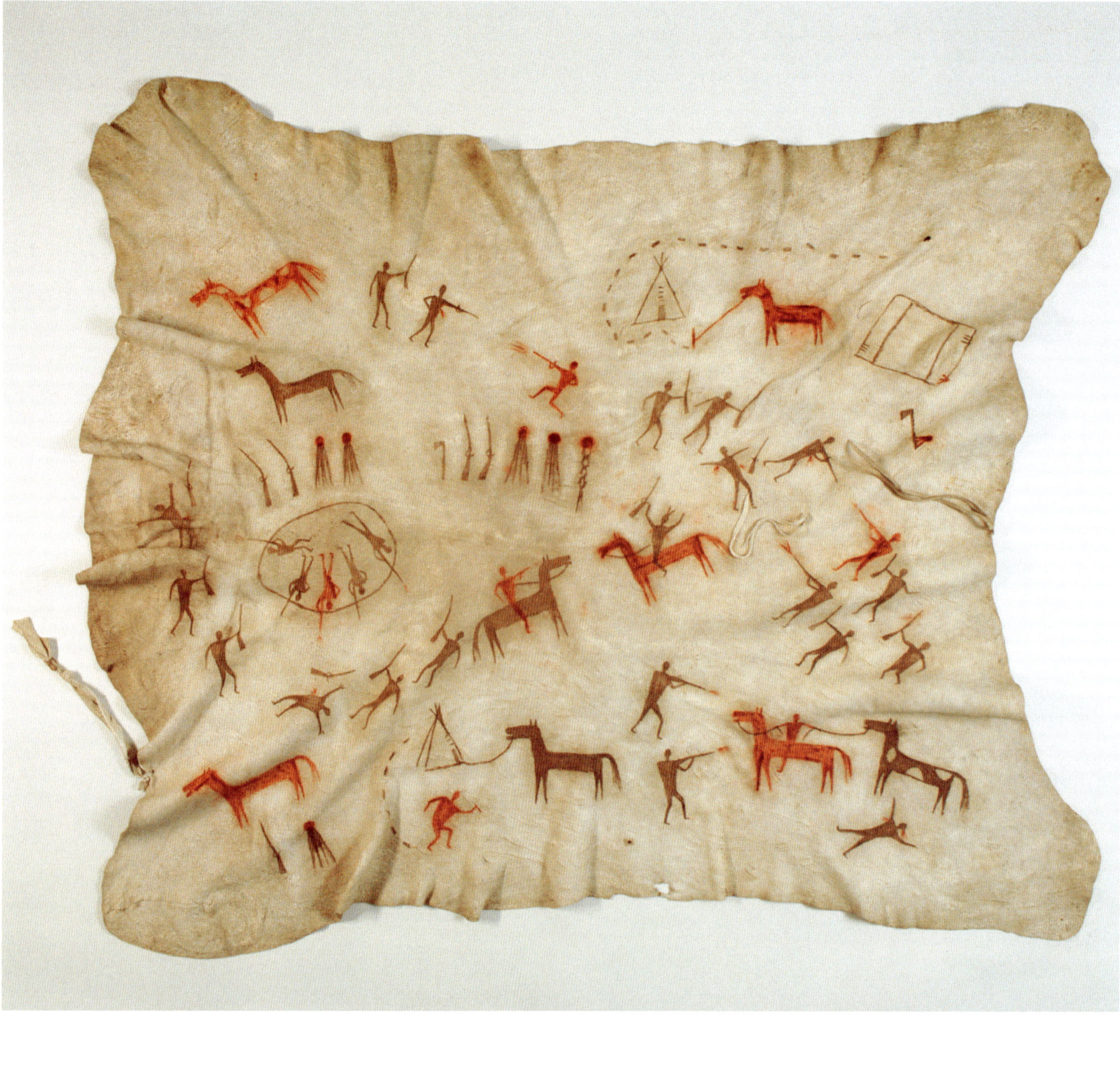

Raw Eater / *Story Robe*, late 1880s / paint on bison hide / Glenbow Museum, Calgary

THE HISTORICAL PERIOD TO 1920

Patricia Ainslie

The First Artists of the West

For thousands of years, the First Peoples of the Plains carved and painted images on cliffs and rocky outcrops throughout the region. With these images, First Nations recorded their visions and chronicled their history. Often found in sacred places, these rock carvings and paintings represent the intimate connection between First Nations and their spirit world. Hundreds of rock art sites have been recorded in Alberta, the most well-known of which are at Writing-on-Stone in south-eastern Alberta. Most sites predate the arrival of Euro-Canadians. The petroglyphs, engravings incised or pecked into rock using stone, bone, antler, and later metal tools, range from representational to abstract.

The prominent tribe living in southern Alberta were Blackfoot who followed a nomadic life based on the horse and the buffalo. In such nonliterate societies, traditions and histories were passed from one generation to the next through the telling of stories. Sometimes these stories were recorded pictorially on rock faces and story robes. As well as the ceremonial tradition of rock art, inter-tribal conflict and war exploits were the prominent subjects of Blackfoot pictographic art recorded on tipis, rock faces, and skin robes. A man's status was linked to his willingness to risk his life for the safety of his camp. This art was a public demonstration of his achievements by which the brave warrior attained political and social prominence. There is a strong relationship between the designs, symbols, and iconography of rock art and the painting on Blackfoot story robes.

First Nations art is the result of a long period of development in which capable artists devoted all of their inventive skill to perfecting specialized techniques and styles. This vital and living art not only has aesthetic qualities, it is infused with cultural and spiritual meaning. Change and adaptation has been part of this tradition.

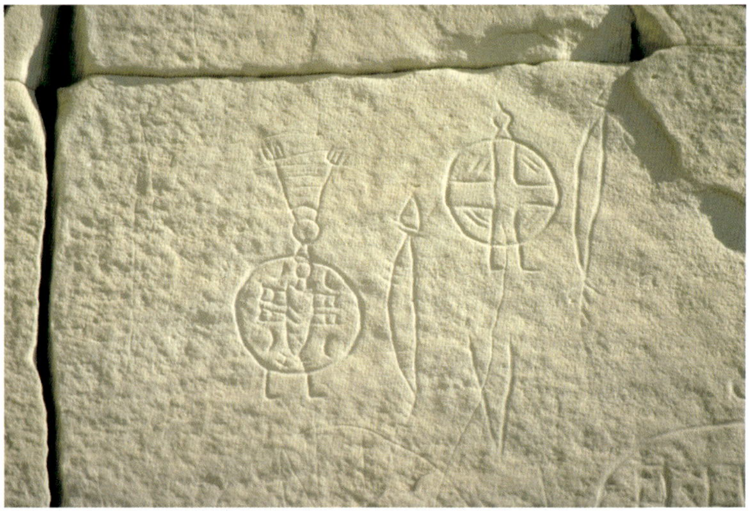

Artist Unknown

Petroglyph at Writing-on-Stone, Alberta, Late Prehistoric (AD 250–1700)

Photograph courtesy of M. A. Klassen

This small group of loosely associated figures suggests a symbolic relationship. The two schematic figures are shield-bearing warriors whose shields have figurative and geometric designs received in a vision. It is this design that protects the owner in battle, rather than the physical shield. The figure on the left wears a "stand-up" headdress common among the Blackfoot. They are each flanked by a long bow-spear with a large point at one end and feathers at the other. The forms are simple, but the meaning and significance is not. These petroglyphs are pictorial manifestations of the medicine powers that protected warriors in battle and gave them status in the community.

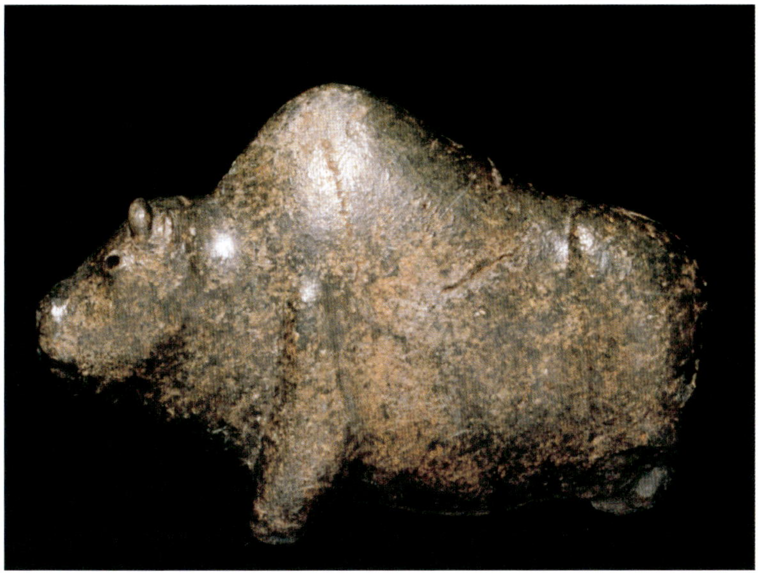

Artist Unknown
Bison Effigy, 1000–1500
green quartzite
Glenbow Museum, Calgary

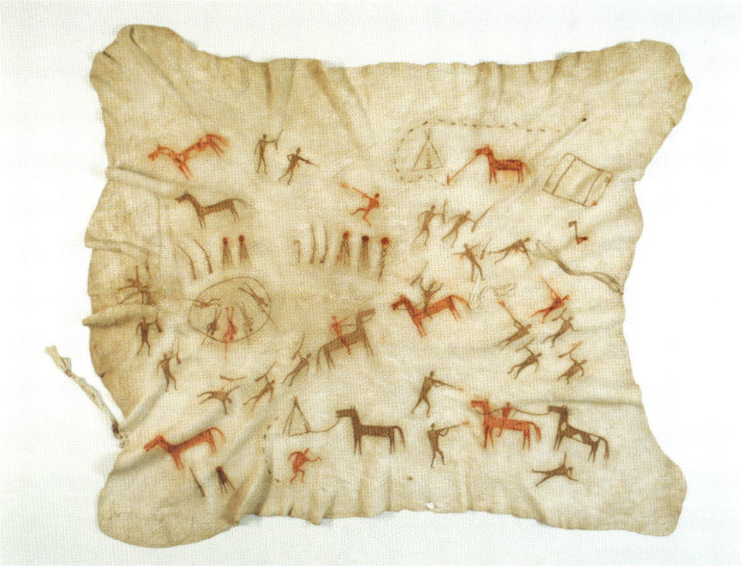

Raw Eater
Story Robe, late 1880s
paint on bison hide
Glenbow Museum, Calgary

The buffalo, roaming in huge herds across the western plains of North America, were essential to the Plains people, providing meat for nourishment, hides for clothing and shelter, and bone for tools. Widespread images of the buffalo are found in pictographs but three-dimensional images such as this are rare. This one was found in central Alberta in 1960. Though its exact purpose is unknown, it was likely sacred and used ceremonially to promote successful hunting. It was carved from a single piece of green quartzite using stone tools. The hunter-artist's keen observation of the mass and weight of the buffalo is evident in this small, twenty-five-centimetre animal. With great accomplishment, the massive bulk of the body, the distinct shoulder hump, and the huge forms of the legs have been represented in a strikingly economical way. The vitality of the animal is expressed through the large, structural, volumetric forms.

Raw Eater was a highly respected leader among the Siksika during the late 1880s, and this robe is an important public record of some of the significant episodes of his life. Its complex scenes embrace several events in which the hero, Raw Eater, executes brave deeds. "The Blackfoot (top right) were camped on the Elbow River. Raw Eater picketed his favourite horse beside his tipi at night, with a rawhide line linking his horse to his wrist while he slept. Awakened by a tug on the line, he rushed out to find a Cree attempting to steal the horse. He chased the Cree and ran into the other raiders. A battle followed between Raw Eater, his friends, and the Crees. One Cree was killed, and a blanket and a tomahawk were captured. The rest of the Crees escaped."[1] Recorded in the centre are items taken in battle: three scalps, two guns, and a tomahawk.

Such a pictograph is a public record of personal achievements that can be understood by all members of the community. The robe needs to be rotated to "read" the action. The treatment of space is two-dimensional and flat. Figures are uniform in size and are grouped evenly over the surface. They are schematized into simple shapes and rendered in outline: most of the men are firing or carrying guns, blood pours from figures being shot, a few lie wounded, some are astride their horses, shown in profile. The colour palette, drawn from charcoal and rocks, is red ochre and black, with Raw Eater and his horse painted red and the Crees black. A wedge-shaped implement, carved from the spongy part of the buffalo's scapula bone, was used to apply the paint.

Paul Kane's Western Travels

Paul Kane was the first European artist to make a comprehensive record of the Canadian West and his work, seen through European eyes, is fundamental to our understanding of the early West. His was a monumental, romantic quest in search of exotic subjects. Inspired to record the appearance and customs of Aboriginal people, he created a key historical record.

Leaving from Toronto, he made three trips to the western regions of Canada between 1845 and 1849. He penetrated a wilderness known only to fur traders and First Nations, where travelling was gruelling and required great stamina and determination. On his second and most extensive trip from May 1846 to October 1848, travelling by canoe, on horseback, and on foot, he crossed present-day Alberta into British Columbia and then into Oregon. Visiting the Hudson's Bay Company (HBC) forts along the way, he met First Nations coming to the forts, but he also travelled to their camps to meet and paint them. His drawings and watercolours produced on-site demonstrate his powers of careful observation in capturing the topographical features of the landscape and important ethnographic details of First Nations. There is a clarity and freshness in the sketches which does not translate into the oil paintings. His large oil paintings, completed later in his studio, often include greater detail, either a composite from several drawings, from artifacts he had gathered on his trips, or from his memory and experience. These finished oils concentrate on a dramatic and romantic mood more in tune with the artistic and academic conventions of the time.

From his heroic second journey, he created more than eight hundred paintings, sketches, and drawings, as well as his narrative, *Wanderings of an Artist Among the Indians of North America*, published in 1859. An extremely popular account of his travels, *Wanderings of an Artist* was published in four languages. Kane's art and writing fed the insatiable demand for information about lands newly penetrated by Europeans. His travels west provided the material on which he based all of his writing and art for the rest of his life and constitutes the basis of his entire reputation.

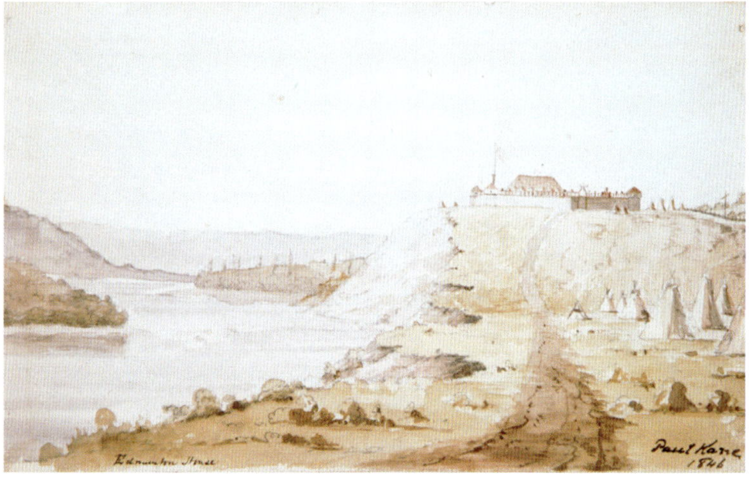

Paul Kane
Fort Edmonton, 1846
watercolour
Stark Museum of Art, Orange, Texas

Fort Edmonton was built in 1832 on the north side of the North Saskatchewan River and was the HBC's main post on the prairies. Kane was at Fort Edmonton from September 26 to October 6, 1846, and then left for the Pacific. This watercolour, sketched on his first visit, is a realistic and accurate depiction of the fort, set on a bluff over the North Saskatchewan River with a First Nation's tipi village in the foreground. It is carefully drawn, showing the topographical detail of the river valley and the almost treeless prairie, with delicate colour washes indicating the tones of the landscape. This sketch is the basis for a finished oil painting now in the Royal Ontario Museum, which is more romantic and dramatic in mood.

On first arriving at the fort, Kane wrote, "Edmonton is a large establishment: as it has to furnish many other districts with provisions, a large supply is always kept on hand, consisting entirely of dried meat, tongues, and pimmi-kon [pemmican]. There are usually here a chief factor and a clerk, with forty or fifty men with their wives and children, amounting altogether to about 130, who all live within the pickets of the fort ... I took a sketch of the fort, and having leisure, I went amongst the Indians, who are constantly about the fort for the purpose of trading."[2] Kane returned to the fort on December 5, 1847, spent Christmas there, and used it as a base from which he travelled to Fort Pitt and Rocky Mountain House. He left finally on May 25, 1848, with the spring fur brigade.

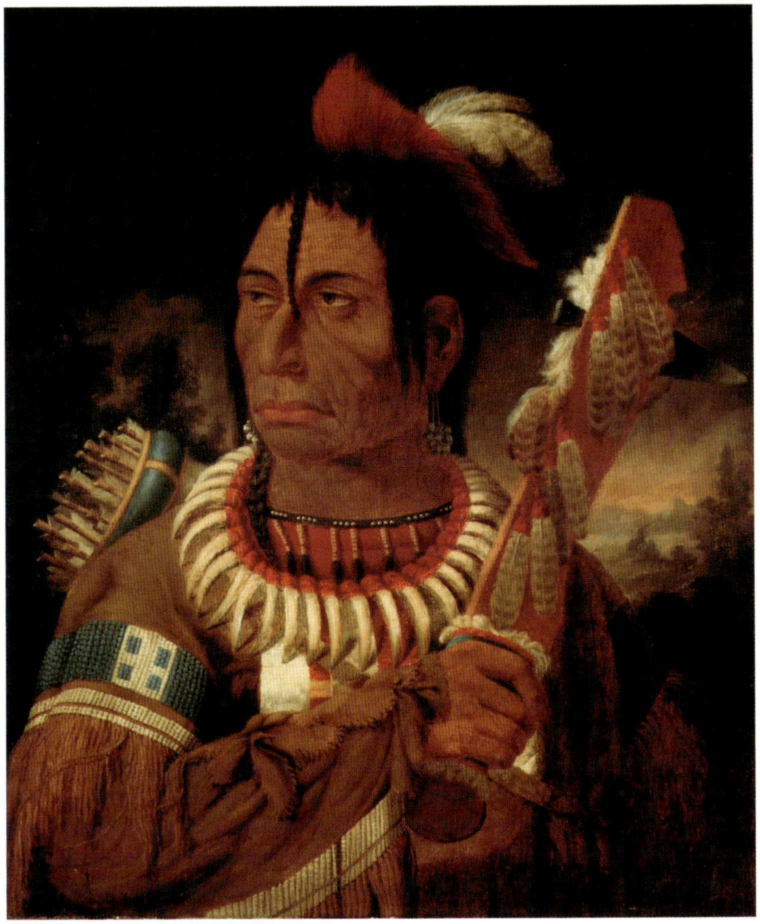

Paul Kane
Mah-Min or "The Feather," ca. 1848
oil
Montreal Museum of Fine Arts, William Gilman Cheney Bequest

This finished portrait was done in Kane's studio once he had returned to Toronto and is based on a sketch done of Mah-Min, Chief of the Assiniboine, at Rocky Mountain House in April 1848. Kane had travelled to Rocky Mountain House from Edmonton eager to meet with tribes gathered there. The original watercolour is simply sketched with summary details of Mah-Min's attire and with no background, but captures the pensive demeanour of the man.

This finished painting shows Mah-Min in full regalia, with a porcupine hair roach, grizzly bear claw necklace, hair lock necklace, war club with feathers, quiver with arrows, and an elaborately decorated shirt with fringes and beaded or quill work details, all authentic Blackfoot adornment. The strong robust forms are both sculptural and full of life. Though the likeness of the face remains, it has been considerably idealized from the sketch. All of the clothing and accoutrements have become much more detailed and sharply defined, and the different textures of leather, beads, and feathers are carefully rendered. Kane based these details on other sketches he had done and on artifacts he had gathered in the field. As well as providing significant ethnographic detail, Kane has created a romantic image of this proud and noble person: an exotic subject. The romantic effect is heightened by setting Mah-Min in a moody wilderness landscape.

Precursors—Explorers' Images of a New Land

Early expeditions to the West often included talented amateur artists who were skilled with pencil and brush. In their heroic journeys, these artist-explorers ran arduous risks and suffered great hardships. They recorded the country they travelled through and provided unique visual records of these vast, unknown regions. Some were military officers, trained in topographical recording at various military academies; others were engineers, who also had technical training in drawing. Topographical images were intended to provide a precise visual description of a particular place. The Romantic era stimulated expansion and exploration, and artists fed the desire for new information about unknown lands and people who were considered exotic. For the British, the pictorial record was tangible evidence of British power.

Watercolour was an ideal medium for landscape painting completed outdoors. The British watercolour tradition became a popular way to record travels. It was used by British artists in Canada and also adopted by Canadians in the nineteenth century for landscape painting in the West. Watercolour equipment was both lightweight and easily transportable: a sketch pad, pencils, brushes, and a watercolour box. A fast-drying medium, watercolour can be used to execute quick sketches, making it ideal for recording images in the field. Most watercolours were done on the spot and because of this have clarity and freshness.

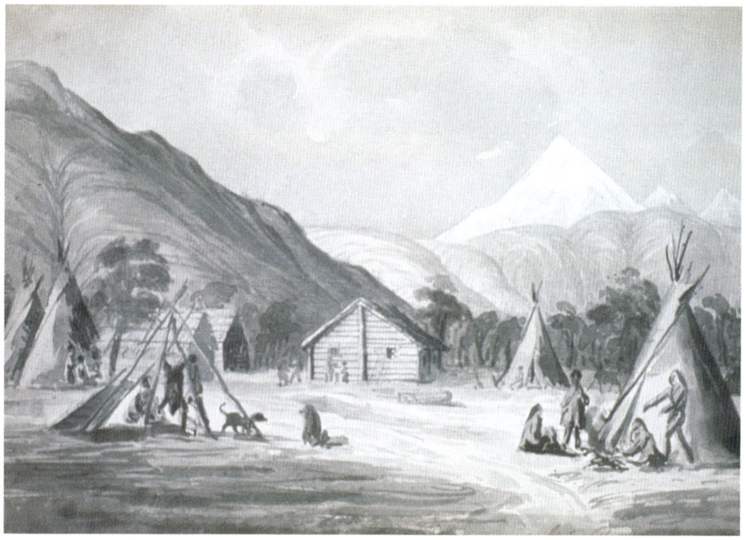

Henry James Warre
Jasper's House, Athabaska River looking West, 1846
watercolour and gouache over pencil
With permission of the Royal Ontario Museum, Toronto, © ROM

This unique image is the first depiction of the settlement at Jasper House, the last stop before the arduous trek over the Rockies. It provides us with substantial information. It shows the pitched-roof log-house construction of the European settlement in a clearing in the woods with mountains in the background. Surrounding these are the skin-covered conical First Nations' tipis. There is lively activity. Women are cleaning skins to the left, figures congregate in front of a tipi to the right, and, in the distance, toboggans await their loads for transportation. All of this is simply rendered with quick watercolour brushstrokes with the immediacy of a done-on-the-spot sketch. The figures are quite rudimentary, yet this topographical view provides a vivid sense of the life about the house.

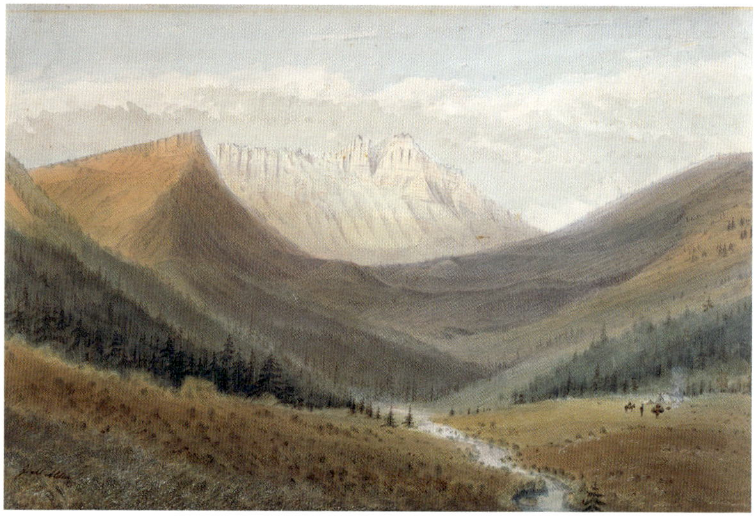

James Alden
Kishenena Pass, ca. 1857–61
watercolour
Glenbow Museum, Calgary

Alden was an accomplished draughtsman and painter capable of rendering the immense landscape of the Rockies. He traversed the boundary area to record the activity of the Northwest Boundary

Survey, through swamps, wide rivers, and unmapped forests. Alden's compositions are topographically correct with accurate perspective conveying the breathtaking landscape. For *Kishenena Pass*, in the Waterton area of south-western Alberta, he has chosen a high vantage point that heightens the grand scale of the landscape. The mountains sweep up from a deep valley with a river threading through it. The physical structure of the craggy mountains is clearly delineated. To the right are the tents of his survey camp and some precisely drawn figures, their minute size creating a sense of scale in the vast landscape. Vertical strokes of the brush depict the densely treed forests in the shaded bowl of the valley. Over these tightly drawn areas, washes of muted colour unify the elements, creating a harmonious composition.

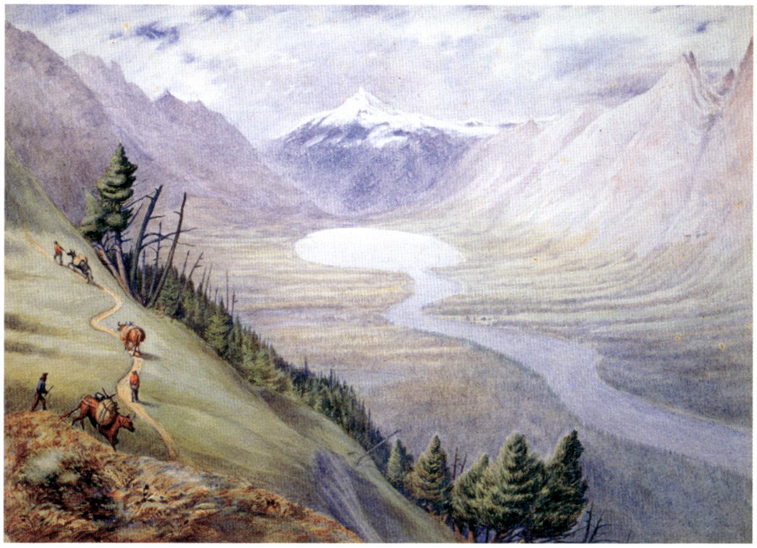

William G. R. Hind
The Leather Pass, Rocky Mountains, 1862
watercolour
McCord Museum, Montreal, M472

This is a refined and delicate composition, charming and somewhat naive. There is a grand sense of scale with the huge majestic mountains lifting up from the deep valley. As with many topographical views, there is a great deal of precise, accurate detail in the foreground trees and the forested slopes, but due to the overall tonality and the strong basic structure of the composition, the detail does not obscure the picturesque effect of the whole. At left are some diminutive travellers with oxen and horses. Rather than showing the arduousness of such a journey, they travel through the garden-like Eden in this serene scene. It is in marked contrast to Hind's sketchbook, which shows the difficulties of recalcitrant horses, carts bogged down, with men and beasts hauling carts up steep slopes and over broken bridges. It is likely that this painting was completed, once he returned east, from sketches done on site when the difficulties experienced had faded from memory.

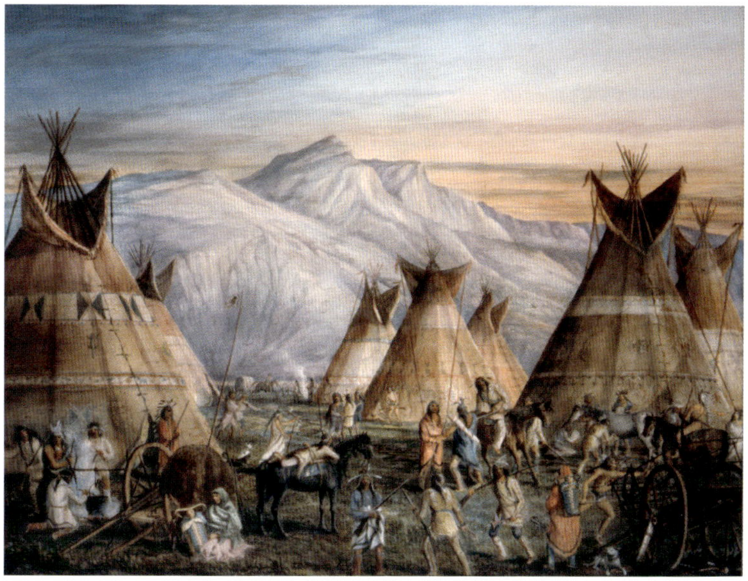

William Armstrong
Blackfoot Indian Encampment, Foothills of the Rocky Mountains, n.d.
watercolour and gouache
With permission of the Royal Ontario Museum, Toronto, © ROM

This is an animated scene in a tipi village set in a broad plain beneath huge, bulky, snow-capped mountains. It may have been completed in 1877, when Armstrong travelled to the Rockies with Sir Sandford Fleming. Groups of First Nations are involved in different activities of daily life. To the left, people are cooking food in a huge pot hanging over a fire, some in the foreground are carrying muskets presumably preparing for the hunt, while others are saddling their horses. However, unlike many of the early topographical drawings, the ethnographic detail here is indistinct, inaccurate, or absent. Some of the items are taken from other First Nations groups: the mother in the foreground watches over her baby in a cradleboard that is Cree and not used by the Blackfoot; two Red River carts in the foreground are unlikely as the Blackfoot did not like either the Cree or Métis coming into their territory; the tipi designs are not Blackfoot and the smoke flaps should all face in the same direction. He has also not been able to render the perspective accurately. The figures in the foreground are too small compared with the figures in the middle-ground, and all of the figures are very small in proportion to the huge tipis. The figures are awkward and poorly rendered. Though this painting gives the viewer the impression of a Blackfoot camp, it is both misleading and inaccurate.

Arrival of the Mounties

The North-West Mounted Police (NWMP) was created in 1873 by the Canadian government to police the vast North-West Territories then recently acquired from the Hudson's Bay Company (HBC). They undertook their famous March West in 1874 and established a fort at Fort Macleod. The force curbed the illegal and deadly cross-border whisky trade to First Nations and was responsible for law enforcement as European settlement increased. Richard Nevitt, assistant surgeon with the police, and also an amateur artist, travelled on the March West and was stationed at the fort for four years. During the time he was there, he was joined by another amateur artist, D. B. Robinson. After they had completed their service, many of the force stayed behind to ranch. Sara Mary Blake, an amateur artist, married one of these officers. Thus a small group of resident artists, living temporarily or more permanently here, began to record the face of Alberta.

None of these artists could be considered professional, though they all had likely received some art training. As talented amateurs whose documentary images give us unique insights in to early settlement on the prairies, they provide key historical visual records of important people, places, and events. There is also considerable charm in their intimate record.

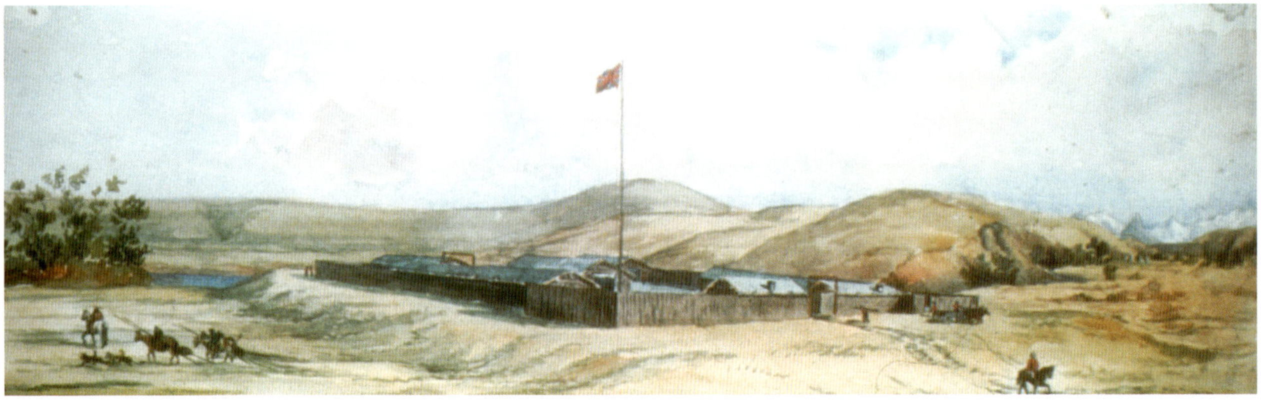

Richard Barrington Nevitt
Fort Calgary in Summer, ca. May 1876
watercolour
Glenbow Museum, Calgary

Fort Calgary was built in late 1875. It is set on a grassy knoll against the bluff of the Bow River in the centre of a broad panorama, with the rolling foothills behind and the snow-capped Rocky Mountains shown on the left horizon. With this narrow horizontal composition, Nevitt provides a sense of the immensity of the land, further emphasized by the small foreground figures, dwarfed against this huge land. There are Mounties at work, their jackets points of bright red against the straw-coloured, almost treeless prairie. To the right are three First Nations people with travois carrying supplies from the fort. The fort is compact with the interior buildings well protected by the sturdy palisade. The tall flagpole flying the red, white, and blue Union Jack anchors the fort to the land and signifies the Europeans' first firm imposition in this region. Nevitt has carefully drawn the buildings, figures, and geographical features and then applied watercolour in a direct and spontaneous manner. These delicate transparent colour washes add volume to the forms and luminosity to the big sky. The harmonious scene is infused with the soft prairie light of spring.

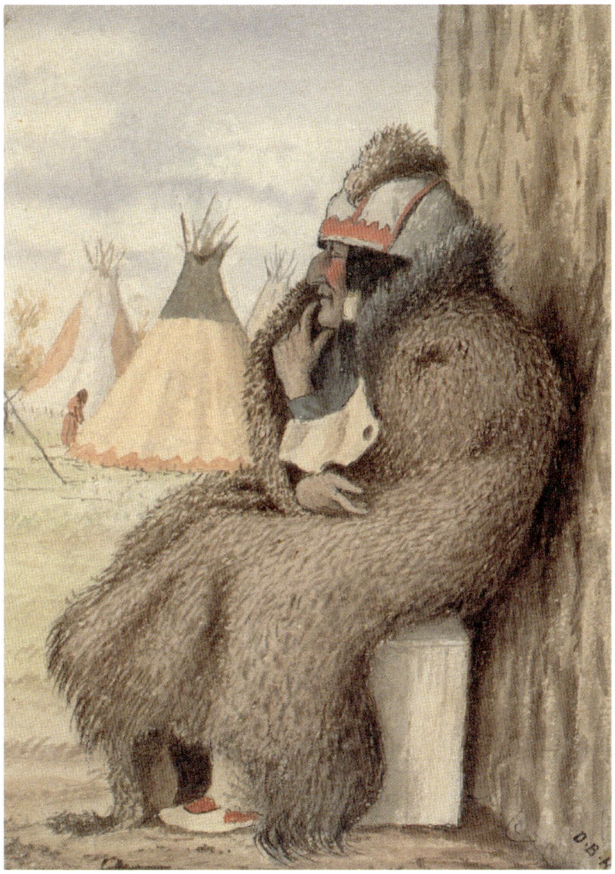

D. B. Robinson
Crowfoot, ca. 1875
watercolour
Glenbow Museum, Calgary

Crowfoot was the head chief of the Siksika and signed Treaty No. 7 in 1877 on behalf of his people. He played a significant role in keeping the peace between First Nations people and newly arrived Europeans. Seated on a box and leaning against a building of the fort, he is wrapped in a buffalo robe that cocoons him protectively. In the background are some tipis with traditional Blackfoot designs. Robinson has concentrated on Crowfoot's face, carefully delineating his features, his prominent hooked nose, large mouth, and deep-set eyes. This is finely drawn, skilful, and sensitive. Robinson shows him in pensive mood, deep in thought. His hair is bunched, not braided, and tied with a silver hair clasp. The colour is sharp and clear, and the splashes of red on his cheek, hat, and moccasins provide a point of vitality in an otherwise fairly monochromatic painting, with its pale prairie sky.

Sara Mary Blake
The Deer Horn Ranch on the North Fork of the Old Man River, Alberta, 1889
watercolour
Glenbow Museum, Calgary

Blake is the first known woman artist in Alberta, but few of her paintings survive. She painted the landscape around Waterton, scenes on the doors of her house, and cards for parties. This watercolour depicts her brother's new ranch house with its porch and mounted elk horns, various outbuildings for supplies and animals, and a large central corral. Hay is already stacked in a huge pile outside the corral. This detailed composition documents all the elements of the new ranch, identifying its location in the foothills. Drawn with a delicate line, it shows care and attention to detail and is then filled in with colour. By including figures and horses that are too small and not in proportion to the buildings, the image appears naive. A pale light diffuses this orderly, somewhat romantic scene at the end of a hard day's work.

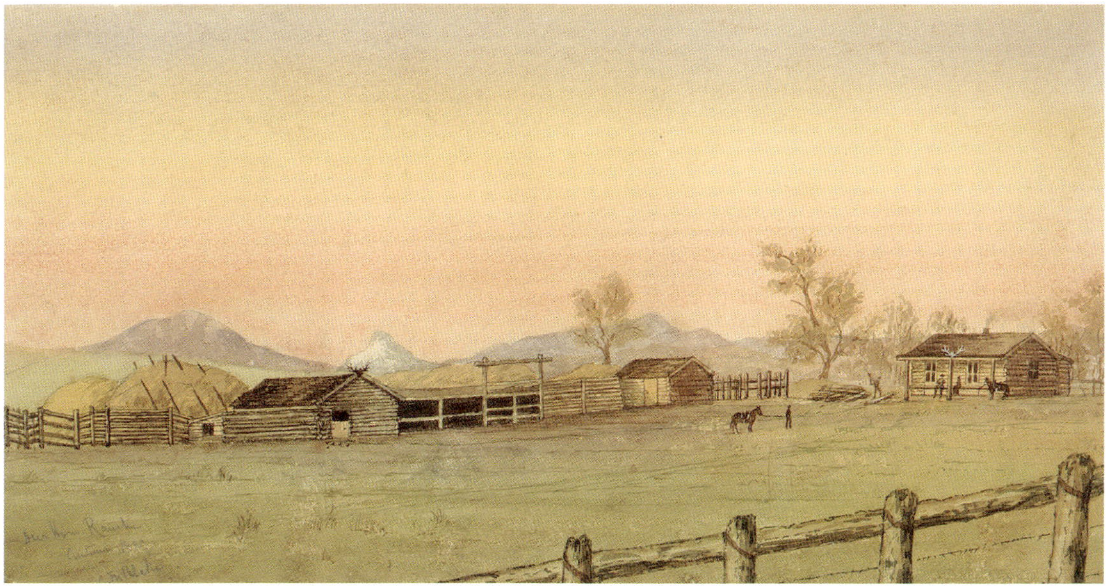

Photographers Document the West

Photography was invented in 1839 and the camera then became a mechanical eye recording a specific place at a specific time. A blend of chemistry and optics, it provided authentic visual information. As early as 1858 there were photographers recording scenes in the West. But it was not until 1871 that photography was first used in Alberta by Charles Horetzky, and by the North American Boundary Commission. That same year, the William Notman photographic studio in Montreal sent Benjamin Baltzly with the first Pacific Railway Survey of the interior of British Columbia. At this time, photographic equipment was large and cumbersome and photographers required strength, stamina, and patience. Many lost equipment during their travels due to the difficult terrain, the rivers, and inclement weather.

It was not until the 1880s, after Canadian Pacific Railway (CPR) had penetrated Alberta, that the photograph was more widely used. Photographers were the first to receive passes from CPR. The most successful photographic firm in Montreal was owned by William Notman, established in 1857 or 1858. Due to his readiness to experiment and introduce new techniques, William Notman excelled in many areas. His work included Canadian scenes and life, portraits, resorts and hotels, industry and trade, and "views" of Canada from coast to coast. He had a long relationship with CPR, starting in the 1880s, producing a huge stock of photographs for their use. His son, William McFarlane Notman, was apprenticed in his father's studio and became a partner in 1882. William McFarlane Notman travelled west in 1884, again in 1886, and made six subsequent trips. Another photographer, Alexander Henderson, who had his own successful photographic studio in Montreal, was sent west by CPR in 1885. (Regrettably all but four of Henderson's photographs from this trip are now lost, and those that remain are views in British Columbia.) This was also the time when photographers began to set up studios in the towns developing in Alberta. William Hanson Boorne was a pioneer, setting up his studio in Calgary in 1885. Most early photographers were self-taught entrepreneurs with a wide variety of clientele. Studio portraits were popular and enabled photographers to make a living in the new communities.

Early landscape photographs were topographical images intended to provide a precise visual record of a particular place, showing the physical features and geological forms. Many of them were destined for official reports or travellers' published journals. Despite its documentary nature, and the belief that the camera captured exactly what the eye saw, photographers selected views from many possibilities. Their selections showed their interest in aesthetic concerns of the picturesque and sometimes the dramatic and exotic quality beloved by the Romantics. There was an ongoing interplay between the convention of photography to record and the tradition of fine art. It took time and patience to get the precise quality of light and atmosphere the photographers wanted, often they had to wait days for special conditions. They were awed by the spectacular mountains, intrigued by the First Nations people they encountered, and intent on capturing not only the reality, but also the mood, emotion, and atmosphere of what they saw.

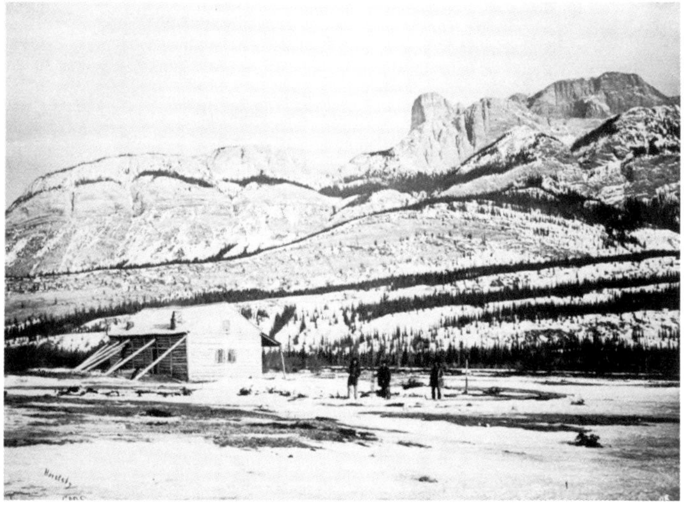

Charles Horetzky
View of Jasper House from the rear, November 1871
photograph
Glenbow Museum Archives, Calgary, NA-1408-72

Jasper House, established in 1800, was the last stop before explorers began the challenging task of crossing the Rocky Mountains via Yellowhead Pass. Horetzky's photograph records the structure and form of the impressive mountains and provides important geological information. He has documented the cabin's position at the foot of Roche Miete in the late fall, showing the structure of the small wooden cabin with its special log construction, chimney, and a porch in front, set on the river flatland with the Athabasca River flowing by. But Horetzky has done more than merely record the scene in front of him. The image gives us a sense of the vast landscape and the extreme isolation of the cabin precariously propped up, dwarfed by the sweep of the mountain behind it. The figures create a sense of scale in the landscape, but they also indicate Horetzky's knowledge of the Romantic artistic tradition in which small figures in nature indicate man's impotence against natural forces.

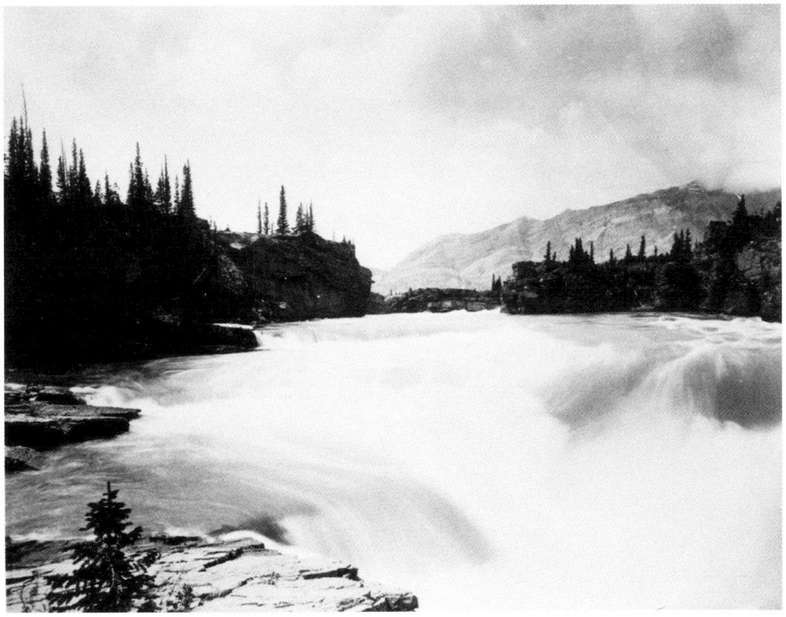

Oliver B. Buell
Kananaskis Falls, Alberta, 1885
photograph
Glenbow Museum Archives, Calgary, NA-4140-12

Buell has captured a sense of the power of nature in this image as he focuses on the energy of the river surging towards us. The composition is anchored and enclosed by the mountains in the distance and the dark banks of the river. The river itself emerges from this darkness and broadens out widely to reach the falls where the impetus and pressure turns the water into a boiling, churning mass. The lowering clouds add a sense of foreboding. Buell chose the vantage point and the weather to create a dramatic image in the Romantic tradition of the sublime—nature as a metaphor for a powerful and vengeful God.

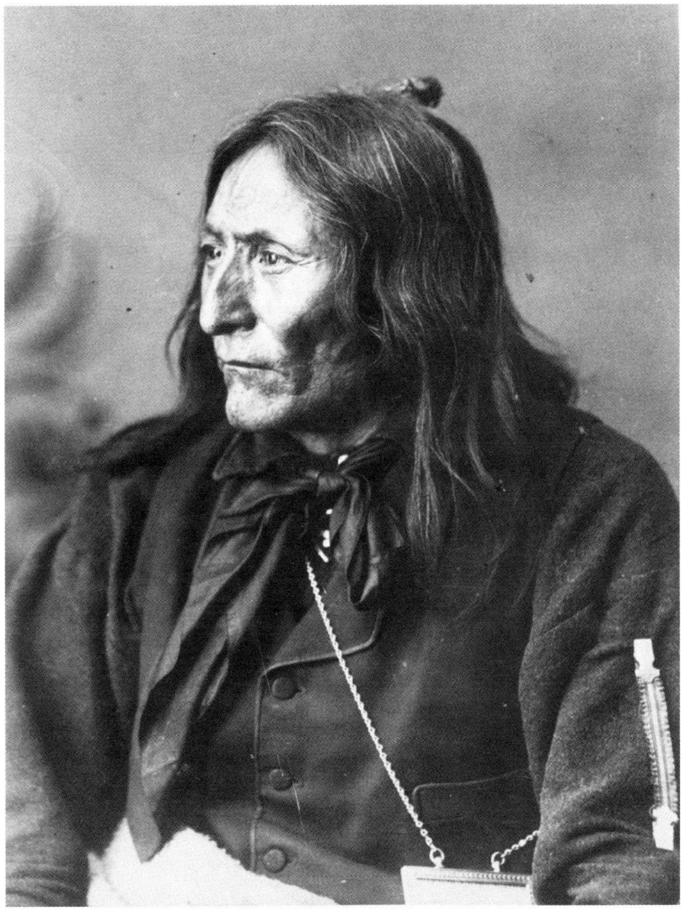

Alexander R. Ross
Chief Crowfoot (Isapo-Muxika), ca. 1885
photograph
Glenbow Museum Archives, Calgary, NA-29-1/PA-10-1

Crowfoot was born about 1830 at a time of tremendous change in Blackfoot society and he lived to 1890. He had established good relations with the newcomers, the missionaries, and the North-West Mounted Police, and was a spokesperson for the Siksika at the Treaty No. 7 negotiations. But he became disillusioned with the Europeans after experiencing the harsh conditions of reserve life. Crowfoot is shown here with his hair loose, with the characteristic topknot, a bird as spirit helper in his hair. He wears a European shirt and kerchief around his neck and a Hudson's Bay blanket wrapped around his waist. From his neck hangs his railroad pass. This is a very sympathetic portrait in which Ross has captured the deep sadness of Crowfoot's expression. His strong face, with prominent nose and set mouth, is careworn and thoughtful, staring off into the distance. This is not a nostalgic view, but a heart-rending portrait of Crowfoot, who witnessed the end of the Blackfoot traditional way of life.

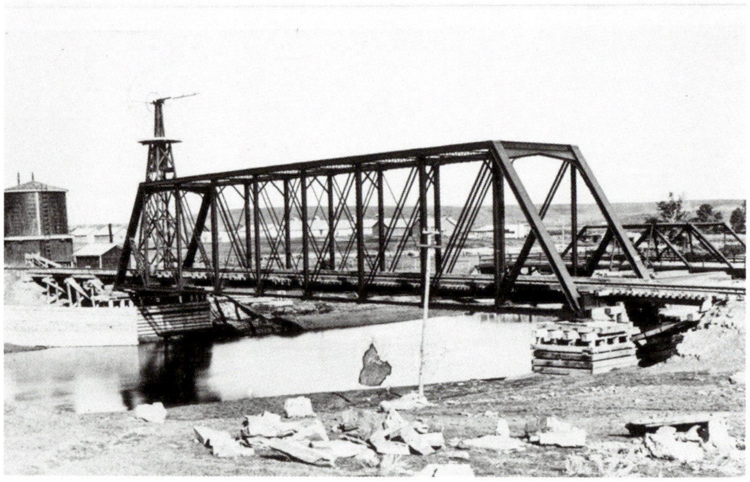

William Hanson Boorne
Canadian Pacific Railway Bridge over the Elbow River, Calgary, Alberta, 1886–89
photograph
Glenbow Museum Archives, Calgary, NA-3026-15

A clear-sighted, objective examination, this photograph documents the new bridge over the Elbow River in Calgary, with the newly laid track that brought the first train to the city in 1883. Calgary can be seen through the rigid geometry of the bridge, a small prairie town on the flood plain of the Bow River. The windmill and water tower provide balance for the composition, adding interest and depth. This is an impressive piece of engineering, and here Boorne shows it rivalling some of the natural landmarks of the region.

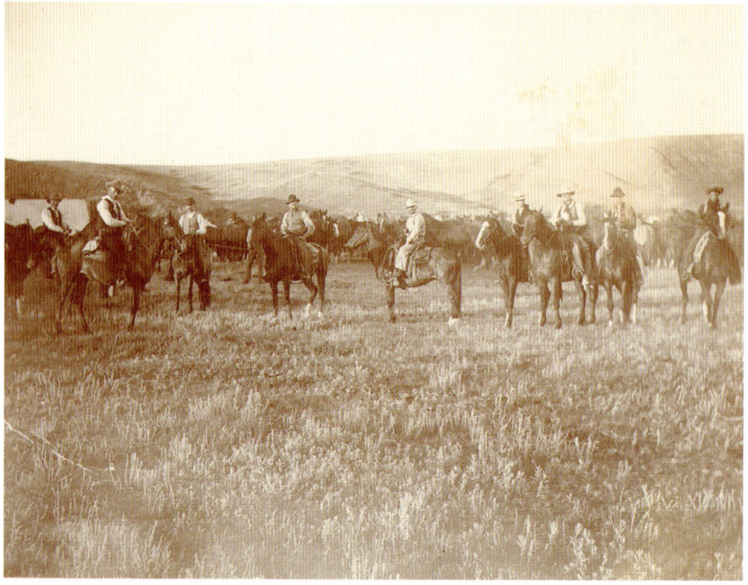

Geraldine Moodie
Cowboys posed on Horseback in Round-up Camp on the Hawke Ranch Southeast of Medicine Hat in the Cypress Hills, ca. 1897–98
photograph
Medicine Hat Museum and Art Gallery, P2.3

Moodie opened a photographic studio in 1895 in Battleford, Saskatchewan. She was the first professional woman photographer on the prairies to do so. Her photographs, some set in Alberta, are primarily documentary in nature, providing an insightful view of early prairie life. Her range of subjects indicates her strong personal independence and is exceptional for a woman at this time. This image documents the roundup. It is a simple composition with a wide foreground, leading the viewer's eye to the cowboys set in the middle distance, with a large corral of horses behind them and the rolling Cypress Hills as a backdrop. The grouping of the figures demonstrates the communal nature of cowboy life, the camaraderie, as they pose, poised for the roundup.

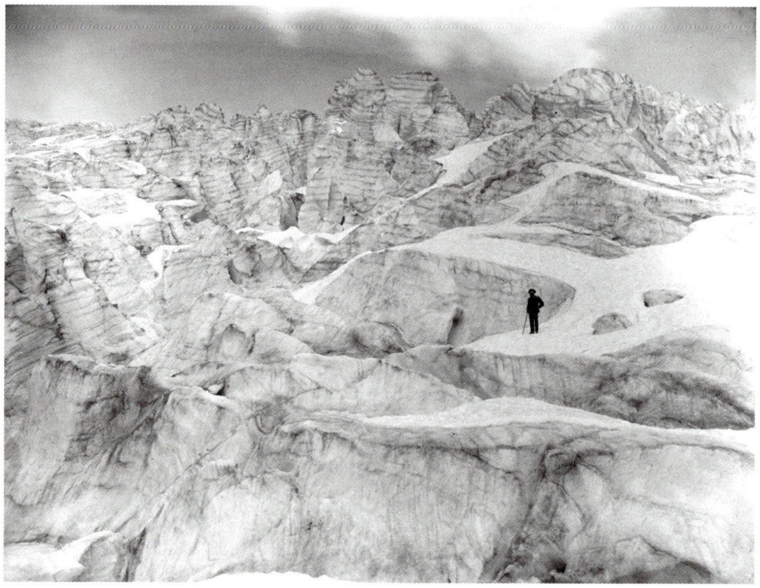

Vaux Family
Seracs, Great Glacier [Illecillewaet], June 29, 1900
photograph
Whyte Museum of the Canadian Rockies, Banff, NG 4-635

The Vaux siblings, Mary, George, and William, were well-educated and widely travelled Victorians from Philadelphia, a major centre for photography in the nineteenth century. They were committed to the study of glaciers and after their initial trip to the Rockies in

1887, spent many summers in Alberta and British Columbia. They recorded the structure and form of the glaciers in their environment, the pressure of the immense weight forcing the pushing and lifting of ice into a craggy mass, demonstrating the extraordinary power of nature. While their focus was on science, their photographs are also beautifully poetic. *Seracs* could be seen as an elaborate abstract composition, with forms repeated and layered one on top of another, with the pressure lines in the seracs forming a striped pattern undulating over the surface. Providing a sense of scale, the figure in the middle distance is completely dwarfed by the environment, a sublime image worthy of the Romantics.

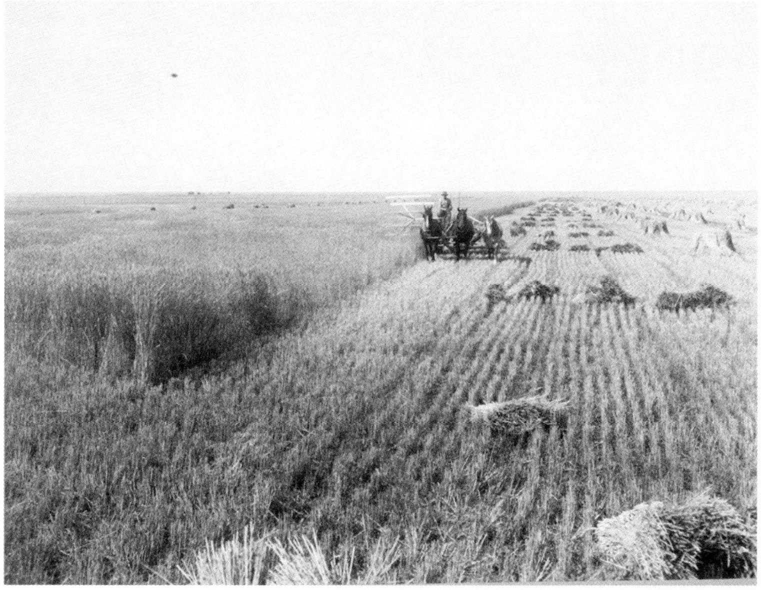

William McFarlane Notman

Harvest of C. James's Wheat, Lethbridge area, Alberta, July 1904

photograph

Glenbow Museum Archives, Calgary, PB-863-10

During his 1904 trip west, Notman spent most of his time recording farming and the growing small towns of southern Alberta. CPR, for whom he was working, had thousands of acres of land it wanted to sell and photographs would help. They had acquired the North West Irrigation Company in the Lethbridge district with the aim of attracting settlers to the area. In this photograph, we see a land of plenty with wheat stretching as far as the eye can see to the flat prairie horizon. C. James is riding on the harvester pulled by three horses as they mow down the tall healthy wheat and stack it in neat piles. The extensive land and the abundant successful harvest are clearly articulated in this photograph. There is no hint of drought, hail, or pests, which often posed a great challenge to prairie farmers. Compositionally, this is a very balanced scene, with the lines created by the already harvested field to the right stretching into the distance and the tall waving wheat an even mass to the left. The farmer is the centre of attention.

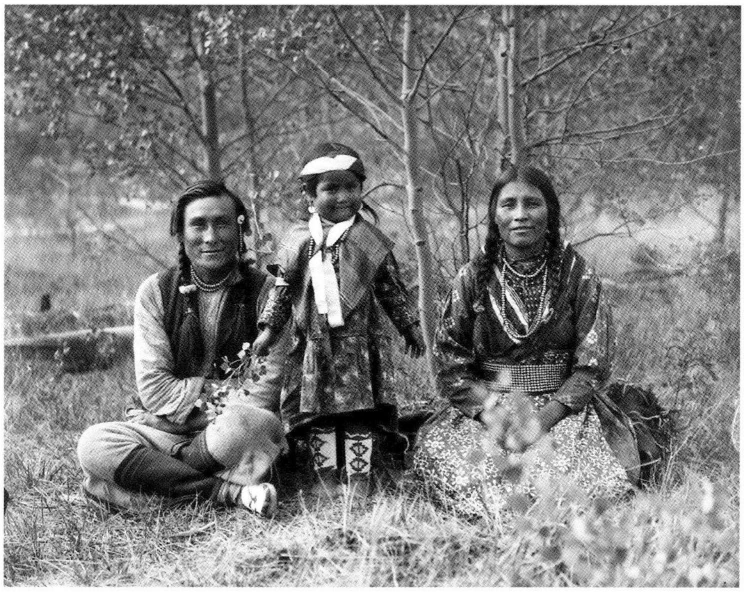

Mary Schäffer

Sampson Beaver's Family, 1906

photograph

Whyte Museum of the Canadian Rockies, Banff, WMCR-V527/NG-124

Author, photographer, and botanist, Schäffer first visited the Rockies with Mary Vaux in 1889 and subsequently travelled annually to the mountains, settling in Banff in 1929. She undertook significant outfitted pack trips throughout her life, and in 1908 she explored Maligne Lake using a map Sampson Beaver had provided for her. This portrait depicts Sampson Beaver, his wife Leah, and daughter Frances Louise, of the Wesley Band of the Nakoda (Stoney) Indians, who lived in the Kootenay Plains on the North Saskatchewan River. Clearly she knew this family well as she has created an intimate and charming portrait. She depicts them looking directly at the camera, their smiling faces open and friendly. Dressed in a mix of traditional and European clothing, the family looks at ease. The soft light picks out the costume details and the features on their handsome faces.

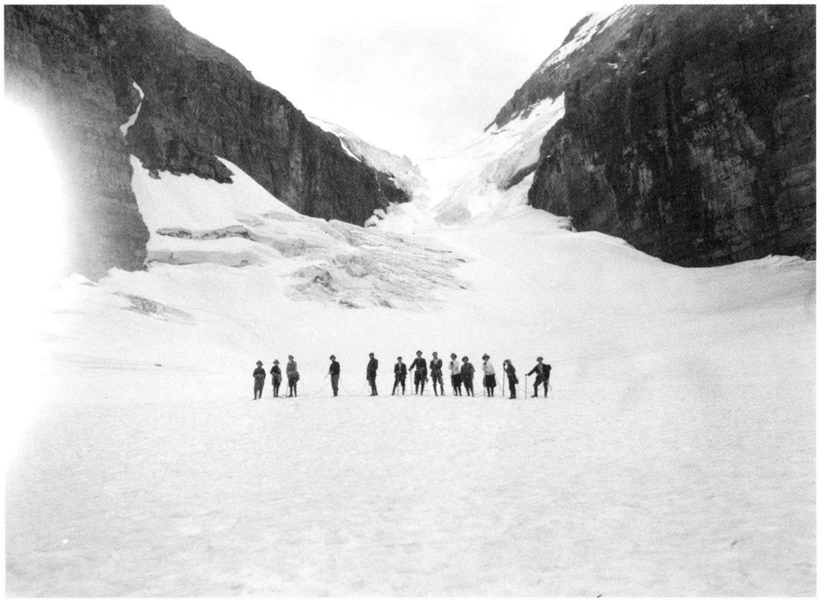

Byron Harmon
Group of ACC climbers ascending to Abbot Pass, 1907 or 1909
photograph
Whyte Museum of the Canadian Rockies, Banff, NA 71-38

Harmon travelled deep into glacier-scoured valleys, over ridges and peaks, and across glacial ice and fast-flowing rivers to capture the unique mountain landscape of the Rockies. In this image, we observe members of the Alpine Club of Canada (ACC), on one of their annual climbing trips. Harmon has framed Abbot Pass between the massive rugged mountains scoured through by the ancient glacier. Only a wedge of the mountains is in view, jutting in from each side of the frame, the dark forms in sharp contrast to the white snow. We comprehend their weight and sense that they loom high above the pass. The figures with all their climbing gear stand nonchalantly, roped together in preparation for their climb. Dwarfed by the wilderness, they appear insignificant in the face of the immensity and terrible beauty of nature.

Harmon became the premier mountain photographer in the Canadian Rockies after his arrival in Banff in 1903 until his death in 1942. He was the first Alberta artist to have an international reputation through the wide distribution and exhibition of his photographs and films in Europe and North America.

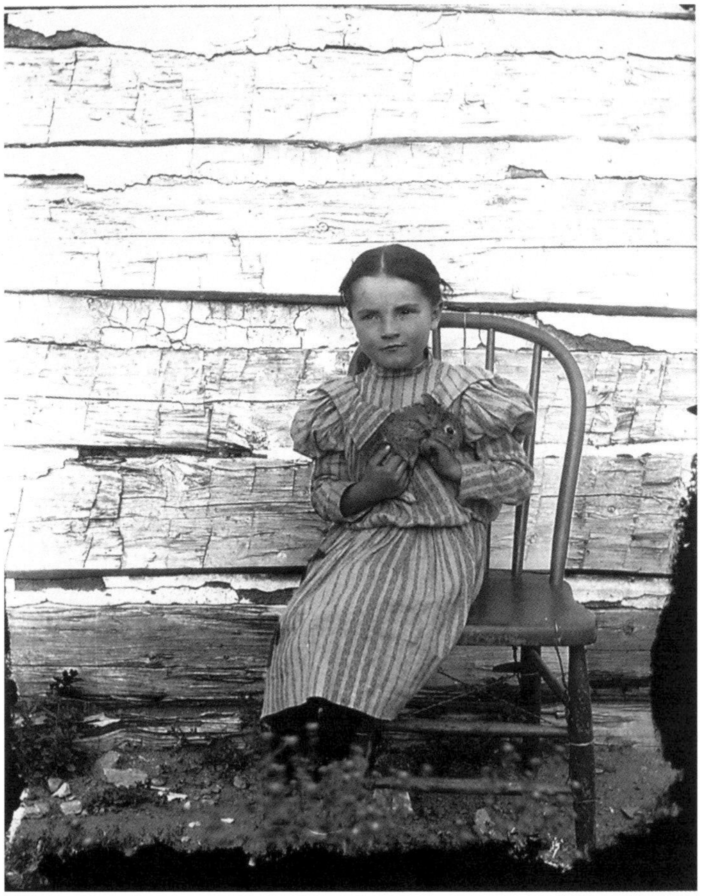

Ella Hartt
Little Girl Holding Rabbit, n.d.
photograph
Glenbow Museum Archives, Calgary, NC-39-296

This is one of many images of childhood photographed by Hartt. It is an insightful portrait of a girl, casually sitting on a chair, hugging her precious rabbit. With its clear and sharp focus, the precision of the image has good contrasts of light and dark with crisp details. The composition is surprisingly modern, partly due to the informal nature of the portrait, but also because of the untraditional off-centred position of the child and the large, what might be considered empty, expanse of white background. She is shown against the chinked wooden wall of the log house, painted white and peeling. The image exudes the charm of simple prairie life.

Canadian Pacific Railway Promotes the West

One of the dreams of my early manhood was to visit and paint the Rockies, about whose magnificence all travellers raved. I dreamed this over and over again until the vision took form in finding myself, very early one summer's morning, at 'The Gap.' Never was a mountain peep-show more appropriately named. Right across an iridescent reach of the Bow River—gold-shotted by the reflections of the mirror sky—stood out boldly the vanguard sentinels of the mountain host. Displaying the glint of their glacier accoutrements, they beckoned the enraptured pilgrim to explore their mysteries and their shrines.[3]

—FREDERIC MARLETT BELL-SMITH

In 1885, the railway stretching across Canada linking east and west was completed. That same year, photographer Alexander Henderson was sent to document views along the line, though all of his negatives and unfortunately all but four of his photographs from this trip are now lost. The following year, Sir William Van Horne, president of Canadian Pacific Railway, gave free passes to artists to travel west on the new railway. Their paintings provided CPR with the means to promote tourism to this newly opened region. For the first time, artists could reach the Rockies and return after a few months work in the summer with many images of the West. Four artists travelled west that first year, including John Fraser and Lucius O'Brien, and more went west in 1887, the most accomplished being Frederic Bell-Smith. These were professional artists, being distinct from most of the talented amateurs who had up to that point represented the West. As well as being used as promotion for CPR, many of their paintings were exhibited in art society exhibits in the East, including in the newly formed Royal Canadian Academy (RCA). Their images popularized the West. For the first time the Rockies became an icon for Canada: an image of nationhood.

Though they travelled through the prairies, the artists painted almost exclusively in the mountainous regions. The irony is that although they depicted the wilderness, they were transported there by train. Artists viewed the mountains through a romantic lens. They were entranced by the sublime landscape of the Rockies, the endless variety of scenes, the great drama of the dizzying heights and cavernous depths, and the awe-inspiring beauty. They focused on the pristine quality of nature, mostly uninhabited. When figures were shown, they were a dwarfed symbolic presence. Occasionally, a diminutive train showed man's intrusion into the landscape. The artists painted predominantly in watercolour and needed few, easily transportable supplies. Due to its quick application, watercolour allowed the artists to spontaneously capture the mood and atmosphere of the mountains. These western paintings were very popular in eastern Canada. Some CPR artists continued to produce romantically inspired mountain scenes well into the twentieth century, long after they ceased being relevant in art circles.

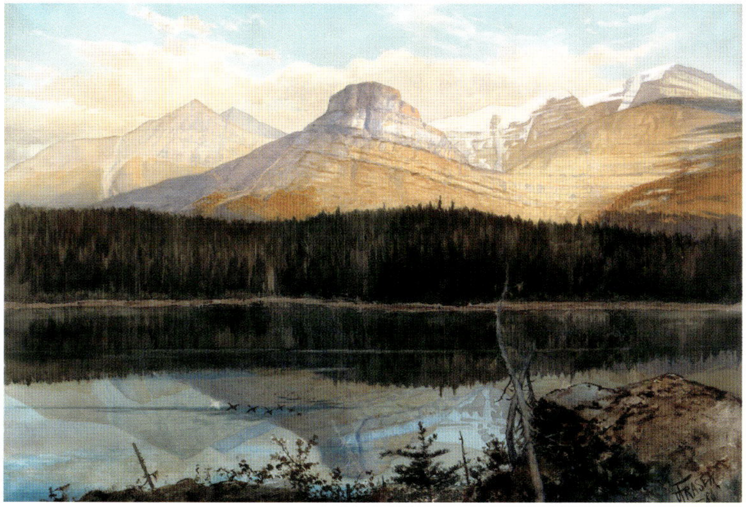

John Arthur Fraser
Summit Lake near Lenchoile, Bow River, Canadian Pacific Railway, 1886
watercolour
National Gallery of Canada, Ottawa

To promote CPR, in January 1886, Van Horne offered Fraser a commission to paint three large watercolours from Alexander Henderson's black and white photographic prints, for exhibition at the Colonial and Indian Exhibition in London, England, in May of the same year. As the commission came so late, Fraser, who was living in Boston, did not have the time, nor was the season suitable, for a painting trip to the West. It was only later that Fraser was able to travel to the Rockies, though he had travelled as far as Calgary, Alberta, the end of the line, in 1883. It is very likely that this image is one painted from Henderson's photographs. Fraser has depicted the impressive bulk of the mountains, the sombre dark forests below and the broad tranquil river in the foreground. This is a beautiful picturesque scene with which to lure travellers west. But it is not an accurate rendition of the mountains. Taken from a photograph, it lacks animation and the depth of field of the layered mountain ranges. In addition, the fast-flowing Bow River is shown uncharacteristically mirror-smooth. The colour is crisp and bright, but the river is too blue, rather than the real emerald-green colour of the silted Bow. As well, the tawny, rust-coloured mountains do not reflect the massive grey forms we know. It is Fraser's best attempt, having not actually seen the mountains. Correspondence exists between Fraser and Van Horne at the time of the commission over Fraser's difficulty in representing the colour of the scene: he had to rely on Henderson's notes for this.

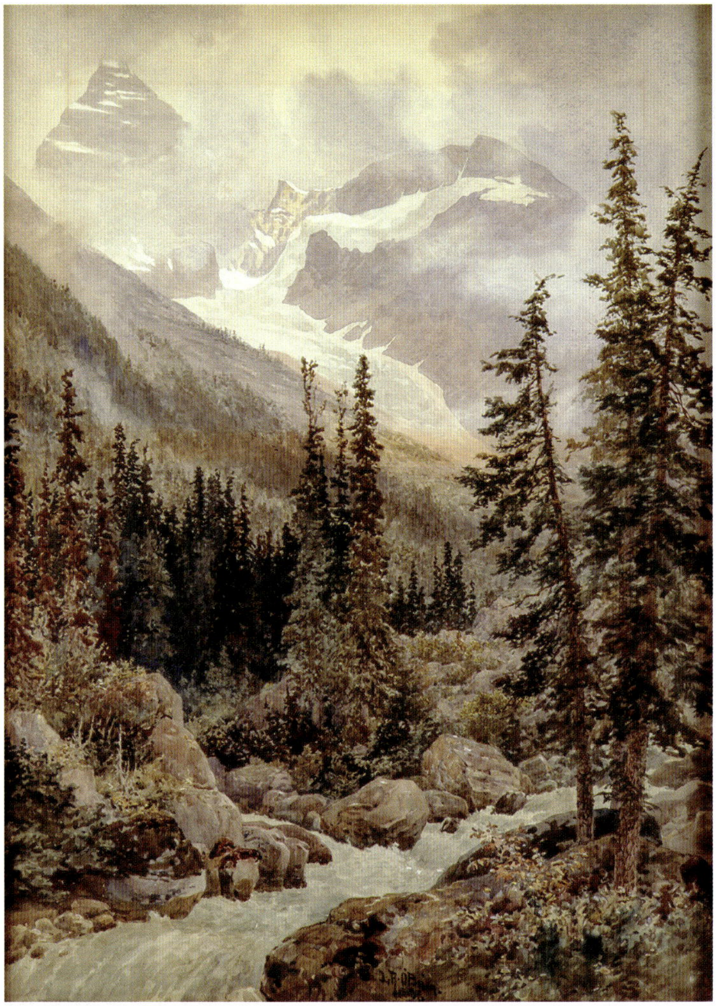

Lucius O'Brien
Cloud Capped Towers, 1886
watercolour
Glenbow Museum, Calgary

O'Brien travelled west the first year the CPR passes were offered. This dramatic image shows the grandeur and power of the mountains. O'Brien pays close attention to the composition. With the precision of meticulous drawing, the composition is carefully recorded. The moody, stormy sky envelops the mountains. The peaks, cut through by the age-old glaciers, tower above this. Making this a vertical composition heightens the effect of these very tall mountains. A grey-green, silted mountain stream cascading through rocky terrain widens as it flows towards us. O'Brien provides a detailed representation of trees, foliage, and underbrush in the foreground, while the background is more generalized—increasing both distance and perspective. In the middle distance is a tree-covered slope, which slices the composition at a sharp diagonal, creating two distinct zones of middle-ground and background. This diagonal increases the impact of the height of the mountains but also cuts off and isolates the distant mountains, increasing their inaccessibility, awe, and mystery in this dramatic, romantic image.

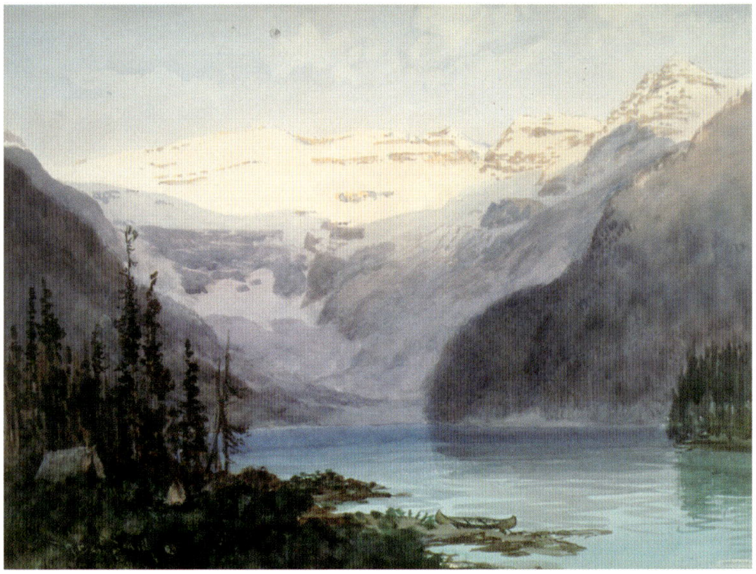

Frederic Marlett Bell-Smith
Morning, Lake Louise, 1889
watercolour
Glenbow Museum, Calgary

Bell-Smith was entranced with Lake Louise on his first trip to the Rockies with the American artist Alfred Bierstadt in 1887. Here he paints it as the early morning light catches the tops of snow-covered Mount Victoria in dazzling white, in vivid contrast to the rest of the scene bathed in a soft glow of reflected light with an azure sky overhead. The high mountains tower up from the lake creating a bowl-shaped cirque for the deep glacial lake in the centre. This enclosed protective space adds to the harmony of this peaceful scene. In the dark foreground, a figure in front of a fire with a tent behind is barely discernible. A lone canoe is pulled up at the water's edge. Bell-Smith has used a very fluid, wet watercolour technique in which forms soften and blend together. No detail or activity disturbs the conception of the still, serene composition. This harmony in blue and purple is a tour de force.

Robert Gagen

Rainstorm, Great Glacier, B.C., 1901

watercolour

Glenbow Museum, Calgary

This is a stormy, turbulent scene, with a snow-laden sky and wildly swaying trees. The mountains, seen through a veil of misty vapours, are only barely discernible at a great distance in the background. The drama is heightened by the contrast of the dark mass of the forest against the lighter, mist-shrouded mountains. The vertical composition accentuates our sense of the height and power of the mountains. A glacial stream, an icy emerald green flecked with white spray, emerges from the darkness of the forest below the mountains, cascading towards us through the rocky moraine. All of the forms have been rendered with quick, spontaneous brushstrokes, making them quite generalized, conveying a sense of the vitality and energy of a forbidding nature. This scene, with its brilliant rendition of atmosphere and light, is romantically charged and captures the terrible power of nature: wild, untamed, and dangerous.

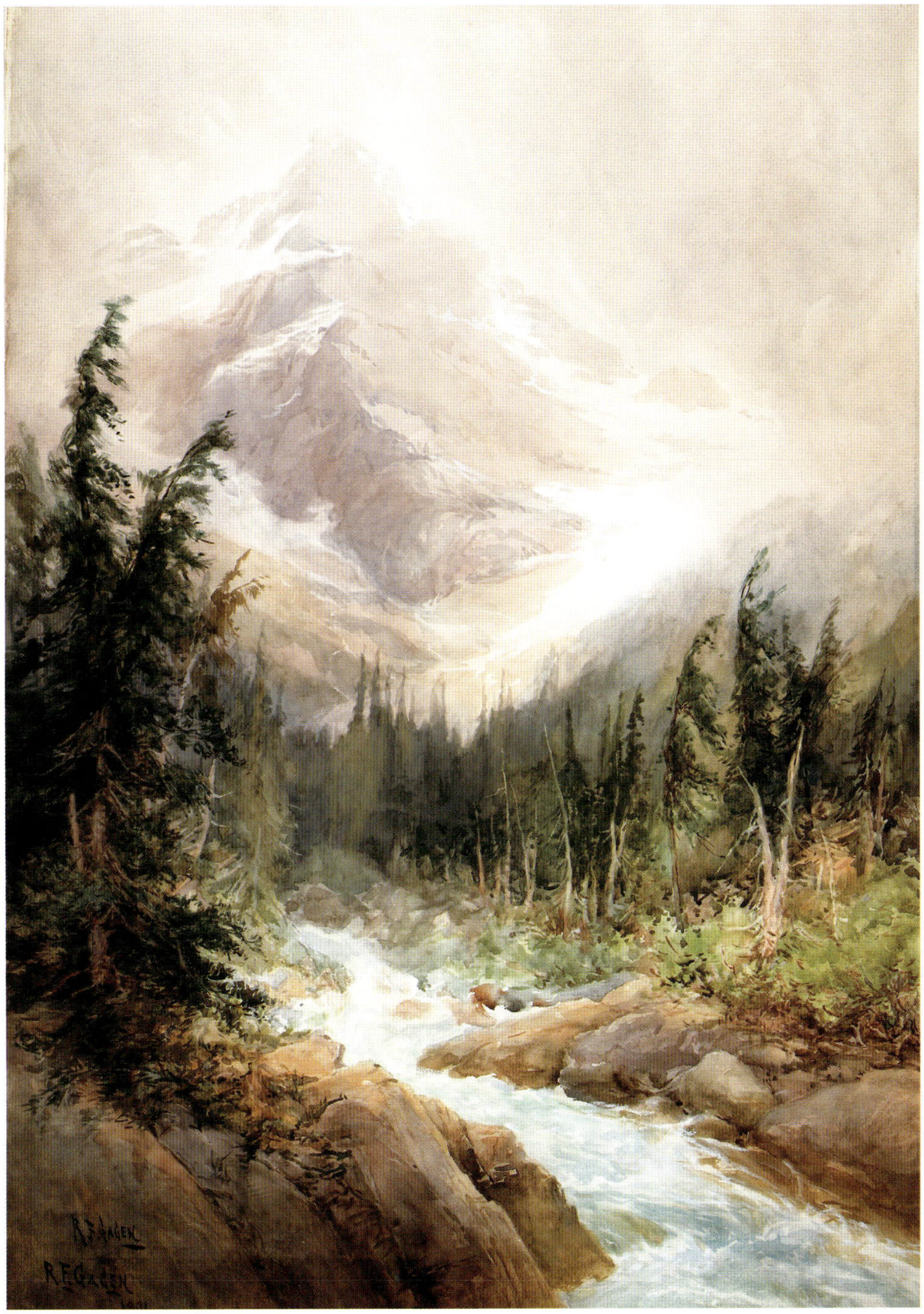

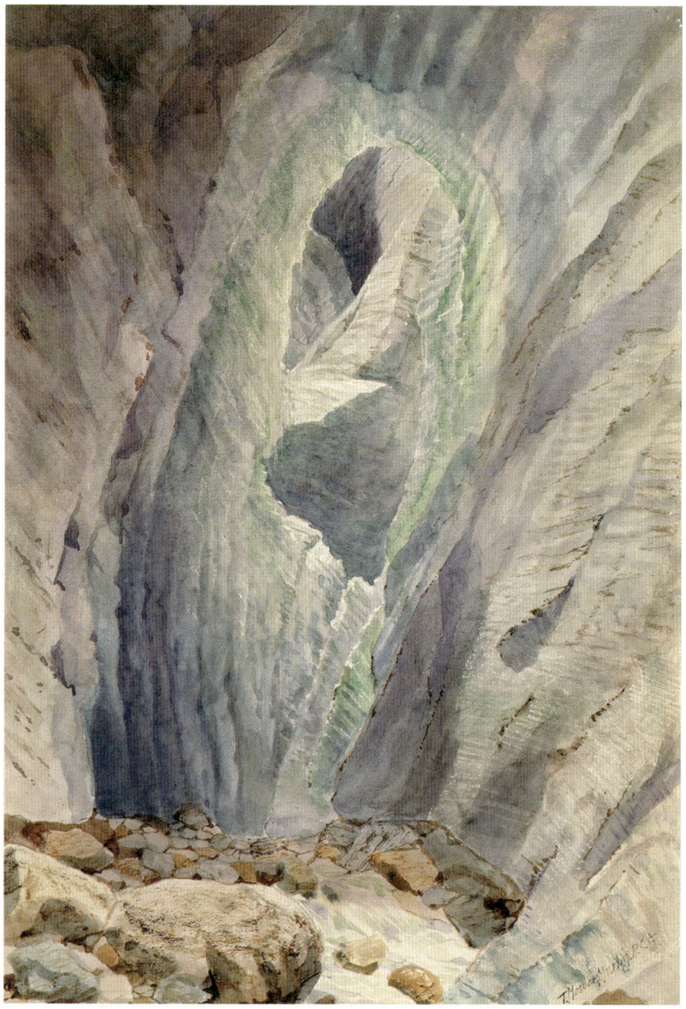

Thomas Mower Martin

Interior of the Great Illecillewaet Glacier, n.d.

watercolour

Glenbow Museum, Calgary

Martin's painting was often pedantic and contrived, but this is a unique and original image brilliantly rendered. It is complex to "read," appearing almost abstract in conception. The ice cave narrows at the far end to a strange vertical form in which there is a yawning cavern, revealing further openings into an abyss. Deep wedges are cut into the ice walls of the cave creating dark voids, mysterious and ominous. The forms are sketched in layered folds with a tight repetitive rhythm. There is no reference point to enlighten us as to the scale of the cave. The extraordinary colour of the translucent ice is a vivid emerald green painted with light transparent colour washes. This is an enigmatic, dramatic scene.

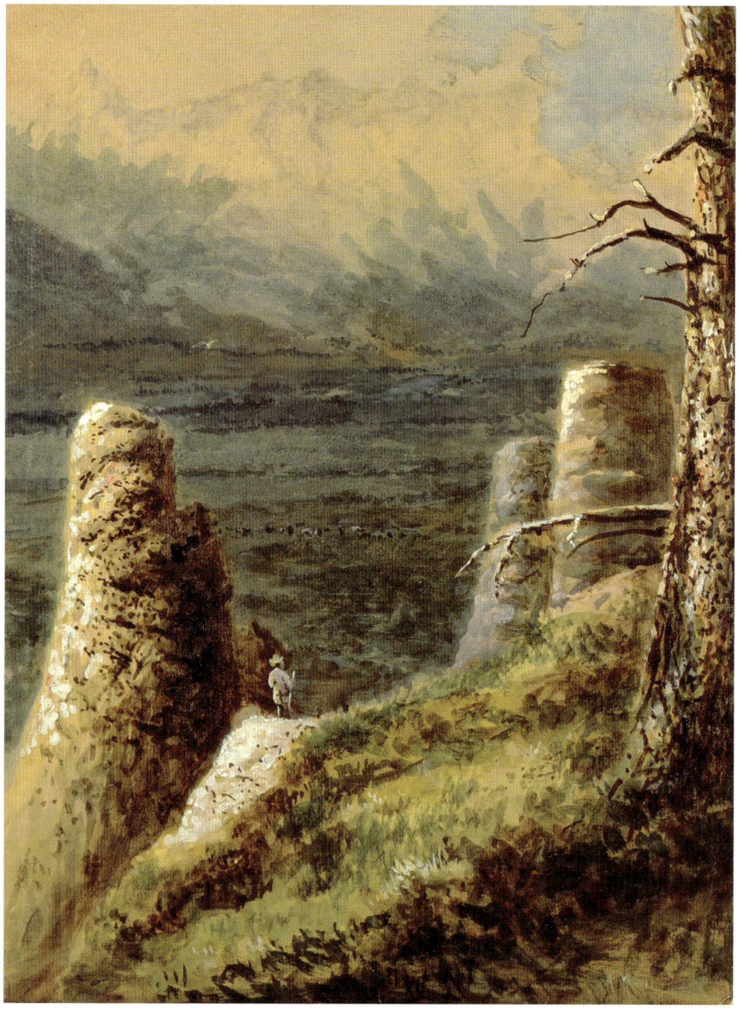

Marmaduke Matthews

Sunrise in the Hoodoos, Canmore, n.d.

watercolour

Glenbow Museum, Calgary

Matthews has depicted the strange forms of the eroded sandstone hoodoos along the Bow River. A pale early morning light highlights the hoodoos and grassland in the foreground. Between them, on a rocky outcrop, stands a melancholy man dwarfed by the landscape, contemplating the deep, dark, wide valley below him. There is only a faint outline of distant mountains. This is a romantic notion: diminutive man overawed by nature with its terrible forces. Despite Matthews's lofty intentions, this painting is rather poorly rendered. Some of the painting is overworked and laboured, while in the foreground the busy flicks of paint do not provide a coherent articulation of the forms. Matthews has used opaque paints, which deaden the surface compared with the usual transparency possible with watercolour.

John Hammond
The Three Sisters, ca. 1895
oil
Glenbow Museum, Calgary

In the 1890s, Hammond was commissioned by Van Horne to paint large murals depicting CPR's role in the West. This painting hung in CPR's Palliser Hotel in Calgary for many years until 1957 and was later purchased by the Glenbow Museum in 1960. The three mountain peaks tower above the surrounding landscape, thrusting upwards sharply from the earth, creating a strong visual rhythm. They are bathed in a soft, diffused evening light, which enhances their remoteness and inaccessibility. The strong diagonal of the dark low mountain in the middle distance creates even more space. A tiny plume of smoke to the left represents a train, labouring through the immense landscape—man's intrusion in nature as yet insignificant. The light plays delicately on the river and mud flats in the foreground. There is a stillness and momentary quietness in nature in this majestic and inspiring conception.

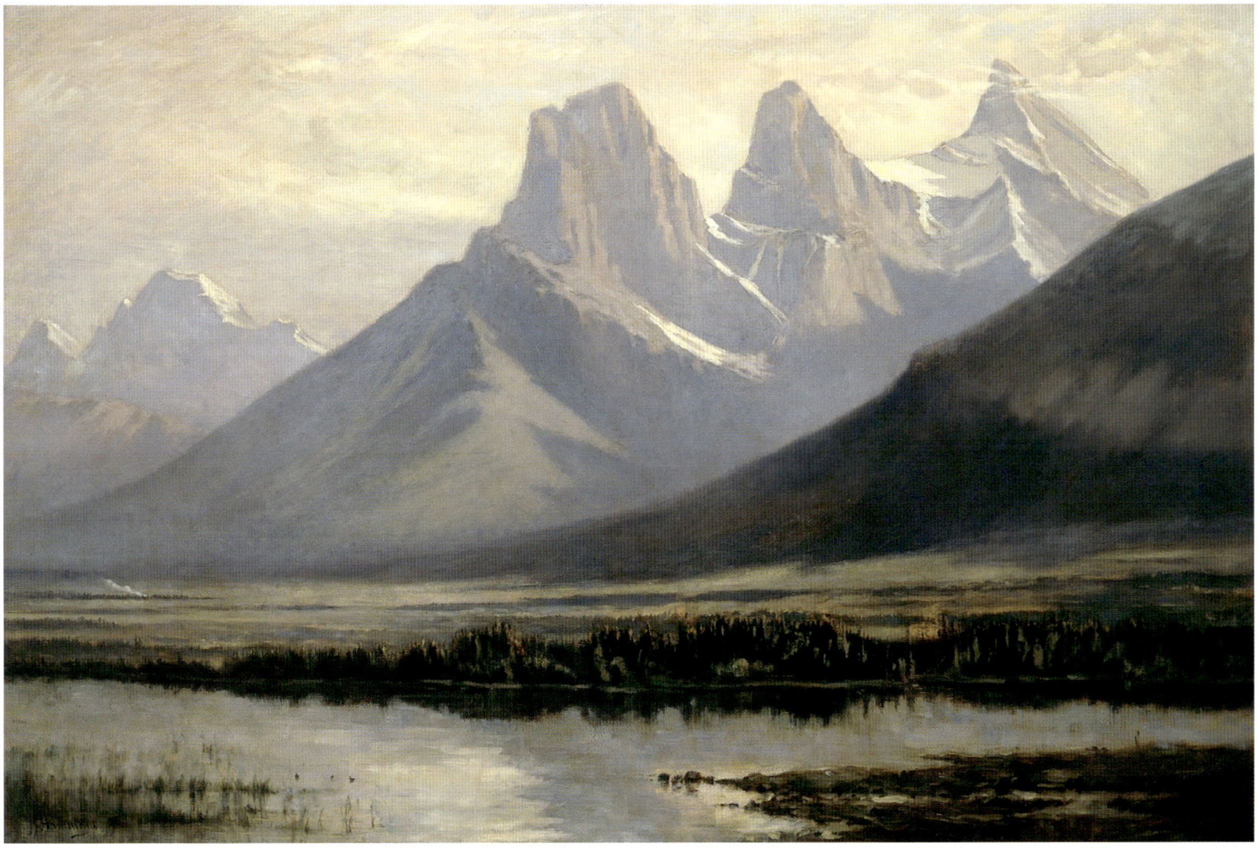

Other Visitors

A variety of visitors continued to be drawn west by the spectacular scenery, the Indigenous inhabitants, and the new communities opening up, especially once the railway was completed. Professional artists and talented amateurs made insightful records, and illustrators provided images for wide distribution to a receptive audience. Canadian illustrator Charles Jefferys, who worked in Toronto and New York, made six trips west between 1901 and 1924 and many of his illustrations of the West were published. Melton Prior, who worked for the *Illustrated London News* as a reporter-artist, visited the West twice, in 1888 and 1901. As a professor of geology at various universities in Ontario, Arthur Coleman started to explore the Rockies in 1884 and published books on his western research. Robert Rutherford was a member of the Royal Canadian Artillery, which mounted a campaign in the West in 1885 during the Riel Rebellion. As a member of the United States Coastal Survey, Cleveland Rockwell was involved in surveying large areas of Oregon and travelled throughout the West, producing significant visual records.

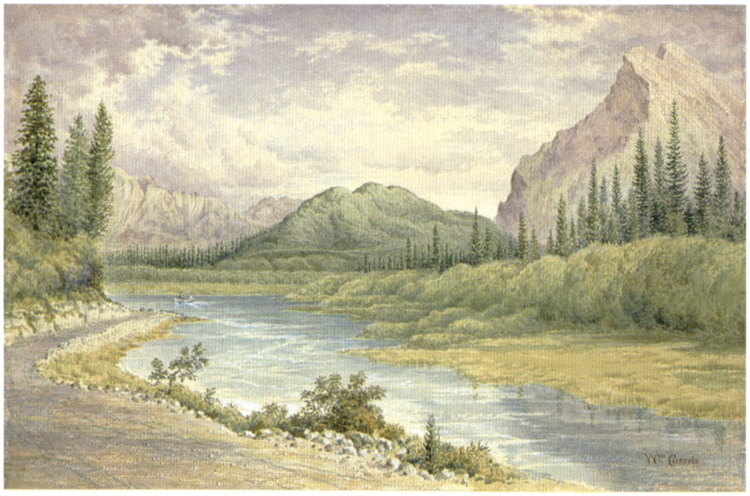

Walter Cassels
View of Mount Rundle, ca. 1860–70
watercolour
Glenbow Museum, Calgary

The artist has carefully delineated extensive detail in this charming topographical view. He has given us precise information about the view across Vermilion Lakes with the peak of Mount Rundle to the right and Tunnel Mountain in the centre.

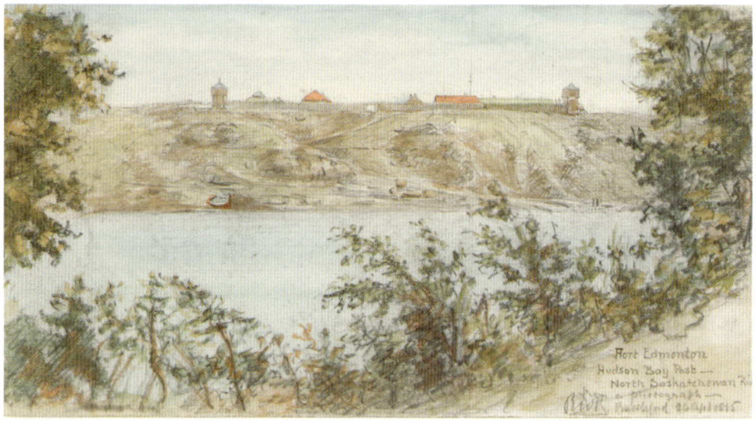

Robert Rutherford
Fort Edmonton, Hudson's Bay Post, 1885
watercolour and pencil
Glenbow Museum, Calgary

More than just a topographical view, this lively energetic sketch is quite impressionistic. The fort sits high up on the opposite bank, and the shrubs and trees on the riverbank in the foreground are simply rendered with quick pencil and brush marks: a very naturalistic effect of the tangled, vital growth. This image is based on a photograph by Cornelius J. Soule, taken in the summer of 1884.

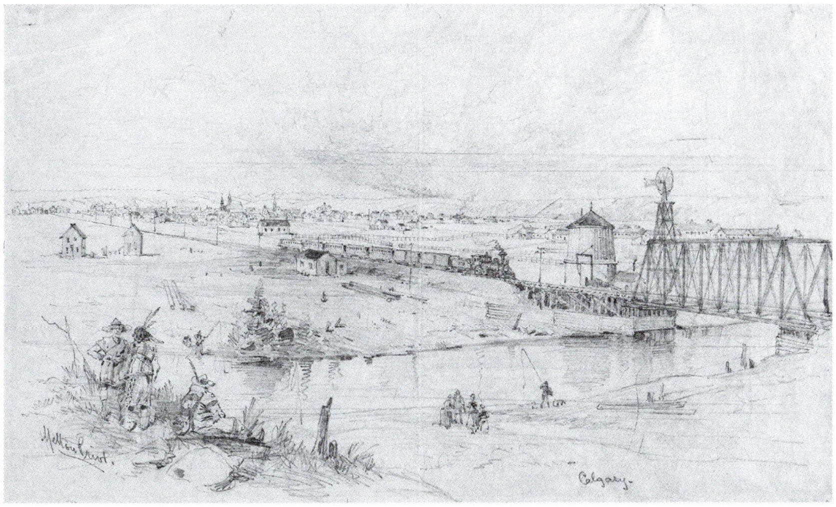

Melton Prior
View of Calgary, Alberta, ca. 1887
pencil
Glenbow Museum, Calgary

This drawing was the basis for an illustration that may have appeared in the *Illustrated London News*, bearing the title: "Calgary at the Foot of the Rocky Mountains, 2,262 miles west of Montreal." This is a delicate drawing taken from a hilltop showing the Elbow River spanned by the new CPR bridge with a train chugging toward it. The small town is shown to the left, the North-West Mounted Police barracks to the right, and the smoke, from the Eau Claire Mills on the Bow River, appears in the distance.

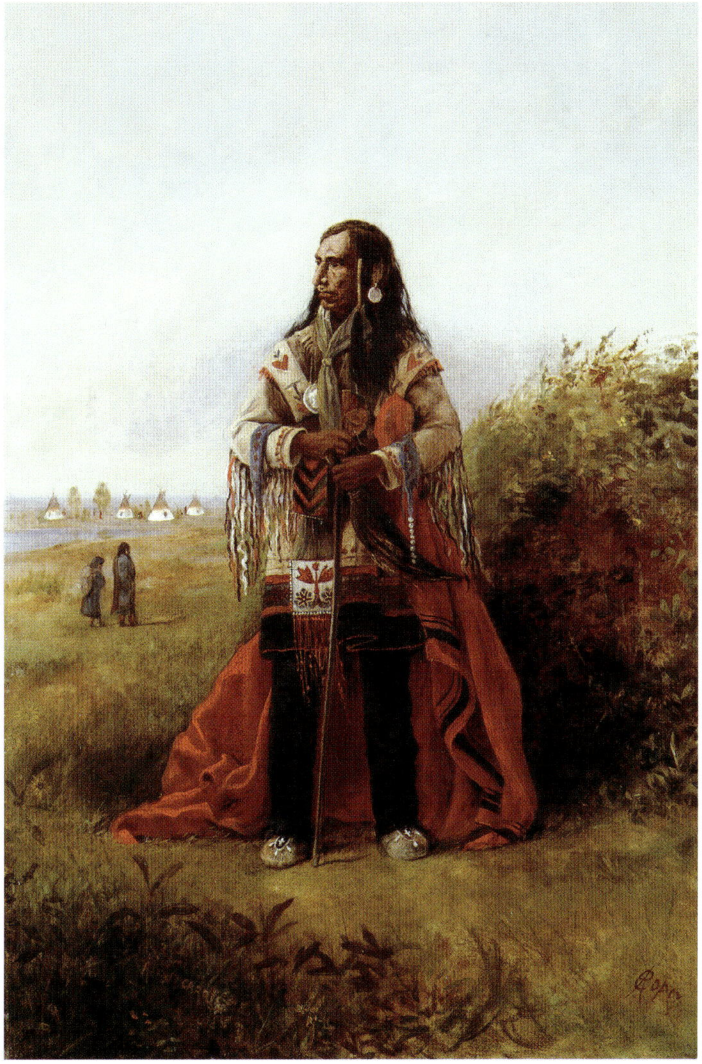

Edward Roper
Rabbit Carrier, Blackfoot Chief, ca. 1887
oil
Glenbow Museum, Calgary

Rabbit Carrier was a minor chief of the Blackfoot at Gleichen and a signatory to Treaty No. 7 in 1877. Roper depicts him in a blend of traditional and European attire. He wears a capote made from a Hudson's Bay blanket, and there is a treaty medal around his neck. He carries a fan and holds a chief's staff given to him at the treaty signing. He also wears a hair pipe and a large shell earring. By 1887, tribes were confined to the reserves and not allowed to hunt. The only hide items Rabbit Carrier still has are his pipe bag and moccasins. The cloth trousers are not traditional leggings. Roper has chosen to portray Rabbit Carrier as large and imposing in the foreground, staring nostalgically into the distance, implying his link with the past, eliciting the romantic view of the dying race, a popular notion in the nineteenth century.

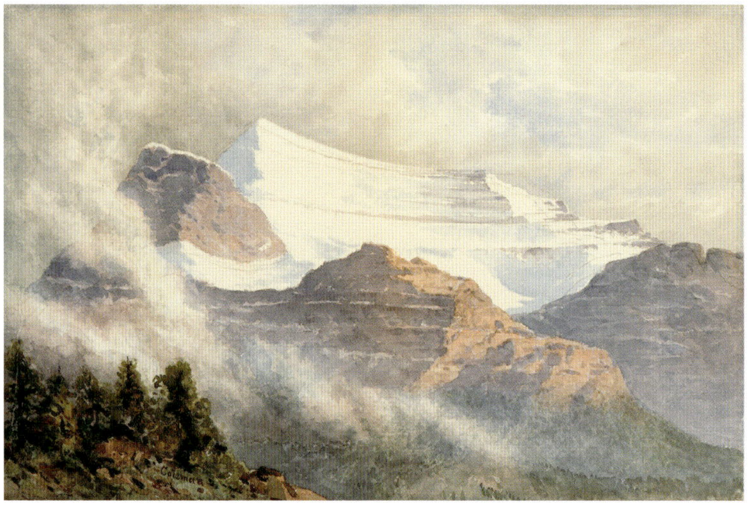

Arthur Coleman
Saskatchewan Mountain, n.d.
watercolour over pencil
Glenbow Museum, Calgary

Coleman had an intimate knowledge of the mountains through his scientific research and his climbing activities. This quickly made sketch, using a very fluid watercolour technique, captures the rugged mountain atmosphere.

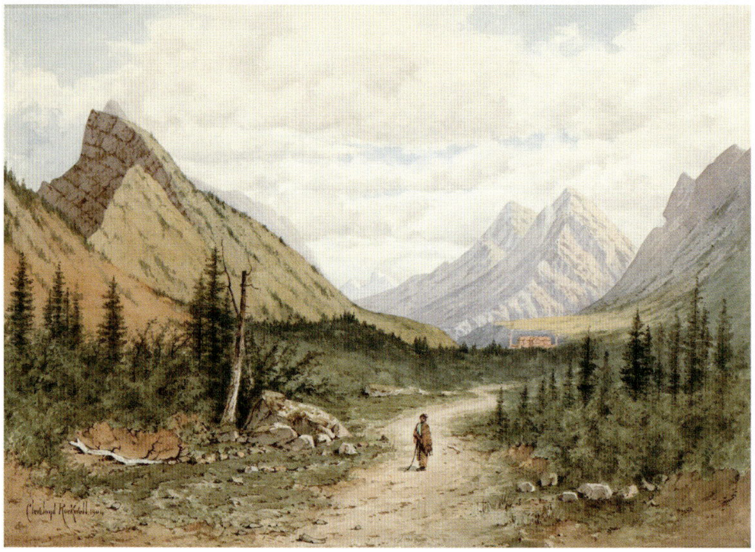

Cleveland Rockwell
Banff Springs Hotel, 1904
watercolour
Glenbow Museum, Calgary

This is a romantic early view of the hotel, nestled in the imposing mountains, with a lone figure in the foreground. The arc of the mountains draws the viewer's eye to the tiny hotel in the centre of the composition.

Edmund Morris
Bad Boy, Blood Indian, 1907
pastel
Glenbow Museum, Calgary

Morris was commissioned by various Canadian governments to produce portraits of First Nations individuals. This is a realistic, accurate, sensitive, and insightful portrait of Bad Boy, a young man in his prime, strong and healthy. The black pastel is carefully used to model the strong volumes of the face and applied heavily to the hat and black braids, dramatically framing the face. Fast drawing with summary detail of the figure brings full attention to the face, which is rendered in greater detail and with a thoughtful gaze.

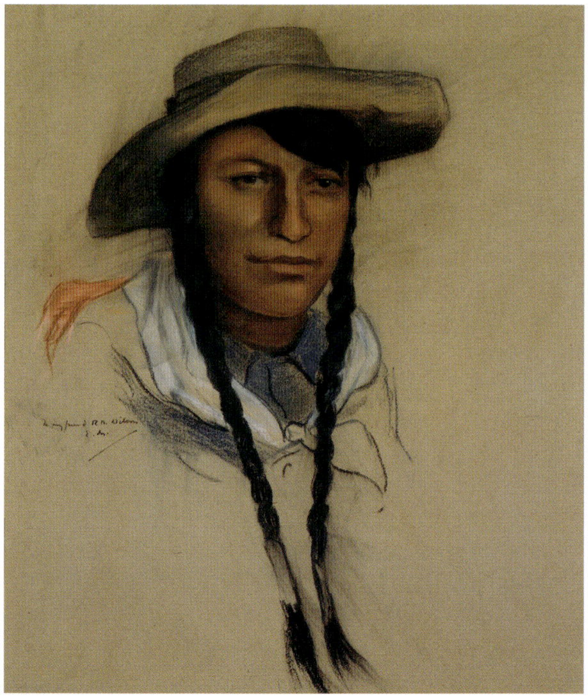

Charles Jefferys
Untitled (Western Town: Grain Elevators and Wagons), n.d.
watercolour and gouache
Glenbow Museum, Calgary

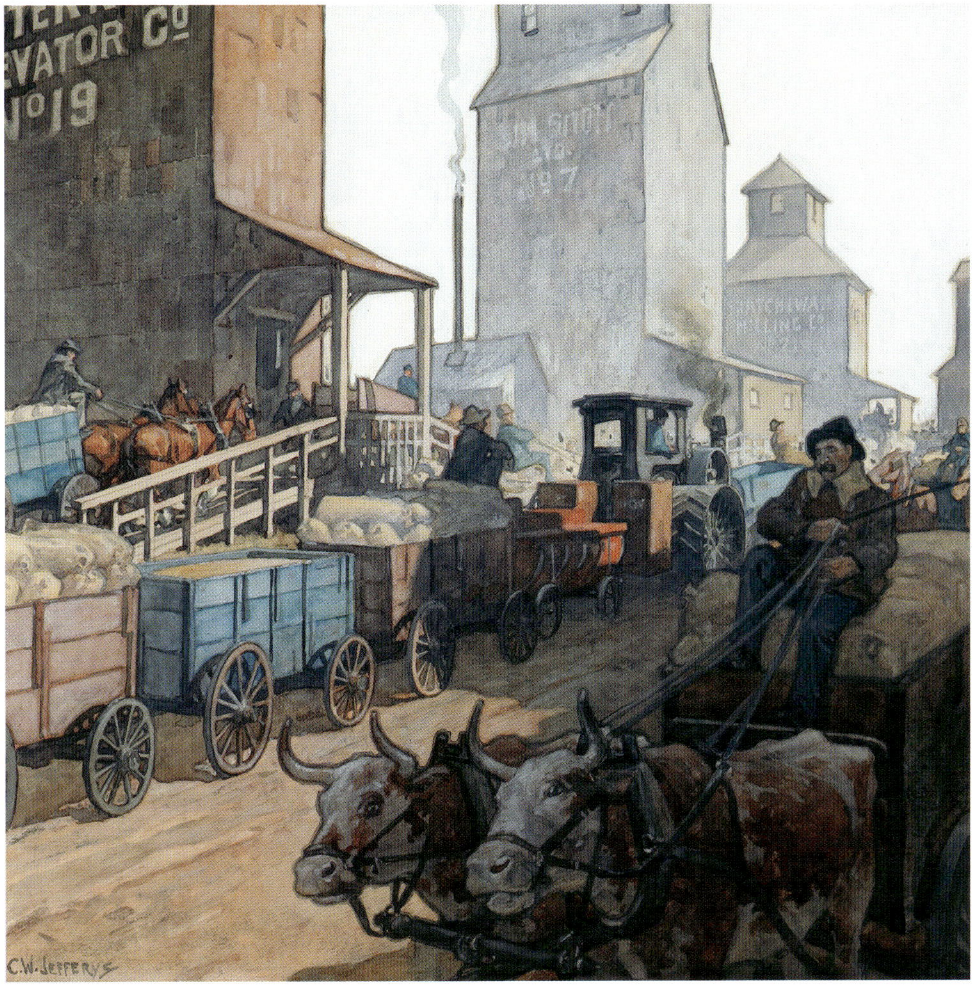

Canadian illustrator Jefferys was unusual at the time for his strong attachment to the prairies rather than the mountains. He produced paintings alive with the brilliant prairie light, which truly reflected the subtle beauty and simplicity of the prairies. He had done a number of fine landscape paintings of grain elevators and here combines this artistic approach with that of the illustrator to tell a story. There is a tremendous bustle as farmers bring their grain to the tall, impressive elevators. Oxen and horses strain to pull the heavy loads, but Jefferys also shows that farming is in transition, with a tractor pulling a string of carts. The well-composed elements and heavier lighting in the foreground imbues the scene with a dramatic intensity in this evocative image.

Notes: The Historical Period to 1920

1. Text courtesy of the Glenbow Museum, interpretation by Rosie Runner, 1957.
2. Paul Kane, *Wanderings of an Artist Among the Indians of North America* (London: Longman, Brown, Green, Longmans, and Roberts, 1859) 83.
3. F. M. Bell-Smith, *Macleans Magazine* xxv: 2 (December 1912).

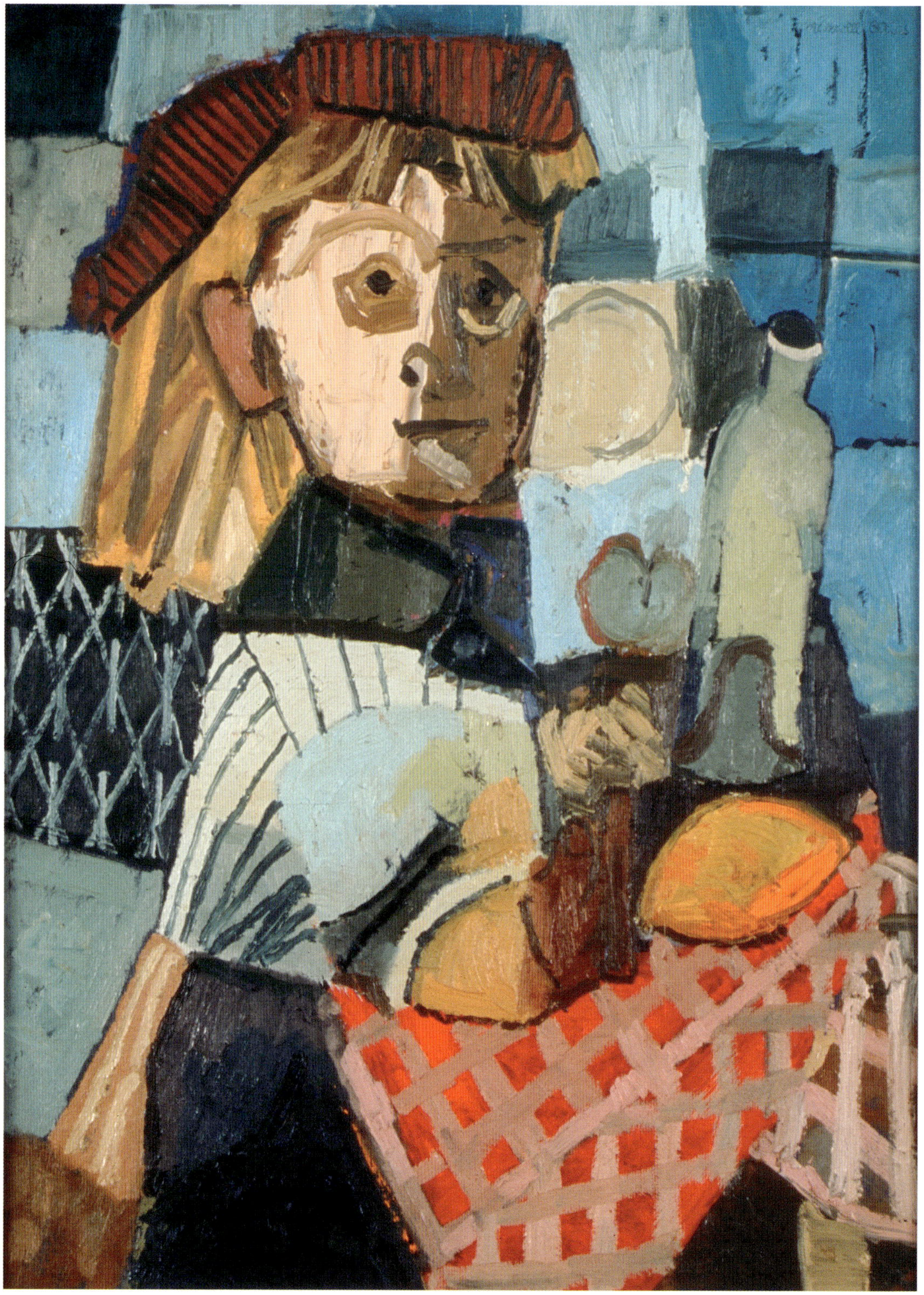

Maxwell Bates / *Girl with Yellow Hair*, n.d. / oil / Glenbow Museum, Calgary

A SENSE OF PLACE: MODERN ART 1920–1970

Patricia Ainslie

Establishing a Place for Art

It was not until the 1920s that art gained a foothold in Alberta. The first full-time art classes in Alberta began in 1927 at the Provincial Institute of Technology and Art in Calgary. A two-year program was offered, with courses in fine and applied art, including oil and watercolour painting, decorative design, and lettering. Previous to this, from the institute's inception in 1916, art was limited to technical drawing classes. Art courses for teachers were introduced in 1921. Lars Haukaness, a Norwegian artist who had been influenced as a student by modern art movements, including Impressionism, began to teach full-time at the institute in 1927. He introduced his students to modern art and had a significant impact on two of them: William Stevenson and Maxwell Bates.

After Lars Haukaness's untimely death in 1929, the accomplished British artist Alfred Leighton took over the art department. Leighton provided a rigorous academic training for his students with an emphasis on draughtsmanship. Leighton committed considerable energy to the growth of the school, teaching both day and night classes, but he left the institute in 1935 due to ill health. Both Leighton and Haukaness laid the first solid foundations for professional art instruction in Calgary.

Prior to the 1920s, there had only been amateur art groups operating in Alberta. Some exhibitions were held at agricultural fairs, and the 1912 Calgary Stampede included an exhibit of the work of Montana cowboy artist Charles Russell. In Calgary, the formation of a sketch club, first started in 1909, led to the short-lived Calgary Art Association that existed from 1912 to 1914. The Calgary Art Club, which held workshops and exhibitions, was established in 1922. The Edmonton Art Association was established in 1914 and the Edmonton Museum of Arts in 1924. After initiatives by various groups, Leighton founded the Alberta Society of Artists in 1931, drawing members from earlier art associations created in the province. This prestigious society set high standards through its selective membership and regular juried exhibits. In 1933, and from 1948 until the late 1960s, the society published *Highlights* magazine to foster communication about Alberta art. The society established links with the national Royal Canadian Academy. Leighton initiated summer art courses at Seebe, Alberta, in 1933, which led to the formation of the Banff School of Fine Arts.

With Leighton's illness, Henry Glyde, his colleague from Britain, took over the art program at the institute in Calgary in 1936. He trained a new generation of artists, many Alberta-born, including Stanford Perrott and Luke Lindoe. Dedicated to education, he spent the next thirty years teaching in the province, making a lasting contribution. He spent a decade building the fledgling art program at the institute, as well as art programming at the Banff School of Fine Arts and widespread communities across the province. He moved to Edmonton in 1946 to develop the art program at the University of Alberta. He was a disciplinarian who provided a thorough grounding in technique and urged students to see and think for themselves.

In southern Alberta, the first art teacher in Lethbridge was Edith Fanny Kirk, who arrived there around 1916. Jessie Ursenbach was one of her pupils and a founding member of the Lethbridge Sketch Club in 1936. The club held regular exhibitions and in 1950 became part of the Western Canada Art Circuit, showing their circulated national and international exhibitions. A number of artists, including Ursenbach, won scholarships over the years to attend the Banff Summer School. In 1938, the first regular summer classes offered by the University of Alberta Extension Department were held in Lethbridge. Most of the classes were taught by Henry Glyde, but after 1943 Walter Phillips taught some. The Sketch Club was very active through the 1950s.

A. Y. Jackson, a founding member of the Group of Seven, made a contribution to the development of art in Lethbridge when he made summer visits to his brother Ernest during the 1930s. Sketch Club members were entertained in Ernest's home and Jackson showed them his latest work. He also accompanied club members on local outings. Another important contributor to art in Lethbridge was engineer Frederick Cross, an accomplished watercolour artist, who had exhibited internationally. Though not a member of the Sketch Club, he offered valuable criticism to club members, who often gathered in his home.

In Lethbridge, full-time visual arts education was not available until the 1960s. It was not until 1966 that Pauline McGeorge, a graduate of the University of California at Berkeley, was hired as the first full-time instructor in the art department at the Lethbridge Junior College. She transferred to the University of Lethbridge when it became independent from the college in 1967. In the late 1960s, other instructors joined the staff of the university: Alfred Gimse taught sculpture and ceramics; Herb Hicks taught painting and design; Larry Weaver taught ceramics; and Charlie Crane taught art history. A small art gallery was set up as a teaching gallery in 1967, which had a schedule of fifteen exhibits during the 1968–69 year. Early gifts to the collection included works by Sorel Etrog and A. Y. Jackson. Students also had access to the Roloff Beny collection of modern European art, including Picasso, Braque, and Matisse.

In Medicine Hat, the art club was established in 1945. Early visiting instructors included Henry Glyde and Walter Phillips. Hope Johnson was the club's local instructor. A number of artists from the club, including John Barrie and Roloff Beny, studied at the Banff School of Fine Arts. However, it was not until the late 1970s, when the Medicine Hat Museum and Art Gallery opened, that there was a permanent place to exhibit. Medicine Hat's most famous son, Roloff Beny, left the city immediately upon graduation from high school to study in Toronto, Iowa, and New York. He went on to build an international reputation as a photographer, with residences in Lethbridge, New York, and Rome.

The City of Red Deer's Art Club was formed in the late 1940s. It benefited from the University of Alberta Extension program when professional artists like Henry Glyde and Harry Wohlfarth came to town to teach. But development was slow and mainly amateur and, apart from printmaker James Agrell Smith, there were no significant artists working in Red Deer until the 1970s. It was not until 1973 that Red Deer College had an art department—established by Ian Cook. Before that, Red Deer College provided community interest courses through continuing education and some diploma credit courses in painting and drawing.

Meanwhile, back in Calgary, the institute continued its art program through the 1930s. During the Second World War, the art department at the institute was relocated to the large Coste House in the Mount Royal neighbourhood. An exhibition program was started in 1942. After the war, Glyde spearheaded the establishment of the Calgary Allied Arts Centre at Coste House in 1946, directed by Archie Key. It embraced various cultural groups, including artists, writers, and the Calgary Civic Theatre. It proceeded to play a major role in the arts in Calgary, organizing classes and workshops and hosting exhibits. The Calgary Allied Arts Centre moved downtown in 1960 and remained active until 1969.

An important contribution to the Calgary art scene was the establishment of Canadian Art Galleries by John and Grace Turner in 1945, the first commercial gallery in Calgary. The gallery provided important support and encouragement, supplied artists' materials, and showed the work of local and national artists. After the war, artists from outside of Alberta infused new energy into the community. Vancouver artist Jock Macdonald taught at the institute in both 1946 and 1947, and his idea of automatic drawing had a significant impact on Calgary artist Marion Nicoll. In 1947, Macdonald was succeeded by Illingworth Kerr, who had trained in the 1920s with the Group of Seven artists and then in the 1930s in London, England, and came to Calgary from Vancouver. He was head of the school for twenty years. With the influx of war veterans, the school grew quickly and soon there were four staff members by 1948. Luke Lindoe taught painting, sculpture, and ceramics; Marion Nicoll taught design and craft; Stanford Perrott taught life drawing, design, and art history; and Stanford Blodgett taught commercial art. The art department at the institute was renamed the Alberta College of Art in 1960.

In September 1960, the University of Alberta at Calgary was established with an art division run by Helen Stadelbauer, assisted by Eric Dodd. Harry Kiyooka joined the division in 1961. In 1966, the university achieved autonomy from the University of Alberta in Edmonton and was renamed the University of Calgary. The following year a faculty of fine arts was established for art, music, and drama with a four-year bachelor of fine arts (BFA) program. The department of art, headed by Eric Dodd, grew rapidly, with new programs and workshops. In 1968, new professors were hired: Ken Esler for printmaking and Ronald Spickett for painting.

Though the Calgary Allied Arts Centre built a collection of art, primarily works by local talent, another significant development for the future of art in Alberta was the creation of the Glenbow Foundation. In 1954, wealthy oilman Eric Harvie established the Glenbow Foundation in Calgary, and began an international collection. The art collection focused on western Canadian art, including works by Paul Kane, Emily Carr, and Walter Phillips. When the Calgary Allied Arts Centre closed in 1969, their collections were transferred to Glenbow. In 1969, the Glenbow Art Gallery opened with three exhibition spaces and over fourteen thousand works of art. In 1978, it was consolidated with a museum, library, and archives at its current location on 8th Avenue, SE.

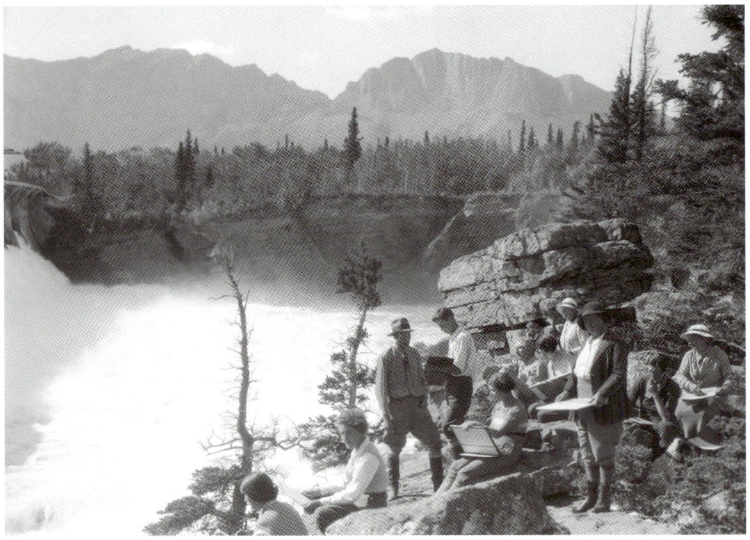

Byron Harmon
A. C. Leighton art class near Seebe Dam, ca. 1935
photograph
Whyte Museum of the Canadian Rockies, Banff, NA-71-4292

Leighton is shown standing with his back to the river.

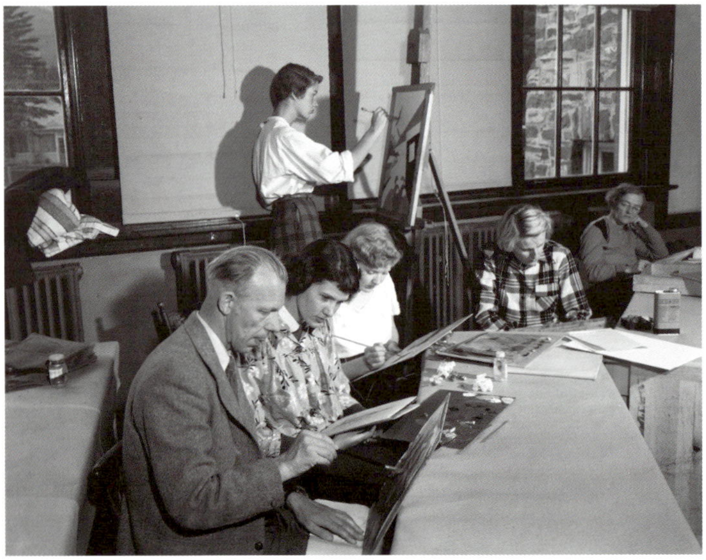

Bill Gibbons
Glyde's Studio, ca. 1949
photograph
Whyte Museum of the Canadian Rockies, Banff, V227/2563

In Banff, Glyde worked both outdoors and indoors with his students.

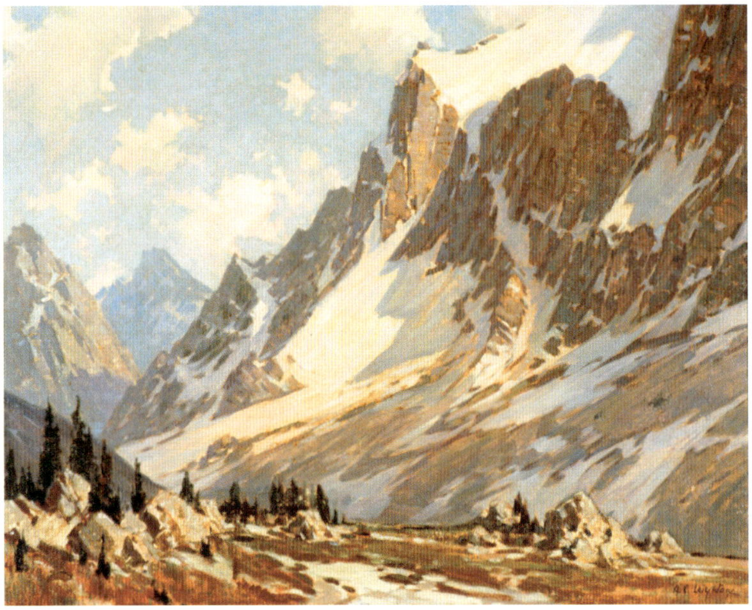

Alfred C. Leighton
Goodsir Plateau, ca. 1955
oil
Alberta Foundation for the Arts, Edmonton, Alberta

Leighton was a master draughtsman and here has caught the brilliance of the spring light on a clear bright day, with impressionistic sun-speckled clouds in this naturalistic scene. The majestic, craggy mountains tower above the valley where most of the winter snow has melted, revealing the red tones of both the earth and the dogwood. The sun illuminates the mountainside with its dazzling snow, casts long shadows, and picks out the fissures in the rock. He has counterpoised the flat, insignificant foreground with the impressive sweep of the mountains, enhancing their bulk and power, creating a great sense of depth and distance.

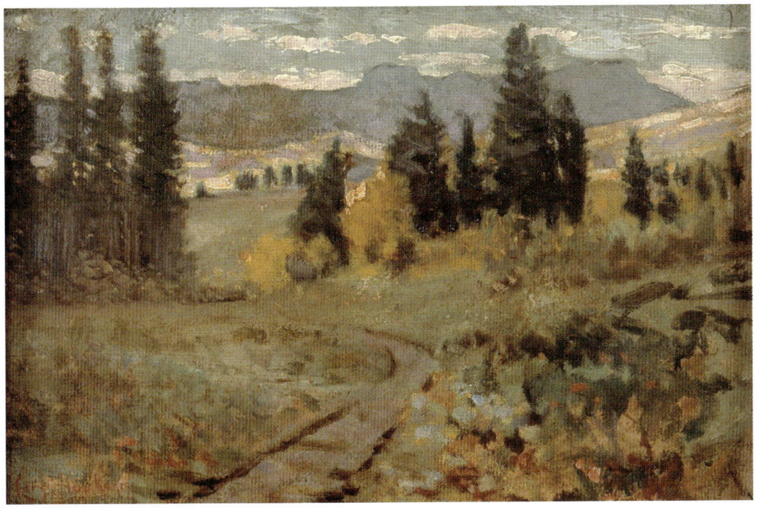

Lars Haukaness
Bow Valley at Morley, n.d.
oil
Glenbow Museum, Calgary

Despite the influence of modernism on his work and the use of loose brushstrokes here, this painting remains somewhat heavy and dark, a contrast to Impressionism's intense study of light and colour. Haukaness has built the basic structure of the composition with broad colour areas. Over this he has laid quick brushstrokes that provide nuance and detail, with thick white impasto representing the clouds in the sky. The foreground surface is broken up in an impressionistic manner with small dabs of colour juxtaposed for the eye to fuse at a distance.

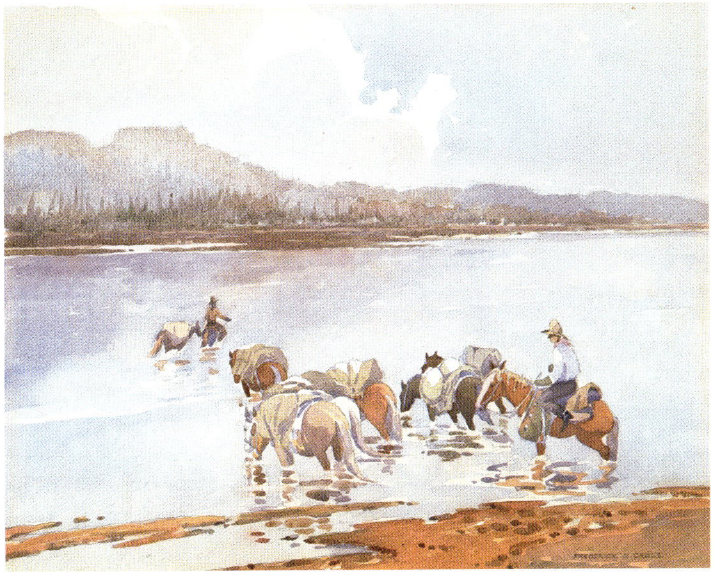

Frederick Cross
Fording the River, 1935
watercolour over pencil
Glenbow Museum, Calgary

An accomplished watercolourist, Cross has applied extraordinarily delicate, thin watercolour washes. He has captured the essential details in the work with an economy and brevity of mark-making. He has laid in the broad areas of the water, distant hills, and sky, and then with great visual acuity has painted in the precise details of the horses and riders. Their reflections are small pools of paint. Though precise, the elements are never laboured. He has used the white of the paper effectively, and the paper's texture creates a slight stipple effect. This is a harmonious integrated composition.

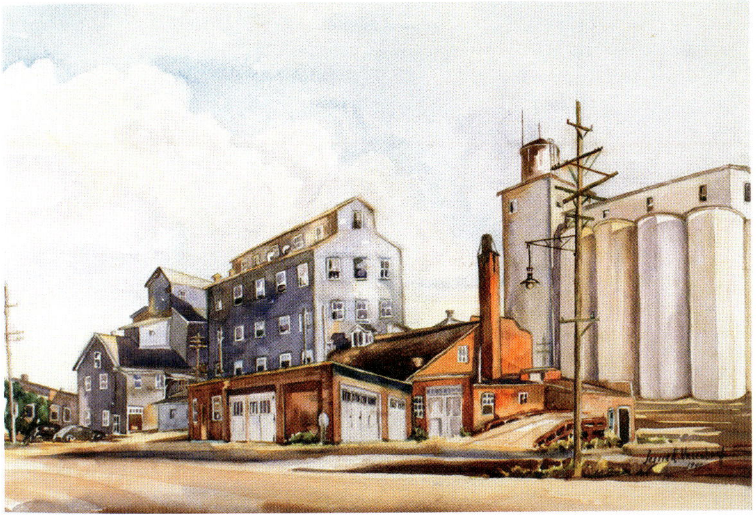

Jessie Ursenbach
Ellison Mills, 1940
watercolour
Alberta Foundation for the Arts, Edmonton

This industrial image is unusual in Alberta art. It features both the grain elevator with its concrete silos and the mill that processes the grain. It is a carefully delineated composition, which effectively represents the bulk of the buildings, and is filled in with thin colour washes enhancing the volume of the structures. In places, the watercolour pools add texture to the forms. This is a strong cogent image, showing an important aspect of Alberta's industrial life.

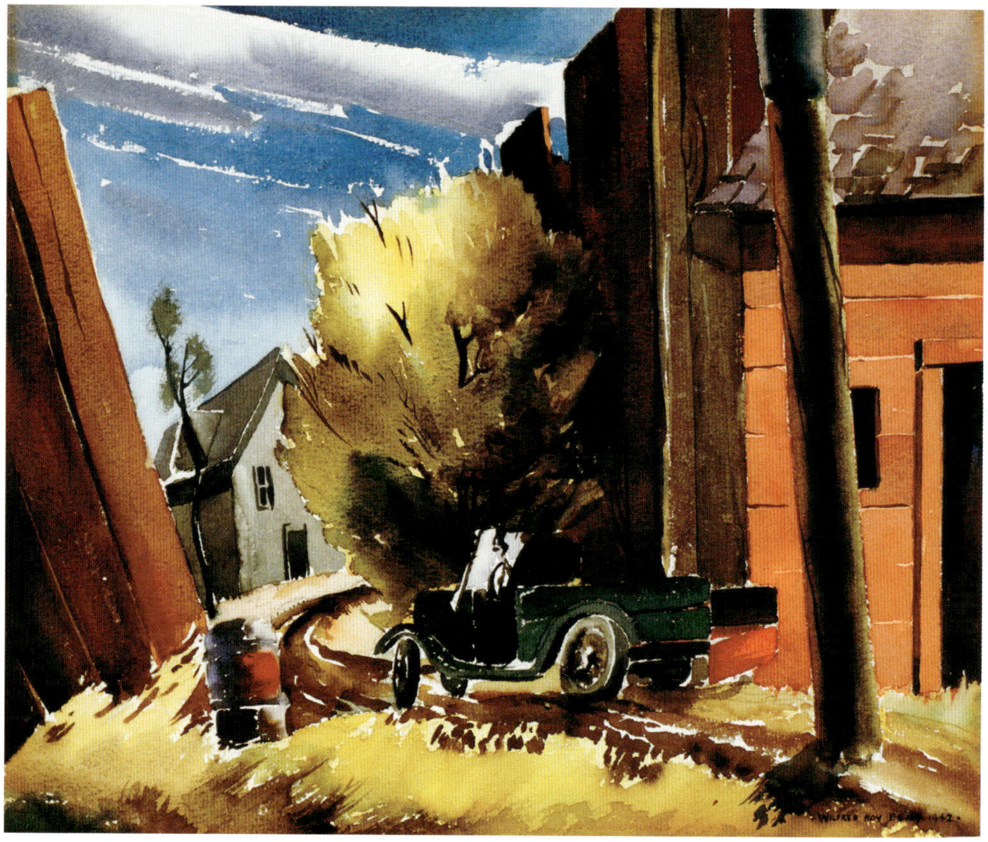

Roloff Beny
Unruly Corner, March 1942
watercolour over pencil
University of Lethbridge Art Gallery

Eighteen-year-old Beny produced this exceptional, dynamic work. The title is witty with the 1940s-style truck approaching a dangerous corner in the road in this well-structured composition. His technique with watercolour is quickly rendered and light. Fast, transparent watercolour washes are applied, pooling in places to create shadow and texture. Strong colour adds vitality to this imaginative watercolour. This work was selected by the National Gallery of Canada for an exhibit that toured nationally with the Canadian Society of Painters in Water Colour.

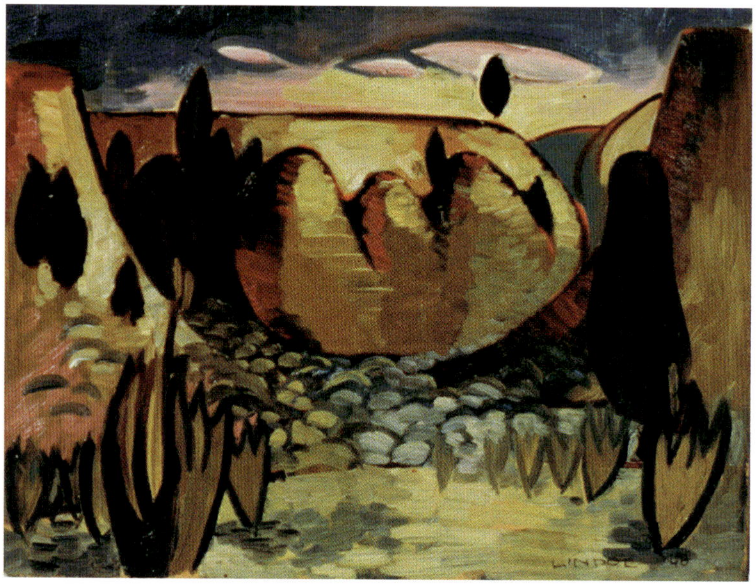

Luke Lindoe
South of Kamloops, 1948
oil
Alberta Foundation for the Arts, Edmonton

Lindoe takes a modernist approach in the way he simplifies all of the elements of the composition. The hills are rounded and modelled, the distant trees simple ovoid shapes, flames of energy and growth, while those in the foreground are graphically rendered in outline. The forms have heavy, black, expressive outlines. The dark oppressive sky, illuminated from behind the mountains, gives this scene a sense of foreboding. Animated brushwork portrays the energy of nature.

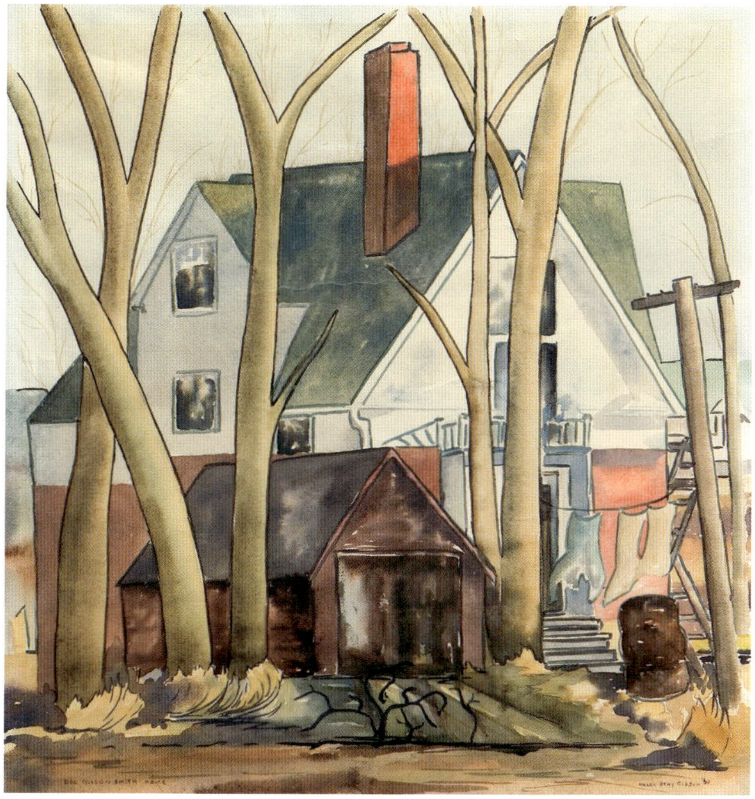

Helen Beny Gibson
Doc. Alison Smith Home (Medicine Hat), 1960
watercolour
Medicine Hat Museum and Art Gallery

This painting may be loosely based on one by Winnipeg artist LeMoine FitzGerald, entitled *Doc Snyder's House*, from 1931. It has a similar composition with the house seen through a screen of trees, though Gibson focuses on only one house, rather than on the group as in FitzGerald's work. Yet she uses the same stark bare trees as a compositional device to denote the foreground, with the big house behind. The composition is strongly structured with the forms carefully delineated to create volume and mass in space. Using a very light touch, she has applied fluid watercolour washes, some thin and transparent, others heavier and dark, full of pigment.

Hope Johnson
Untitled (South of Suffield), 1963
oil
Medicine Hat Museum and Art Gallery

Johnson's work fuses many interests in art, geology, and palaeontology. With her practice of careful scientific observation, she shows her visual experience of the badlands of Alberta with their strata of alternating layers of shale and sandstone, worn down by wind and water erosion over the millennia. She includes botanical details of tiny native plants in the foreground. This is a carefully structured composition of the characteristic stark, barren landscape. The colour reflects the sun-bleached forms of this arid area.

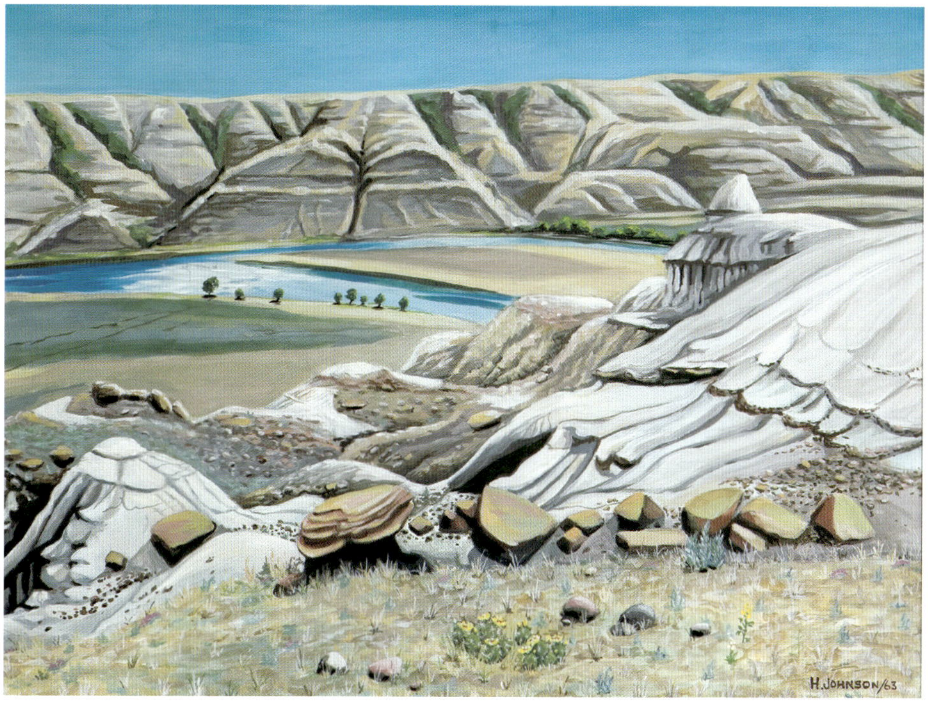

Banff Art and Artists

Banff's unique mountain environment has been a magnet for artists. Initially they just passed through, recording the spectacular scenery. CPR brought trainloads of tourists and developed the Banff Springs Hotel. Trail Riders of the Canadian Rockies and Skyline Hikers were set up and made annual trips into the mountains. Skiing became popular. Indian Days with a rodeo was advertised in Banff. The annual winter carnival in February featured outdoor activities.

As the small settlement of Banff grew, artists began to settle there. The first to arrive in 1903 was photographer Byron Harmon. Harmon was followed by Carl Rungius in 1910 and photographer Mary Schäffer in 1912. In 1930, Catharine Whyte, newly married to artist husband Peter Whyte, arrived, along with Charles Beil. They created a tight-knit supportive artistic community. Peter Whyte was born in Banff in 1905, the first native of Banff to become an artist.

Banff became a magnet for other artists in the province. With his strong commitment to fostering the development of artists, A. C. Leighton initiated summer art courses at Seebe, Kananaskis, in 1933, attended by Marion Nicoll and Stanford Perrott. This opportunity to work out of doors, guided by Leighton's instruction, enhanced the artists' study of nature. In 1935, Leighton moved classes to Banff and shared facilities with the fledgling theatre school. Henry Glyde took over from Leighton in 1936. That year, the art, drama, and music administrations were combined under the title the Banff School of Fine Arts, directed by Donald Cameron and under the aegis of the University of Alberta Extension Department. Students came from the Provincial Institute of Technology and Art, the University of Alberta, and from across Canada. Additional artists were brought in to teach, including Walter Phillips in 1940, and A. Y. Jackson in 1943. After the Second World War, following a dramatic increase in enrolment, international artists were invited to the Banff School of Fine Arts, including Frederic Taubes from New York, who taught there from 1948 to 1950, and William Townsend from England. Townsend first came in 1951 and in many subsequent years until his death in 1973.

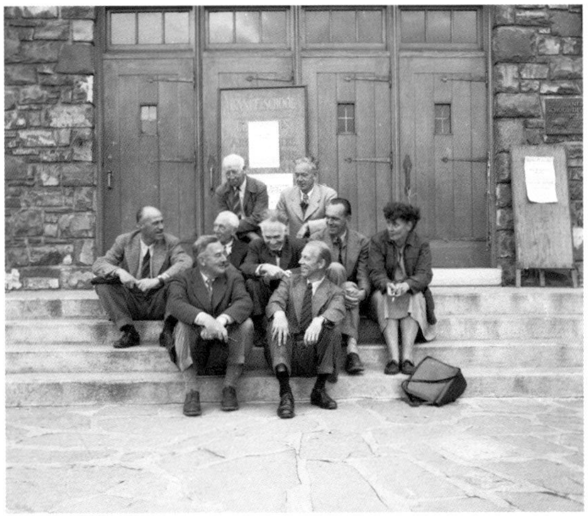

Bill Gibbons

Henry Glyde and colleagues at the Banff School of Fine Arts, ca. 1947

Whyte Museum of the Canadian Rockies, Banff, V227-2469

Back row (left to right): A. Y. Jackson, J. W. G. Macdonald; middle row (left to right): George Pepper, James Dichmont, André Biéler, Murray MacDonald, Marion Nicoll; front row (left to right): Walter Phillips, Henry Glyde.

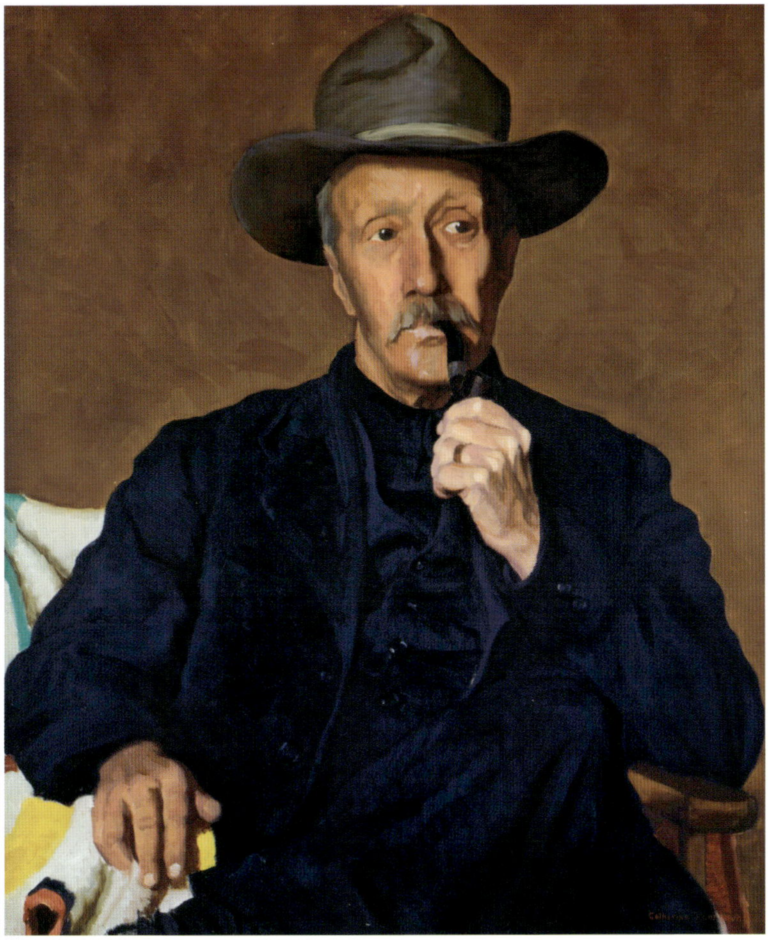

Catharine Whyte
Tom Wilson, 1932
oil
Whyte Museum of the Canadian Rockies, Banff

Tom Wilson, a guide and outfitter, was a friend of the Whytes in Banff. Here he is shown in a pensive mood smoking his pipe. The volume and mass of his face are carefully modelled and his features delineated, his rugged workman's hands accentuated. The folds of his clothes follow the slump of his body as he relaxes in the chair. The lack of detail in the background brings full attention to the figure. Catharine Whyte has not only captured his likeness, but also his character. He bears the stoic calm of a man of the mountains.

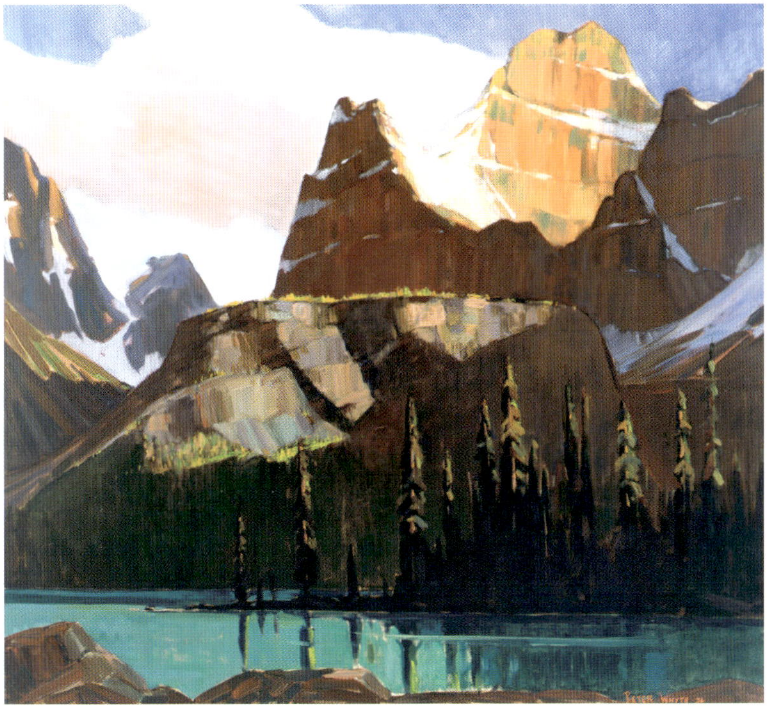

Peter Whyte
Lake O'Hara and Mount Biddle, 1937
oil
Whyte Museum of the Canadian Rockies, Banff

Peter and Catharine Whyte spent many hours outdoors, often working together on the same scene, studying the landscape and producing small oil sketches capturing the exact light and atmospheric conditions at a given time on a given day. These sketches, such as *Lake O'Hara*, were worked up into large finished canvasses in the studio. In this finished work, the horizontal scene is compressed, accentuating the high impressive peaks. The powerful geometric forms of the mountains, with their facetted angles, soar upwards, bathed in the brilliant sunlight. The upright trees fringing the lake mimic this vertical thrust. Forms are sharply delineated in the crisp mountain air against the luminous blue sky. This is a vivid image of great clarity.

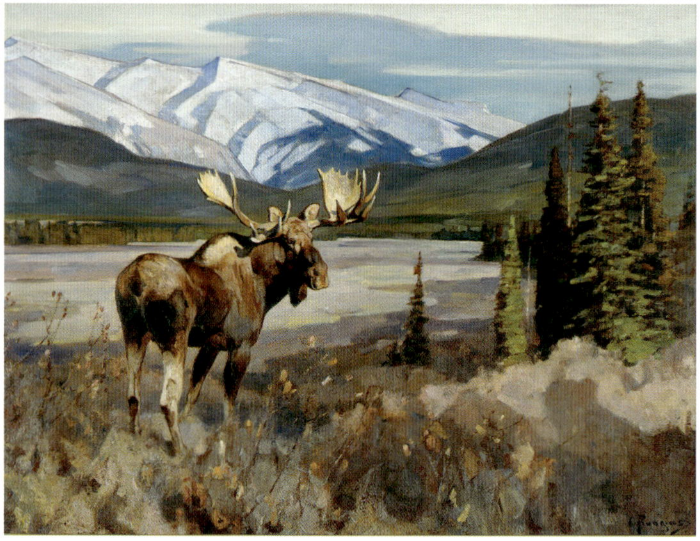

Carl Rungius
Late Fall on the Clearwater, ca. 1946
oil
Glenbow Museum, Calgary

An avid sportsman and hunter, Rungius was the greatest big game painter in twentieth-century North America. He merged rigorous academic training with a belief in extensive fieldwork, producing hundreds of drawings, oil sketches, and photographs to document wildlife in their natural habitat. He increasingly incorporated modern elements into his work: cubic structure and impressionistic rendering.

Here, the moose is caught, pausing, before disappearing into the brush. Clearly delineated with a crisp line, the three-dimensional structure and solid mass of the animal is realistic and convincing. The moose is illuminated by the waning sun, his pelt brilliantly rendered with dabs of brush-tip on canvas. The landscape is simplified into broad areas of colour, blocks of form and mass. The distant mountains are structured with geometric, faceted modelling. The grass in the foreground is quickly rendered, with dabs of impressionistic colour over it to denote other plants. Rungius has captured the crisp clean air and the clarity of light with a light palette and bold emphatic strokes.

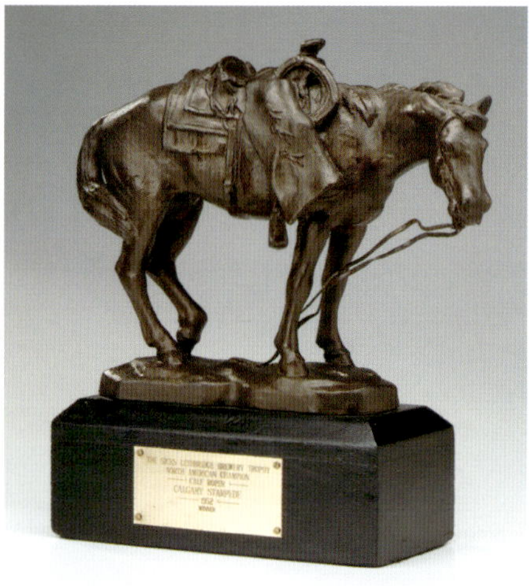

Charles Beil
Horse, 1952
bronze
Glenbow Museum, Calgary

Beil produced this sculpture for the Calgary Stampede in 1952 as a trophy for calf roping. The realistic rendering of the horse, saddle, and other accoutrements has been carefully modelled with great attention paid to the correct details of all of the elements. The process involves producing a model in clay, worked by hand. From this a plaster cast is made and a wax model developed. A composite mould is built around the wax model, the wax is melted out, and molten bronze poured in—the so-called "lost wax process." After cooling, the bronze is sandblasted, hand-tooled, and oxidized to produce the desired colour.

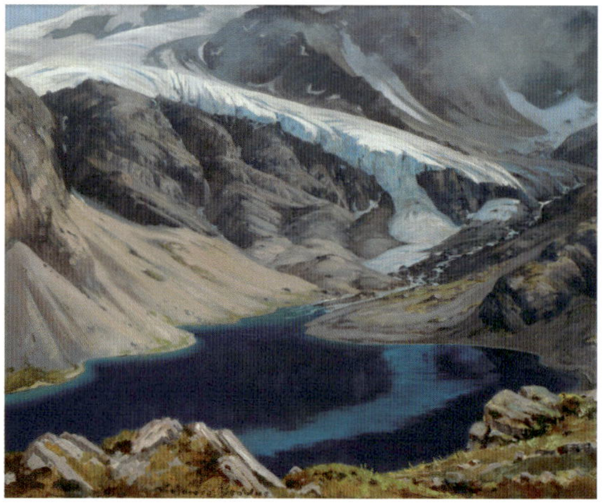

Belmore Browne
An Echo of the Ice Age, n.d.
oil
Glenbow Museum, Calgary

The high vantage point, looking into the deep valley, adds to the drama of this scene. The impressive weight of the tongue of the glacier is still at work as it descends into the cirque, adding water and silt to the blue-black lake. The desolate rock faces carved by the ancient glacier give a sense of geological time in this remote and inhospitable landscape.

Consolidation: Edmonton and the North

Organizations in Edmonton were key to the development of art in Alberta. The Edmonton Art Association was established in 1914 and offered lectures and courses, and staged exhibitions. The association was replaced by the Edmonton Art Club in 1921. Its first president was William Johnstone, who had trained as an artist in Edinburgh, Scotland, and was the only professional artist in Edmonton at that time. Florence Mortimer, who arrived in Edmonton in 1926, was a member of the club and gave private art classes to aspiring artists, such as Thelma Manarey. The Edmonton Museum of Arts, established in 1924 with Johnstone serving on the board, became the Edmonton Art Gallery in 1956.

Although the University of Alberta did not establish an art program until the 1940s, it played a seminal role in other ways when it came to establishing a place for art in Alberta. In 1933, the university extension department received a grant from the Carnegie Foundation in the United States in support of adult education fine arts programs. With this the department established a summer school for drama in Banff. Leighton's summer art classes moved to Banff in 1935 to share facilities with the young theatre school. In 1936, art, music, and drama were combined into the Banff School of Fine Arts, coming under the aegis of the University of Alberta Extension Department. The university also began extension courses in towns around the province, starting in 1937 in Vegreville with Henry Glyde as the first instructor. Until the 1960s, Glyde taught many of these classes, which were the first available to many aspiring artists in small communities. Some continued their studies at the Banff School of Fine Arts and developed professional careers.

In 1946, Glyde became head of the first department of fine arts in the province at the University of Alberta in Edmonton, which included theatre, music, and art. He was joined by Jack Taylor in 1947, Alison Forbes in 1949, and Norman Yates in 1956. These four guided the program for over a decade. In 1953, the first full four-year diploma program was established, and in 1962 this became a bachelor of fine arts degree. In 1966, Glyde retired. In 1967, Ronald Davey was appointed department head and implemented a more comprehensive program and in 1970 hired more teachers.

Developments north of Edmonton were fostered by two pioneer artists of the Peace Country area in northern Alberta, Euphemia McNaught and Evy McBryan. From 1942 to 1944 they travelled together along the Alaska Highway as far as the Sikanni River in northern British Columbia, east of the Rockies. Their art documented the construction of the highway—the United States Army camps and newly constructed roads and bridges—but they also focused their attention on the remarkable landscape of the country.

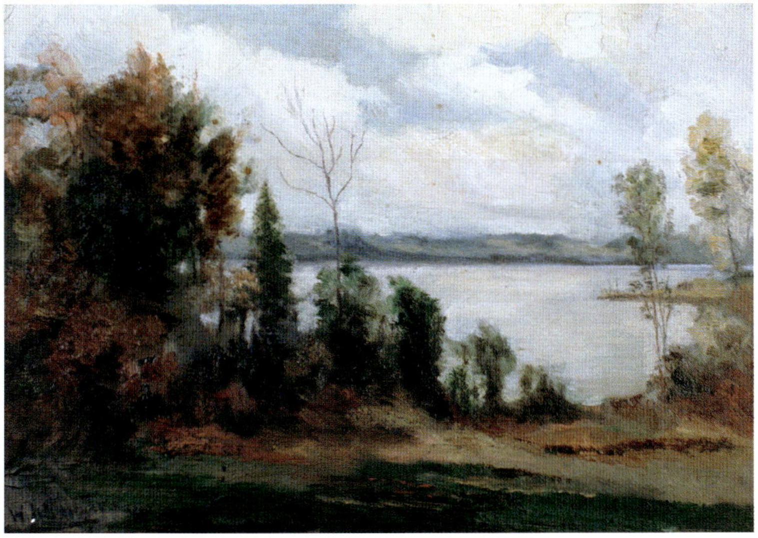

William Johnstone
Untitled, ca. 1920s
oil
Alberta Foundation for the Arts, Edmonton

A well-composed harmonious scene, painted in a realistic style, this work is typical of traditional, picturesque, late nineteenth-century British landscape painting, not yet impacted by modernism. This style of painting served as the early model for Edmonton painters.

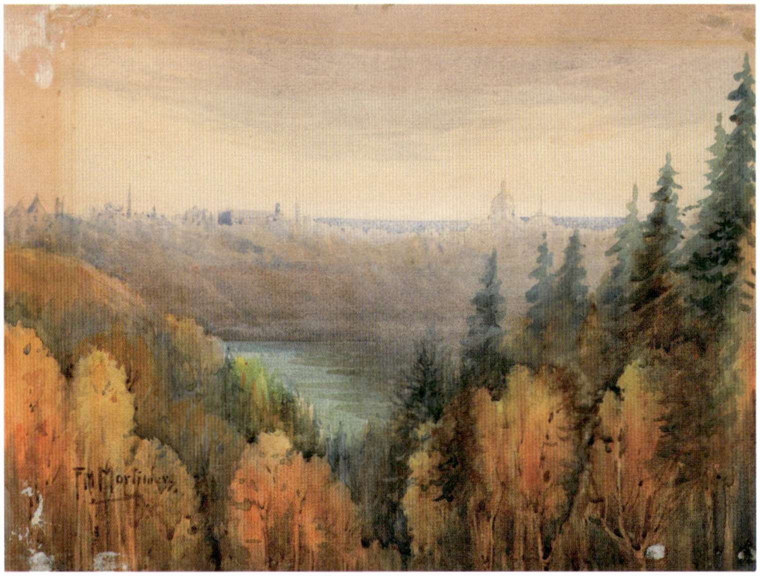

Florence Mortimer
Valley of the North Saskatchewan Looking towards Edmonton, 1928
watercolour
Glenbow Museum, Calgary

Using a very wet technique, Mortimer has applied broad washes of thin paint fused with other colours, and then added details. The distant view is hazy and atmospheric, with light, subdued colour. The foreground is painted in brilliant autumnal hues of red, orange, and yellow against a vivid, contrasting, turquoise river. Greater detail in the foreground elements, compared with those in the distance, provides a sense of deep perspective in this energetic and vital work.

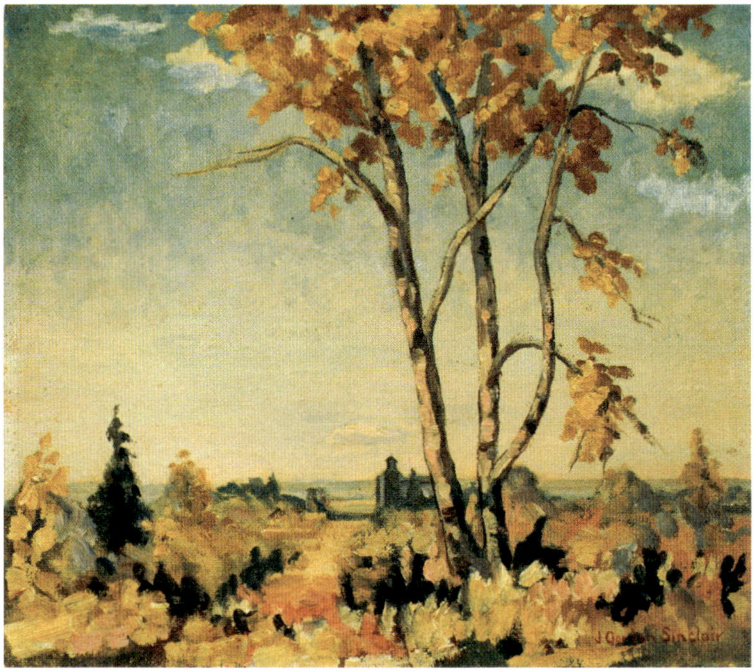

Gordon Sinclair
On the Trail to the Elevator, 1947
oil
Alberta Foundation for the Arts, Edmonton

This work evidences the light, fresh, and quick paint handling of modernism. The autumn colours are vivid with dashes of yellow and orange amongst the ochres and greens. The sky is full of light.

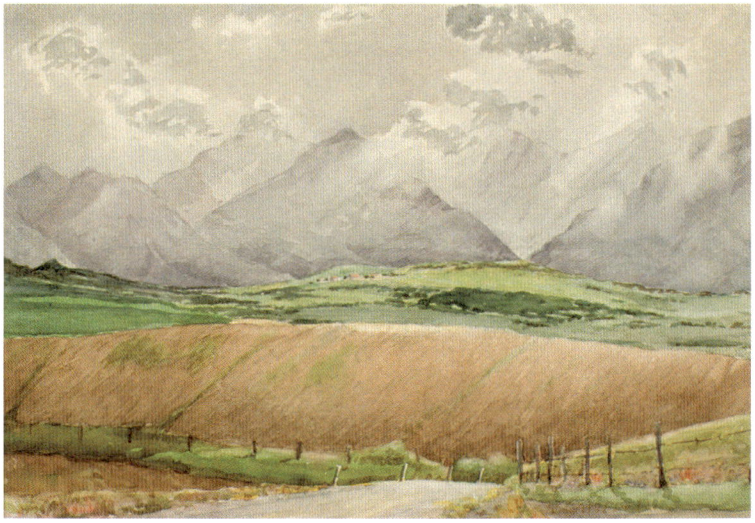

Robert Campbell
Near Waterton, 1932
watercolour
Alberta Foundation for the Arts, Edmonton

Watercolour continued to be a favoured medium for many twentieth-century artists in Alberta, who continued working in a naturalistic style. This is a carefully rendered view of the mountains, seen through a sun-infused, cloudy haze. The foothills and cornfields are clearly delineated in this crisp, bright watercolour.

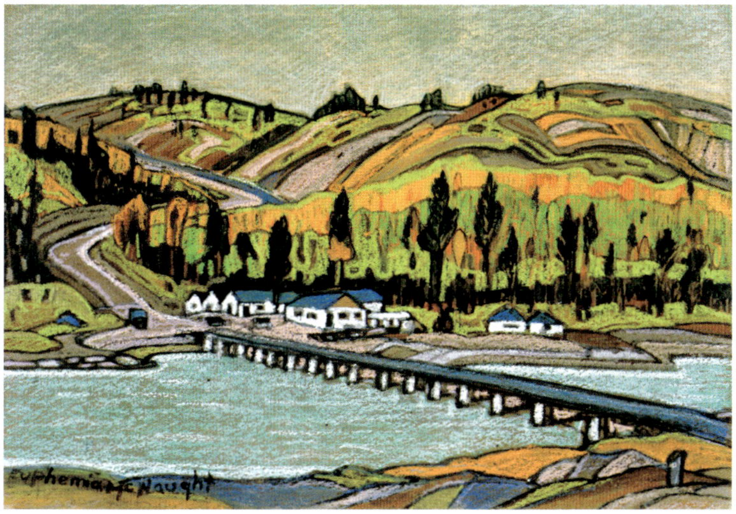

Euphemia McNaught
Army Camp, Temporary Bridge, ca. 1942
oil pastel
Alberta Foundation for the Arts, Edmonton

Though McNaught chose to depict the building of the Alaska Highway, this image is almost pure landscape, with the small work camp appearing insignificant in the distance. The rhythm of the rolling landscape with its patchwork of fields is depicted in rich greens, yellows, and earth colours, all rendered in thick pigment-laden strokes of oil pastel in this vividly coloured harmonious scene. The rhythmic composition recalls the work of the Group of Seven artists with whom McNaught had studied.

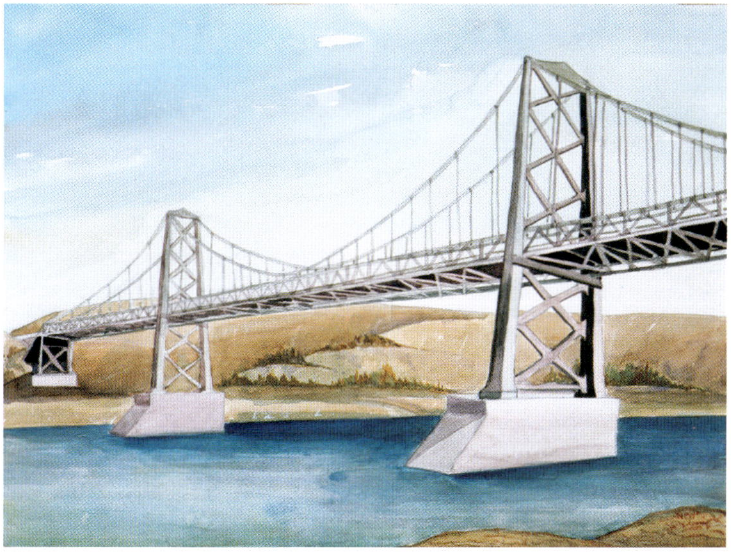

Evy McBryan
Suspension Bridge over the Peace at Taylor, ca. 1942
watercolour
Alberta Foundation for the Arts, Edmonton

The bridge dominates the scene, a symbol of power and progress. The rolling landscape is insignificant behind the dominant bridge, and the smooth broad river flows quietly beneath it. Shown at an angle, the bridge is dynamic and wields authority over the landscape. The details of the structure with its beams and supports are carefully delineated in this dramatic image.

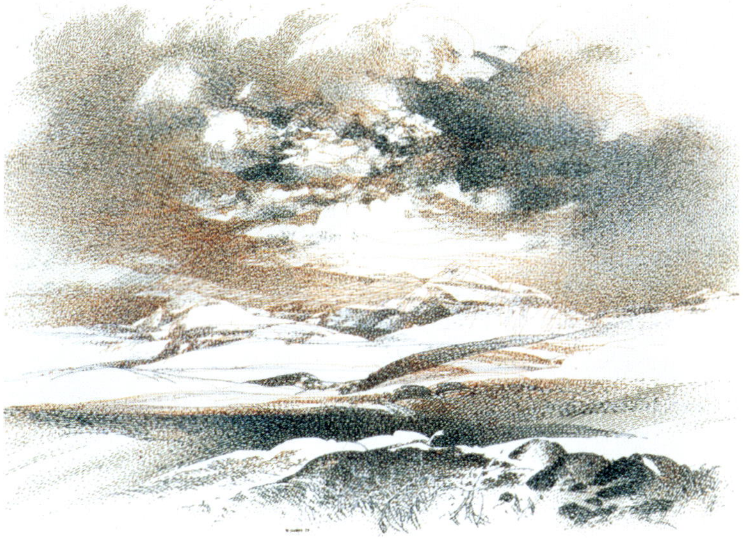

Robert Guest
Wilderness in Three Colours, 1973
pen and ink
Alberta Foundation for the Arts, Edmonton

Thin veils of colour create this simplified atmospheric landscape. With extreme economy, Guest has captured the essence of this panoramic northern land, the lake and moody sky.

The Group of Seven in Alberta

Canada's most important association of artists in the early twentieth century was the Group of Seven. Living initially in Toronto, these artists forged a national identity based on their representation of Canada's diverse natural landscape. Their modernist art was expressive, employing brilliant colour and dramatic lighting. All but two of the group (Franklin Carmichael and Frederick Varley) worked in the Rocky Mountains and were given free Canadian Pacific Railway passes to travel west. Most of the Group's images of the mountains presented a pristine, unspoiled wilderness: iconic images for the nation. A. Y. Jackson, the only one in the group to do so, also focused on the prairies. They were all established artists by the time they travelled west, but none of them actually settled in Alberta.

Jackson was the first to travel west in 1914, when he worked in the Yellowhead Pass, west of Jasper. He visited again with Lawren Harris in 1924, and they hiked and sketched in the Jasper area. Jackson found the high mountains, with their rugged and angular forms, a great challenge and in time preferred painting the rolling foothills of the prairies. Harris, on the other hand, was inspired by the mountains and returned for many subsequent summers. J. E. H. MacDonald travelled to the Rockies in 1924 and made subsequent trips every summer until 1930, inspired by Lake O'Hara. Other Group of Seven artists spent less time in the mountains: Frank Johnston came west in 1924 and 1930, and Arthur Lismer made only one trip in 1928.

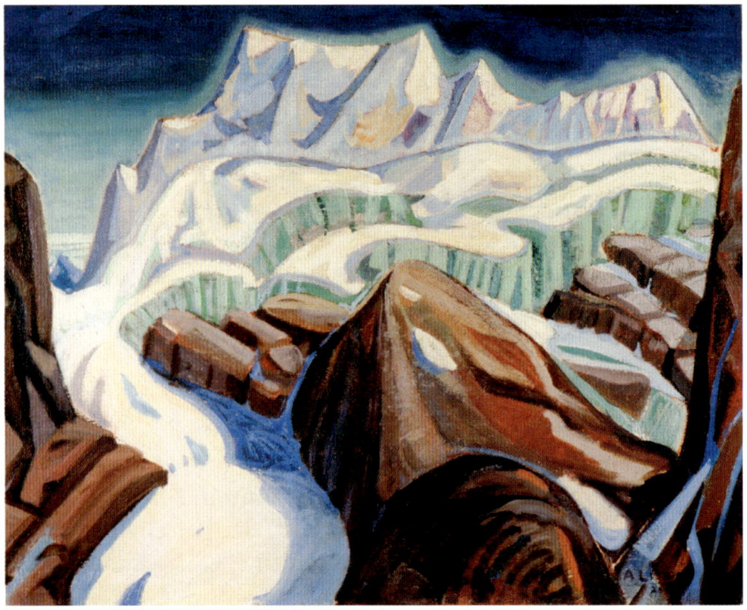

Arthur Lismer
The Glacier, 1928
oil
Collection of the Art Gallery of Hamilton, 1960

This painting depicts Mount Fay above Moraine Lake near Lake Louise. Lismer was awed and felt the omnipotence of the soaring mountains. In *The Glacier*, the power of the glacier is as formidable as the mountains themselves as it grinds and forces its way through the rock with intense pressure. Through his dynamic construction of the forms of glacier and rock, Lismer conveys the tremendous power of nature. Glowing with brilliant light and translucent colour, the thrust of the rugged mountains and the heavy slow movement of the glaciers, this image is cold, remote, and awe-inspiring.

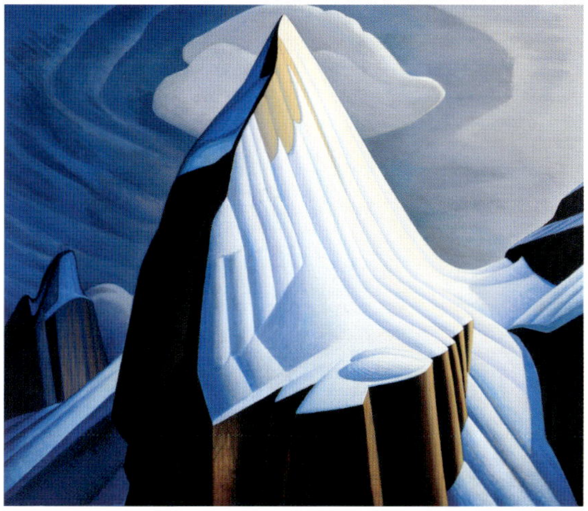

Lawren Harris
Mount Lefroy, 1930
oil
McMichael Canadian Art Collection, Kleinburg

Harris's landscapes reached their deepest spiritual intensity in the Rockies, and the mountains inspired his pursuit of abstraction. He was searching for universal forms and spiritual truths, and simplified nature to symbolize archetypal forms. In *Mount Lefroy*, the mountain has a central emblematic position. Its triangular shape is accentuated, reinforcing its power, verticality, and upward thrust. The mountain marks the point of transcendence between the natural and divine world. Brilliant light, symbolizing enlightenment, illuminates the white snow on one side of the mountain, in startling contrast to the dark shadow on the other side. The aura of the white cloud surrounding the apex of the mountain-triangle emanates in concentric circles through the sombre sky. Harris's limited use of colour creates a dramatic, austere, and timeless effect. Details have been eliminated, creating an image of spiritual force and power.

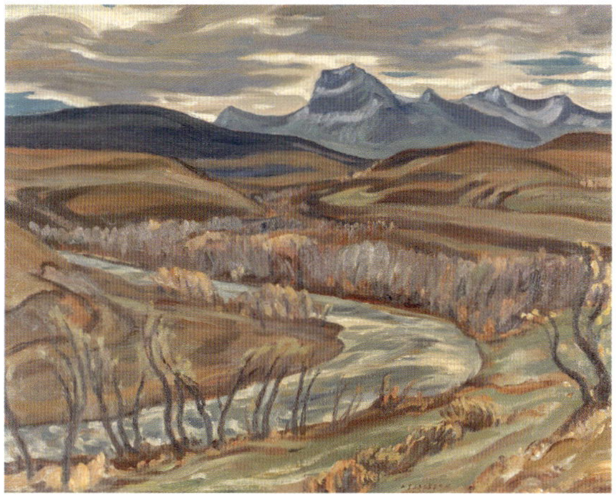

A.Y. Jackson
Chief Mountain from Belly River, ca. 1947
oil
Lethbridge Community College
Copyright Courtesy of the Estate of the late Naomi Jackson Groves

Though he had travelled to Alberta a number of times, Jackson only started to paint the prairies in 1937. They continued to inspire his art during his annual visits to the West until 1957. He felt the vast space of the prairies was an escape to freedom, a place of renewal. Here he depicts the great vistas of the undulating hills and deep coulees of the southern Alberta foothills. A vital rhythm flows through the entire composition, from the foreground river and scrubby brush to the rolling hills, and the distant mountains. The mountains loom stark and impressive, defining the space. The land is golden with the brilliant colours of the fall. The cool moody sky presages the onset of an icy winter.

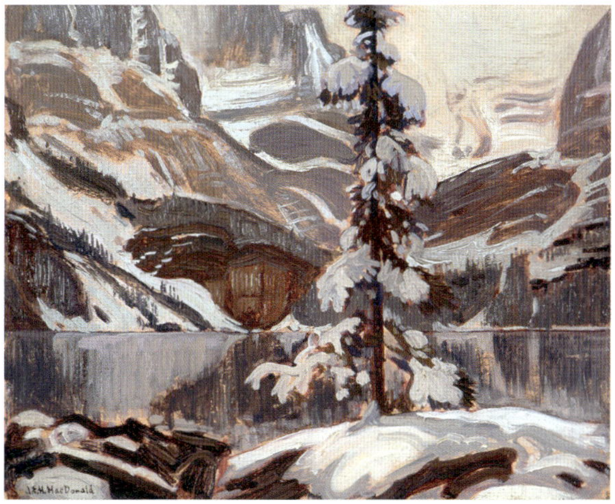

J. E. H. MacDonald
Lake O'Hara with Snow, n.d.
oil
Glenbow Museum, Calgary

MacDonald made his first trip to Lake O'Hara in 1924. This small oil painting has the vitality and economy of means of a quick sketch, providing an intimate view of this beautiful lake scene. The off-centre tree in the foreground anchors the composition. The image is framed with the lower mountains wrapping around the lake, creating a shallow, enclosed space which enhances the impressive bulk of the mountains. The early snowfall weighs down the branches of the foreground tree and is caught in the undulating declivities of the mountains. He has captured the effect of the light on an overcast day, with its rich, subdued colours.

The Lure of the Land

From the 1920s, artists living in Alberta and those settling here continued to be drawn to the beauty of the land. Nature could provide an immediate and inexhaustible fund of visual riches. Working directly from nature, artists spent time out of doors closely observing nature with serious intent and application. The focus was no longer just on the mountains; artists were interested in the prairies, foothills, and developing towns. This was nature increasingly marked by human intervention. The sensational scenery enabled artists to express deeply felt emotions about nature. Paintings are often not purely visual descriptions of visual appearance, but sensory and resonant.

Most of the early work was representational with a quiet naturalism, an objective and unsentimental examination, literally depicting the artists' precise experience of the land. But it became increasingly expressive and abstract over time. Some artists, such as Walter Phillips, painted in watercolour in a naturalistic style, providing poetic, luminous images of the region. He saw nature as redemptive, pure and free. Some, like Illingworth Kerr, worked in oil and became more interested in abstracting from nature, or, like Maxwell Bates, providing expressive images that evoked a sense of the land. For them, the landscape became a work of the mind, a world of associations, built from a stratum of memory, as well as the literal scenes. Henry Glyde's images evoked the fears of the Cold War era. Industrial imagery, like James Nicoll's *Shacks and Refinery* (ca. 1950), was rare. First Nations artists, like Gerald Tailfeathers, began to work in the European tradition of two-dimensional painting, producing poignant images of their own communities.

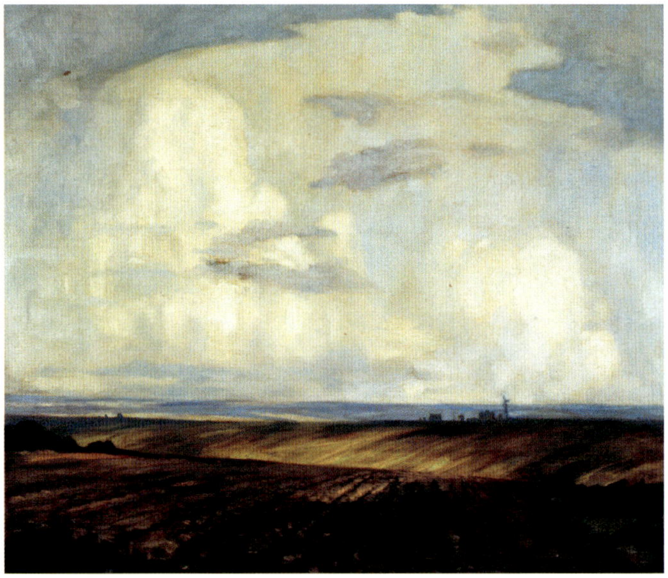

Roland Gissing
Clouds over the Prairie, ca. 1925
oil
Alberta Foundation for the Arts, Edmonton

This is a classic prairie scene: big sky country. The prairie sweeps away before us, and the slight undulations increase the impact of distance in this limitless, flat land. Over this hangs the great sky with its massed cumulus clouds as impressive as mountains. The parallel ploughed furrows converge in the distance increasing the sense of space and perspective. By depicting the land as about a third of the image, Gissing has emphasized the huge prairie sky.

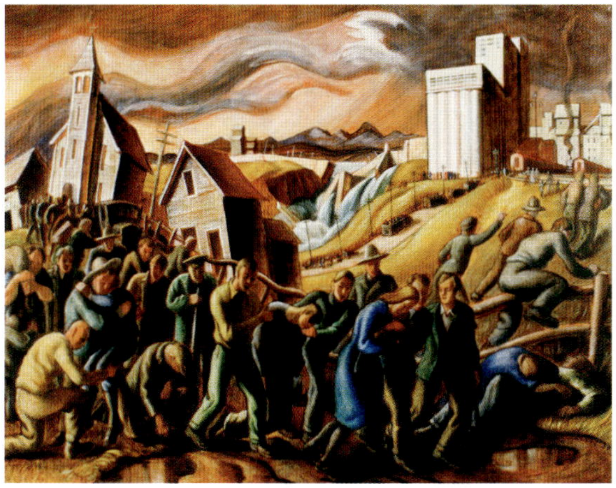

Henry Glyde
Exodus, 1941
oil and tempera
Alberta Foundation for the Arts, Edmonton

Glyde had studied mural painting in England and the idea of the mural as a vehicle for epic themes carried over into his easel painting during the 1940s. *Exodus* is a biblical theme set in contemporary Alberta: a prairie landscape with grain elevators and distant Rocky Mountains. A dam has broken and water surges into the valley. The heaving landscape, with tilted buildings, mirrors the trauma of the displaced people who move forward awkwardly, injured and distraught, some fleeing into the distance. The rhythm and energy flowing through the figures enhances their turbulent movement, adding to their agitation. The drama is enhanced by the composition, with the unstable angles of leaning buildings. A low prairie light illuminates the buildings and figures, and the sky is heavy and ominous in this dramatic scene.

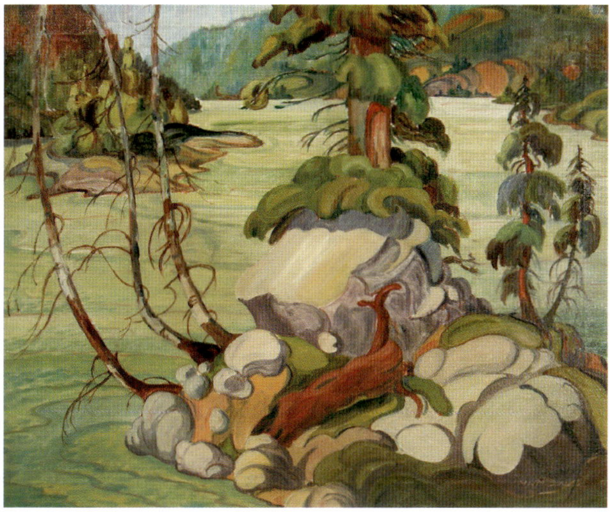

Murray MacDonald
Lower Maligne, 1942
oil
Art Gallery of Alberta, Edmonton

Murray MacDonald was a student of A. Y. Jackson's. *Lower Maligne* shows MacDonald's debt to the Group of Seven. It is a very accomplished, carefully conceived composition, with the wide open lake fringed with forested mountains stretching into the distance. We view the deep space of the landscape through a screen of trees on the island, which anchors the composition. Rhythms flow through the rocks and trees in the foreground and are echoed in the distant forest. MacDonald has used fluid and painterly brushwork and rich colour harmonies with red for emphasis, which enlivens the surface.

Martha Houston
February Thaw (West of Okotoks), n.d.
watercolour over pencil
Glenbow Museum, Calgary

A classic Alberta landscape composition, repeated many times over by other artists, *February Thaw* depicts a road going straight towards the distant foothills and the stark mountains beyond. The forms in the work are carefully delineated. Houston has provided minimal information, yet there is a great sense of the depth of the landscape. Her use of watercolour is extremely delicate and light, and she has very effectively left the white of the watercolour paper unpainted to represent the snow. From the sharp edge of the chinook cloud, the sky is carefully modulated. This clear image is infused with the crisp Alberta winter light.

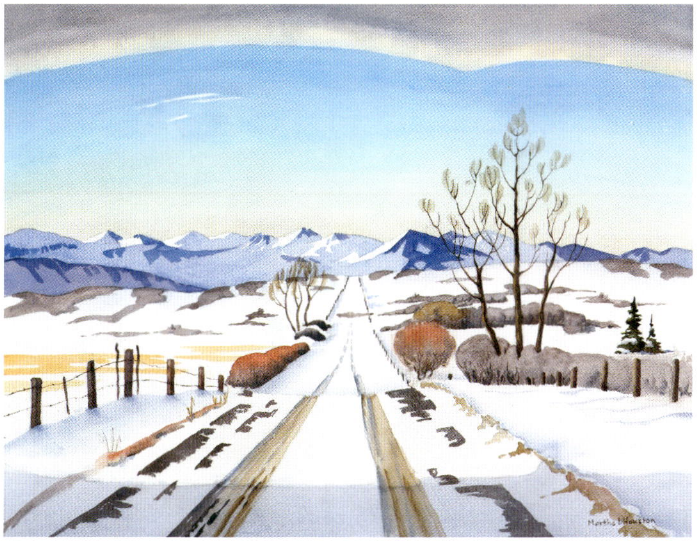

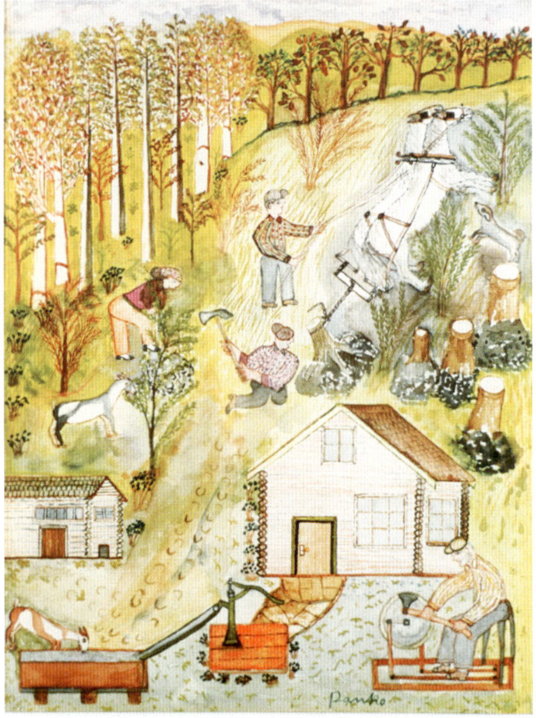

William Panko
Homesteading, 1943
watercolour and pencil
Alberta Foundation for the Arts, Edmonton

With no formal instruction, Panko began painting with Marion Nicoll's encouragement. This charming, vibrant scene is painted from Panko's memory. It is a composite view of many homesteading activities, all given equal importance in this composition. The initial drawing has been filled in with delicate watercolour washes. Minute details have been carefully added: the leaves on the trees, the patterns on the men's shirts, the horses' harnesses. Typical of a naive, untrained artist, the perspective is flattened. Buildings and figures are drawn in profile and are not in proportion. It is a charming idyllic view with no sense of the laborious and strenuous work to clear the land.

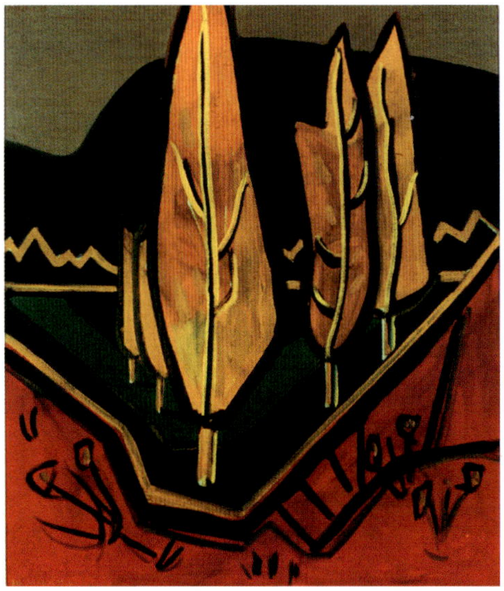

Janet Mitchell
Tribal Lands, 1948
oil
Alberta Foundation for the Arts, Edmonton

Like other artists in Alberta at the time, Mitchell experimented with abstraction in her early work. Here, the elements of the landscape have been abstracted and dramatically simplified into a red foreground zone, a treed middle distance, and the smooth arc of the mountains in the background. The flame-like trees reveal their trunks and major branches like spines. Bold dark outlines mark trees and other forms in this graphic decorative painting.

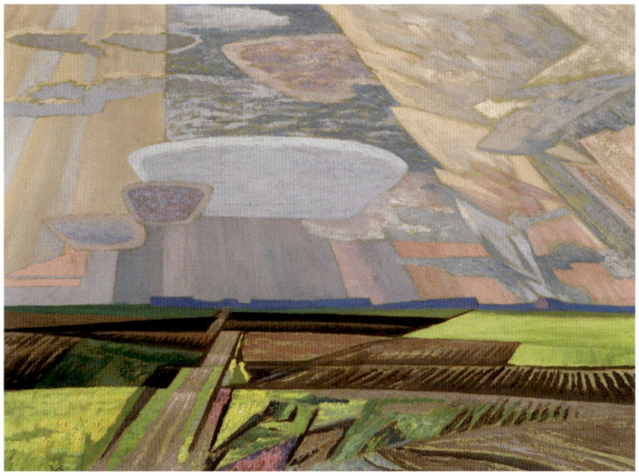

Illingworth Kerr
Oblique Fields, 1949
oil
Glenbow Museum, Calgary

Kerr loved the Alberta landscape, the combination of prairie, foothills, and mountains. He has formalized the broad open prairie into a series of angular shapes, a patchwork to represent the cultivated fields stretching to the horizon. Over this grid he has brushed in the furrows of the fields and the brilliant colours of the crops. Slicing through this is a long straight road, diminishing into the distance, adding to the great depth of space. The sky is a symphony of faceted shapes like beams of light in a prism, creating deep corridors of space, radiating from the horizon. Rounded clouds float over this. Expressively painted with loose brushstrokes in pale pastel colours, the sky has the appearance of a spiritual realm, in contrast to the vibrant, earthy land below.

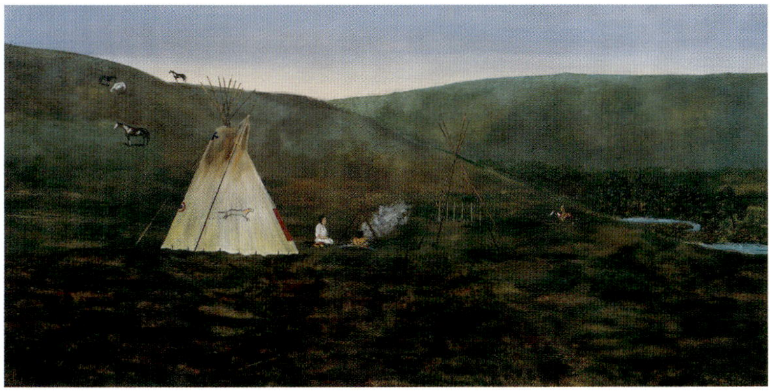

Percy Two Gun
Landscape with Tipi, 1949
oil
Glenbow Museum, Calgary

A self-taught artist, Two Gun represents First Nations life. He depicts the wide open prairie and gentle rolling foothills of his experience. A lone tipi painted with the owner's motifs of the otter, otter's den, and butterfly stands in the distance. A woman sits in front of a fire as a man approaches on horseback. Nearby, a tipped-up travois has been set up with supporting poles for hanging things to dry. Pinto horses, integral to Native life, graze in the distance, all represented in profile, rather like pictographs. This simply conceived image has a naive charm.

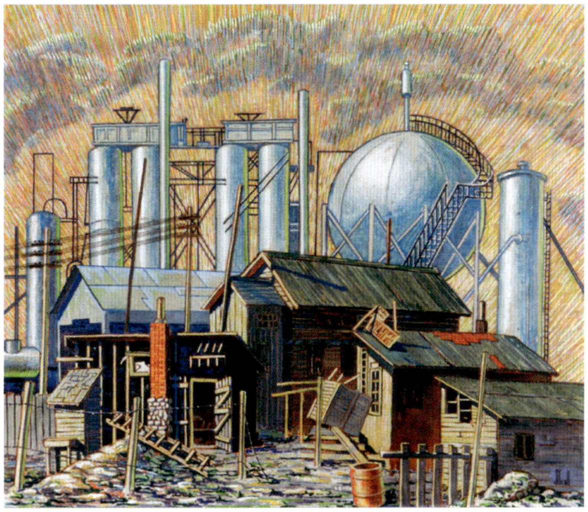

James M. Nicoll
Shacks and Refinery, ca. 1950
oil
Government House Foundation, Edmonton

Nicoll has juxtaposed the gleaming steel of the new refinery buildings with the dilapidated shacks and junk nearby. This heightens the impact of these modern progressive buildings, crowding out the past, in this poetic, nostalgic image. The warm tones of the wooden buildings and sky are in marked contrast to the hard metallic steel of the refinery. The structures are carefully and sensitively drawn with attention to the accuracy of the details, showing the influence of Nicoll's engineering training. A pale low prairie light illuminates the sides of the buildings, enhancing the details and shafts of light radiating from behind, creating a vivid sky.

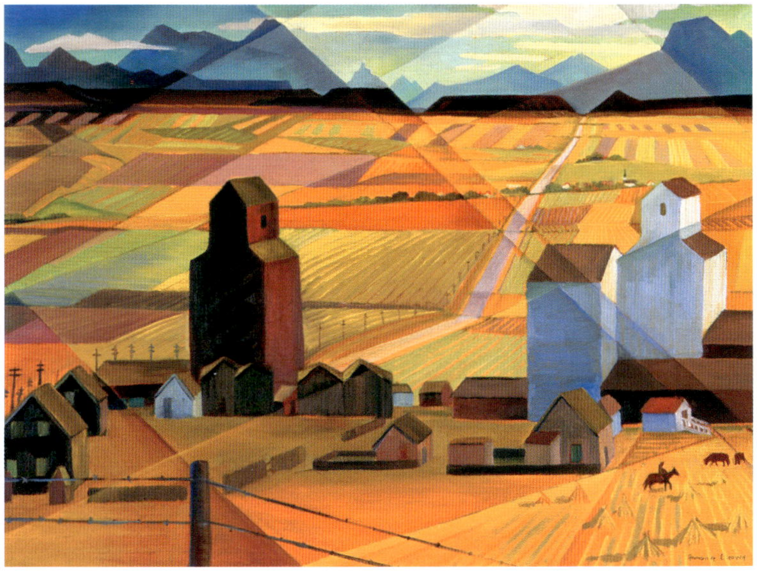

Annora Brown
Foothills Village, ca. 1950s
oil
Glenbow Museum, Calgary

Brown, an artist from Fort Macleod, Alberta, depicted this scene from a very high vantage point, with the prairie laid out below her, providing a long view to the mountains in the distance. A typical long straight road leads the eye to the distant horizon. The agricultural patchwork of fields and the rectilinear buildings of the town in the foreground lend themselves to a geometric approach. Overlaying this, Brown has placed diagonals from the peaks of the mountains faceting the surface with shafts of light. This could have been the start of a more fully cubist approach, however the artist did not follow that path.

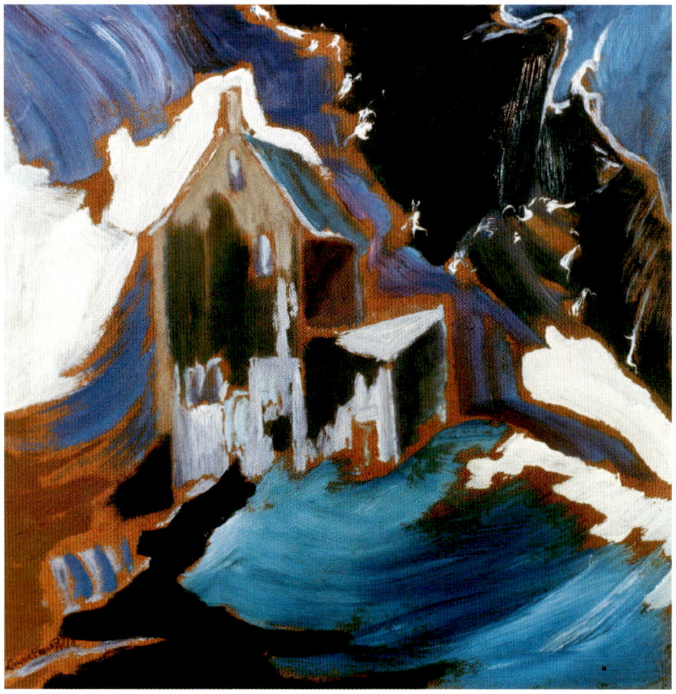

Laura Evans Reid
Eerie Encroachments, 1951
oil
University of Alberta, Edmonton

This is an extraordinary work with an amazing economy of means painted in the year of Reid's death. Concerned with a transcendental vision rather than depicting actual reality, she explored abstract elements for their symbolic and emotive qualities through the expressive use of colour. Rather than being about landscape, this work is expressive of mood. Quickly rendered animated brushwork provides a strong emotive image of haunting melancholy. Paint is quickly applied directly on the brown masonite, which forms part of the background colour of the composition. The absolutely simplified forms of the landscape around the house are merely suggested, not described, with fast gestures of colour. Catalyzed by avant-garde American art in the late 1940s, Reid was one of the first artists in Alberta to embrace such an expressive, abstracted style. Her untimely death cut short a promising career.

Walter J. Phillips
Rundle Through a Screen of Poplars, 1952
watercolour
Glenbow Museum, Calgary

Phillips had an international reputation before he arrived in Alberta in 1940. The translucency of watercolour demonstrates his mastery of the technique, which inspired many other Alberta artists. The composition has been carefully delineated and then filled in with thin transparent washes of harmonious colour using a very wet brush. In some areas wet paint has been infused with pigment creating a rich tonal variation. To achieve depth of tone, some colours are layered but never laboured. His extraordinarily keen eye for detail, in the trees and in the folds of the mountain, never detracts from the overall harmony of the concept. The delicacy of the foil of the foreground trees, bathed in brilliant golden sunlight against the impressive thrust of rugged Mount Rundle, is in exquisite balance.

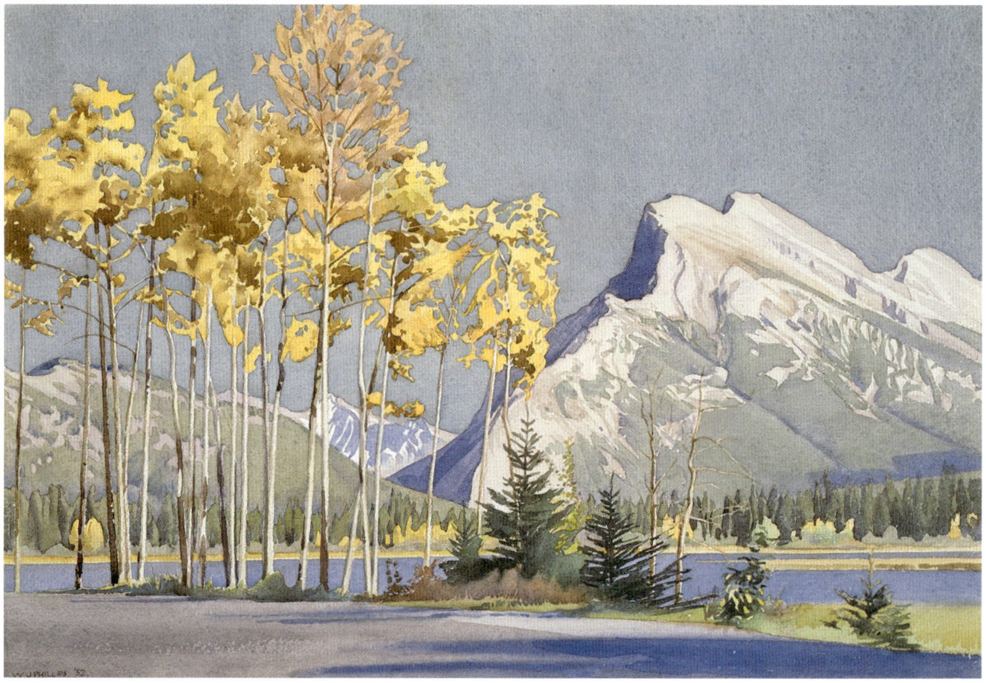

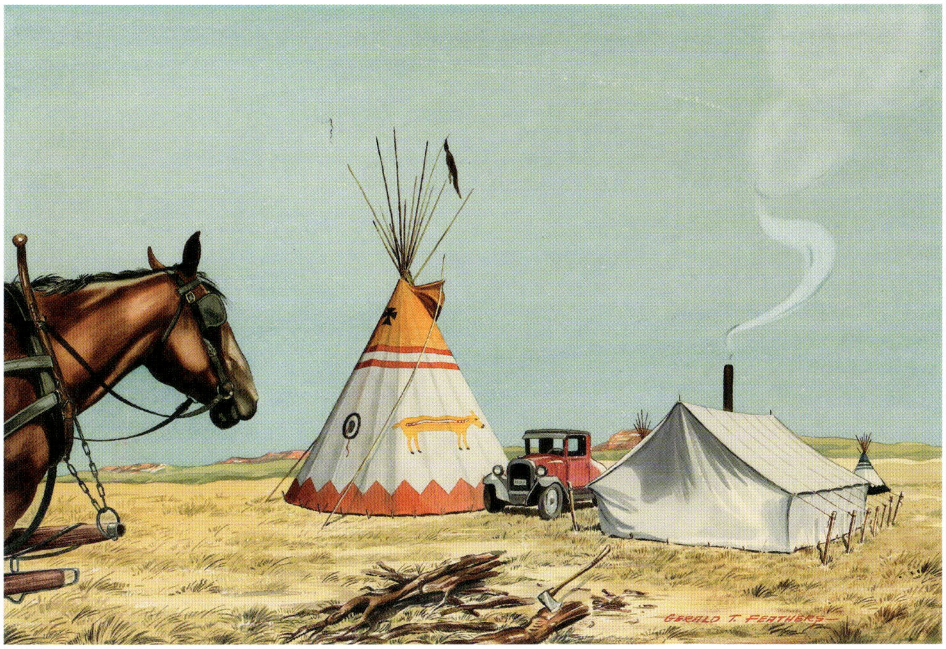

Gerald Tailfeathers
Blood Camp, 1956
watercolour
Glenbow Museum, Calgary

Born on the Blood Reserve near Cardston, Alberta, Tailfeathers was trained in the European tradition of art. He represents First Nations life but does not integrate this with traditional First Nations imagery and beliefs, except in such things as his use of symbols on the tipi. This scene is a representation and juxtaposition of the old and the new in the Blood camps of southern Alberta: the traditional Blood tipis and the European tent, the horse harnessed to a cart and the contemporary car. The tipi carries the symbolic designs of the owner. The scene is carefully drawn and then rendered with delicate watercolour washes, showing his mastery of this technique learned from Walter Phillips. The horse's head jutting in from the margin is a compositional device derived from Japanese prints as taught by Phillips.

Henry Glyde
End of the Prairie, 1957
mixed technique
University of Alberta, Edmonton

In the 1950s, Glyde experimented with abstraction, manipulating form and shape, as well as different kinds of painting techniques—impasto, stippling, knife work, and mixing sand into his paint. But his abstraction remained tied to the world around him. Here he depicts the oil refineries east of Edmonton at night. The composition has a formal and coherent structure, set up on a geometric grid system with facets, angles, and different planes illuminated. The human figures have been reduced to statuesque robotic forms in a deep illusionist space. A rich surface is created by layering and stippling of one colour over another, in a highly worked, dappled manner. The eerie, quivering light from the lamps pervades this haunting scene, giving the composition a surreal, neo-Romantic effect.

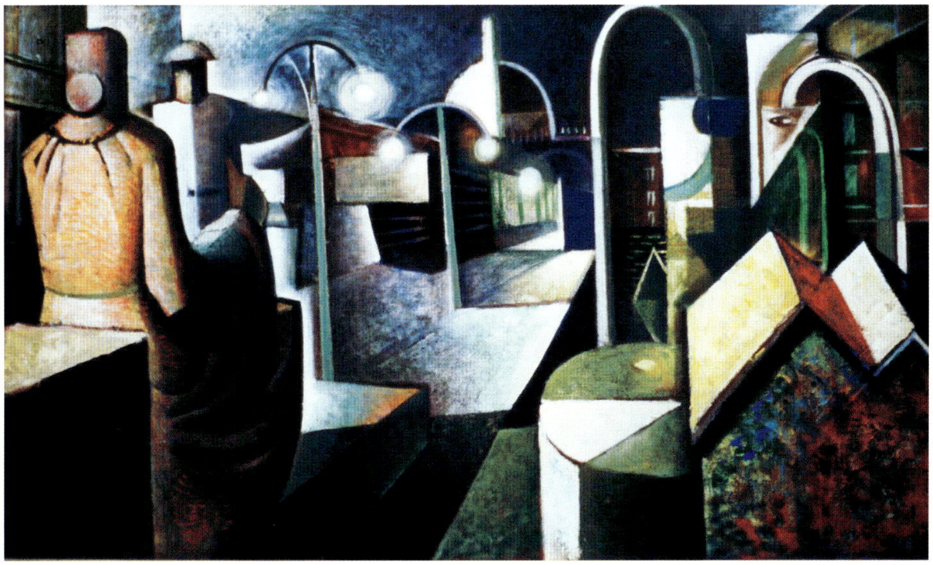

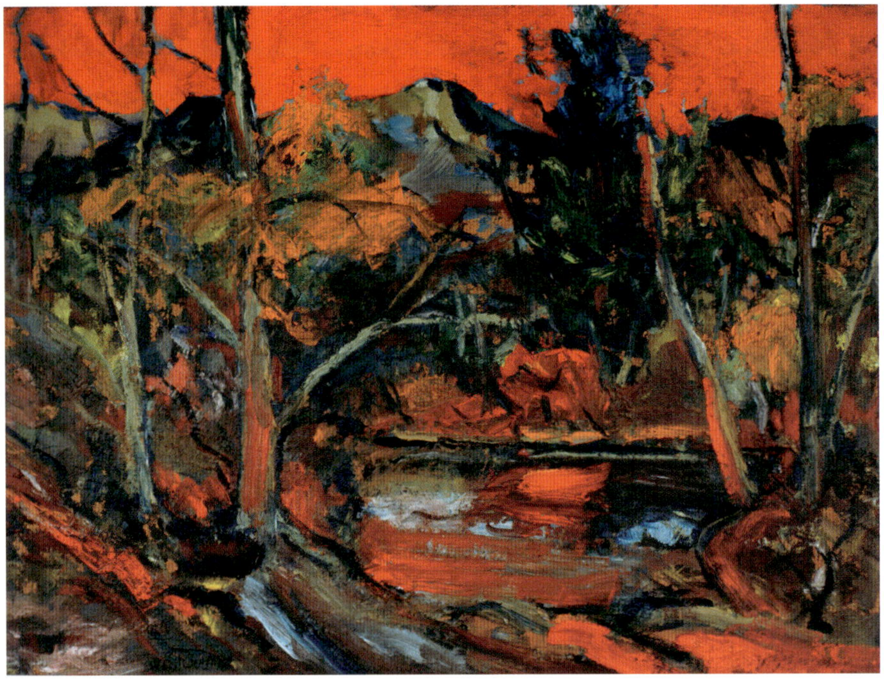

William L. Stevenson
Sun's Brilliant Glow, n.d.
acrylic
Alberta Foundation for the Arts, Edmonton

Stevenson had travelled to Chicago in 1929 to see impressionist and post-impressionist art and his work remained deeply influenced by this early experience. For him, nature remained a framework on which to act, rather than a model to be depicted. With a vigorous brush, he has captured the vitality of nature and her fleeting moods. Over the basic compositional structure, he has laid in minimal, almost abstract features of the landscape, which gives the impression of forest and mountain but without the detail. The foreground trees on rocky outcrops grow in their untidy, natural way. The distant mountains with their impressive bulk are roughed in with quick brushstrokes. Like the Fauves, modernist artists active in France from 1905 to 1910 who found new ways of communicating emotion with discordant brilliant colour and simplified design, he does not use representational colour. His colour is emotional: the sky is red and hot. Stevenson expresses his inner experience in this extraordinarily vibrant image.

Maxwell Bates
Landscape near Victoria, B.C., 1965
oil
Alberta Foundation for the Arts, Edmonton

Bates was one of the most accomplished modern artists in Alberta. This simplified composition is divided into two zones, the earth and sky separated by a diagonal line of trees which adds a dynamic visual force. The tall, corn-yellow grasses in the foreground are rendered with quick, parallel brushstrokes coalescing into a harmonious whole, the sky with quick overall strokes creating a luminous heaven. The rocks in the lower right-hand corner of the work and the screen of branches in the upper left anchor and "frame" the composition and bring attention to the centre. The tree to the left is made up of twists and flicks of paint rapidly applied to represent bunches of leaves. With great economy of means based on abstract principles, Bates has created a dramatic image expressing the vitality of nature, vivid with light and energy.

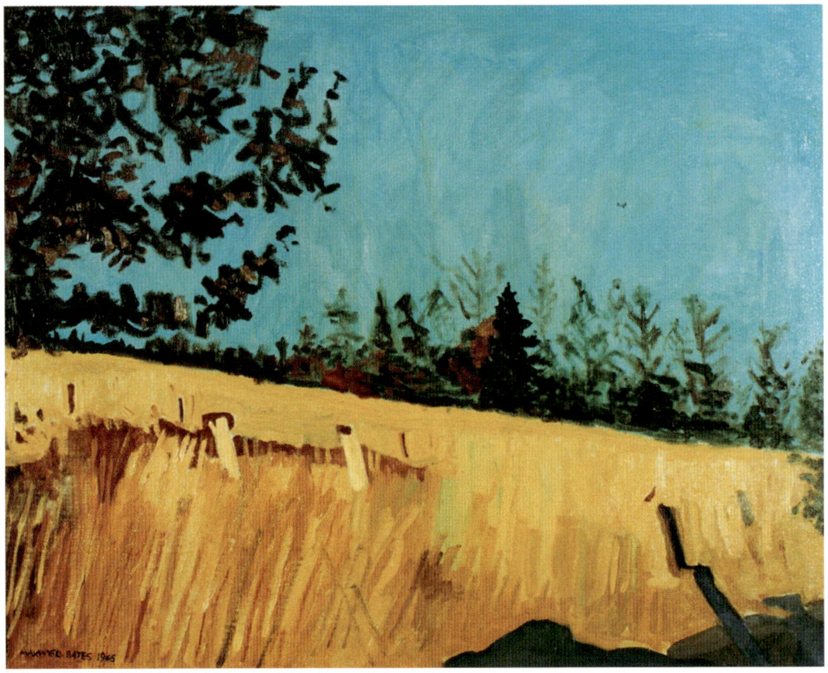

Representing the Figure

In Alberta, the landscape remained the primary inspiration for artists of the modern period from 1920 to 1970. However, there were notable artists here who used the figure for expressive and symbolic purposes. Representing the figure was an urban subject. Portraits could be penetrating characterizations that revealed the personality of the subject through the intensity of the artist's vision. Based on different aesthetic theories and political ideologies, subjects ranged from the naturalistic portraiture of James Nicoll and Nicholas de Grandmaison to the expressive and metaphysical compositions of Maxwell Bates, Henry Glyde, and Ron Spickett. Bates, Glyde, and Spickett used the figure to explore complex human relationships, their struggles, fears, and foibles, in iconic images that express the psychological drama of the human condition. A unique project by Kainai artist White Wolf, which continued the traditional Blackfoot story robe in a modern context, was a series of murals commissioned for display at the Prince of Wales Hotel in Waterton Lakes National Park.

White Wolf
War Pictograph, ca. 1926
trade paint over pencil
Glenbow Museum, Calgary

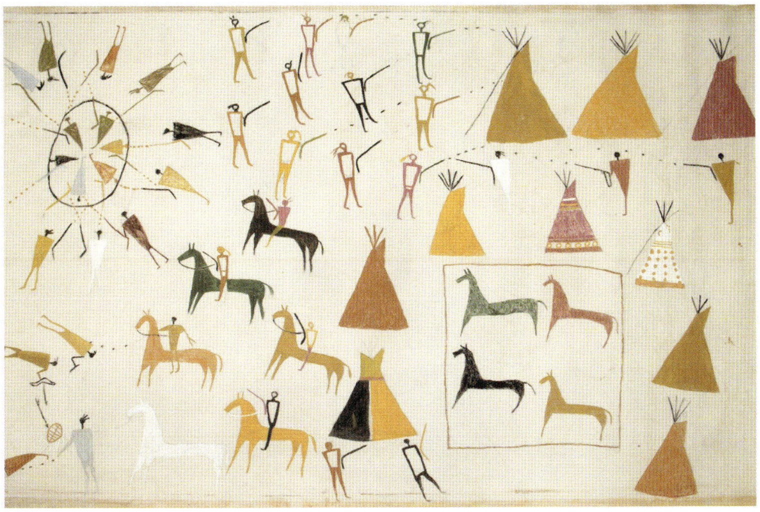

This mural shows the war adventures of White Wolf. Recounted accurately, White Wolf's status and role in the community derived from his personal achievements. He defends the camp under attack (upper right), captures four horses from an enemy corral (lower right), kills three enemies (lower left), and during a battle he is surrounded in a pit by the enemy (upper left). The central area shows various tipi designs he owned.

This mural continues the use of the traditional designs and symbols of earlier rock art and story robes, while incorporating modern elements. Historically, First Nations artists show horses with two legs, the other two being behind, whereas here the running horses are shown with four legs. Likewise, the Y-human figures traditionally have one leg, some here have one, some two. Like tipi designs, forms are outlined in pencil and then filled in with vibrant colour. The narrative is conveyed through simple schematized figures shown in profile, with the narrator painted red, and appears surprisingly modern in form and design. A balance of interest and activity across the surface creates a strong, dynamic composition and bold graphic effect.

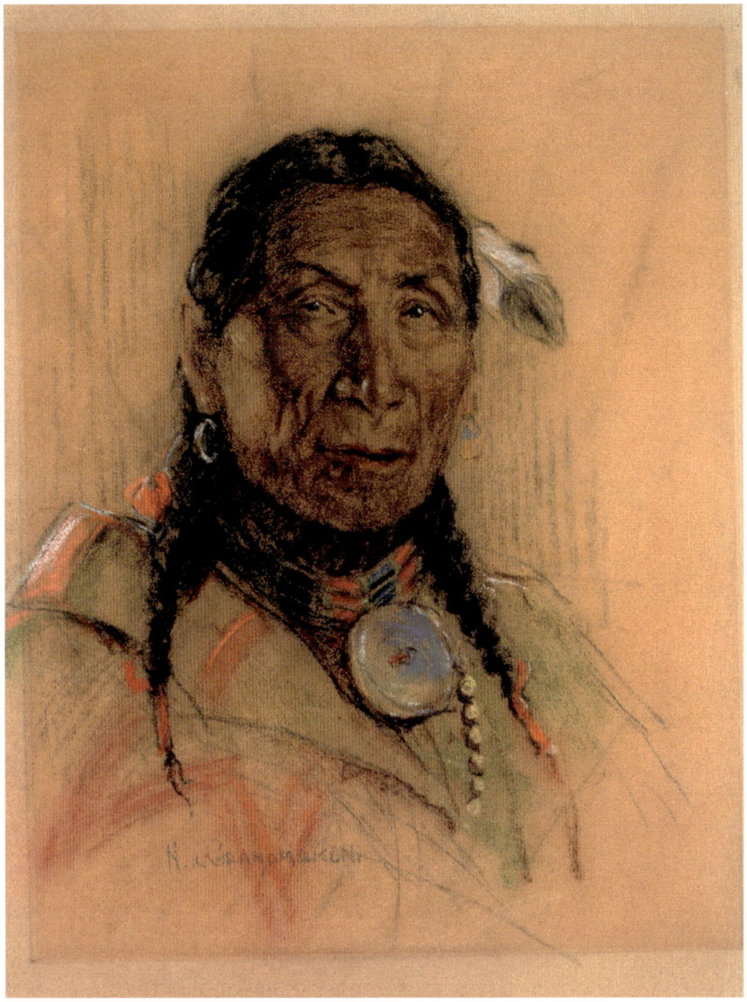

Nicholas de Grandmaison
Many Turning Robes, ca. 1930s
pastel
Glenbow Museum, Calgary

Working from life, with First Nations individuals posing for him, de Grandmaison completed hundreds of First Nations portraits. Many Turning Robes was Siksika from near Gleichen, Alberta. His face is modelled with quick gestures of pastel crayon capturing the overall structure, with highlights adding volume to the forms. de Grandmaison had sound technical ability to capture character, though his approach was traditional and conservative. These portraits are nostalgic in mood, consistent with nineteenth-century romantic ideas.

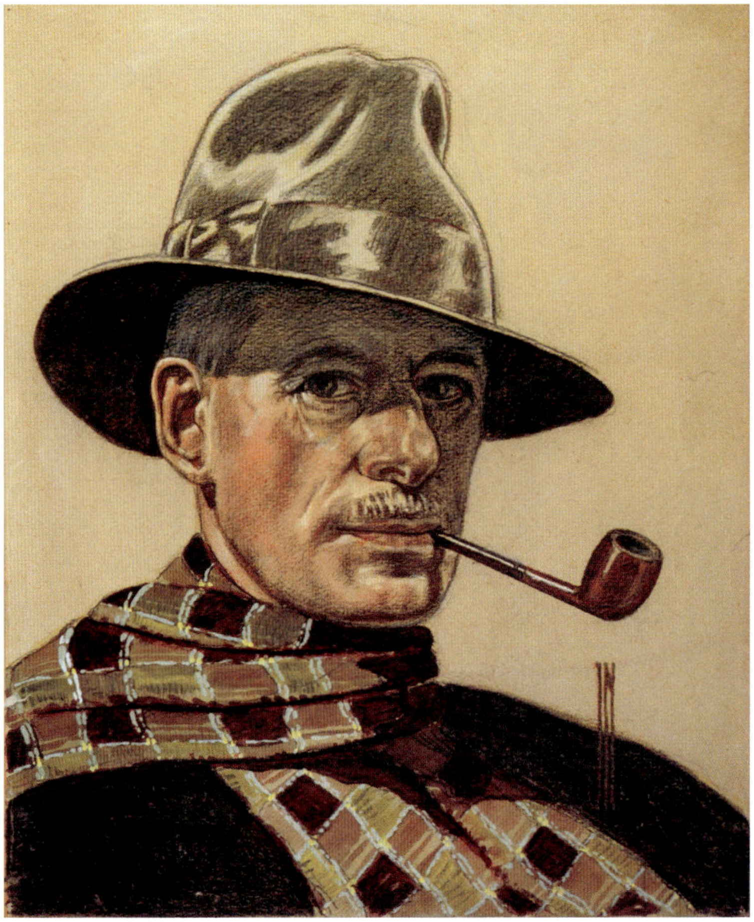

James M. Nicoll
Self Portrait, n.d.
watercolour
Alberta Foundation for the Arts, Edmonton

Nicoll's acutely keen eye has captured the character of his own handsome face, realistically rendered, crisp and incisive. The strong face is carefully modelled showing its structure, the prominent nose, pursed lips holding the pipe in place. The nuance of highlights and colouring amplifies the articulation of the volumes of the face. The lines around the piercingly blue eyes, mouth, and forehead add to the individuality of the subject. The brim of the hat frames the face, which is further emphasized by the scarf thrown jauntily over his shoulder. Full attention is thus drawn to the intense face, to his personality in this sensitive, insightful portrait.

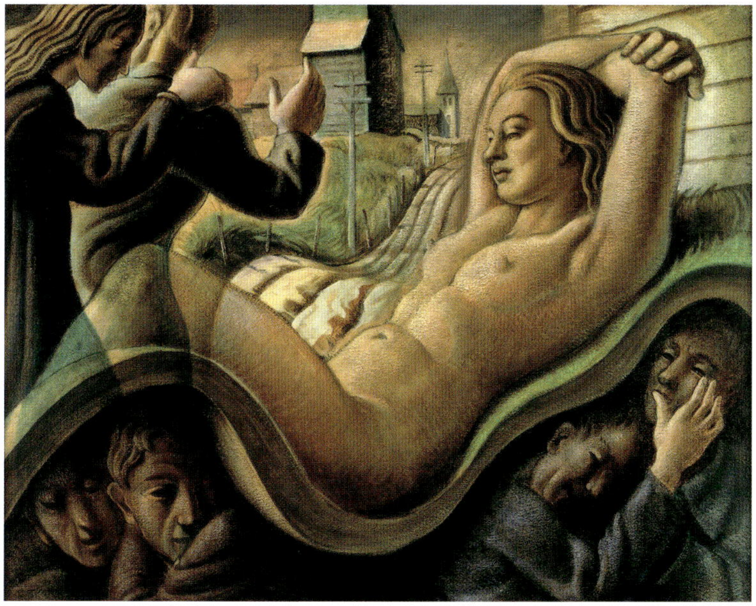

Henry Glyde
She Sat Upon a Hill Above the City, 1949
mixed media
Glenbow Museum, Calgary

This work exemplifies Glyde's lifelong interest in the figure and epic, though often enigmatic, allegories. A languid voluptuous nude in a classical pose rests on the ground of an undulating prairie landscape. Ghostly figures pass her by and appear underground, insubstantial and partly transparent. Influenced by visionary English artist Stanley Spencer, Glyde has set this biblical theme in a contemporary prairie town. The nude figure is brilliantly rendered and projects a calm, ethereal quality. The modelling of the volumes of full-rounded forms is cross-hatched and built up in layers. This is comparable to his mural technique, and gives translucence to her skin. There is a disconcerting tension between the serene nude and the other animated, baroque figures. This enigmatic scene is pervaded with an aura of mystery, eluding specific interpretation.

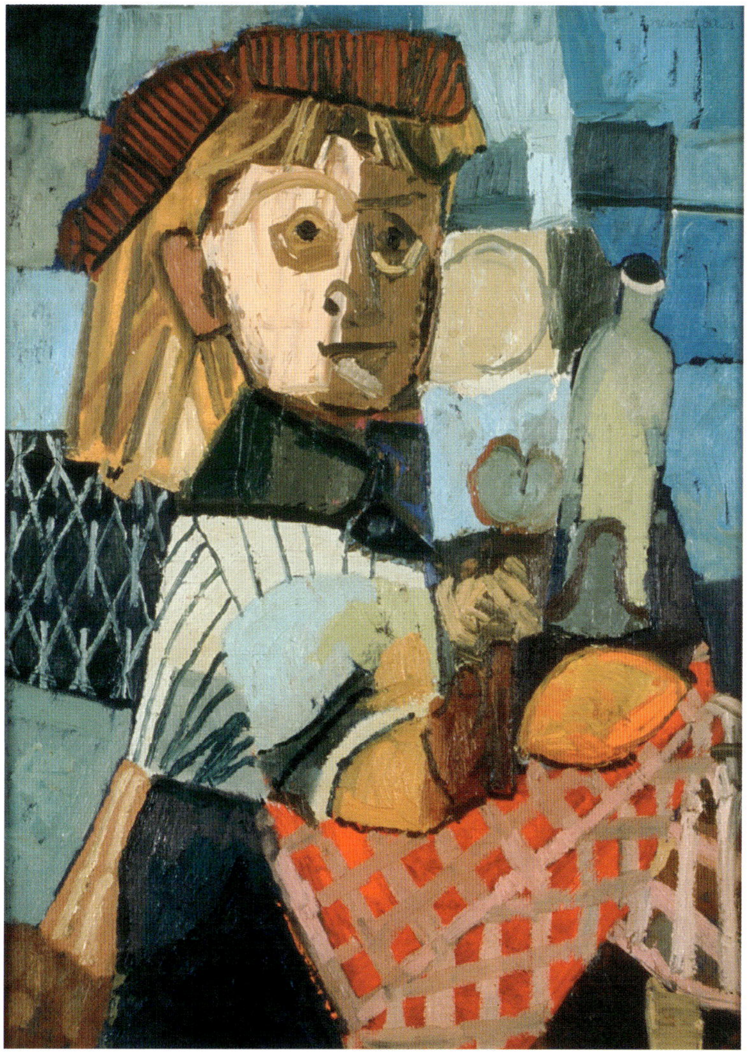

Maxwell Bates
Girl with Yellow Hair, n.d.
oil
Glenbow Museum, Calgary

This painting, with its distorted abstracted forms and harsh abrupt modelling, is infused with Bates's understanding of European modernism. He has systematically altered perspective, titled planes, flattened volumes, expanded spaces, and dislocated symmetry. Using the cubist device of combining several points of view, he creates disruption and a nervous energy through the abstracted rhythms. Expressing a poignant image of childhood innocence and vulnerability, the girl turns towards us, her features summarily drawn and asymmetrical, her heavily outlined eyes looking intently at us with a quizzical look. Her hair and clothing, angular and heavily outlined, is laid in with a few quick brushstrokes. The table is tipped up with an awkward perspective and the background is divided into geometric shapes, creating a flat, shallow space. The bright colour, symbolic rather than naturalistic, is discordant and jarring. The compositional and figurative distortions and expressive power of colour, shape, and brushwork delivers an emotionally charged image, intensely alive.

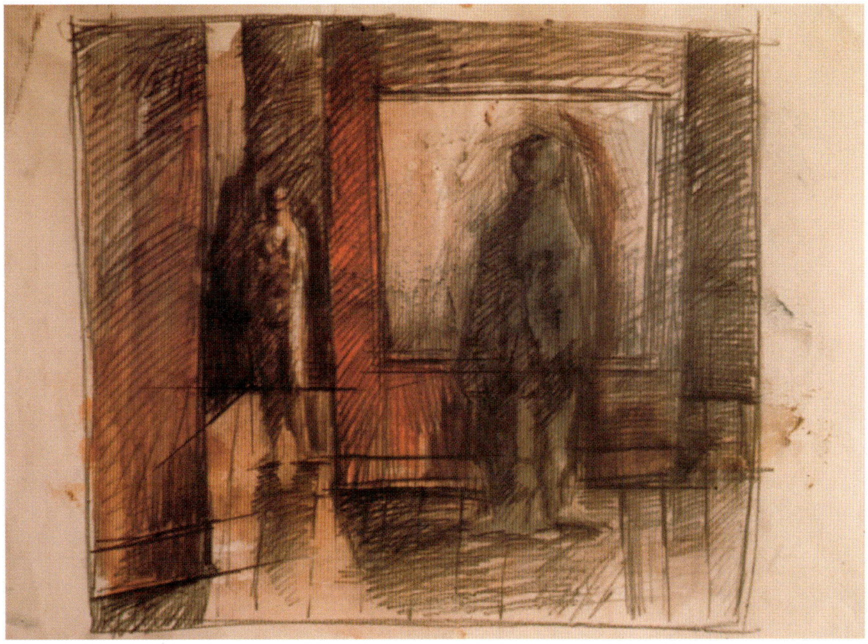

Norman Yates
Two Figures in a Space, 1960
watercolour and pencil
Collection of the artist

The summarily rendered male and female figures set in a stage-like space are like statues and stand apart, alienated, hallucinatory, and pathetic. Yates was interested in the dynamic relationship between space and figures rather than the figures themselves. Space is thus the main element of this composition, both in content and structure. The formal, classical setting is undermined by the animated fast drawing, which creates a nervous agitation. The sharp light and dark contrasts heighten the expressive power of the human psychological drama. The formal compositional means of disruption and edginess reflect the anxieties of our time.

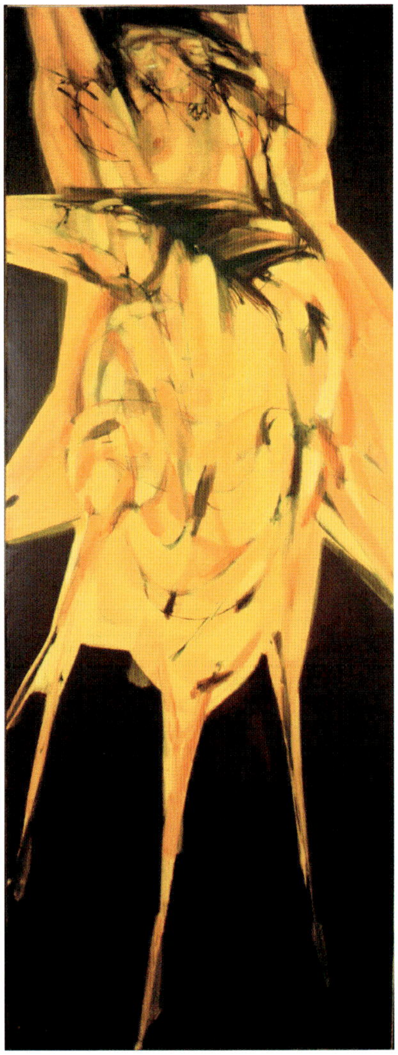

Ron Spickett
Fancy Flight, 1965
acrylic
Alberta Foundation for the Arts, Edmonton

For Spickett, painting is a philosophical quest. Here, the abstracted figures retain human and animal armature, the nuance of muscle and bone. Summary gestural marks indicate only the bare essentials of muscle and bone, yet denote the inner structures of man and beast. The figure on horseback merges into the horse, a continuous flow of body and limbs, inseparable and starkly silhouetted. Outlined against a dark background, they are isolated from the outside world and convey a mood of troubled anxiety. In his search for universal truths, Spickett uses the formal conventions of abstract art to express metaphors of the human condition through emotive colour and the expressive line.

Modernists: Embracing Abstraction

In the early twentieth century, social, political, and economic changes paralleled scientific and philosophical developments. This directly impacted the visual arts and led to a passion for change and renewal. European modernism was an explosive, liberating force, characterized by an enormous complexity, multiplicity, and simultaneity of ideas. Given impetus by the impressionists in the 1860s, modernism in Europe evolved through the post-impressionists to the cubists and German expressionists of the early twentieth century. After the Second World War, there was a further rupture with traditional values in culture and the arts. Experimentation became a driving force, with avant-garde movements rapidly superseded by newer ideas.

Despite the passion for change and new ideas elsewhere, in Alberta, early forays into modernism were met with disapproval. In 1928, both Maxwell Bates and William Stevenson were banned from exhibiting with the Calgary Art Club because their paintings were considered too "modern." Abstraction was slow to develop in Canada. It took hold in eastern Canada in the 1940s and became more widespread in the 1950s. In Alberta, landscape was considered regional, whereas abstract art was international. In post-war Alberta, artists looked increasingly to New York City, considered the centre of art, for inspiration. A number of artists, including Marion Nicoll and Stanford Perrott, studied there in the 1950s. Abstract expressionism was in full spate.

Starting in 1955, Alberta artists had opportunities to study closer to home at the Emma Lake summer workshops. Critical to the development of abstraction in the west, these workshops held north of Saskatoon were mainly led by American critics or avant-garde artists such as Will Barnet and Barnett Newman. A group of abstract artists in Saskatchewan, the Regina Five, was consolidated in the early 1960s into a national force in art through these workshops. Artists from Alberta attended the workshops and explored the formal or expressive aspects of painting and the problems of pictorial space. Alberta artists were also inspired by the proliferation of art magazines, which demonstrated the pervasive practice of abstraction. Most Alberta artists felt compelled to experiment with abstraction, but few maintained their commitment to it. Still, their exploration of purely formal concerns was evident in their subsequent work. No group of artists forged a coherent "movement" in Alberta in the 1950s and 1960s. There was no support for abstract art in Alberta and most artists became disillusioned and gave up. Marion Nicoll was exceptional in her ongoing dedication to abstraction and she became one of the most influential artists and teachers here.

Abstract work moved away from the traditional representation of illusionistic space in which the frame was a window through which to view the world. Artists sought to work on the two-dimensional picture plane itself, with colour and form articulating the dynamic push-pull of space. Abstract art ranged from the spontaneous, intuitive, and gestural, to the more intellectual, premeditated, and formal approaches.

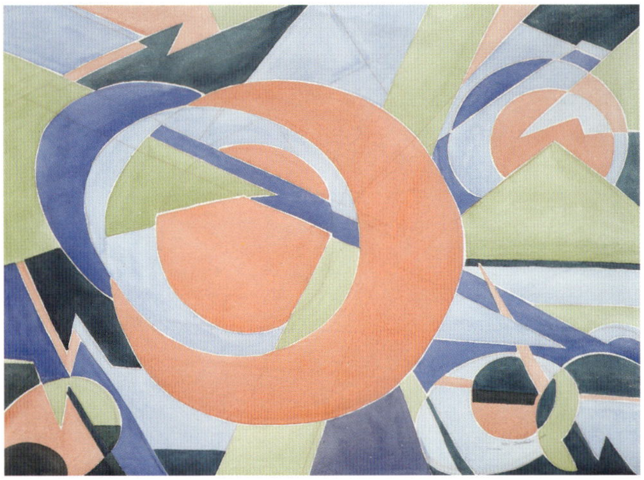

Helen Stadelbauer
Breaking the Atom, 1946
watercolour
Glenbow Museum, Calgary

This is one of the earliest abstract paintings in Alberta, and likely one of the first by Stadelbauer, who before and even after 1946 worked in a naturalistic style, often showing the influence of Henry Glyde. Here, the formal arrangement of concentric circles, pierced through with ziz-zag forms and triangles, creates hard-edged abstraction. Through colour and form, a deep space is implied. Fields of light and transparent watercolour are carefully modulated. Despite the abstract forms, there is a suggestion of triangular mountain forms and faceted fields. It is likely this was abstracted from nature.

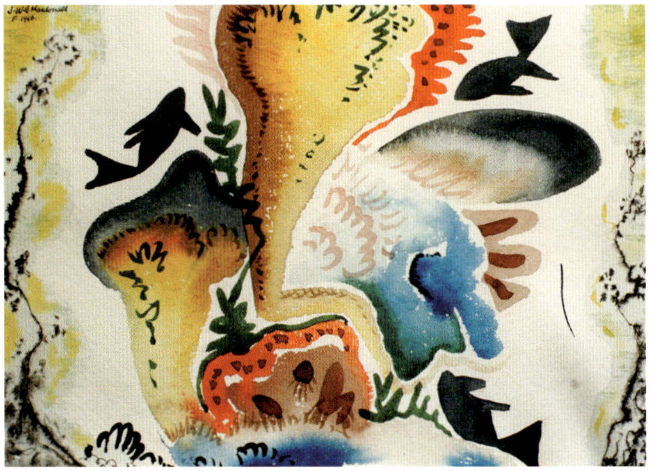

Jock Macdonald
Fish playground, 1946
watercolour
Alberta Foundation for the Arts, Edmonton

Macdonald, who taught at the Provincial Institute of Technology and Art in 1946, had practised automatic drawing since 1943. Born of French Surrealism and Freudian psychology, automatism sought to tap the unconscious and bring submerged feelings and forms, suppressed by the conscious civilized mind, to the surface. Automatic works possess a vitality not attained in any other way. Through quiet concentration, Macdonald has allowed his brush to move of its own accord to lay in amorphous forms in transparent, vibrant, colour washes overlapped with graded halo-like edges. Embellished with his personal vocabulary of hieroglyphic symbols, simplified fish forms were added to these dream-like images, creating an underwater fantasy vibrant with spontaneous power.

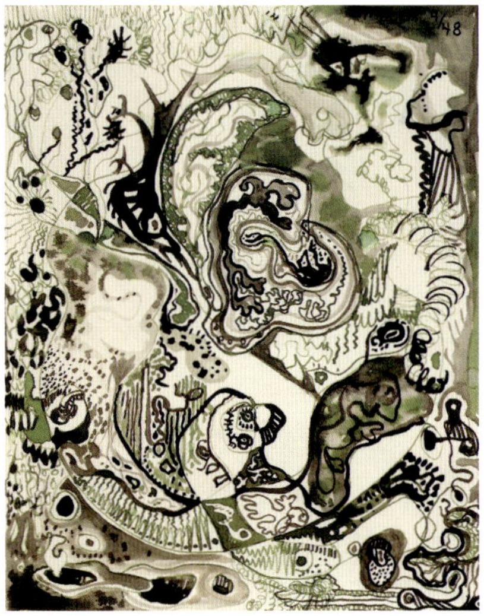

Marion Nicoll
Untitled, April 1948
brush, pen, and ink
Glenbow Museum, Calgary

After Jock Macdonald introduced her to the automatic process, Nicoll practised automatic drawing almost daily for over a decade, producing a huge number of enigmatic drawings in her notebooks. She considered these a studio exercise, like doing scales, and did not exhibit them. She believed in Carl Jung's theory that no human experience is forgotten. She explored the amazing wealth of subconscious imagery that sprang from her pen and brush. Freeing her conscious mind enabled her to reach something more intuitive in her art. Automatism also freed Nicoll from a representational approach and prepared the way for her later exploration of pure abstraction.

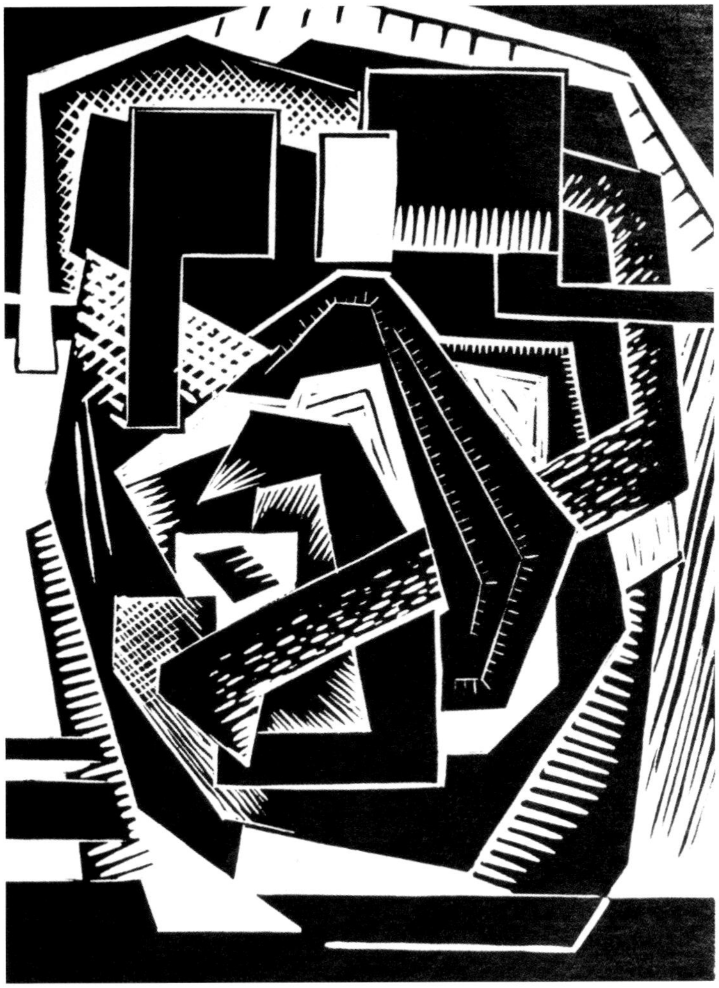

Doug Motter
Forward Pass, 1949
linocut
Alberta Foundation for the Arts, Edmonton

This blockprint was included in the December 1949 issue of *Highlights* magazine, published by the Alberta Society of Artists from 1948 to the late 1960s to foster communication about Alberta art. Working from an idea about basketball, Motter has constructed a bold abstract image in which there are minimal references to life: the suggestion of the upheld arms of a figure and a basketball board. Some areas of the block have been completely cut away resulting in areas of white alternating with sharply contrasting black forms. Different patterns of cutting within the forms create tones of grey. Complex interlocking shapes emanate from a central core of articulated forms, creating a lively rhythm across the surface.

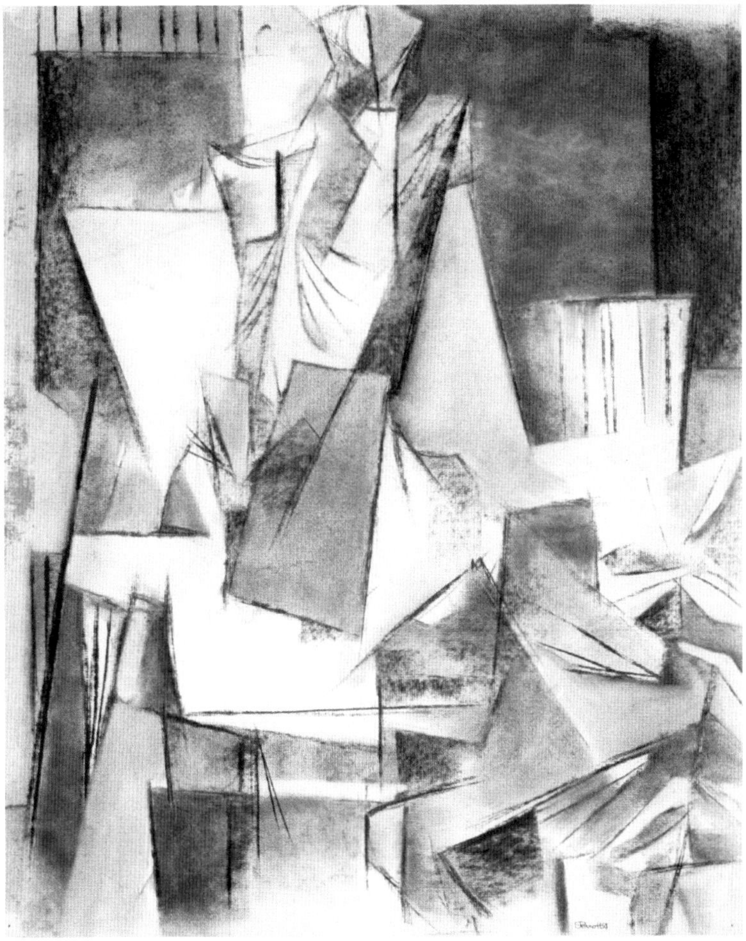

Stanford Perrott
Untitled, 1954
charcoal
Alberta Foundation for the Arts, Edmonton

Perrott's studies with Hans Hofmann in Provincetown, Massachusetts, in 1954 had an immediate impact on his work. A major force in American art, Hofmann absorbed first-hand the experience of European modernism, especially cubism and expressionism, which he synthesized into an ideology for American abstract painting. Here, Perrott has used principles of cubism to abstract from life. Forms are tipped up on a table with background forms merely suggested. Various sides of the different forms are shown, allowing you to see both around and through them—you can see not only two but three dimensions. Sensitive yet emphatic, clear lines articulate the forms in a summary manner. Shading indicates different planes of the forms, all woven into a complex cubic structure. Other works by Perrott at this time became completely non-objective.

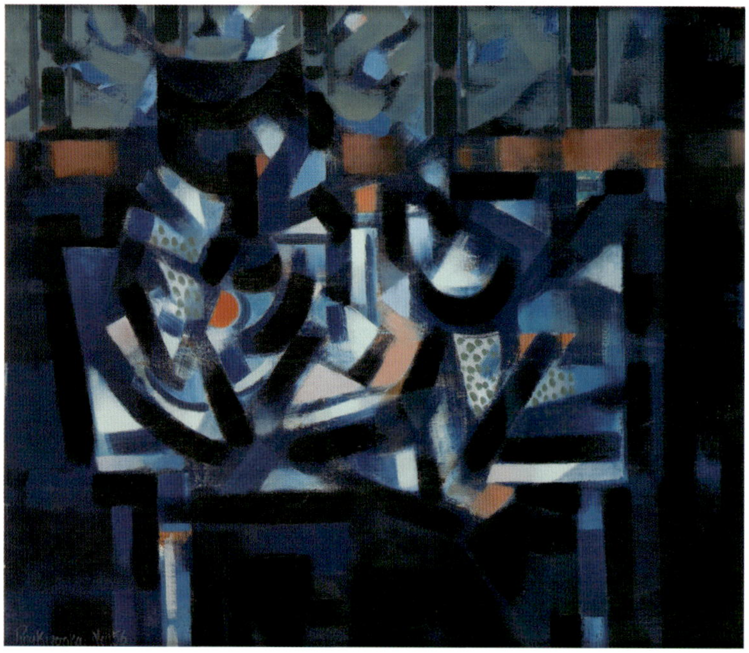

Roy Kiyooka
Blue Still Life, 1956
oil
Glenbow Museum, Calgary

Though this work is still recognizable as a still life taken from daily life, Kiyooka reveals his debt to late cubism in the way he has abstracted the forms and tipped them up on the table creating an awkward perspective. In the background are five panels of an abstract painting. In the foreground, forms on the table have been abstracted and painted in light colours, some with patterning. Over this, bold, quickly rendered fat, dark blue brushstrokes partly obscure the painting underneath, negating representational elements. These expressive slashes of paint set up a lively articulation of interrelated forms creating a rhythm across the surface. Monochromatic ranges of blue create a vivid colour harmony and are enlivened with dashes of white, orange, and pink. This painting shows Kiyooka moving away from a representational style, which preceded his move into pure abstraction.

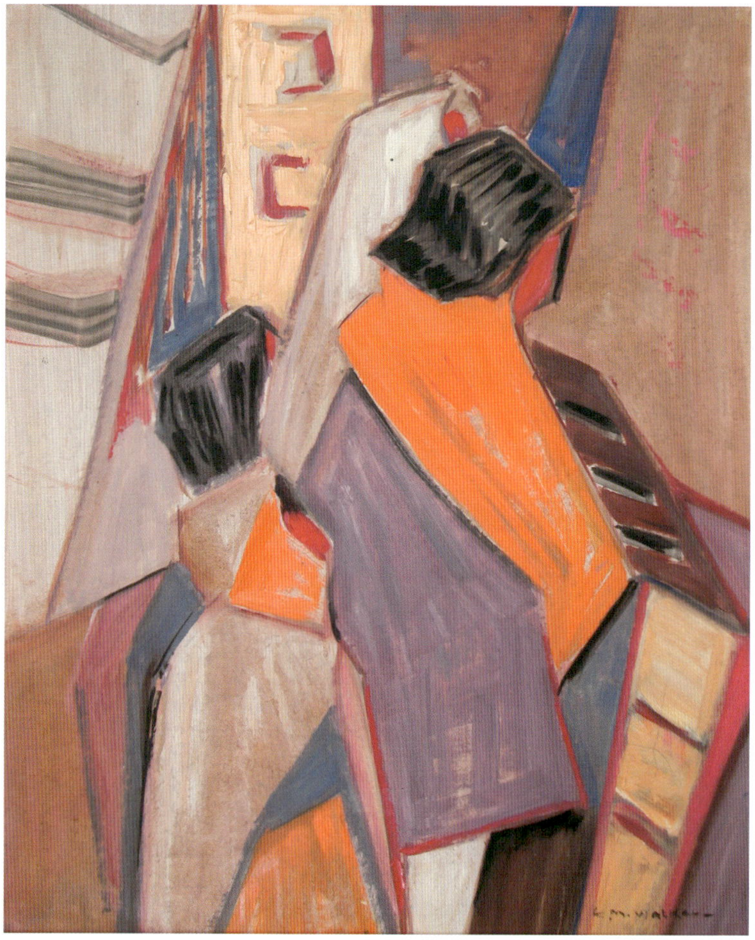

Ella May Walker
Untitled, 1957
oil
Art Gallery of Alberta, Edmonton

This work was created in the same year that Walker attended the Emma Lake workshop in Saskatchewan with Will Barnet. She has abstracted from life, though there are only slight clues as to her objective sources. Large forms, some heavily outlined for emphasis, have been assembled and arranged around a central structure, set against a background as though in a room creating an illusion of space. Using a very painterly technique, the forms are roughed in. Walker's work is concerned with solving the pictorial problems of organizing forms in space.

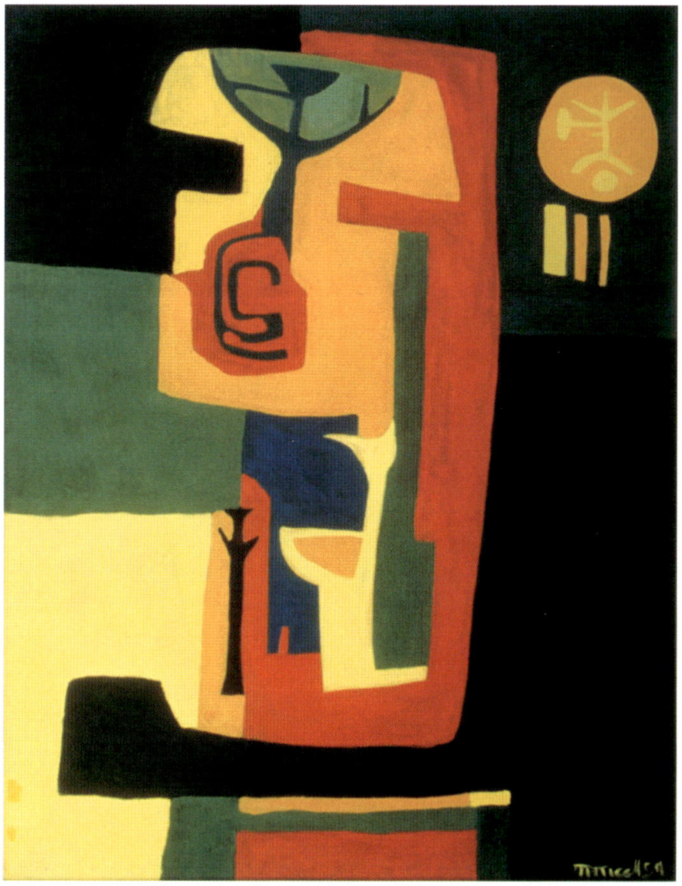

Marion Nicoll
Spring, 1959
oil
Glenbow Museum, Calgary

Nicoll was the most significant abstract artist in Alberta. After her studies with Will Barnet at Emma Lake and then New York, Nicoll's work became increasingly simplified and abstract, a more intellectual and formal approach after she abandoned the intuitive approach of automatism. Initially she abstracted from life, seeking the essence of form, but increasingly objects became just the starting point from which to develop compositions. In numerous preparatory sketches, ideas were reworked and pared down in a continual reassessment of form.

Spring is a transitional work between her objective and non-objective painting. Simplified tree and plant forms are still present and an orange disc represents the sun. But spring is even more strongly referenced in Nicoll's symbolic use of colour with its subliminal psychological power. Brilliant yellows, oranges, and reds denote sunshine, life, and growth. Green describes new growth. Nicoll said, "Painting for me is all on the picture plane, the actual surface of the canvas, with power held in the horizontal and vertical movements of the expanding colour shapes."[1] She was no longer interested in creating perceptual reality or illusionistic space. She has used a compositional scheme derived from classical sources, in which scale, position, and the balance of horizontal and vertical flat forms are carefully worked out. The interlocking pattern of symbolic shapes and the articulation of colour create a visual rhythm across the surface. The outer dark forms anchor the composition, and the intense warm colours and smaller shapes of the central section create a sense of depth. Nicoll has achieved a pure, well-ordered composition in this formal abstract work.

Kenneth Sturdy
Autumn Nocturne, 1959
oil on plywood
Alberta Foundation for the Arts, Edmonton

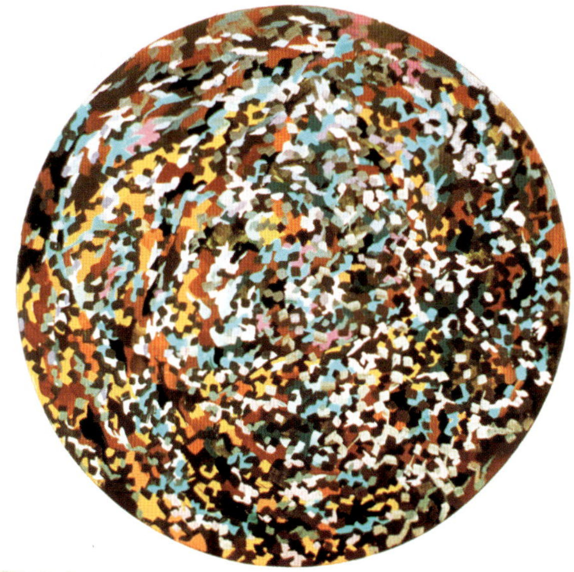

Sturdy produced a series of circular paintings in the 1960s, some dripped and poured, others painted like this one. In an act of pure painting, he has painted layer upon layer of small coloured marks, building up a rich tapestry of colour. No mark is the same, each agitated mark adding to the lively surface. There is a complex spatial tension with the colour creating spatial depth.

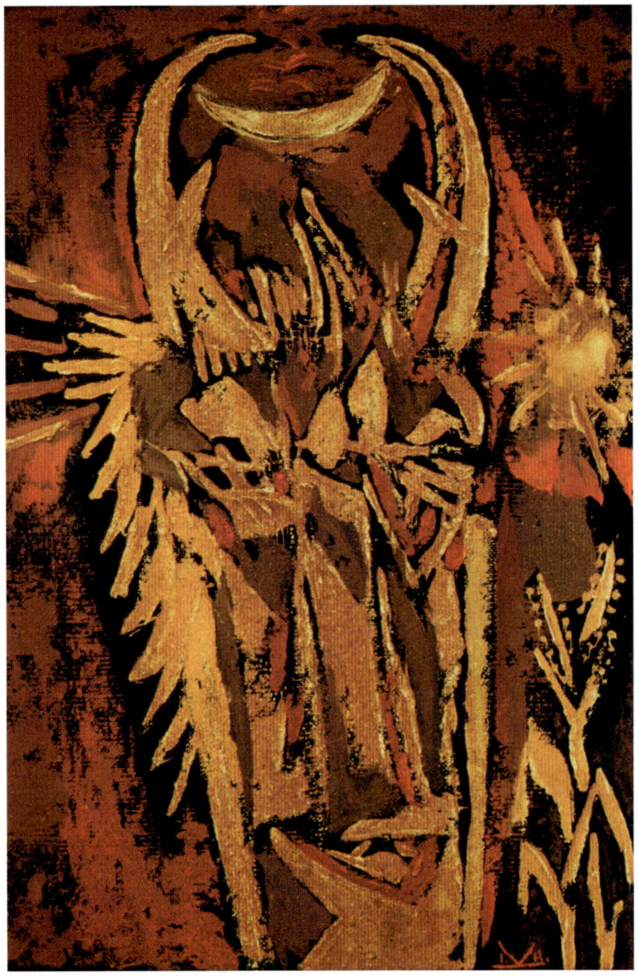

Illingworth Kerr
Drought, 1960
oil and sand
Alberta Foundation for the Arts, Edmonton

During his stay in England (1960–61), Kerr began experimenting with mixing sand into his oil paint to create a more three-dimensional surface. *Drought* draws on these experiments and his studies in Massachusetts in 1954 with Hans Hofmann, who instructed artists to build up the composition with planes to achieve a new reality, free from imitation. Working intuitively on a dark ground, he has dashed in the horned, mask-like shape, the sun and plants positioned to the right, and then filled in and around this with quick strokes of green and red. The paint and sand mixture is laid in with a palette knife, dragged and spread across the surface, creating areas of thicker and thinner paint. This gives it a textured, layered, relief effect. Though a semblance of the image emerges, the method is subconscious and spontaneous. It is about the action of painting.

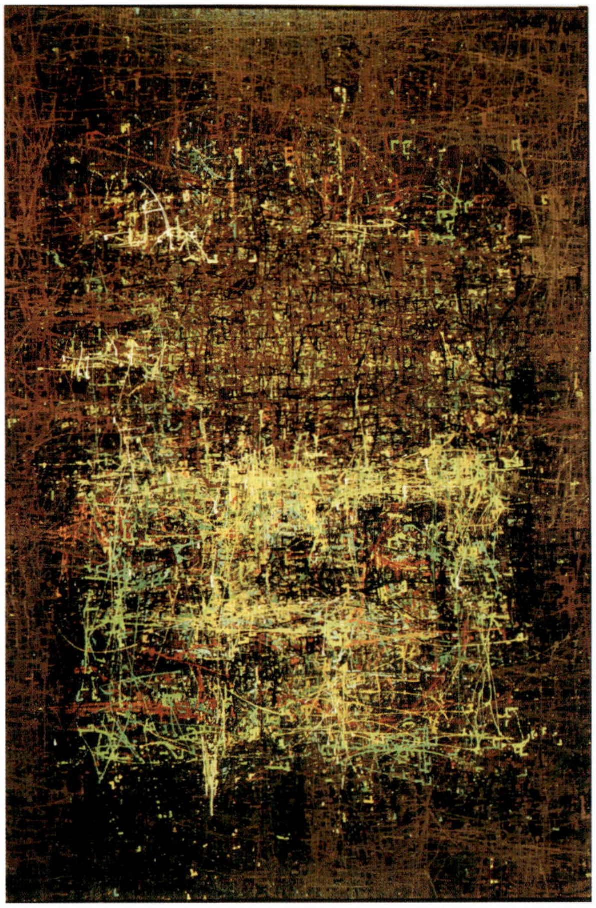

Ronald Spickett
Enamel Grass, 1960
enamel
Alberta Foundation for the Arts, Edmonton

Searching for both inner and outer harmony, Spickett experimented with pure abstraction in the early 1960s. Here, working spontaneously and fast, he has built up layer upon layer of threads of paint, dribbled, spattered, and thrown onto the masonite surface. Starting from a dark ground, he has built up these layers of paint, getting ever lighter, with touches of orange enlivening the surface. Each new layer still reveals the one beneath it, creating a delicate tracery of lines with a complex web of paint in an all-over design. The overlapping skeins of paint hover on the picture plane creating a sense of space. In this expressive and intuitive work, inspiration is drawn from the subconscious mind, with no deliberation and erasure during the process. The flow of energy provides a unifying principle. The action of producing the painting is the driving force and intent. This method is akin to that of the American abstract expressionist Jackson Pollock.

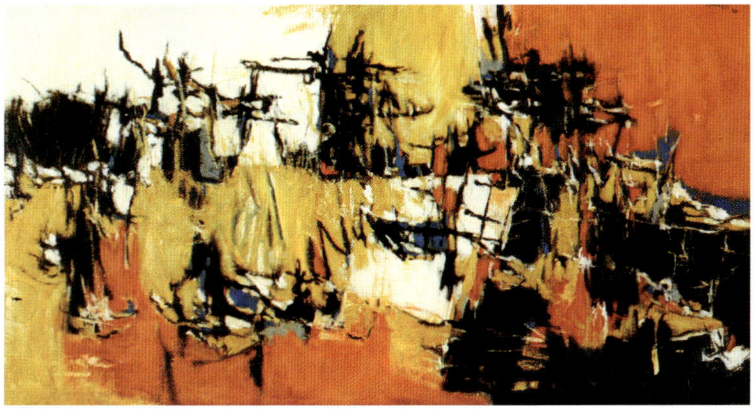

Thelma Manarey
Untitled, 1960
oil
Alberta Foundation for the Arts, Edmonton

In this painting Manarey has created zones of black, yellow-ochre, and brick red. Over the black, she has worked cream, ochre, and red. She leaves some of the black revealed, creating an armature that provides a strong structure for the composition. Over this she has worked fast calligraphic marks with vigorous energy. Patches of intense blue enliven the surface. The alternating layers of colour articulate back and forth, creating spatial depth and a dynamic rhythm across the picture plane.

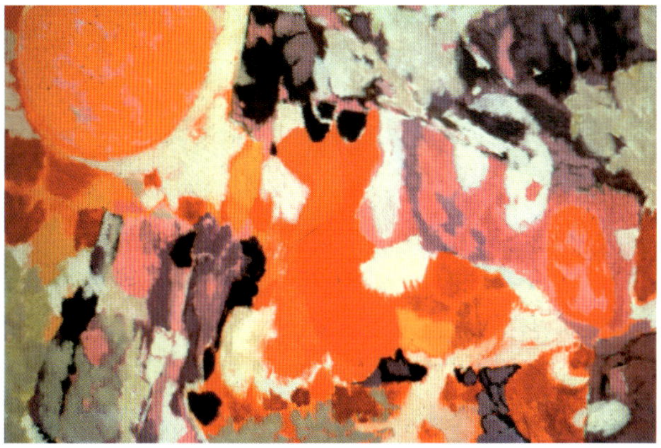

George Wood
Painting A53, 1962
acrylic
Collection of the artist

Some of Wood's paintings during the early 1960s were inspired by microcosmic designs in nature. These designs denoted organic life and growth, especially the designs in birds and insects together with cellular structures and crystals. These were starting points for abstractions of softly painted forms of many thin layers of vivid colour, creating fields of resonant atmospheric shapes with chromatic sensations that arouse a visual and emotional response. Forms radiating luminous auras drift across the surface and diffuse shapes coalesce into others, edges blurring. These are not explicit symbols, but abstract pictorial elements.

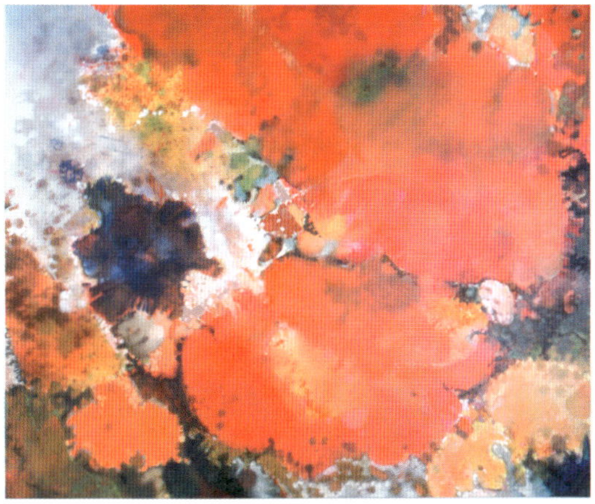

Ted Godwin
Red Grew, 1961
oil
Glenbow Museum, Calgary

This painting developed from Godwin's explorations after being inspired at a workshop at Emma Lake by Barnett Newman, a Colour Field painter and central figure in the development of abstract expressionism in New York. After the workshop, Godwin began painting in oils on stretched canvas, working on a much larger scale. The inspiration for *Red Grew* came from organic and microscopic images in *Scientific American* magazine and this initiated a series of paintings that grew organically from the artist's process. Godwin poured thin stains or drips of paint onto the canvas as it lay on the floor. Further painting was done with the canvas hanging on the wall. Using glazes, he built up layers of thin colour washes, some impregnated with contrasting colour, bleeding out into other colours. Seemingly free, it has a carefully orchestrated harmony of light and dark tonalities and blazing colour. The result is a glowing luminous canvas of sensuous colour with vigorous organic forms that looks like the surface of the moon. The process was an improvisation akin to the jazz music he loves. This painting was exhibited in the *Five Painters from Regina* show at the National Gallery of Canada in December 1961, which brought the group national attention.

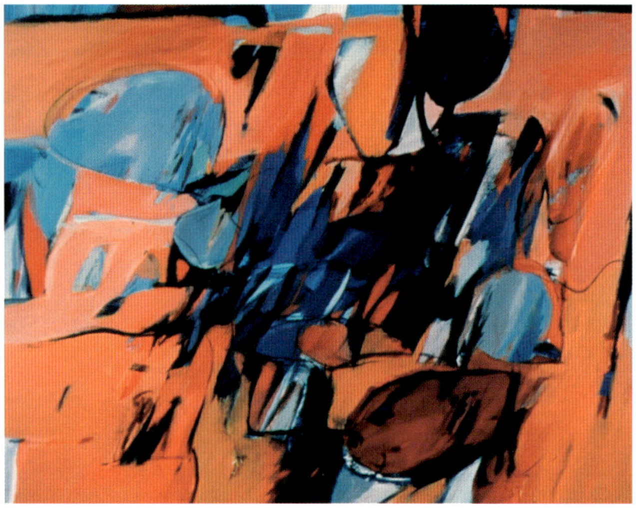

George Mihalcheon
Composition RBB #5, 1962
acrylic
Glenbow Museum, Calgary

When the influential New York art critic Clement Greenberg came through Calgary in 1962, he said Mihalcheon and Ken Sturdy were the only Calgary artists whose painting approached New York "flashiness."[2] This painting is an act of pure abstraction, of bold gesture and vibrant colour, which creates the dynamic push–pull of space. The artist has worked from a blue underpainting and layered a range of hot red to orange colour over this. Painting quickly with a heavily laden brush and slashes of heavy paint (or dragging thin paint across the surface), he has created a rich-textured painting. Black is used over this to delineate shapes and add calligraphic detail and expressive gestures to this vigorous composition.

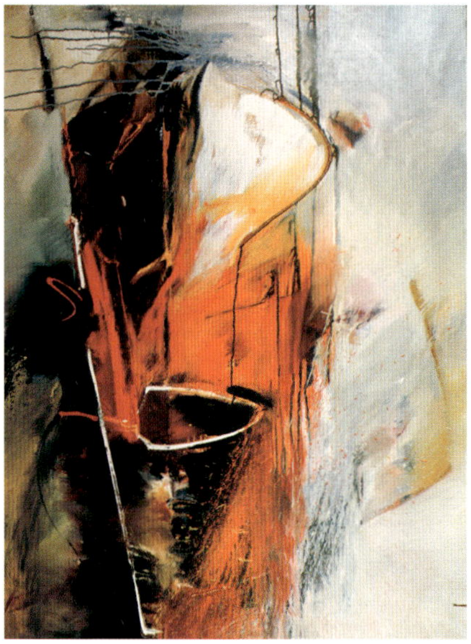

Les Graff
Untitled, 1962
oil
Alberta Foundation for the Arts, Edmonton

Working on a light background, Graff has applied fast vigorous brushstrokes and spattered paint in a rapid intuitive act of painting. In some areas, paint has been thinned and runs down the canvas, creating a grid of drips. Into this he has "drawn" abstract shapes, with some graphic marks squeezed directly out of the tubes of paint. By manipulating pigment, he has created a variety of textures. This is dynamic, passionate action-painting with a hot pulsing central core of saturated colour.

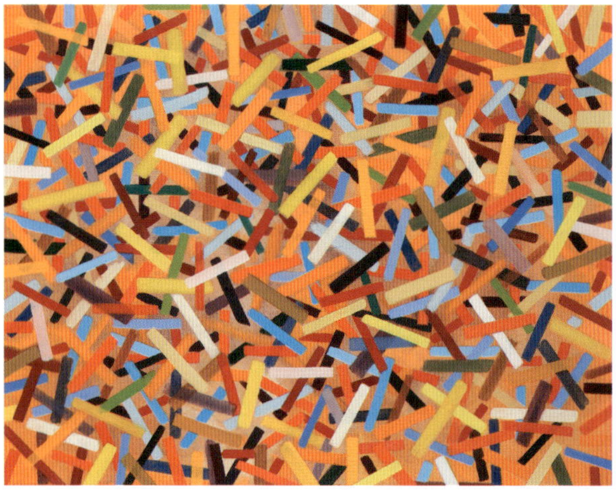

Harry Kiyooka
Orange Jam, 1964
oil
Glenbow Museum, Calgary

Kiyooka's early work was inspired by abstract expressionism. This painting is one of a series done after his return in 1961 from studies in Europe. Inspired by his observation of a log jam during the spring runoff on the Fraser River in British Columbia, Kiyooka has arranged strips of hot, brilliant colour, with brushstrokes clean and squared off, on an orange ground. Optically dynamic and apparently random, they are placed at all angles, creating a lively alternating rhythm dancing over the surface. The web of marks moves in and out and floats to the surface of the picture plane with a sense of infinity behind it.

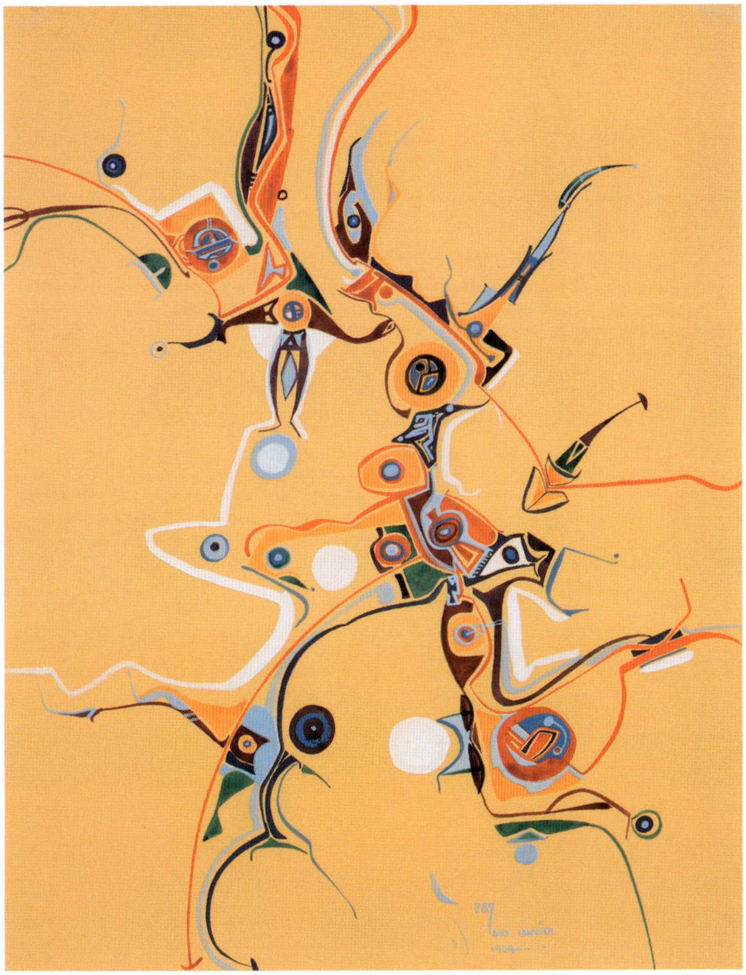

Alex Janvier
Walking in Snow, 1964
tempera
Glenbow Museum, Calgary

Janvier has melded his training in modern European art with his traditional Dene First Nations heritage, imagery, and beliefs. His work is impacted by the energy of the natural world—he thinks of the wind as the Great Spirit talking to him. His stylized linear motifs relate to traditional geometric designs found in First Nations beadwork and clothing decoration. In this work, his fluid, attenuated calligraphic lines swirl energetically across the surface in constant motion, enclosing geometric symbolic elements. Flatly painted forms build from the central core, enclosed in repeated bands of different thickness and colour, like echoes making a complex pattern. Bold primary colours create a lively articulation of the space. The orchestration of line, colour, and form creates a dynamic spatial effect in this abstract painting.

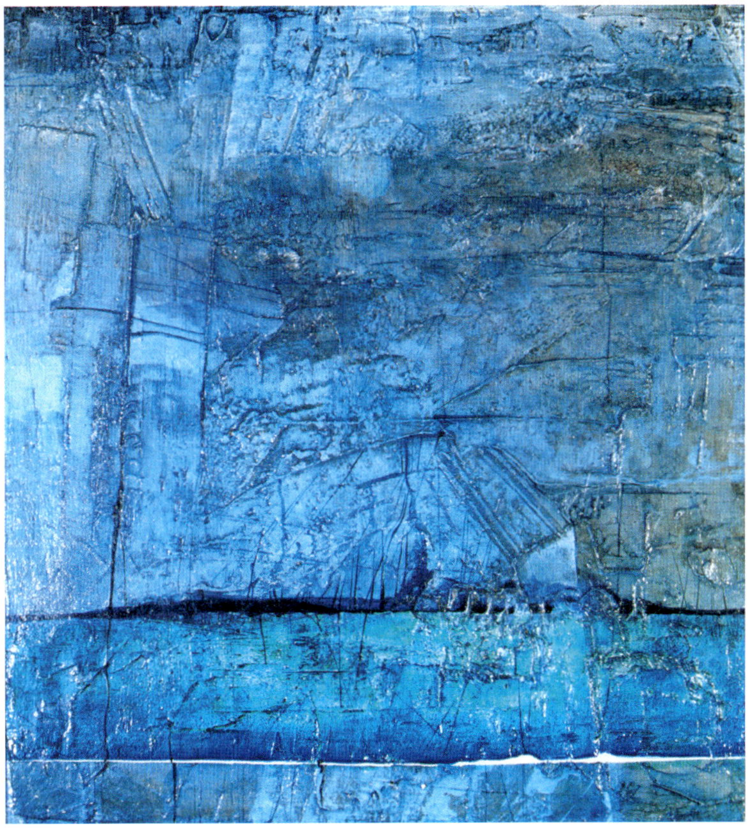

Jack Taylor
Composition #2, 1968
acrylic and gesso
Government House Foundation, Edmonton

Even in his most abstract work, Taylor continued to be inspired by nature in his search for an uncomplicated statement about the natural environment. His intent was to work on the picture plane and manipulate the surface to reflect his analysis of the underlying structure of rock and ice related to his study of glacial formations. Here, he has first applied a thick medium of gesso to the surface, which he has worked with a palette knife to create a shallow textured relief. Over this he has applied three bands of colour in thin luminous veils and then glazed the surface. The translucency of paint in close-valued blues is in a rich, harmonic key.

Art for the People

Few prints were made in Alberta before the 1930s.[3] After 1931, the annual exhibitions of the Alberta Society of Artists (ASA) provided an important outlet for printmakers. Henry Glyde taught linocut printing at the Provincial Institute of Technology and Art in Calgary from 1936 and introduced a full printmaking course in 1942. His student, Margaret Shelton, became the most prolific early printmaker in Alberta. Walter Phillips was a pioneer of the colour woodblock print in Canada. As a mature artist with an international reputation for his prints when he settled in Alberta in 1940, he was an inspiration to Alberta artists. In 1953, Maxwell Bates and John Snow became pioneers in lithography in Calgary using two presses they had salvaged from a commercial printing company, learning by trial and error.

The publication of the ASA newsletter, *Highlights*, spurred interest in printmaking. From 1948 until 1962, artists contributed original prints, which were "tipped into" the newsletter. Editions of up to one hundred prints were made of each image. Further impetus for printmakers was the Alberta College of Art's annual Calgary Graphics exhibition from 1959 until 1974.

Up north in Edmonton, George Blair Brown made etchings and exhibited them with the Toronto-based Canadian Society of Graphic Art in the 1930s. Starting in the late 1940s, George Weber championed the introduction of serigraphs in Alberta: he gave lectures, wrote articles, and taught workshops at the Edmonton Museum of Art and the University of Alberta. Weber organized an important exhibition of western prints called the Western Printmakers Exhibit at the University of Toronto's Hart House in 1957.

Starting in the 1960s, there was greater experimentation in printmaking and new well-equipped facilities were set up. Student enrolment in printmaking increased dramatically. Artists worked on a larger scale and used mixed techniques. The first printmaking course at the University of Alberta was set up by Helmut Becker in 1966 and expanded in 1969 by Roger Silvester. A graduate program was established in 1970, and Walter Jule and Lyndal Osborne arrived to teach in 1971. Private print workshops were also set up to provide a cooperative atmosphere in which to produce prints.

If there was one individual who played a pivotal role in printmaking in Alberta it was John Kenneth Esler. His teaching created a fertile environment for printmakers here, first at the Alberta College of Art from 1964 to 1968, and then at the University of Calgary from 1968 to 1980, where he set up the printmaking program. Over the years, he brought in international printmakers to run workshops: Toshi Yoshida in 1967; Shane Weare in 1968; and Andrew Stasik in 1969. When the two national print societies, the Canadian Society of Graphic Art (CSGA) and the Society of Canadian Painter-Etchers and Engravers (CPE) established in the 1920s in Ontario, joined forces in 1976, Esler became the first chairman of the new organization, the Print and Drawing Council of Canada, and organized the first exhibition in Calgary in 1978.

What is a Print?

A print is an image that has been pulled from a wood, metal, or stone surface, and is then produced in multiple copies. A design is created on the print surface and this surface or plate is inked and an impression is made on paper, often using a printing press. Original prints are works of art printed in editions set by the artist. An average edition runs at around fifty prints, although this is not set in stone (or wood or metal!). Confusion arises when reproductions are labelled "prints." However, reproductions are paintings that have been photographically copied and mechanically printed—they are not original prints, even if they are hand-signed by the artist.

Print Techniques

As there is considerably more confusion about prints than most other art processes, we have provided a description of the main print processes below to aid the reader. The main print techniques fall into the following categories:

Relief or Block Printing—A design that is carved into the surface of a block of wood. Ink is applied to the surface of the block and transferred to paper by applying light pressure. Examples of block printing include:

woodcut—cut from a plank of fairly soft wood usually one inch thick
wood engraving—cut across the grain using very hard wood
linocut—produced as an industrial floor covering since the 1860s, linocut is made up of a thick layer of oxidized linseed oil, rosin, and fillers on a hessian backing, which is a quarter to half an inch thick. Artists began using it for prints in the twentieth century by cutting into its soft pliable surface.

Intaglio—An image that is printed from a metal plate, usually copper or zinc, about a quarter inch thick. Incisions are made on the plate. When it comes to printing, the plate is warmed and the surface is inked up so that the ink penetrates the incised lines. The excess ink is then cleaned off the surface of the plate and it is put through a press with considerable pressure, printing from the incised lines. Examples of intaglio include:

engraving—lines are carved directly onto the plate surface with a V-shaped cutting edge
drypoint—a form of engraving using a sharp-pointed tool, which creates a small burr of metal that holds extra ink and gives the line a soft character
etching—a ground- or acid-resistant material is applied to the surface of the plate; a design is incised onto this; and the plate is then immersed in an acid bath that etches the incised lines onto the plate
soft ground etching—the soft ground enables the transfer of impressions of textured materials onto the plate's surface
aquatint—etchings made with a porous ground, which results in tonal areas.

Lithography—An image that is printed after marks are drawn with a greasy medium onto a printing surface, either stone or metal. The marked surface is dampened with water, which settles only on the unmarked areas. Greasy ink is then applied to the plate, which adheres only to the greasy design marks. The plate is then run through a press.

Serigraph—Also called a "silkscreen," a serigraph is a stencil that is applied to a silk fabric stretched onto a frame. Ink is then squeegeed through the screen. Where there is no stencil to block the ink, it will pass through onto a piece of paper.

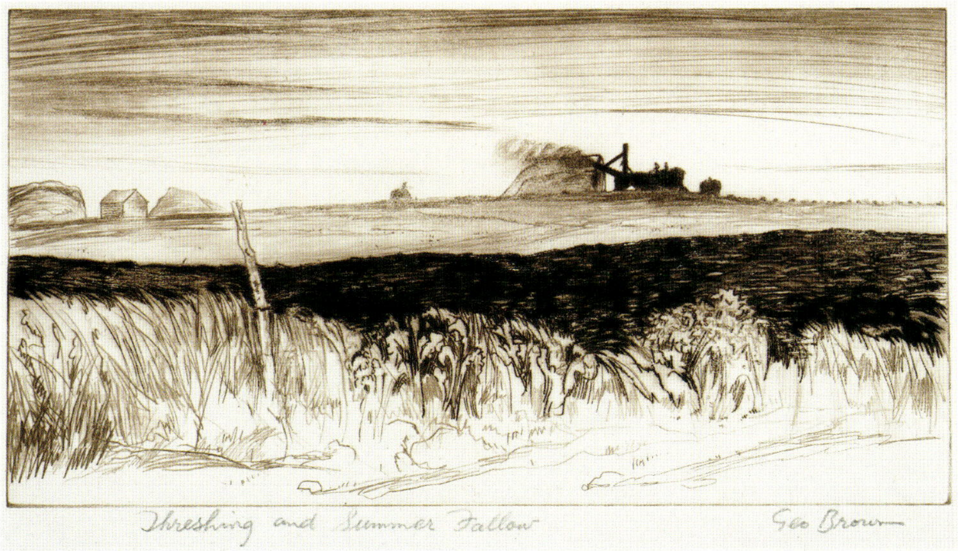

George Blair Brown
Threshing and Summer Fallow, n.d.
etching
Glenbow Museum, Calgary

By using a horizontal format, Brown emphasizes the broad expanse of flat prairie with its straight horizon line. Using the etching technique effectively, he has placed light against dramatic dark areas of tone. Quickly drawn, delicately etched lines delineate the foreground grasses, the distant fields, and the sky and are produced with a shallow etch onto the plate. The upturned sod of the fallow field is deeply etched, producing an intense, dark area.

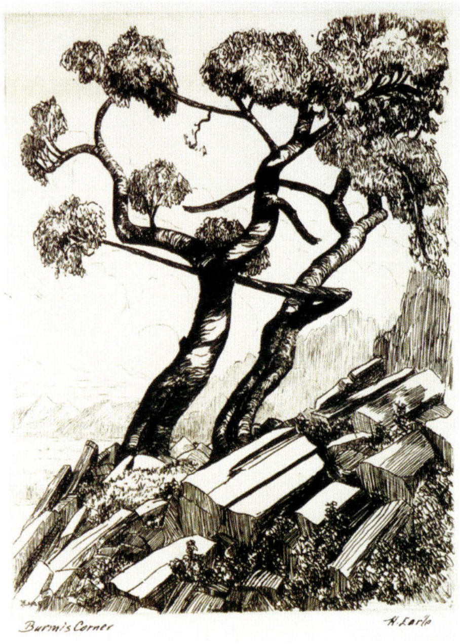

Herbert Earle
Burmis Corner, 1950
soft ground etching
Alberta Foundation for the Arts, Edmonton

This print was included in *Highlights* magazine in December 1950. Earle has built up the composition using the fine lines made possible with the etching needle to create a carefully observed and delicately drawn image. The gnarled trees, the dominant compositional element, have been deeply etched, while the distant landscape has been very lightly etched, providing an animated image of subtle, tonal contrasts.

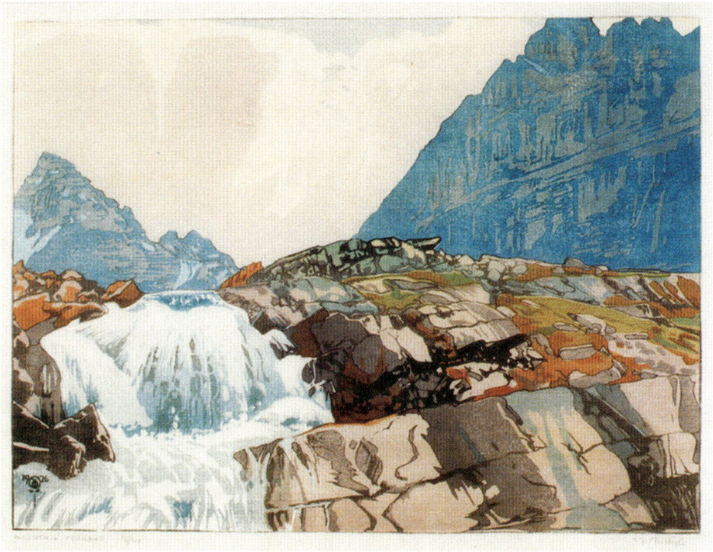

Walter Phillips
Mountain Torrent, 1926
woodcut
Alberta Foundation for the Arts, Edmonton

Through his exceptional woodcuts, Phillips influenced a generation of Canadian printmakers. In his work, he adopted ideas from traditional Japanese prints, which employ unusual viewpoints, tonal gradation, subtle colour harmonies, and outlines in black. This image has an unusual vantage point from below the falls, looking up towards them. The volumes of rocky terrain are rendered with broken-up segmented forms and complex overlays of colour. Further layering of colour provides a convincing representation of gushing water. This characteristic of the colour woodcut, building up the surface with repeated overlays of transparent watercolour, provides a rich luminous effect. The wood grain texture from the block accentuates the texture of the craggy mountains. Inspired by nature, Phillips produced vigorous, naturalistic prints.

Walter Phillips
Vista Lake, 1932
wood engraving
Glenbow Museum, Calgary

In addition to woodcuts, Phillips also produced black and white wood engravings of consummate skill. This dramatic composition is made more intense through the large area of rich velvety black of the mountains offset by the brilliant white of the lake. Details are picked out with fine and delicate cutting of the block and white twinkles against the rich black.

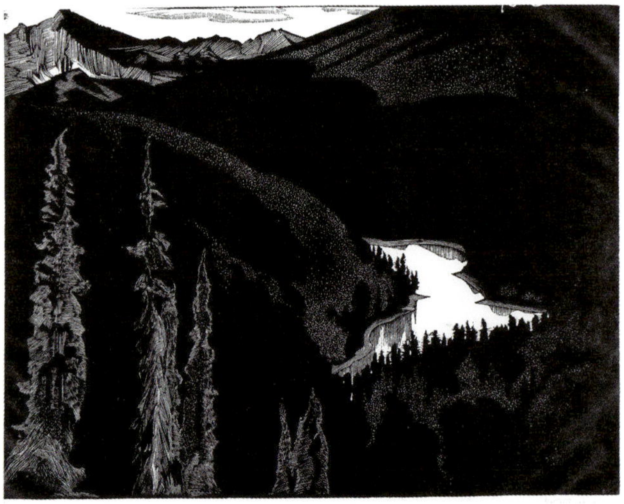

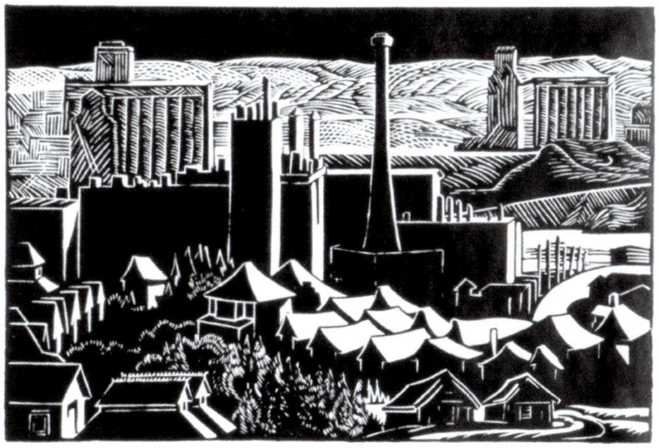

Margaret Shelton
East Calgary, 1940
linocut
Alberta Foundation for the Arts, Edmonton

As well as the natural landscape, Shelton had a keen interest in city scenes and industrial subjects. *East Calgary* shows her mastery of form and design. It demonstrates a refinement and technical brilliance unusual for a linocut. Shapes are simplified to their barest essentials. Hatched lines merely suggest trees in the foreground; rhythmical lines describe the undulating foothills. White has been used to pick out the buildings where the light strikes them, making intelligent and economical use of cut-out areas. Bold lines and flat masses of black and white create a dramatic, geometrically abstracted image. A rhythm flows through the print, particularly the roofs of the houses, creating a visual dynamism. Shelton was exceptional in Alberta: she was one of the very few artists making a living solely from her art production. She produced 174 block prints and numerous drawings and paintings in her lifetime.

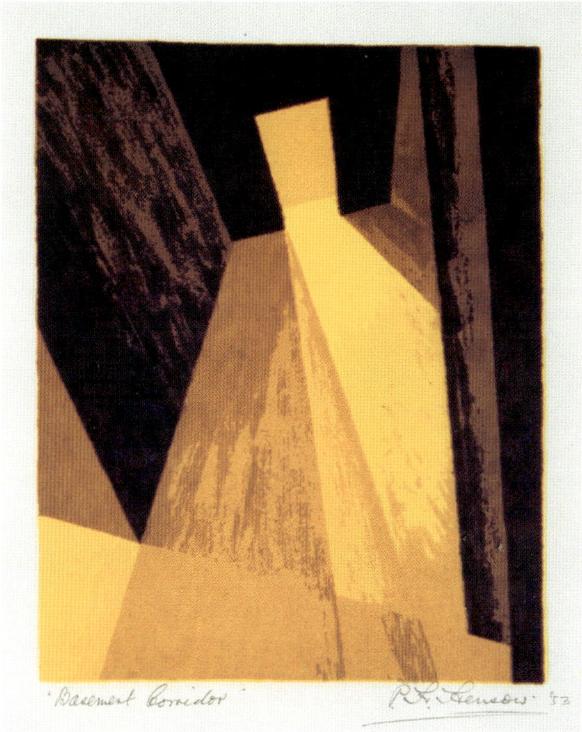

Percy Henson
Basement Corridor, 1953
serigraph
Alberta Foundation for the Arts, Edmonton

This print was included in the September 1953 issue of *Highlights*. This is a cleverly abstracted image, using both the light streaming through the doorway and the architecture to create sharp-angled forms. Some texture and overprinting enriches the surface.

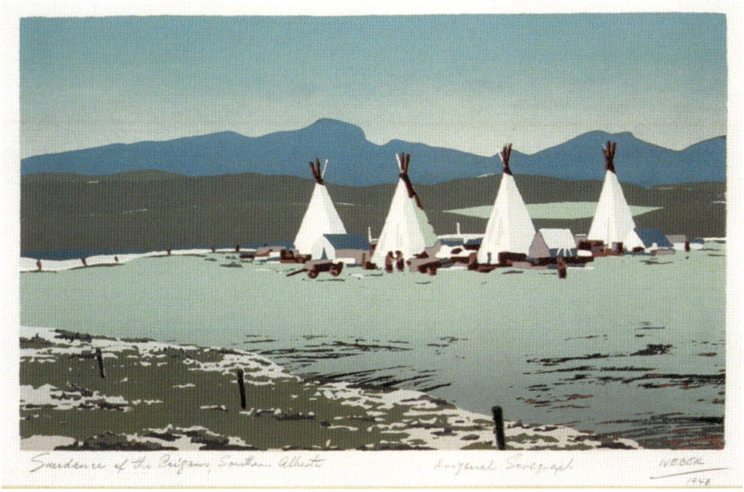

George Weber
Sundance, 1948
serigraph
Alberta Foundation for the Arts, Edmonton

In *Sundance*, Weber uses the broad flat areas of unbroken colour typical of the serigraph to denote the prairie, foothills, and mountains. The conical, vertical tipis and the small details of the surrounding village break up these flat surfaces and enliven the composition. In the sky, Weber uses the graded colour blend of the serigraph, giving the effect of the sunlight emanating from behind the hills.

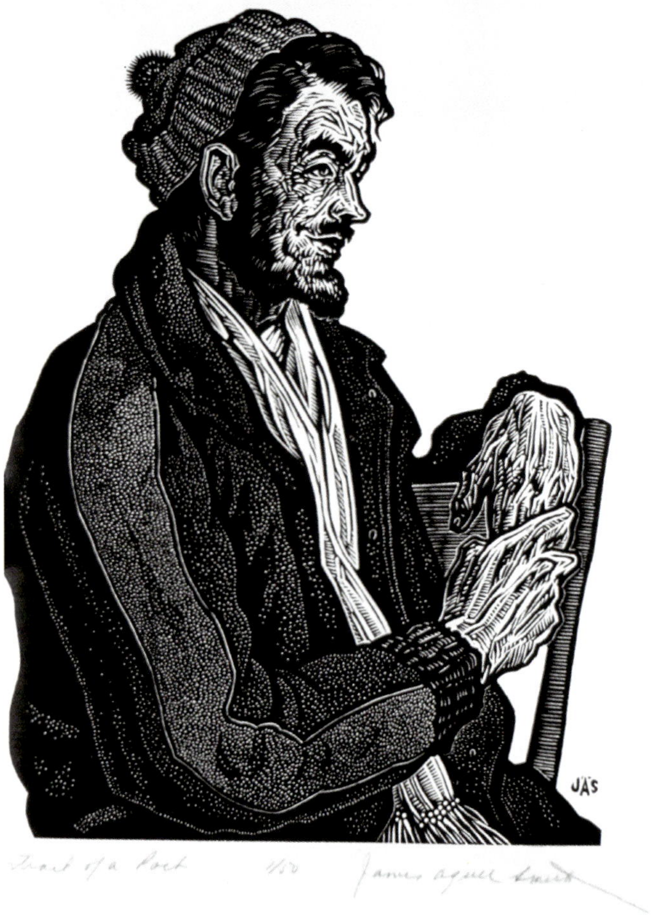

James Agrell Smith
Portrait of a Poet, 1956
wood engraving
Alberta Foundation for the Arts, Edmonton

Smith was a perfectionist in the craft of wood engraving, producing powerful and expressive prints. The boxwood he has used here was first blackened with ink. The sketch was then traced on it and engraved. By cutting the background away completely, he has created a stark white background which emphasizes the figure. Energetic cuts in the face and hands give great character and expression to the man. Finely incised marks denote the different texture of the clothing.

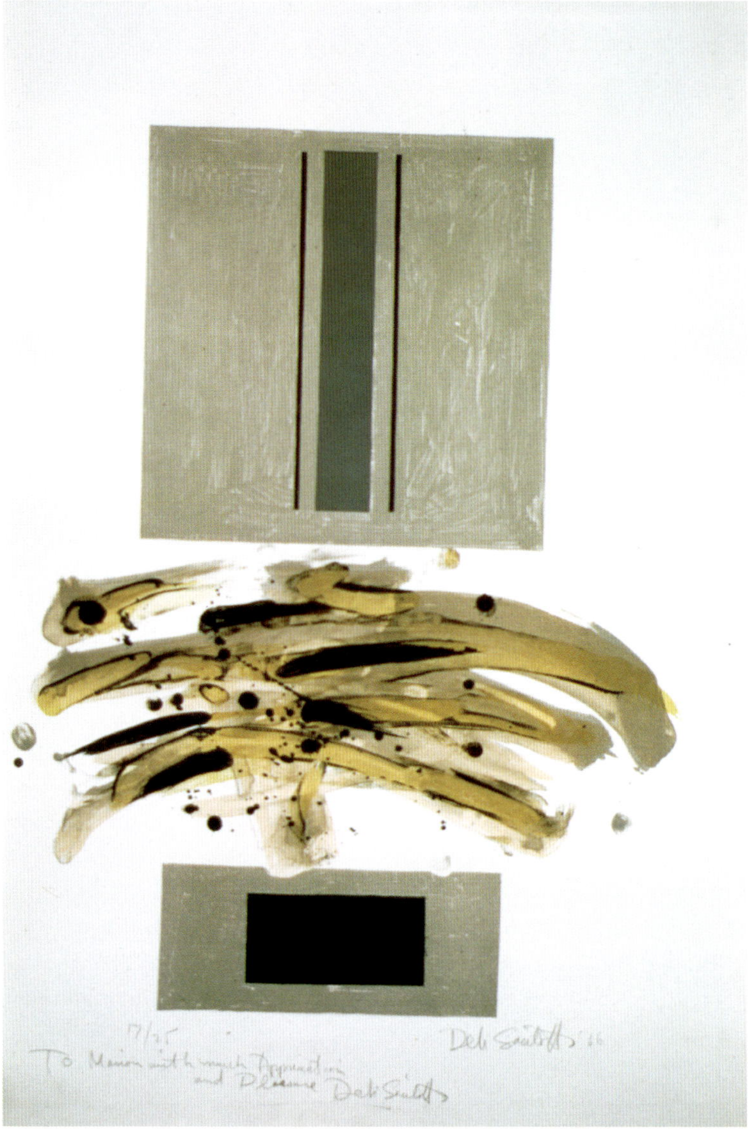

Deli Sacilotto
Untitled, 1966
lithograph
Alberta Foundation for the Arts, Edmonton

Sacilotto's interest in technique is evident in this formal work. Here he has combined two approaches: the geometric forms of hard-edge abstraction and the gestural marks of abstract expressionism. The forms are painted with tusche washes on the plate. Within the geometric forms the surface is quite painterly. The limited tonal values are close: pale grey to ochre, blue to black.

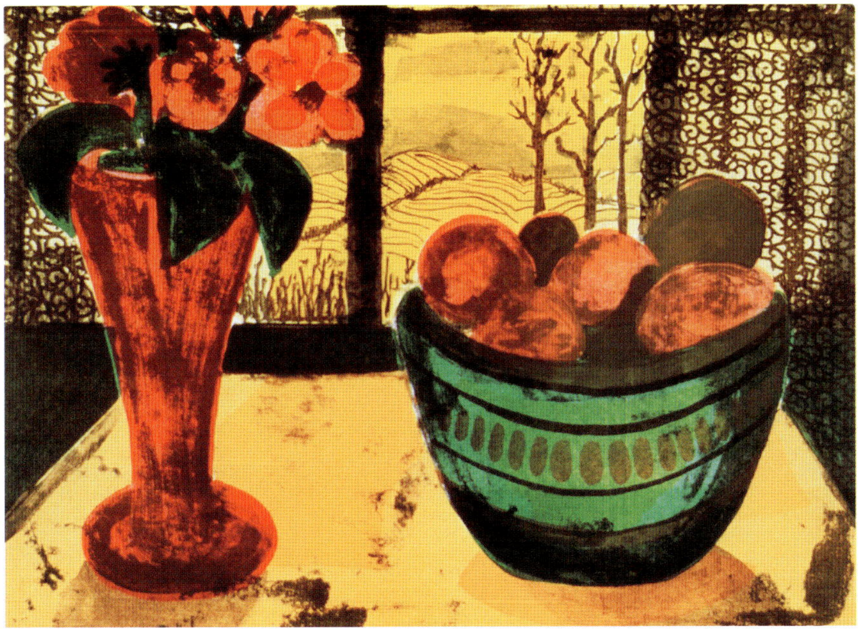

John Snow
Limoux, 1971
lithograph
Alberta Foundation for the Arts, Edmonton

A pioneer in lithography in Alberta, Snow had an expressive and decorative approach, and he used rich colour overlays. *Limoux* is a strong, simple design with the dominant still life on a table against a window with curtains partly drawn revealing a landscape beyond. In the shallow space, the vase and bowl of fruit are quickly rendered with graphic marks and decorative details. The radiant colour, warm yellows and reds contrasting with the green fruit bowl, creates a vivid harmony.

J. K. Esler
Relic of the 20th-century (Lunch Kit), 1973
intaglio
Estate of the artist

Esler played a seminal role in the development of Canadian printmaking. He had an outstanding technical facility and used both traditional and experimental techniques in his work. Here he has used a flattened object, a real lunch kit found in the street. This was first produced as a one-colour print in 1965 and then as a two-colour print in 1973. The found object was an important device for sculptors in the twentieth century, and printmakers often used found materials to create texture in their prints, though they seldom used the complete object. The flattened, corroded, indented surface of the lunch kit acted like an etching plate, which he has inked and printed. With it he has created a sculptural, heavily textured, monumental image.

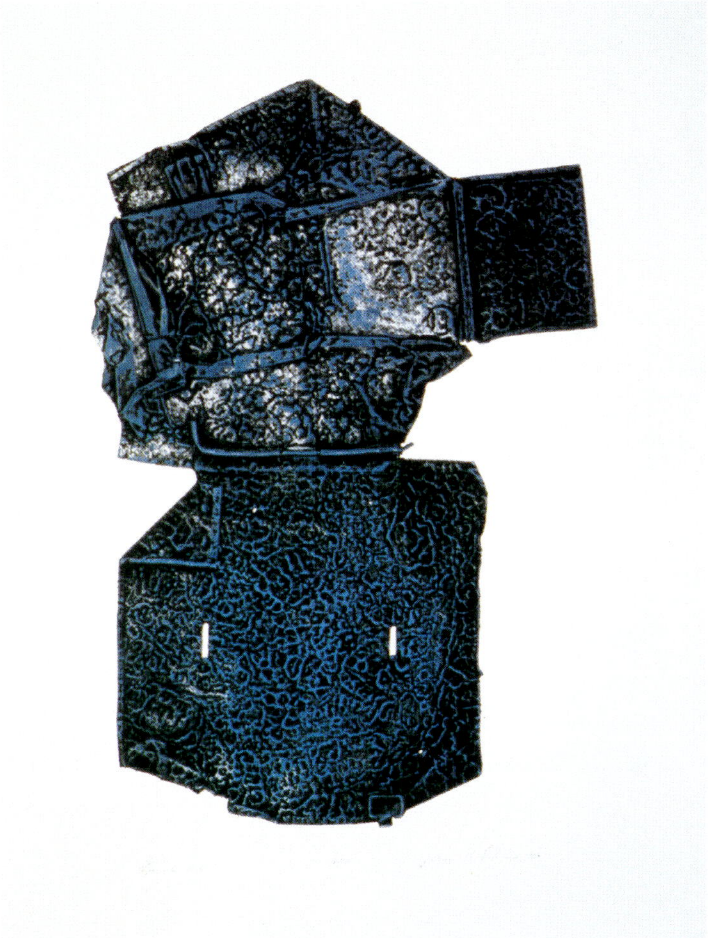

Modern Photography

Initially, photographers in Alberta recorded a vast, sparsely populated land and the spectacular mountain scenery, but they became increasingly concerned with documenting the growth of settlements and towns, and the development of industry and agriculture. After the 1910s, photographers focused on a wide variety of subjects: rodeo, ranching, and the Calgary Stampede; irrigation and new agricultural methods; small settlements around the stately grain elevators; the oil and gas and coal mining industries; and increasing urbanization—city streets and stylish architecture, cars, roads, and bridges. Daily life, leisure-time pursuits, sports and the growing interest in skiing and fishing became of increasing interest. Throughout the modern period, First Nations portraits, villages, and ways of life were an important subject for many photographers.

After the Second World War, many photographers, such as Nicholas Morant, earned their living as photojournalists with large companies like CPR or worked for newspapers and magazines. Because of this, picturesque views remained popular, and colour photography was increasingly used. But photographers also produced dramatic action shots of important events, such as Harry Pollard's view of the oil strike at Leduc, Alberta. Although Alberta photographers did consider formal, compositional issues, they did not take a fully modernist approach and explore aspects of abstraction prevalent in painting. Later, in the 1960s, photographers, such as Ed Spiteri, began to consider the photo essay as a way to document various aspects of a subject. Once their careers were established, a number of Alberta photographers, including Morant and Pollard, travelled widely and photographed outside of Canada. Roloff Beny developed as a photographer long after he left Alberta and gained an international reputation for his photographs.

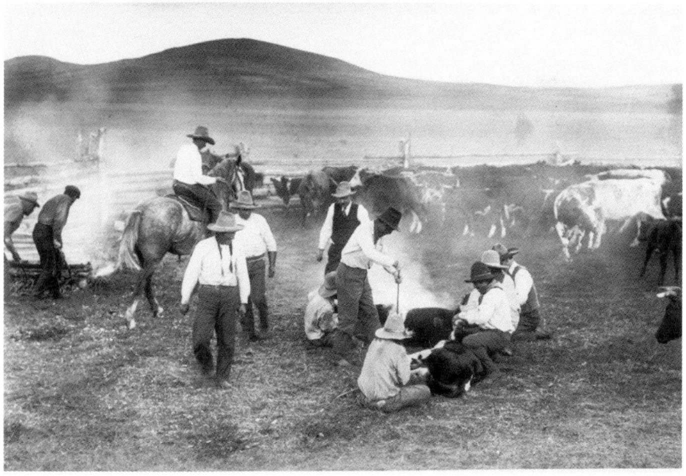

William Oliver
Branding at the Bar U Ranch, ca. 1919
photograph
Glenbow Museum Archives, Calgary, NB-16-260

Outdoor photography was Oliver's forte, and due to his knowledge of ranching and the quality of his photographs, he became the official photographer to the ranching community of south-western Alberta. Here, Oliver has caught the dust, heat, and even smell of the prairies. A group of men in the foreground are holding an animal to the ground as one cowboy impresses the brand. Two men to the left are keeping the fire stoked and burning to keep the brands red hot. Alex Fleming, the Bar U Ranch's general manager, is on horseback ready to capture the next in the herd, while others gather around watchfully available to assist at a moment's notice. The cattle huddle nervously against the corral in the middle distance, and the foothills rise in an arc on the horizon. The evening light provides a strong light-dark contrast, which adds to the dramatic intensity of this scene. This photograph tells of the collaborative nature of ranching, of cowboys working together, of the hard work and concentration required.

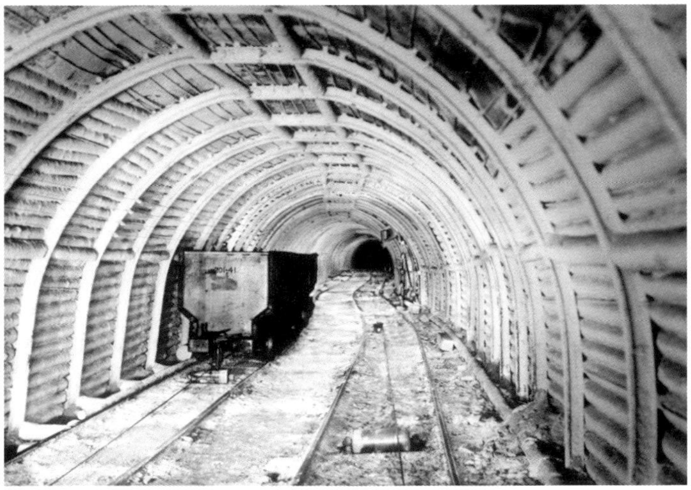

Thomas Gushul
Mine Tunnel, Blairmore, Alberta, ca. 1941
photograph
Glenbow Museum Archives, Calgary, NC-54-2899

Gushul had worked in the mines and excelled at capturing the industrial, social, political, and personal aspects of the coal mining community. He featured the raw industrial imagery, seldom softened by the spectacular scenery of the area. *Mine Tunnel* shows the structure of an underground tunnel, spot-lit and dramatic, the ribs of the arches repeating as they stretch into a yawning hole in the interminable distance. There are no miners present to make this an inhabited, human space. The repeated forms create an almost abstract image, broken only by the railway car on its tracks. As well as presenting a structured, abstract image, this is a powerful emotional image in which the tunnel leads into an ominous, fearful abyss. Mining at this time wreaked huge environmental and personal damage with the creation of slag heaps, contaminated rivers, black lung disease, and cancer. It was extremely dangerous work, where serious accidents were still commonplace.

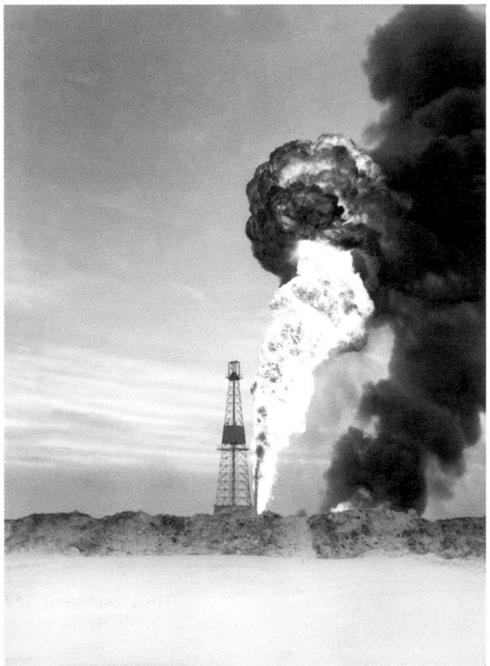

Harry Pollard
Leduc No. 1, 1947
photograph
Provincial Archives of Alberta, Edmonton, P2719

On February 13, 1947, the spectacular gush of the Leduc No. 1 well "blowing in," marked the beginning of Alberta's post-war boom. Fortuitously, Pollard was on-site and captured this important event in this stunning action shot. The oil derrick is starkly silhouetted against the huge prairie sky as the hot flare surges upwards with a roar in this dramatic composition.

Alfred Blyth
Edmonton Oil Refineries at Night, 1951
photograph
Provincial Archives of Alberta, Edmonton, BL1959/2

After the Second World War, longer exposures with faster film made night photography more effective. Though the refinery was likely in operation and staffed, Blyth has captured a sense of the stillness of the night, as though no one was around. Security spotlights sparkle against the gloom in this dramatic industrial image. The light reflects off the snow on to the lower levels of the buildings.

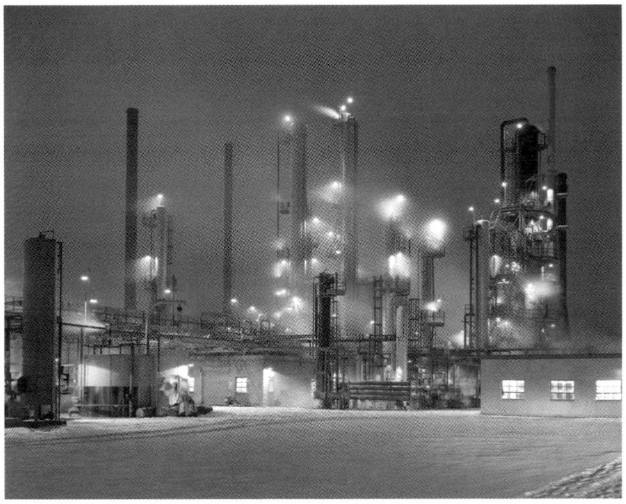

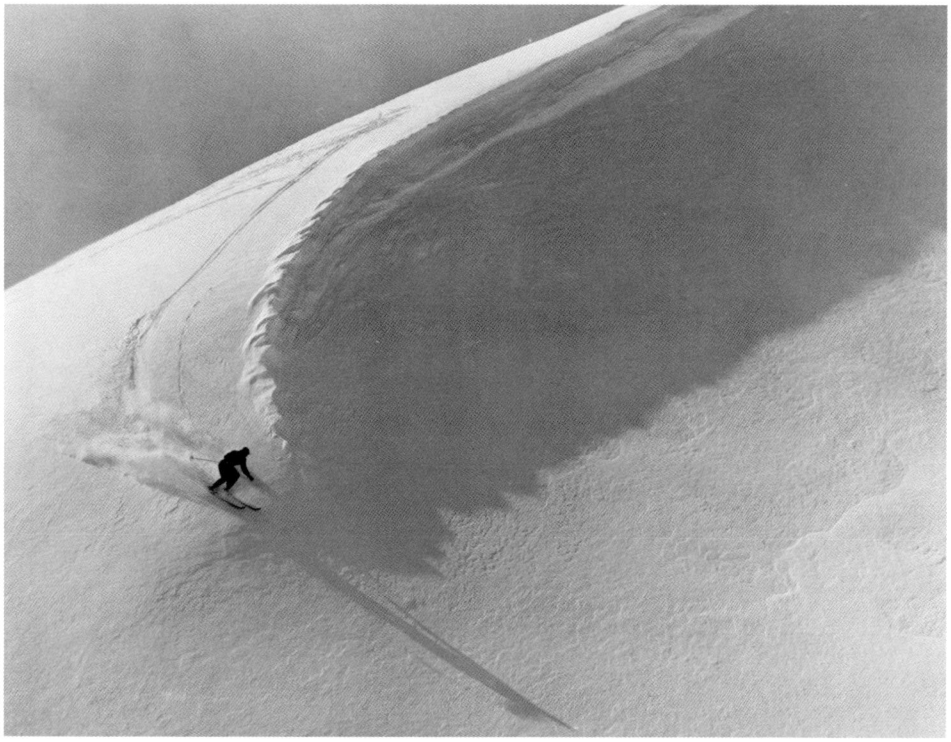

Nicholas Morant
Skiing in the Banff area, ca. 1960s
photograph
Whyte Museum of the Canadian Rockies, Banff, V500 Nicholas Morant Fonds

Achieving such an image takes great patience, as Morant had to wait for this precise moment. The skier races down the untouched snow bank, his trail creating a huge arc. Morant has carefully selected this simple composition, just the slope of the hill against a triangle of sky, and the deep shadow of the gully. Against this, the sweep of the skier's path and the dark figure against the white snow creates high drama. Though his photographs are always carefully composed, this formalized, almost abstract composition is unusual for Morant.

Ed Spiteri
Jail Series, ca. 1970
photograph
Collection of the artist

This potent image gives us an insight into prison life. It is an intimate view into lives being lived, despite being restrained behind bars. The unusual viewpoint shows us the players' hands seen from above emerging from the bars engrossed in the play. By not showing us the inmates' faces the image could have been depersonalized, yet the gestures of the hands have personalities of their own. The stark white bars and the play of light on the hands enhance their prominence in the composition. The composition is dramatic and abstracted, with all of the action in the upper half of the image. This is a unique and powerful image.

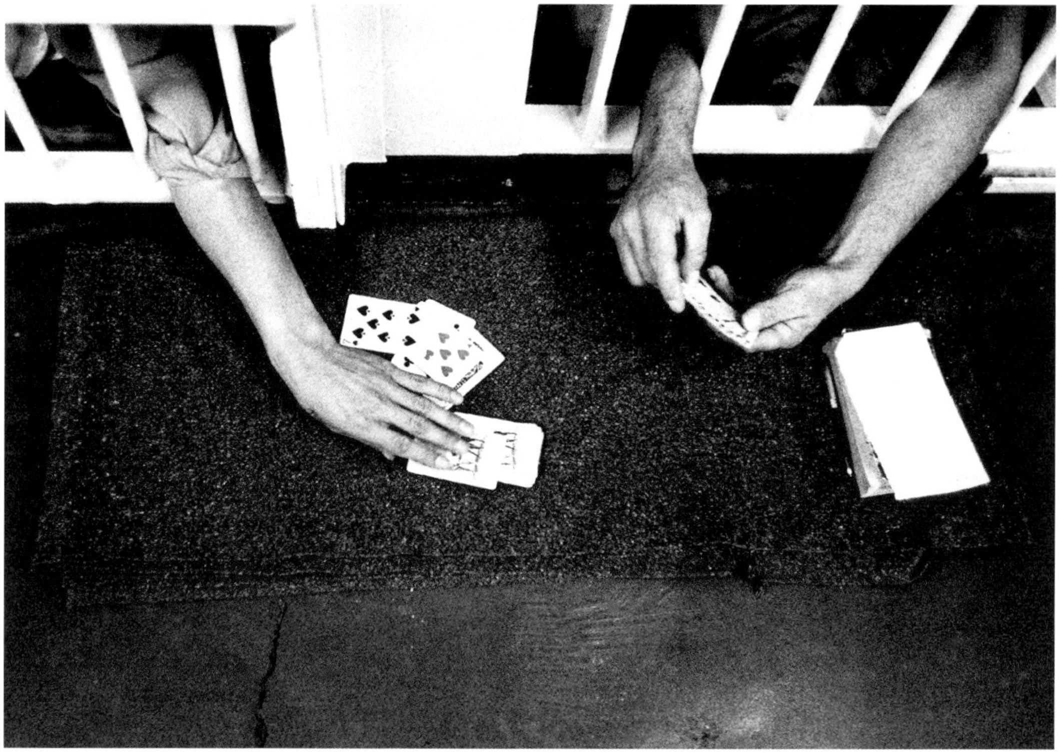

Art in Three Dimensions: Ceramics and Sculpture

Ceramics got its start in Alberta in 1946 when Marion Nicoll lobbied for a ceramics studio at the Provincial Institute of Technology and Art and new equipment was acquired. Luke Lindoe established classes working with stoneware clays and one wheel and gas kiln. In Edmonton, the Potters' Guild was established and began classes in 1953, taught by Bauhaus-trained Sybil Laubenthal, the only artist who had any prior experience in ceramics to draw upon. Lindoe and Laubenthal were key to the development of a vigorous ceramics tradition in Alberta. In time, courses were taught at the Calgary Allied Arts Centre, and by the early 1960s, in city parks and recreation classes. In 1960, ceramics were included in the fine arts course at the University of Alberta.

Initially there were tremendous challenges to producing objects from clay: there was virtually no information about ceramics, methodology, and techniques, and artists had to procure raw materials locally as they experimented with clays, glazes, and different firing techniques. There were few wheels to throw pots on, so artists made hand-built objects, working with coil, slab, and modelling and cast clay methods. Lindoe initially bought clay from Medalta Potteries in Medicine Hat, but soon artists dug their own clay in the Cypress Hills. Glazes were made from local clays. Edmonton students mixed their own glazes, using clay slip from the McLeod River and oxides from Marble Canyon.

The Lindoe Studio, established in 1955, became Ceramic Arts in 1957 and was one of the first commercial pottery studios in Canada. Graduates from the institute, Walter Drohan, Katie Ohe, and Rolf Ungstad, worked there at various times. In 1957, Walter Drohan took over the ceramics program at the institute, which he ran until 1986. In the early 1960s there was an improved market for ceramics and Ed Drahanchuk, widely admired for his technical ability, established a successful commercial studio in Calgary.

There was no guidance for sculptors in Calgary until O. W. Holmsten founded the sculpture program at the Alberta College of Art in 1964–65. Katie Ohe joined him as an instructor in 1970. Ohe initially worked in clay and cement. Few artists worked in metal until the 1970s, except for trailblazers Ohe, Roy Leadbeater, and Charles Beil in Banff. Metal sculpture was technically complex, required expensive equipment, and there were no workshops geared to artists' needs. Ohe and Leadbeater trained in welding at Dominion Bridge in Calgary in the early 1960s, but it took years for their metal sculpture to evolve.

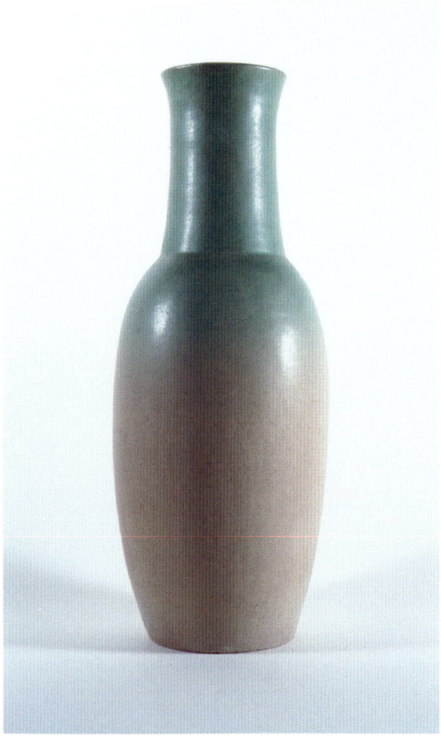

Greg Arnold
Vase, 1951
stoneware
Alberta Foundation for the Arts, Edmonton

Greg Arnold was considered an outstanding designer-craftsman. This vase shows the great simplicity and purity of Arnold's design and his aesthetic pleasure in the handling of clay. Thrown on a wheel, likely in two parts, the body and the neck then joined, the clay has been pulled up and attenuated to form a tall slim shape. A celadon green glaze wash has been overlaid with a transparent glaze. This very subtle glazing accentuates the clean simple form.

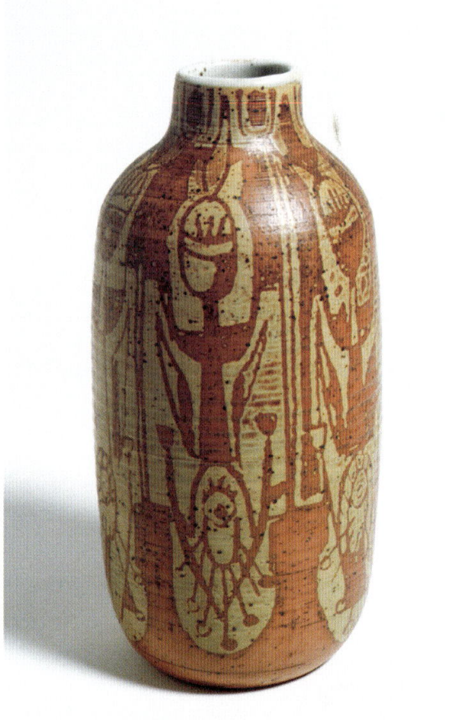

Rolf Ungstad
Bottle, 1953
stoneware
Alberta Foundation for the Arts, Edmonton

Thrown on the wheel, Ungstad's *Bottle* has an elegant, classical, simple shape. Onto this he has painted a design in wax-resist, a graphic child-like image, repeating the design around the bottle. He has then dipped the bottle into a slip glaze, which resisted the wax and formed the background of the design after firing. Ungstad used a different heavier glaze on the inside. Versatile and sensitive, *Bottle* demonstrates Ungstad's strong technique.

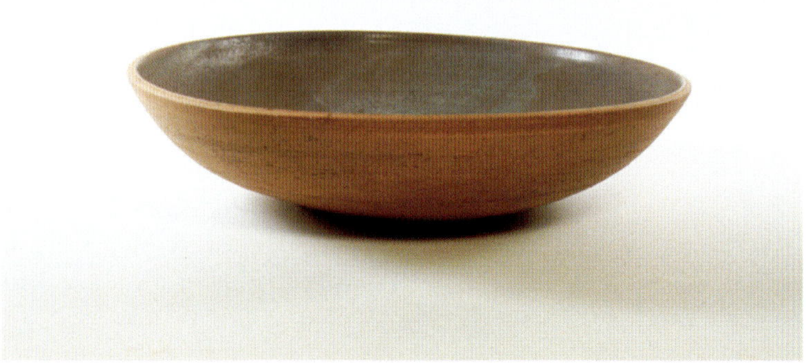

Sibyl Laubenthal
Plate, ca. 1950s
stoneware
Alberta Foundation for the Arts, Edmonton

Reflecting the Bauhaus tradition, this plate is perfectly proportioned and simple in form, with a vitality and natural flow. The glaze, applied only on the inner surface, is simple and understated. Technically extremely accomplished, this is a pure, faultless form.

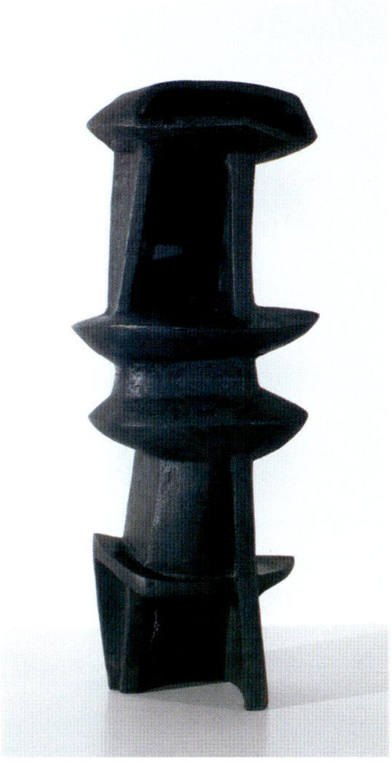

Katie Ohe

Portuguese Woman, ca. 1960

stoneware

Alberta Foundation for the Arts, Edmonton

This is one of Ohe's earliest sculptures in which she was experimenting with formal elements. She has made the concave shapes by draping clay over rocks and then removing the rock supports once the clay has dried. This hand-built work is a composite, built up of parts, and demonstrates Ohe's focus on form, mass, and structure. From a strong central core, she has built up alternating horizontal shapes, section by section, with some inner hollow forms, creating a dynamic rhythm through the piece. The columnar structure is abstract, yet appears totemic. It was fired and then painted with a dark stain. This early exploration led to a series of totemic figures, some of which were cast in bronze and aluminium, during her studies in New York from 1961 to 1963.

Walter Drohan

Bottle #1, 1971

stoneware

Alberta Foundation for the Arts, Edmonton

The bottle has likely first been thrown on a wheel and then flattened into an oval shape. Over this, a large thin piece, richly textured and covering most of the surface, has been applied. Narrower pieces have been layered and intertwined over the body and neck of the bottle. This emphasizes the sculptural quality of the form. A lustre glaze with metallic components has been applied, creating a subtle sparkling surface. The result is an imaginative relief sculpture rather than simply a ceramic bottle.

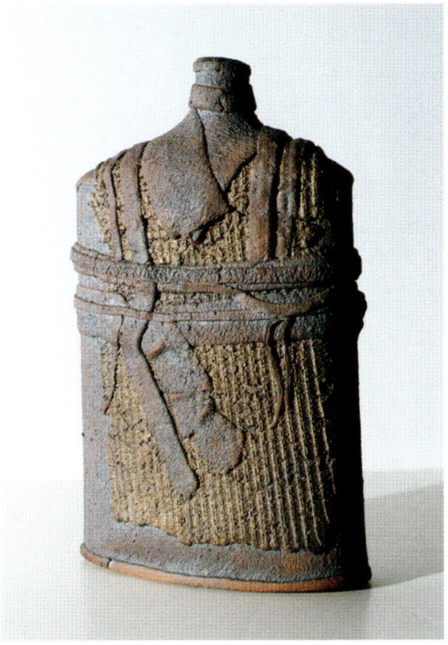

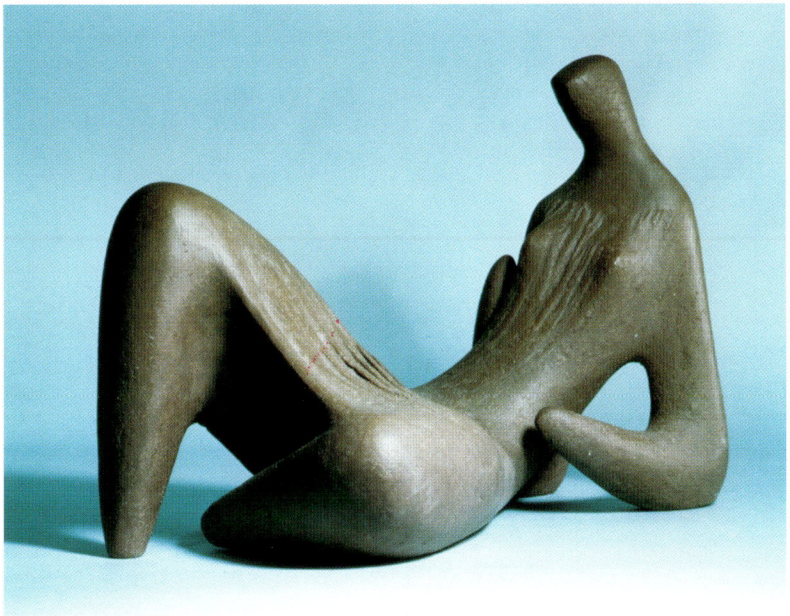

Luke Lindoe

Figure, 1962

stoneware

Alberta Foundation for the Arts, Edmonton

Lindoe had a profound knowledge of clay and glazes and made his own clays. Here he has worked the clay into a massive sculptural form of a reclining female figure, iconic and symbolic, which recalls the work of British sculptor Henry Moore. The simply modelled masses are organized into abstract volumes and planes in an integrated structure with a vigorous rhythm flowing through the forms. He has used dense vitrified brown stoneware with no glaze, but the surface was likely polished with a spoon and is enlivened with texture. Paying meticulous attention to proportion, contour, and surface, the artist's concern here is with formal problems involving the geometry of the human figure.

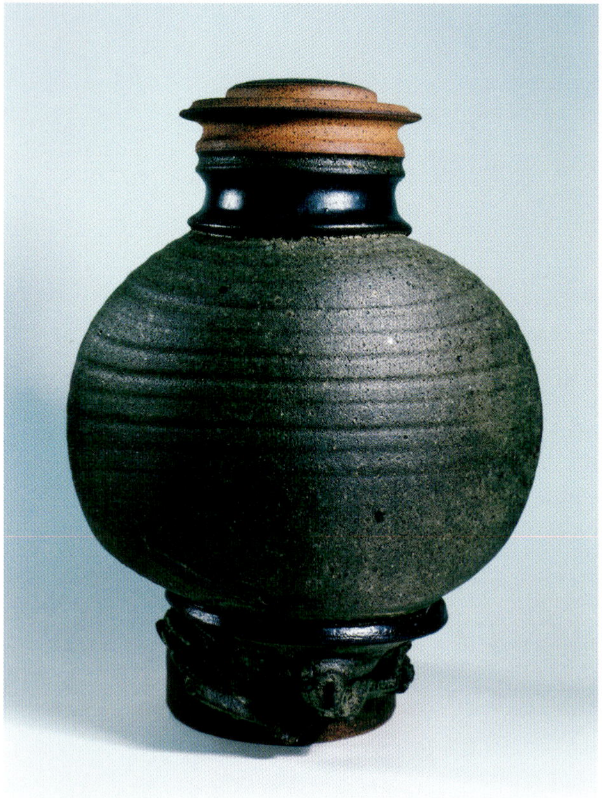

Ed Drahanchuk
Vase, 1969
stoneware
Alberta Foundation for the Arts, Edmonton

This almost spherical, though not symmetrical, pot has been made from an open, porous stoneware and sits on a deep pedestal base with an indented neck typical of Drahanchuk. A slip (a thin slurry of clay, a different colour from the clay body, mixed with water), possibly of manganese, has been applied to the round body. The semi-gloss of the neck and base is likely a clear glaze over the slip. An unglazed brown lid fits into the neck, creating an echo of the base. Squeezed clay with free-form modelling has been wound and coiled around the base. The only details on the round body of the vase are the subtle horizontal incised lines made after throwing the pot while the clay was still wet. The purity of the profile of concave and convex shapes is extremely refined in this elegant vessel.

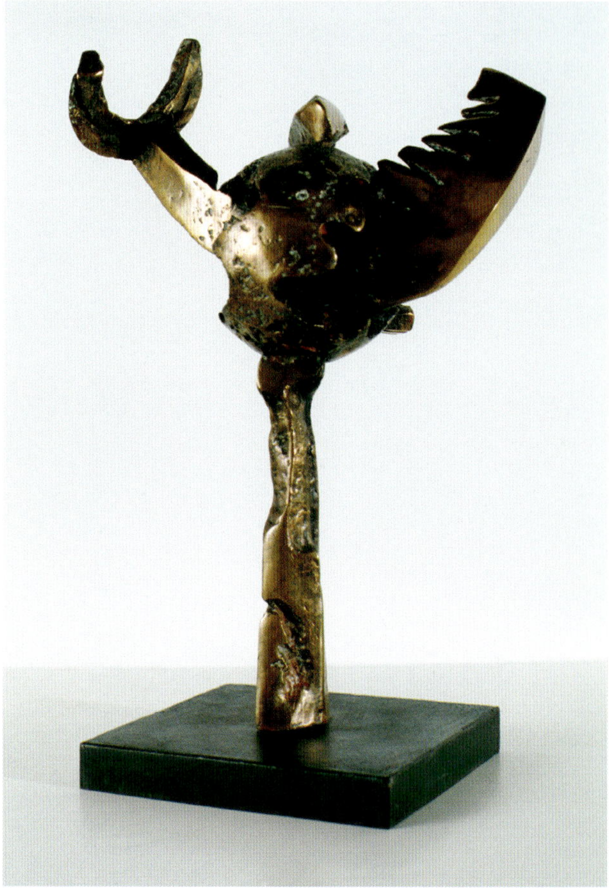

Roy Leadbeater
Caesar, 1969
cast bronze
Alberta Foundation for the Arts, Edmonton

Leadbeater considered *Caesar* symbolic of bravery. A hollow orb, broken and indented, has been cut through with a sickle-shaped element. With an organization of abstract volumes, he has constructed forms and volumes in space balancing weight and mass with nervous energy. The contrast between the corroded mat surface and the highly polished areas creates a lively, dynamic surface. Leadbeater produced a plaster model, worked by hand, which has been cast in bronze using the so-called "lost wax" process at the Morris-Singer Foundry in Basingstoke, England. After cooling, the bronze has been sandblasted, hand-tooled, and oxidized to produce the desired colour. It was exhibited along with seventeen other British and French sculptors, including Henry Moore and Barbara Hepworth, at the Alwin Gallery in London, England, in 1976 to celebrate Britain's entry into the European Common Market.

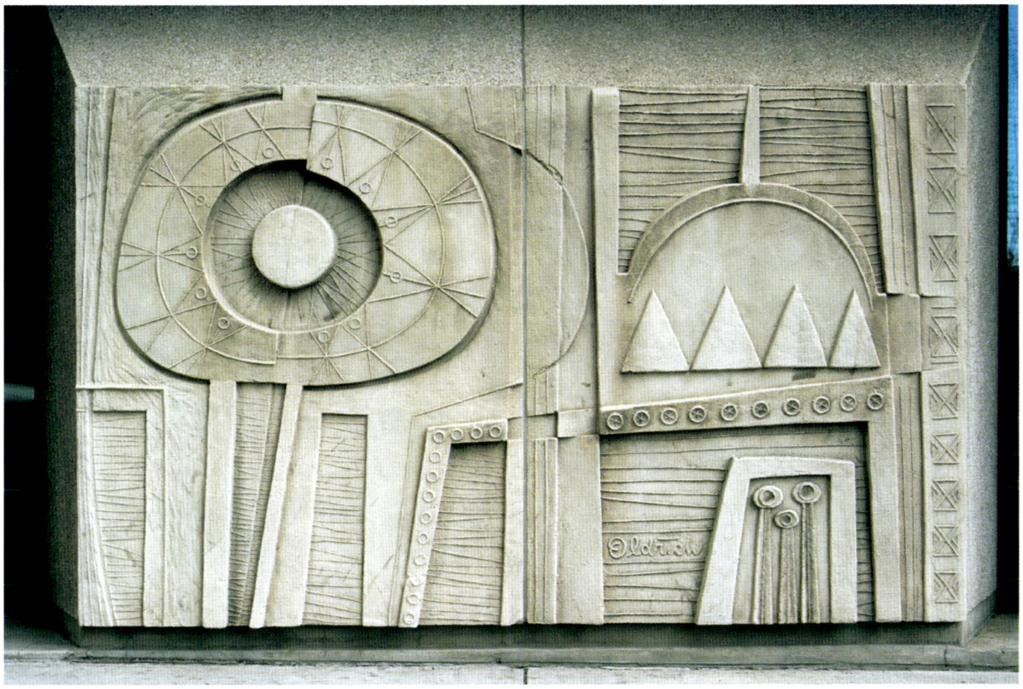

Robert Oldrich
Mural, 1976
concrete
Province of Alberta

A three-panel mural, depicting aspects of Alberta's history and culture, can be found on the south outer wall of the Glenbow Museum. Cast in concrete in relief, Oldrich has used abstracted, geometric symbols to represent this history. The left side of this panel depicts a disc representing the sun, and a tipi circle and a tree. The right side shows a chinook arch, mountains, prairie, snowflakes, and plants. Cast in relief to different depths, the forms cast varying shadows creating a lively surface pattern of simple, dramatic shapes. This mural was another of the public mural commissions Oldrich had begun in 1959 with the Alberta Wheat Pool mural in Calgary.

Notes: A Sense of Place: Modern Art 1920–1970

1. Marion Nicoll, *A Retrospective* (Edmonton: Edmonton Art Gallery, 1975).
2. Clement Greenberg, "Clement Greenberg's view of art on the prairies," *Canadian Art* no. 84 (March–April 1963) 96.
3. One of the earliest prints in Alberta was a woodcut, *Siesta* (1927), by Maxwell Bates.

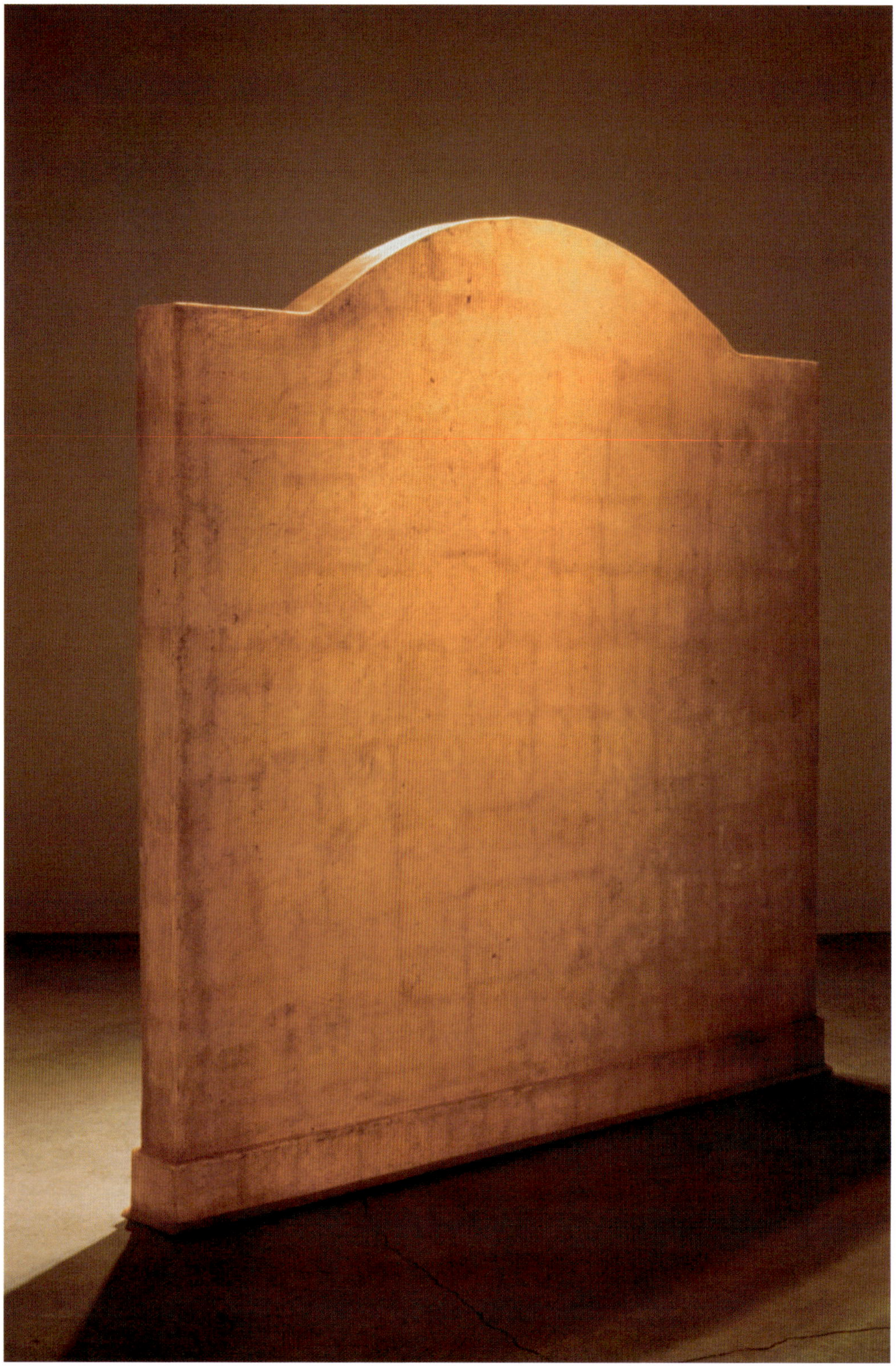

Blake Senini / *The Shape of The Light*, 1996 / polyester resin / Alberta Foundation for the Arts, Edmonton, Alberta

A NEW ERA FOR ALBERTA ART: 1970–2000

Mary-Beth Laviolette

New Bricks and Mortar for Art

Prior to the 1970s, it was often assumed that important new art could only be created in large cosmopolitan centres like New York, London, Paris, and Los Angeles. If it came from anywhere else, the art was deemed likely to be imitative or provincial. But with the surge of new art movements in the 1960s—pop, conceptual, photorealism, funk, earth art, and so on—contemporary art could no longer be defined by only a few styles coming from within the parameters of only a few centres. As one critic wrote about the period, "Art history seemed to be in a shambles ... what had been thought of as the great river of art has become a delta of many streams."[1] The effect of these new currents on smaller, less-developed communities has been inspirational and challenging, reshaping, but in some cases reinforcing what is already in germination.

In Alberta, this art world expansion in the 1960s coincided with the emergence of a new generation of homegrown artists (baby boomers), many of whom, like Calgary's Don Mabie, had "the attitude that you were going to 'do your own thing,' no matter what ... there was a feeling of possibility everywhere."[2] In addition, buoyed by the economic prosperity of the era and political change, a more substantial arts "infrastructure" was developed to support the efforts of these newcomers. This included a circuit of new public art galleries, new teaching facilities, a growing commercial art market, and the new kid on the block: artist-run centres. Rather than art being your life's "calling," art could now become a "career," a profession where even nontraditional mediums and styles outside of landscape painting could flourish.

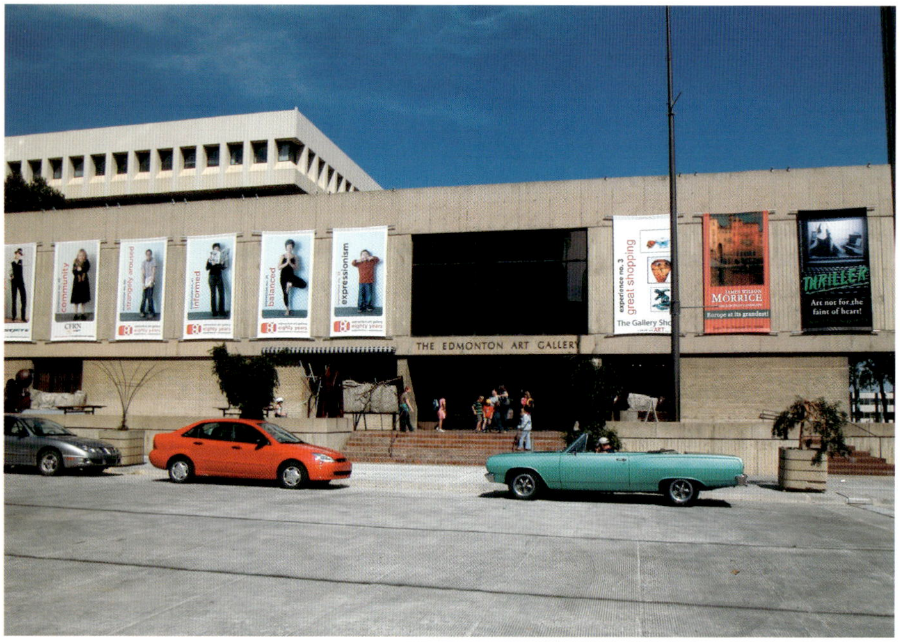

The Edmonton Art Gallery, circa 2004
Photo by Pamela Clark

The Edmonton Art Gallery (or as it is now known the Art Gallery of Alberta) is the senior sister of public art galleries in the province. Its first exhibition was in 1924 in the Palm Room of the classy Hotel Macdonald. On view for patrons and the public were twenty-four paintings from local collectors and the National Gallery of Canada. Despite this promising debut, it was not until 1969 that a permanent home opened for the gallery. Situated in the city centre next to Sir Winston Churchill Square, the gallery's Arthur Blow Condell Building was designed to house a significant collection of art, present larger exhibitions, and provide more space for educational programs.

It was also a new era for Calgary's Glenbow Museum, which enlarged its presence with a new building and a new professional director, Duncan

Cameron. Following the legacy of lawyer Eric Harvie, the Harvie family, other donors, and a dedicated staff, the Glenbow became a multi-faceted entity with an impressive collection ranging from the truly grand to the frontier humble. In its coffers are thousands of historic photographs, First Nations art and artifacts, objects of the fur trade and pioneer era, books and historic documents, arms and armour, rock and mineral specimens, and artworks and curiosities from places around the world such as Asia and Africa, To showcase its Canadian and American art collection, the Glenbow-Alberta Art Gallery opened in 1969 at 902–11 Avenue SW. Then in 1978, the entire Glenbow operation was consolidated under one roof. With a focus on establishing a professionally operated museum, the Glenbow has since operated out of its downtown facility, an eight-storey structure with three exhibition floors and a library and archives floor. By 1991, its holdings contained some five hundred contemporary artworks, many by nationally recognized Albertans.

Besides these changes for the two large institutions, smaller-sized public galleries also came onto the scene during the 1960s and 1970s. Some were connected to educational institutions like the Banff Centre's Walter Phillips Gallery (1976), the University of Calgary's Nickle Arts Museum (1979), and the University of Lethbridge Art Gallery (ca. early 1970s). Other public art gallery operations were attached to museums. Two examples are the Whyte Museum of the Canadian Rockies (1968) and the Medicine Hat Museum and Art Gallery (1967). The Southern Alberta Art Gallery (1976, Lethbridge), the Art Gallery of Calgary (founded as the Muttart Art Gallery in 1977), the Prairie Art Gallery (1985, Grande Prairie), and the Triangle Art Gallery (1988, Calgary) were opened as publicly supported venues without any strings attached. Not all of these smaller operations had a mandate to collect, but what made their appearance in the province so important was their curating and documenting of historic and contemporary developments in Alberta art.

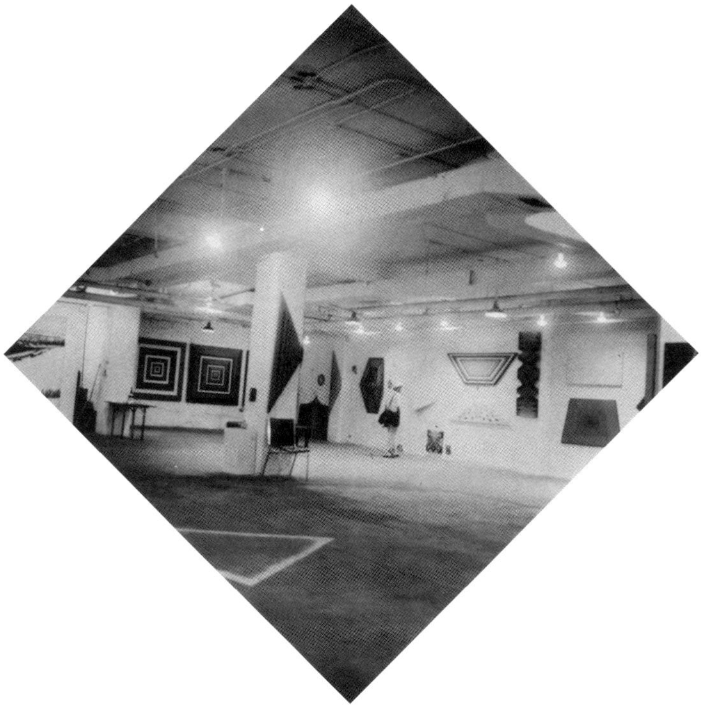

Interior view of Latitude 53, November 1977
Courtesy of Latitude 53

Another phenomenon of the post-1970 period in Canada was the opening of exhibition spaces like Edmonton's Latitude 53 (1973) and Calgary's Clouds n' Water Gallery (1975, now The New Gallery). Known in their early years as "parallel galleries" and later as artist-run centres (ARCs), these grassroots venues position themselves as a feisty alternative to the so-called "art establishment"—art museums, commercial art galleries, academia, and anything associated with the mainstream of Canadian art.

Somewhat similar to the post-war efforts of Calgary's artist-run Coste House and later the Allied Arts Centre, ARCs were a distinct development "infused with the rebellious spirit and experimentation of the 1960s."[3] They are places where the untried and the emerging can innovate, subvert, collaborate, and blur the boundaries of art. The use of nontraditional art materials is encouraged and unconventional practices like video, performance (including poetry and experimental music), installation, and mixed media art are promoted. In many cases, the attitude espoused at ARCs is anti-(high) art, anti-commercial, and critical of social and political norms. Irreverence and humour is very evident, and women artists are also more visible. But most important about ARCs is the opportunity they provide for new artists to exhibit. In Alberta, the development of an urban alternative arts scene added an important new layer to the post-1970 period, with Calgary experiencing the most success provincially.

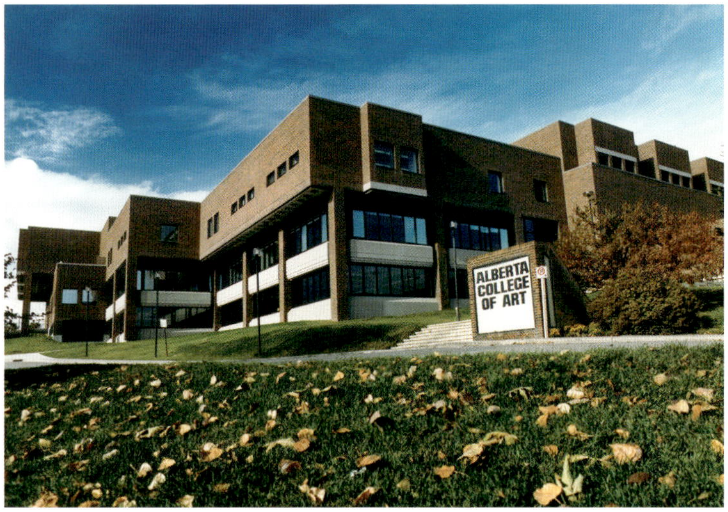

Alberta College of Art and Design, ca. 1973
Courtesy of the Alberta College of Art and Design
Photo by Chris Milejszo

For the aspiring student artist, new doors and new opportunities also started to open up during the post-1970 period in the province's post-secondary institutions. Diploma-granting institutions, like Red Deer College and Edmonton's Grant McEwan Community College, started to offer studio-based instruction. New degree programs became available through university art departments. Choice, it seems, was now everywhere. Along with the more traditional pursuits of painting, drawing, craft, and design, institutions started to expand or develop new programs in printmaking, photography, sculpture, ceramics, glass, metalsmithing, textiles, art education, and art history. (By the end of the century, new media, such as video and digital technology would be added to the mix.)

The veteran Alberta College of Art and Design opened the doors to its new facility in 1973. Located since 1927 on what is now Calgary's Southern Alberta Institute of Technology campus, the case for building a new art school was successfully clinched when the then head of the school, Stanford Perrott, was able to show the provincial government that at least three-quarters of its graduates had "gone on to art or art-related careers."[4] Now one of the largest of Canada's four art colleges, with a four-year studio-based curriculum, the number of instructors at the Alberta College of Art and Design is targeted to grow from twenty-nine to fifty by the end of the decade with a projected enrollment of six hundred students.

The Banff School of Fine Arts is another veteran in the Alberta story of "establishing a place for art," and as the 1970s progressed, it, too, began to alter its horizons. For the first time, in 1973, the historic summer school offered a winter program to young professional artists at a post-graduate level. The vision was simple but enticing: class sizes of no more than ten to twelve people, with participants engaged in their own work. On hand to assist would be instructors, as well as visiting critics, curators, and other professionals. With these changes also came new infrastructure, most importantly Glyde Hall in 1976, outfitted with state-of-the-art studios, workrooms, and professional art gallery space, the Walter Phillips Gallery. Painter Takao Tanabe—who was hired in 1973 as a full-time artist-in-residence and head of the painting division—is credited with turning the painting program "around to face the modern world of art."[5]

From British Columbia, the seasoned Tanabe was one of several Canadians who would come to Alberta starting in the 1970s, not only to teach but to also make new art. Joining him to fill a variety of positions throughout the province would be many more artists and teachers from the United States and Great Britain. Bringing with them new ideas and skills, these immigrant artists would enrich the Alberta arts scene and in turn would not be left untouched by what its people and environment would have to offer.

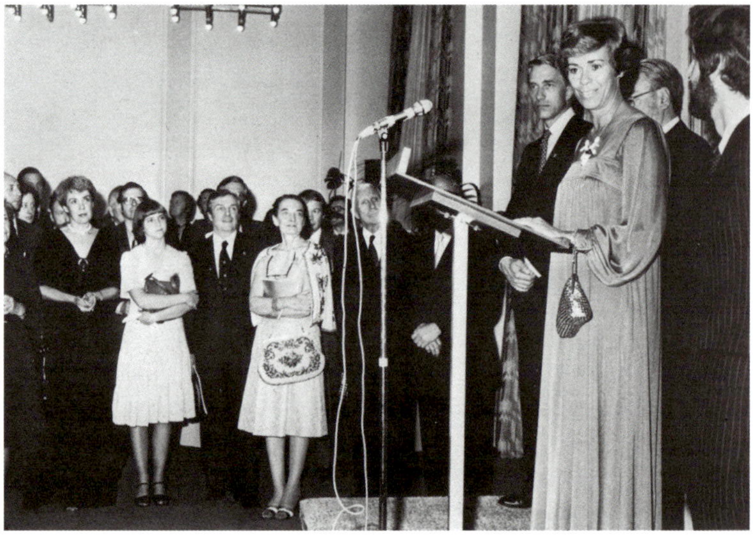

Jeanne Lougheed speaking at the Alberta Art Foundation European Exhibition, 1975
Edmonton Journal

At a 1975 reception at Canada House in London, England, Jeanne Lougheed introduced five hundred people to the paintings and sculptures of seventy-five Alberta artists. Referring to the lively modern content of the collection, she remarked, "We have developed a new self-confidence … a spirit of vitality."[6] Featuring artwork from the fledgling Alberta Art Foundation, it was the collection's first international outing, attracting favourable reviews about artistic individualism. Established in 1972 by the Peter Lougheed provincial government as a collection for the people of Alberta, the Alberta Art Foundation (now the Alberta Foundation for the Arts) and a new separate ministry, Alberta Culture, provided new avenues of support while also raising public awareness. By the end of the last century, building on such early donations by artists like Janet Mitchell, James and Marion Nicoll, and the estate of Group of Seven artist A. Y. Jackson, the collection now boasts over 6,400 paintings, sculpture, drawings, ceramics, fibre art, original prints, and photographs. Acquired through donation or purchase by a jury, the artworks are seen by Albertans in dozens of government buildings and public facilities like libraries and schools. As a result, Alberta art has become more readily available in communities both large and small, nearby and remote.

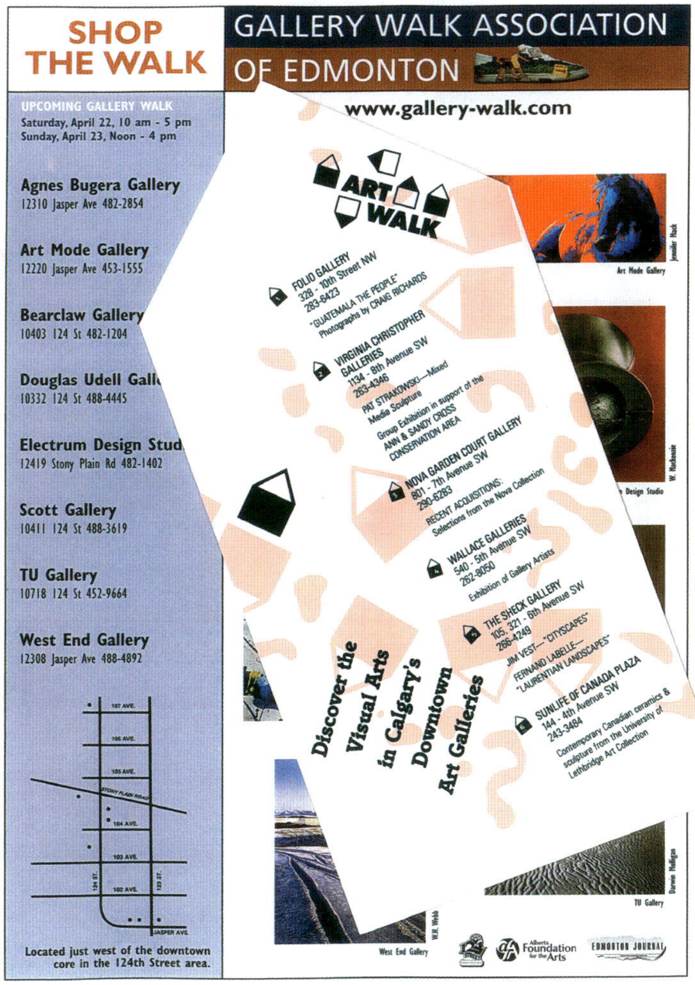

Publicity for Edmonton's Gallery Walk and Calgary ArtWalk

Back in the early half of the twentieth century, the place to buy original art was in framing shops, booksellers, and sometimes retail outlets like Eatons. After the Second World War, selling art in Alberta evolved a little further with the establishment of commercial art galleries that made original art their primary business. An early example in Calgary was the 1945 opening of Canadian Art Galleries by painter Jack Turner and his wife Grace. Not only would the Turners present the art of Albertans like Marion Nicoll and Maxwell Bates, but they would also present the works of artists from farther afield, like Ontario's Group of Seven artists A. Y. Jackson and Arthur Lismer.

In the 1970s, commercial activity took on a whole new momentum with a growing economy fuelling new galleries and the dreams of their owners, who, of course, wanted to sell art but also, in many cases, had a dedication to nurturing a more vibrant arts scene in the province. By the end of the century, the commercial sector had begun to play a key role in making the Alberta arts scene more diverse and better known, locally and nationally. Commercial galleries would never be able to represent all aspects of the creative endeavour, but neither would the publicly funded sector (public art galleries and artist-run centres), whose exhibition programming often depended (and still does depend) on scarce amounts of government funding and/or the preferences of government-appointed juries. Together, both the public and private sectors began to engage Alberta artists and their viewing audiences on different levels, with varying degrees of interpretative and educational outreach as they each began and continue to respond to Alberta's rich visual arts culture.

From Edmonton: A Many-sided Conversation with Abstraction

By the 1970s, abstract art (or "modern art" as it is sometimes called) was neither a new or novel development in Alberta. Still, in the province and elsewhere, it had acquired the status of high art. Abstract art is what glossy art magazines frequently cover and what major institutions often show and collect. In many art circles, abstraction is considered practically a universal language—albeit one with several dialects.

To be an abstract artist means you are "in tune" with modern art's highest aspirations and its most original development. In addition, there are the links shared with New York–based international art and the modernist ideal of "art for art's sake." Referred to as "formalism," this art term implies its adherents regard form, colour, texture, and shape as expressive subjects in their own right. In this type of creative endeavour, it is the basic elements of painting and sculpture that matter, honed into art by those with an artistic vision of how the work should look and feel. At its purest, art need not be about anything else except the expressive potential of both its materials and form.

Post-1970, Edmonton has blossomed into a Canadian hothouse for abstract art, especially acrylic painting and welded steel sculpture. This development has been spurred on by the summer workshops at Emma Lake, Saskatchewan; visits by the influential critic, Clement Greenberg (and others from New York); and by the support of the Edmonton Art Gallery (renamed the Art Gallery of Alberta) and abstract artists who instruct at the University of Alberta's Department of Art and Design. For the Edmonton artists who paint, acrylic colour is often applied in swaths and the canvas is treated compositionally as a single expansive plane, with little or no illusion of depth. As for the sculptors, the name "Edmonton Steel" is often attached to their work. As a type of art, it denotes a type of free-standing, collage-style, constructed sculpture welded from sections of recycled metal to create strong contours, jutting angles, and hard edges.

But the story of abstract art in Edmonton is also more varied. For one thing, there is art being made that despite its strong abstract inclinations stands apart from this much-debated model of the 1970s and 1980s. Examples include Norman Yates and David Cantine, among others. As much as the city is identified with a certain kind of abstract art, even that genre does not stand frozen in time. Artists continue to evolve and redefine their work.

Despite all the promising headlines about abstract art that lasted nearly a decade, by the late 1980s, Edmonton was a split, polarized art community, split between those of the modernist camp and those who worked in other areas, such as installation art and video. Increasingly, too, with new kinds of representational imagery and content about contemporary society in circulation, Edmonton was starting to be considered a provincial backwater stuck in a bygone modern era. It was a black-and-white view of the city's contribution to the art world, with not only its best abstract painters and sculptors "the target of routine scorn by the Canadian curatorial elite," but its entire art scene often overlooked nationally.[7]

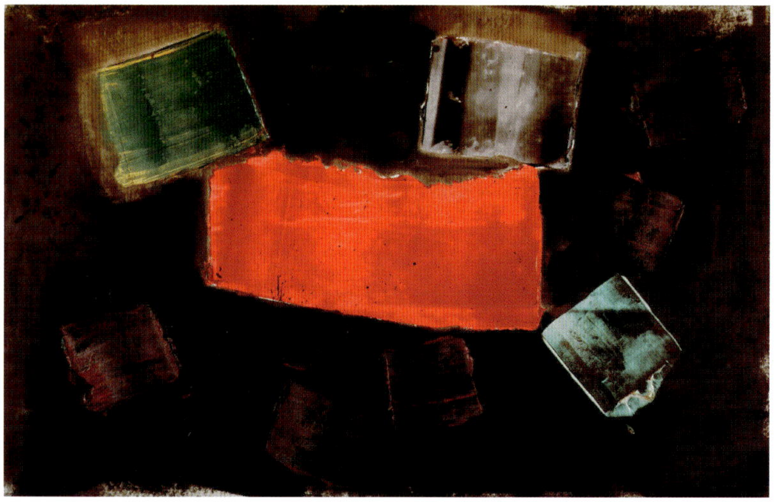

Douglas Haynes
Toledo Series #1, 1988
acrylic on canvas
Art Gallery of Alberta, Edmonton, Alberta

"Breathtakingly simple" is how the much-exhibited Douglas Haynes once described the kind of art he wanted to make—uncomplicated, but rich in both visual and emotional impact. The *Toledo Series* is a body of work inspired by El Greco's thirteen religious paintings for the Spanish Cathedral in Toledo. Working from 1988 to 1990 with blocks of colour—some sumptuously bright, others dark and dramatic—one critic has commented, "It's as though Haynes hoped to reinvent El Greco in contemporary terms."[8] In all, the artist painted about sixty-five pictures to arrive at the thirteen he needed. While there is no one-to-one relationship between his works and those of El Greco's Christ (*El Espolio*, ca. 1577–79) and twelve apostles (*Los*

Apostolados, 1605–10), the artist has suggested in his paintings "the presence of a portrait or figure yet remaining abstract."[9]

As to why abstract art would become a lifetime pursuit for an artist who by then had nearly thirty years of experience as a painter and an art professorship at the University of Alberta, his reply is a youthful one. "In art school we had to paint still life and interiors. And then I'd pick up an art journal and see [an abstract expressionist like] Jackson Pollock—there was the adventure!"[10]

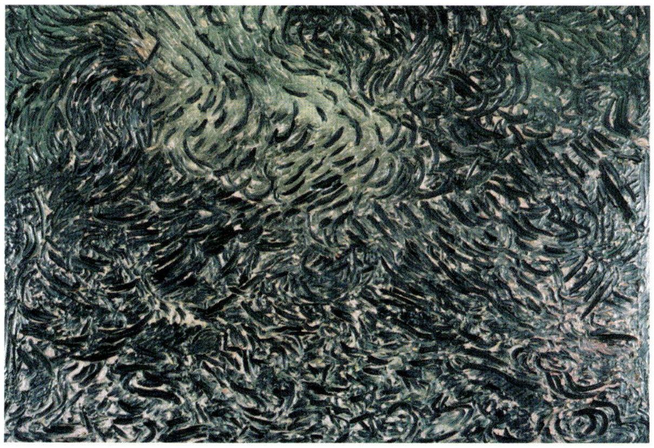

Robert Scott
Black Letter to Theo, 1982
acrylic on canvas
Alberta Foundation for the Arts, Edmonton, Alberta

For sheer impact, a Robert Scott painting, says one critic, can "make you feel like you're being swept away in a sea of paint."[11] And no wonder! The effect is close to pure energy when you see, among other things, how the artist has used his hand to push around thick layers of acrylic paint or exposed underlying colours and textures with his fingers. Add to that, as Scott later did, new materials like grains of shiny black copper slag and larger tools like brooms and scrapers to produce bigger works, and this is painting not only at its most visceral but also at its most expansive. That it should be done abstractly is, for the artist, his "most direct route to seeing." He elaborates further by saying, "I work from an inner source, my statement would be compromised by illustrating the outer world."[12]

But in another sense, the world is not completely shut out. Scott will tell you, for instance, that even as late as the 1980s, "I was still looking at [Jackson] Pollock. I felt he taught me that I must re-invent drawing for myself and set about that task."[13] The making of art for Scott then is a synthesis between his links to earlier modern art and the expressive relationship he himself has to the act of painting. In the darkly coloured and turbulent *Black Letter to Theo* too, another link is evident—this time to Vincent Van Gogh. (The unstable Van Gogh shared a deep bond with his brother Theo.) Uncharacteristically then, for a committed modern painter (also a sessional art instructor at the University of Alberta), Scott's art is said to be "nostalgic—powerfully nostalgic, perhaps even willfully nostalgic. It seems to ruminate over expressionism in all painting, but especially in the painting of Jackson Pollock and Vincent van Gogh."[14]

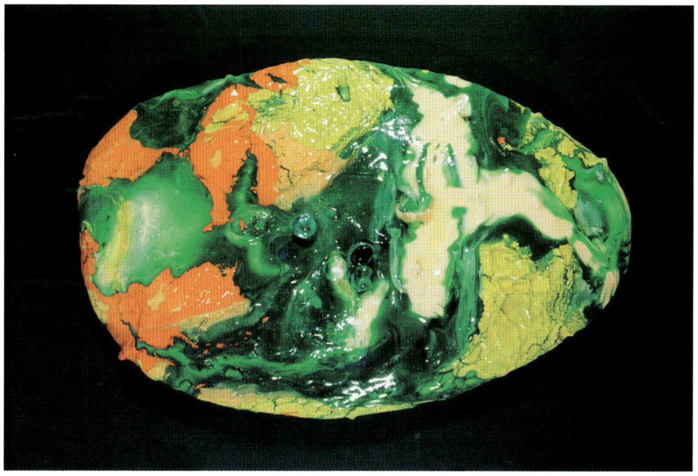

Graham Peacock
Everglade, 1993–94
acrylic on canvas
Private Collection

A radical spirit in Edmonton's modern art scene, Graham Peacock stresses his shaped paintings are "both abstract *and* representational."[15] If they are representational, maybe it is because they remind us of natural phenomena: lava flows, parched landscapes, wilderness topographies, and faraway planets. In the radioactive *Everglade*, the rich green pool meanders as if on an ancient continent.

How are they made? Certainly not with a paintbrush and easel. Looking for a bolder approach to making modern pictures, the University of Alberta art professor developed what is almost an industrial process to render paintings of pigment-rich invention. With his pails of whipped acrylic and troughs lined with canvas, his procedure eschews many of the popular concepts about how a painting is made. (Instead he is a member of the American-Canadian New New Painting, which stresses painterly methods.) What is not so unfamiliar is the reason why Peacock goes to all the trouble. Wanting his art "to be uplifting, joyous and inspiring," the artist views the entire process as a "celebration of life, of creation, an affirmation of the freedom and the boundless creativity of the human spirit."[16]

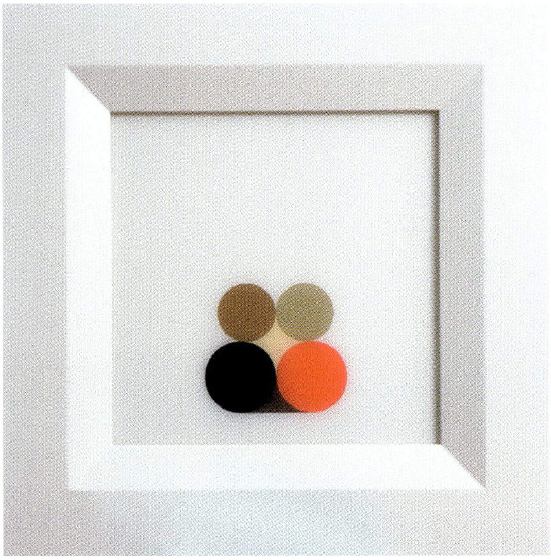

David Cantine
Snow White Six, 2000
acrylic on plexiglass
Courtesy of the Artist

Like all of David Cantine's elegant art, *Snow White Six* has the composure and objectivity of a geometric abstract. But instead of geometry, the roots of this refined work lie unexpectedly in nature: a picture of two apples and their shadows. First painted over thirty years ago, this simple still life has since served as the basis for all of Cantine's pictures: essentially the same composition painted over and over again. In the process of developing this body of art, only the picture's bare essentials have been left. Before painting, there is only the colour to consider, with the artist spending time looking at paint chips to find the right hues. Of this peculiar obsession, now carefully executed on the back of thin sheets of plexiglass (as *Snow White Six* is), one critic has commented, "It is a rare pleasure to stand before one of these eloquent canvases and allow the colour to wash over you; to begin to vibrate, shimmy and dance."[17] Thus in Cantine's rigour to orchestrate colour relationships, a playfully optical and intensely vivid artwork is created.

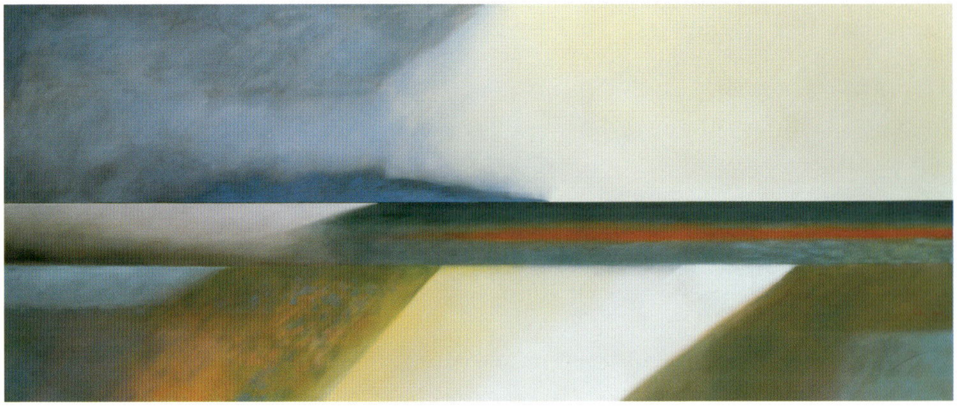

Norman Yates
Landspace Fifty, 1980
acrylic on canvas
Oxford Developments, Edmonton Centre, Alberta

In the 1970s, Norman Yates, among others, inhabited a "space" that few artists before had found scenic or even worth addressing. Flat and seemingly featureless, here Yates has set out to interpret the bald prairie: its light-filled ambience, its difficult-to-describe expanse. To do this, a less literal approach has been taken by Yates and other younger artists, relying instead on the language of abstraction to evoke not only a sense of limitless space but also a volatile climate. Uninterested in depicting "a preconceived slice of landscape," the painter incorporates—as he does in *Landspace Fifty*—several views of the prairie into one picture. Taking the idea even further, Yates adds panels in other works to allow the image, or what he calls "landspaces," to expand in all directions. Full of nuance and invention, *Landspace Fifty* is an example of how, by simplifying and abstracting, the West was finally won.

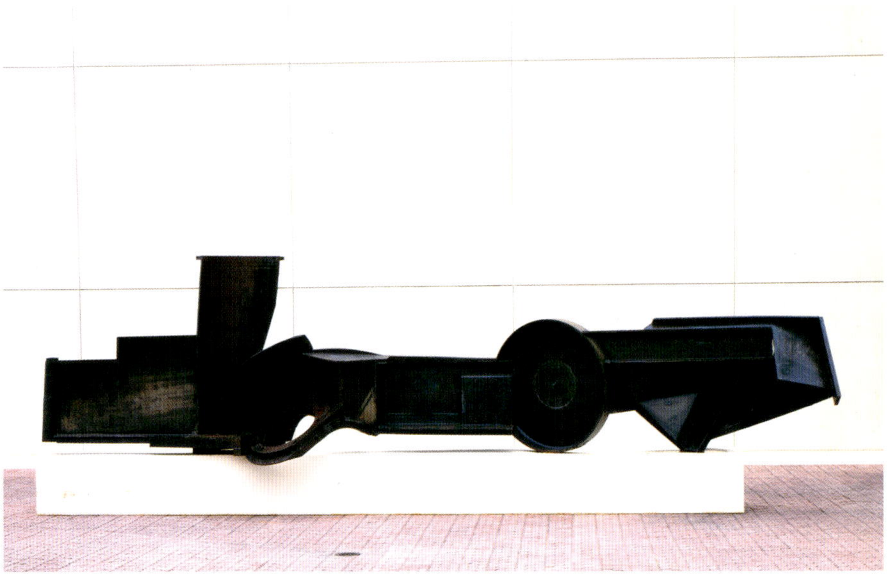

Peter Hide
Malevich Extended, 1990–95
mild steel, welded, rusted, painted, and varnished
Courtesy of the Artist

Once described as "the chief engineer of Edmonton's heavy-metal abstract scene," Peter Hide is one of several artists who, in the 1980s, put the city on the map for a type of "superphysical" artwork known as "Edmonton Steel."[18] Involving professional welding tools, cranes, and even the help of assistants, these substantial works are constructed from recycled fabricated steel. That this kind of artistic and industrial activity would coalesce in "blue-collar" Edmonton was, in a way, no accident, given the city's reputation for being a Canadian centre for steel fabrication. Even in the massive twenty-four-foot long *Malevich Extended*, the city's industrial energy is expressed. As Hide writes, "It was probably inspired by the great processions of CN rolling stock that daily go past my studio."[19]

But aside from the brawn, Hide is also inspired by art history. A full professor of art at the University of Alberta since 1977, he trained in London, England, where historical art is plentiful. *Malevich Extended* reflects the influence of the Renaissance master Andrea Mantegna's horizontal paintings of processions and reclining gods, as well as *After Olympia* (1986–87) by the modern British sculptor, Anthony Caro. Thus, in his more monolithic work, Hide's sculpture is for the Titans. It is also a marker of how this artist of figurative mass and volume departs from the more linear examples of Anthony Caro (a former instructor) and the modern master, David Smith.

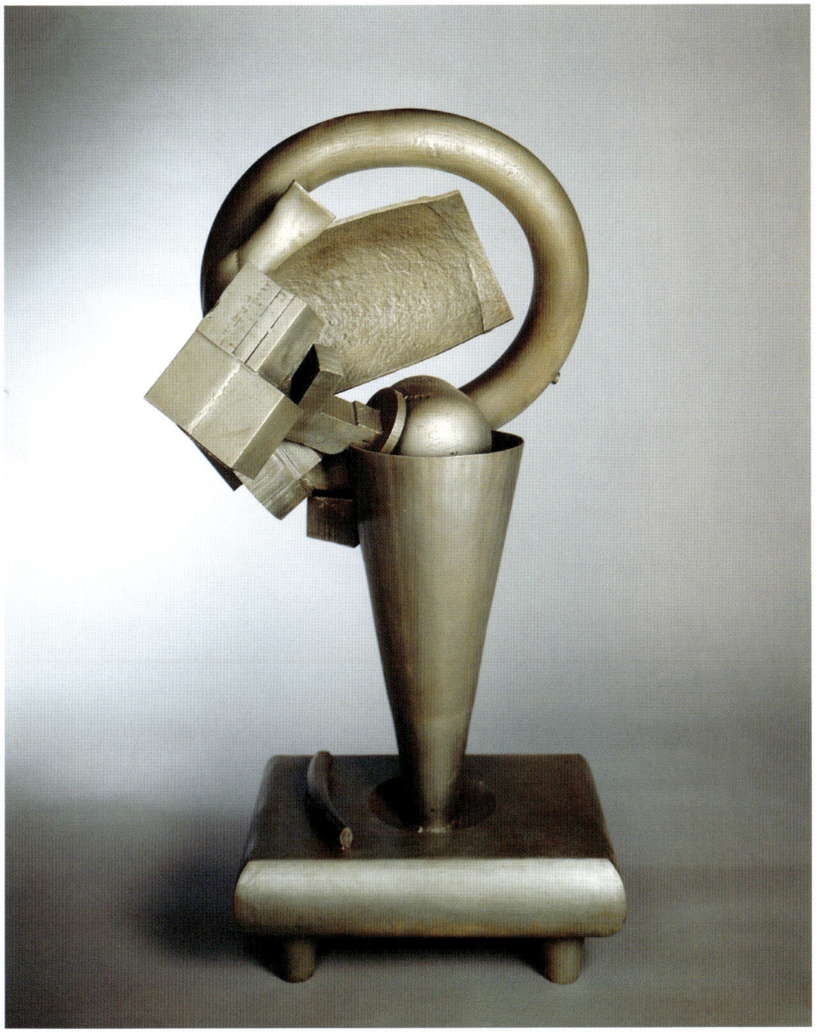

Isla Burns
Offering to Selene from an Elephant God, 1993
steel
City of Calgary Art Collection, Calgary, Alberta

According to Isla Burns, art objects made out of steel don't have to look "aggressive" or "rude." A one-time welder in the oil industry, she is familiar with steel's strength and fortitude. But as a sculptor, Burns has come to know another side to steel, or what she calls its "other personalities."[20] With training and encouragement from Alberta College of Art instructor Katie Ohe, her journey into metal art began in the early 1970s. After an association with Edmonton Steel in the next decade, a new destination was reached when Burns began to cultivate the "soft" and "touchable" side of steel. Two adjectives that are, she admits, a universe away from the material's normally macho reputation in modern art.

Working with a blowtorch and tools to grind and transform the steel's hard surface, Burns became known in the 1990s for a type of lyrical steel sculpture whose finish is warm and burnished, almost buttery in its look. As welded steel sculpture, her art beckons to be touched. But more important, Burns's art of that period gives voice to an unusual subject for the genre: her deep cross-cultural regard for mythology, especially that of India. Enriched by her own childhood spent in Calcutta, Burns has assembled a body of still lifes inspired by Hindu sculpture, especially its gods and goddess. *Offering to Selene from an Elephant God*, with its tall votive-like shape and circular arc, intermingles the creation of the moon by the Hindu elephant god Ganesh with the Greek's own conception of Selene, the moon goddess.

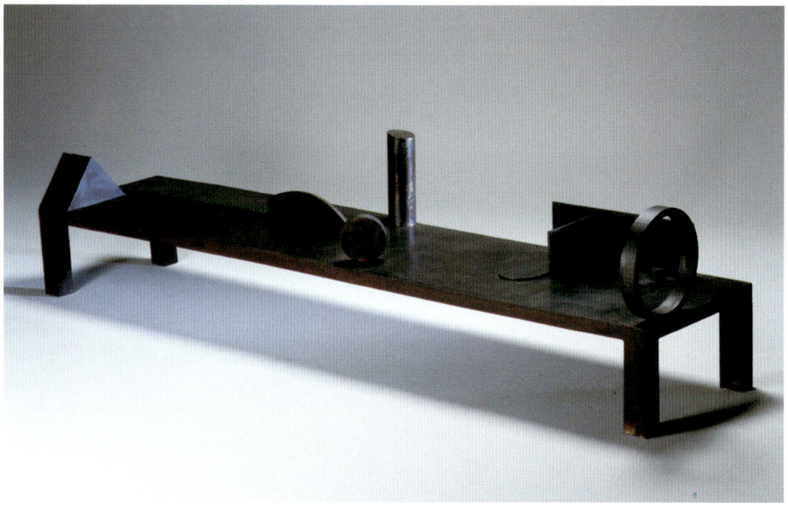

Catherine Burgess
The Story of My Life, 1990
steel
Collection of Kenneth Bradley
Photo by Douglas Curran

In 1985, Catherine Burgess, then already a recognized name in Edmonton, appeared in *Sculpture City: Works by Eleven Artists*. Organized by the Edmonton Art Gallery, *Sculpture City* was a seminal show in a province where sculpture generally receives scant attention. There, in the company of such modernist colleagues as Peter Hide, Isla Burns, Clay Ellis, Blair Brennan, Al Reynolds, and Ken Macklin, Burgess displayed a series of small abstract linear bronzes. In relation to the other larger upright abstract steel pieces in the exhibition, the bronzes signalled a new direction for the artist towards an art more personal, more symbolic, and totally unlike the more rugged monumental steel constructions seen in the city.

In 1990, she created an elegant and understated rectangular table series entitled *Things as They Are*. Entirely fabricated from steel with small geometrically shaped objects welded to their tops, these floor-bound sculptures have been referred to by one writer as "table landscapes," while another has described the small objects as "still-lifes of the subconscious."[21] For Burgess, *Things as They Are* is about "looking back to my past to seek understanding of self."[22] *The Story of My Life* marked the beginning of this memory-laden series.

Clay Ellis
Curtained Sky, 2002
polyurethane on a steel structure
City of Vancouver, BC

Of all the artists once associated with Edmonton Steel, Clay Ellis has evolved into its most idiosyncratic and experimental member. This is partly because he uses a material very unlike the brawny metals of modernist sculpture. Minimally three-dimensional and made out of laminated polyurethane, his new sculptures could easily pass for an abstract painting. If they do, it is no problem for Ellis, who has noted their intentional similarity to painting when they first appeared in the exhibition *Looks Like ...* (Edmonton Art Gallery, 1998).

To blur boundaries between artistic disciplines is a postmodern attitude, but these objects, first fabricated to hang on the wall, are also indebted to Ellis's unique metal art of the early 1990s. In this work, steel, bronze, and cast iron have been shaped, softened, and stained like objects made from moulded plastic. *Curtained Sky*, one of his more recent polyurethane works that puzzles as much as it attracts attention, was installed in downtown Vancouver in 2002. Ellis says his interest is not so much in making sculpture that is recognizable as sculpture as it is "in asking some very simple questions about changing sensibilities, process and creative art."[23]

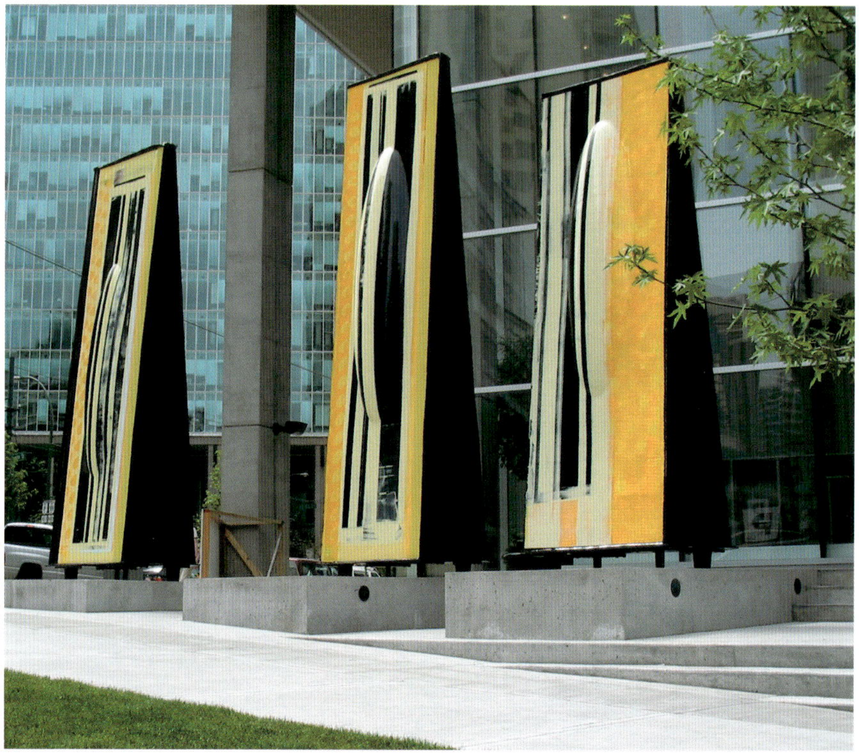

From Calgary (in particular): New Realisms

One avenue to understanding realist art is to consider what the anarchist and artist Gustave Courbet once observed. A mid-nineteenth-century French painter, Courbet is quoted as saying that, having never seen an angel in real life, he would never consider painting one. Instead his allegiance was to the recording of everyday life as he experienced it around him.[24] Fast-forward from Courbet to a 1971 exhibition statement prepared by John Hall, a twenty-eight-year-old Calgary-based painter. "I aspire," he writes, "after an art that is concerned with seeing the world as it is. An art that is non-escapist, non-idealist and non-elitest. An art that sees as its goal the clear communication of the artist's perception of his environment."[25] A fairly innocuous declaration it would seem, but in the context of its time not always a welcome sentiment. In many influential circles, abstract art is still considered the mark of an advanced artist despite the inroads made by 1960s Pop Art and other representational modes developed by artists as diverse as American painter Alex Katz and Britain's Lucien Freud.

In Canada, contemporary forms of realist art date back to the late 1950s and 1960s with Alex Colville, Jack Chambers, Christopher Pratt, Christiane Pflug, and others. Noted for their sharply focused technique, fine brushwork, smooth-surfaced painting, and attention to the familiar, these artists, though categorized as high realists or hyper-realists, would each develop their own personal take on reality. They would never hesitate to visually edit, add to, or heighten what was before them. No matter what the critics thought, it was never as simple as painting a picture to look exactly like a photograph.

In post-1970 Alberta, just as Edmonton was emerging as a Canadian centre for abstract art, Calgary, in a less-recognized fashion, was developing into a hothouse for contemporary realism. Certain artists like John Hall, then of the University of Calgary, and one of his students, Dulcie Foo Fat, would be in the forefront, but there were others, too, who, in reaction to the dominance of abstract art, would aspire to new means of representation. With this focus came subject matter inspired by the environment, the home, contemporary society, and personal life. There would even be content related to the spiritual, the otherworldly, and the eccentric, as in the case of a younger generation of realists like John Brocke and Marianna Gartner. In general, these realists would not just be disinterested observers dealing solely with pictorial matters, but would know instead that "things around us in the world have intrinsic meaning."[26]

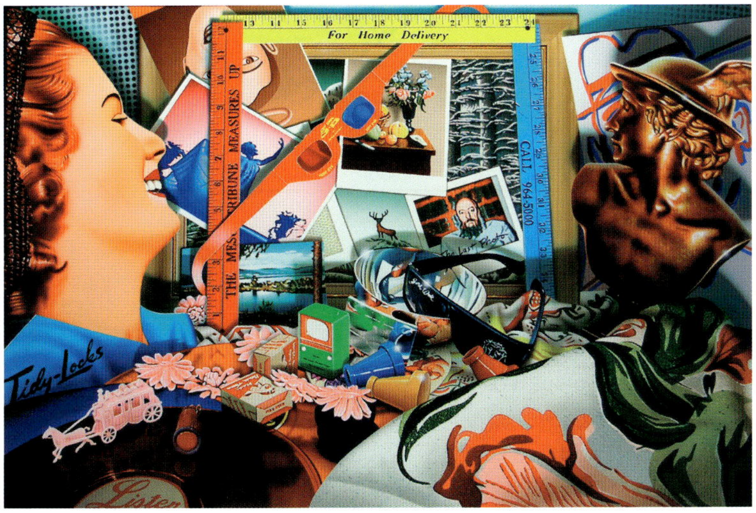

John Hall
Listen (Chris), 2000
acrylic on canvas
Courtesy of the Artist

Hall is one of Canada's premier new realists, and nobody's compositions say as much about the materialism of modern life and all that "stuff" as a John Hall painting. Bright, shiny, and unrepentant in what they depict, his art is sometimes interpreted as an allusion to how social, cultural, and personal identity is reflected in the things we hoard and possess. Hall describes his paintings as still lifes—an apt reference to a genre that took Dutch art by storm in the seventeenth century but has since settled down to a more docile existence (the exception being Hall's work with its ruthless precision). To achieve this rigour, Hall sought the aid of a camera. More recently, as in the still life "portrait" of Calgary-based artist Chris Cran (see p. 108), the digital version downloaded into a computer helps to create the image he will paint.

A student of the Alberta College of Art in the early 1960s, it was Pop Art, according to the artist, "that made it seem possible to make a picture that was representational without being reactionary."[27] Thus, in a Tom Wolfe-like guise, Hall has become something akin to a social observer with a vivid view of his time and place. A view—it turns out—that is also different from a lot of Canadian realism with its more sober, introspective stance. Hall describes his role a little differently: "An urban archaeologist," he writes of himself, "who produces still life paintings that mine the rich complexity of contemporary urban life."[28] But, like advertising on steroids, there is an edge to what he arranges and portrays. The visual overload present in many of Hall's paintings seems to ask: Is it possible to be overwhelmed by contemporary life?

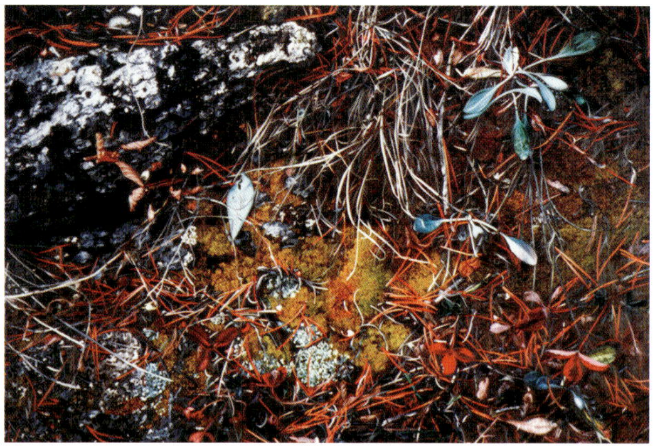

Dulcie Foo Fat
Kananaskis Autumn: Moss and Pine Needles, 1986
oil on canvas
Whyte Museum of the Canadian Rockies, Banff, Alberta

As a landscape painter (and that is only one aspect of her oeuvre), Dulcie Foo Fat generates a magnified, close-up view of the land that is unique in Canada. It has made her art instantly recognizable and different from the standard Alberta panorama. As one Toronto art critic has observed "In the vast spaces of the Alberta landscape, Foo Fat focuses on the small and intimate. She finds a whole universe in a plot of earth no bigger than a placemat."[29] A universe, it should be said, that conveys a lot about the abundance of life and its intrinsic grace.

Described as groundscapes—capable of putting us right there, nose to the terra firma—these works are derived from both the photograph and the experience she brings as a painter. Foo Fat's art is sometimes categorized as photorealist, but its lack of anonymity and more textured surfaces suggest she cannot be pigeon-holed easily. Abstraction is also present in her images in the way in which the landscape seems to dissolve into patterns of colour and form. Because of this, her paintings have been compared to tapestries. They invite us to re-examine not only what is often overlooked but how paint can subtly alter our perception of things.

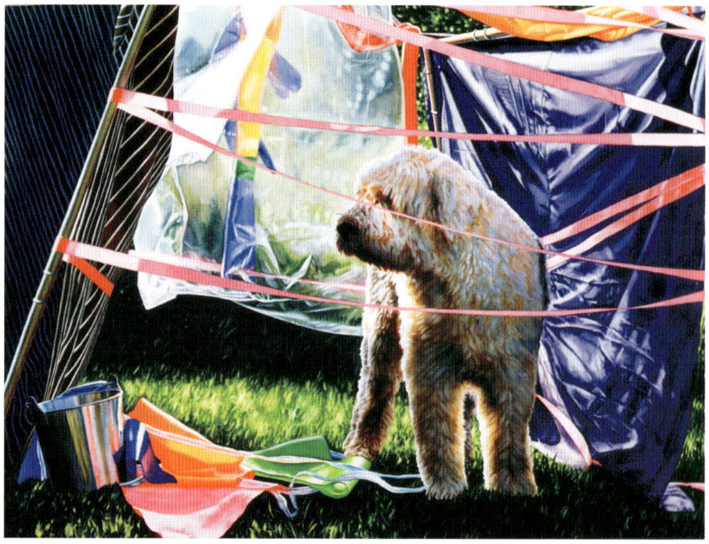

Alexandra Haeseker
Expedition: Surfacing, 1990
watercolour, B.F.K. Rives paper
Private Collection

At the time Alexandra Haeseker created her *Expedition* series—one of four concerning the subculture of dog shows—her realism was as intense and as eyeful as that of her friend and colleague, John Hall. A prize sheepdog in this 1990 watercolour appears to be the subject, which, given the artist's own background in showing dogs, is not unexpected. But surrounded as the animal is by such colour-drenched paraphernalia, it is hard to say what in the picture is meant to be seriously real. In other words, it is hard to say what is a reflection of what Haeseker has actually observed and what is teasingly abstract or added by the artist to heighten the effect of the picture.

By 1990, she was a recognized name in Canadian art for her contemporary treatment of the "figure" (two-legged and four), and Haeseker's artistic excursions had in a roundabout way already taken her through twenty years of painting, mixed media, lithography, and some sculpture. It was in the 1980s that her imagery became more detailed and photo-like as she set to paint pedigree dogs within the strange and peculiar confines of their tarped and beribboned enclosures. Of her work, she writes, "I pick up on what is current and found in my life."[30] When writing about her work, she always bases it on autobiographical sources and yet she is always open to feats of picture-making that take her images beyond the realm of the ordinary.

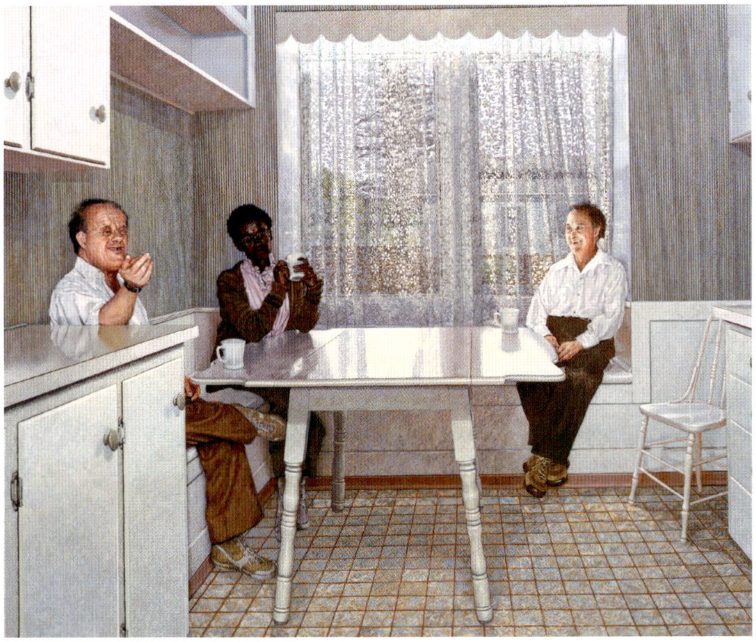

John Brocke
John, Dovie, John, 1985
oil on linen
L'Arche Association of Calgary, Alberta

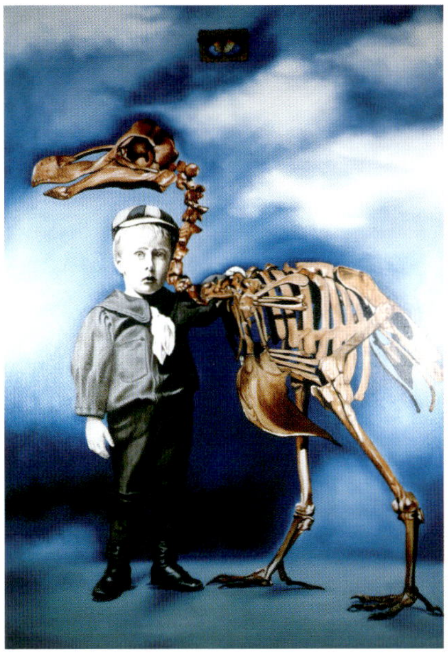

Marianna Gartner
Dead as a Dodo, 1996
acrylic on canvas
Private Collection, Winnipeg

Made only a few years after he was out of art school, this luminous 1985 painting heralds the arrival of John Brocke, one of the best of a second generation of realists then emerging in Calgary. Aside from his technique and the large-scale size of his work, even more compelling is the content of Brocke's imagery, some as informal and straightforward as *John, Dovie, John*, others more complex and improbable if not partly invented.

John, Dovie, John is a commissioned work, featuring John Hautzinger, Dovie Williams, and John Hambrook who, at the time, lived in a group home supported by a Calgary-based handicap association. As in subsequent pictures, the artist has demonstrated just how obsessive the detail in realism can be with his colour applied in tiny textured amounts. Serene and bathed in light, the three sitters are almost three-dimensional in their impact, not flattened against the picture plane as would be the case in a John Hall or an Alexandra Haeseker. Composed from information gleaned from several photographs, *John, Dovie, John* celebrates, as one critic aptly put it, "evidence of the spiritual in the physical world."[31]

A first-year painting student of John Hall, Marianna Gartner developed an approach to realism that, by the late 1990s, was neither hyper-real nor as photo-based as the work of the first generation of Alberta realists. Instead, her images—based largely on vintage photographic portraits she has collected—seem to emanate from a distant time and place. It may be the "past," but it is a past of Gartner's own making. She prefers to say that "[much] of my work deals with life and death, beauty and horror—simple contradictions."[32]

The "old world" seeps from Gartner's art—informed by her own eastern European background and a personal interest in the darker, more grim figurative art of early twentieth-century Europe. This otherness gives her painting a distinctive look and has prompted much comment. "[It] seems as if her visiting of European picture galleries has had a stronger influence on her work than contemporary Canadian art," writes one German critic who considers Gartner to be a "counterpoint" to the Canadian art establishment, "where conceptuality [installation and media art] and the reception of minimal art play such an important role."[33] Also, by composing ambivalent images like *Dead as a Dodo*, Gartner underlines a strong tendency in Canadian realism to act like it is all "normal" but still convey disturbing and even sinister content. Because of the curious subject matter and sheer delicacy of her portraits, Gartner is a one-of-a-kind artist but still an example of how varied contemporary realism is in post-1970 Alberta.

By and About Women

By the 1970s, at least two generations of women in Alberta had contributed to the province's artistic heritage. As much as their circumstances permitted, their commitment to art was no less substantial than their male colleagues. By name, there are too many to list but some of the better known might include Annora Brown, Thelma Manarey, Euphemia McNaught, Janet Mitchell, Marion Nicoll, Mary Schäffer, Margaret Shelton, and Catharine Whyte. In many instances, the subjects they have tackled—landscape, still-life, and the portrait—are the same as the ones chosen by men. Sometimes, though, there are differences in how and what they choose to represent, like Brown and Schäffer's passion for depicting wildflowers. Nonetheless, whether male or female, all of these artists trained and worked in an earlier era when "the very definition of an artist implied he was male."[34]

In the 1960s all of this would change with the women's movement, when introduced "into the male fabric of modern art," comments Lucy Lippard, "[were] the multi-coloured threads of female experience."[35] Put to rest was not only the preoccupation with the achievements of (white) men to the exclusion of nearly everything and everyone else, but also the modernist ideal that art existed in its own universe—untainted by popular culture, social concerns, and other distractions. The very terrain of art became altered and the role feminism played in this multi-faceted and provocative expansion (pluralism) cannot be underestimated. Feminism changed how many women *and* men made work, and how art itself—both past and present—was viewed and studied (or deconstructed). Traditional boundaries between fine art and the so-called crafts became blurred, themes like gender and identity became very topical, and painting was pushed to the periphery of the Canadian contemporary art scene because of its overt masculine past.

In Alberta, though painting was never totally abandoned by up-and-coming younger women, something new did develop about how art can both be conceived and made. This included the use of unconventional materials like fibre or an alternative medium like video; a stress on content over style; an interest in critiquing the depiction of women in society and mass media; the injection of storytelling and autobiographical detail into works of art; and the establishment of collaborative projects and events, such as the annual province-wide Celebration of Women in the Arts (est. 1983) and Calgary's feminist *spin* (1994).

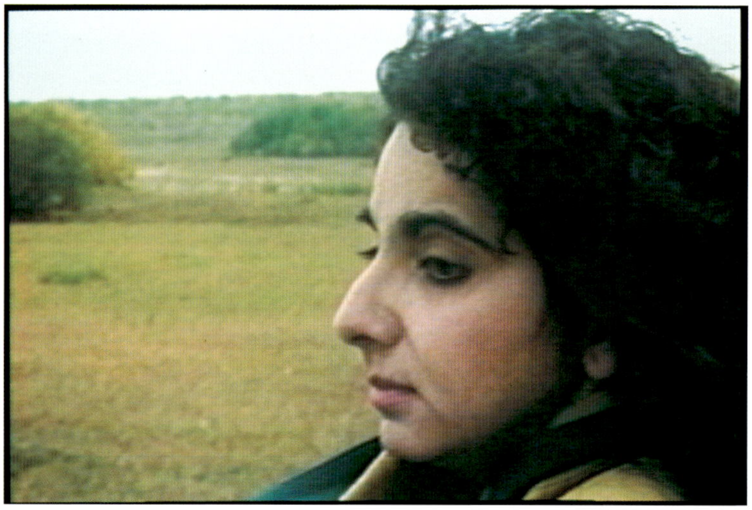

Cherie Moses
Mubarakah, 1994
colour video, twenty-four minutes
Vision TV

Shot in the aspen parkland of the Edmonton area, an unnamed woman is out for a walk. With only her thoughts to keep her company, we hear what she is thinking in the three languages she knows: English, French, and Arabic. Gradually, aspects about her life are revealed, including the dislocation she feels being identified and singled-out as an "exotic-looking" woman in Canada. *Mubarakah* is a fictionalized story told from the point of view of the other.

Earning a five-year broadcast contract for Moses with Vision TV, *Mubarakah* ("blessed") is a multicultural story in which Moses's own cross-cultural background keeps her attuned to such themes as identity, stereotypes, and the social construction of roles played by women and men. Besides video, Moses has produced and presented photoworks, paintings, prints, textile sculptures, audio productions, and live performances like *Brides and Opening Ceremonies* (1981). A pioneer in Edmonton's alternative (avant-garde) art scene, Moses's range of work makes her truly an example of what it means to be a multimedia artist, or what is sometimes referred to as being "multidisciplinary." In 1982, Edmonton's Grant MacEwan College became the first post-secondary institution in Alberta to offer video as a formal part of the curriculum in an intermedia course offered by the fine arts program. The instructor who created this course was none other than Cherie Moses—who had a long association with the college.

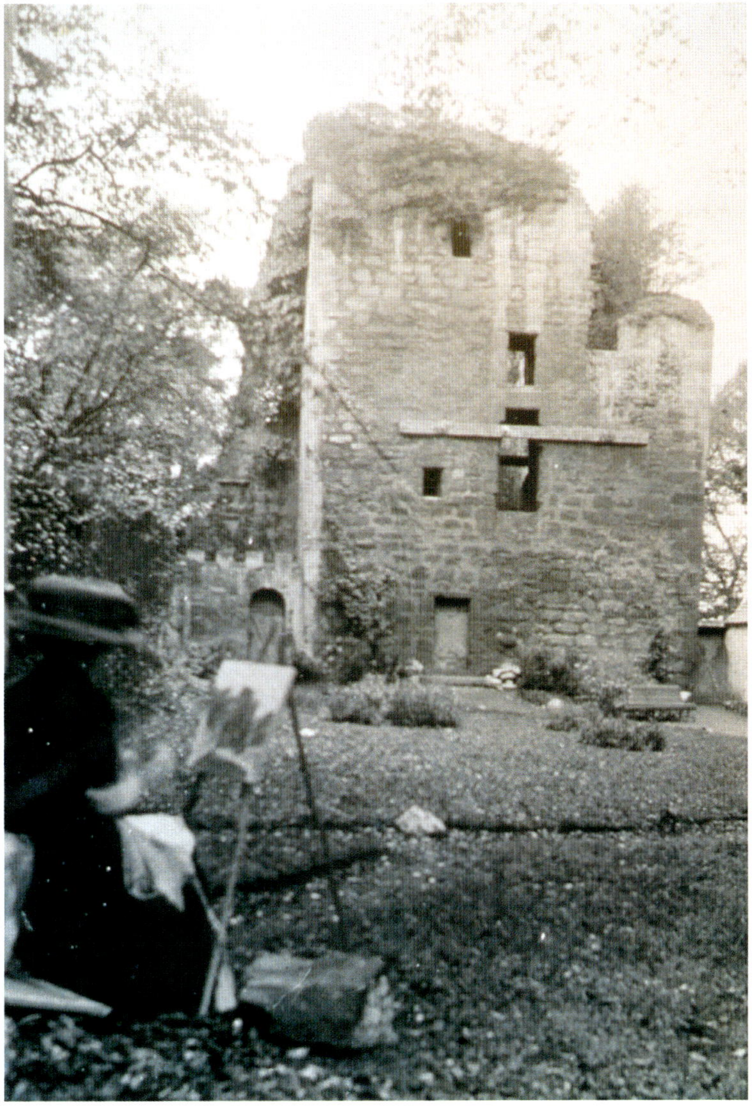

Sandra (Tivy) Vida
"...near where my great- aunt was born," 1992
multimedia installation
Collection of the Artist

In 1990, Sandra Vida spent a summer in Glasgow, Scotland, researching and developing a work about her little-known great-aunt, Jessie Struthers, who lived and worked in the area between 1867 and 1947. Dressing up as her relative and visiting several sites that Struthers may have known both as an artist and a worker in the cotton mills, Vida realized this "imagined mentor came to symbolize for me the women who are erased from a dominant male history [i.e., the canon]."[36]

Blending personal history and fiction, "... *near where my great-aunt was born*" features not only a video of Vida role-playing, but also one of her walking the streets in 1990 "looking" for Struthers. Other real and imagined aspects of Struthers's life are displayed through written text, video loops on two other monitors, and mounted photographs. Created while she was an artist-in-residence at the City of Culture Festival (a European Union event) in 1990, Vida's layered work highlights how personal stories can act as a springboard into larger issues like "the canon."

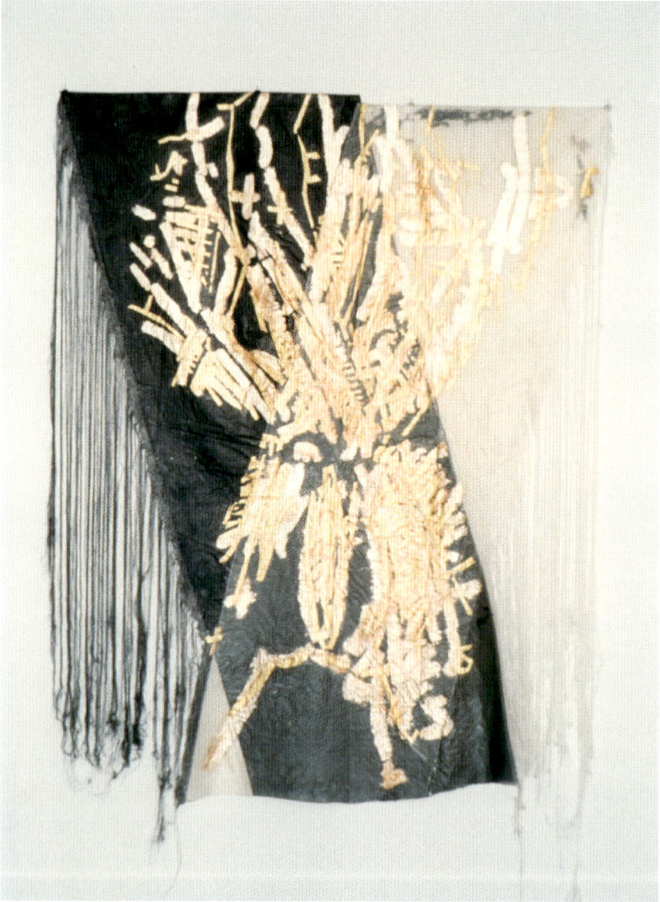

Mary Scott

Imago VII Urverdrangung: refoulement "translatable"<< she is there>>, May 1988
spray paint, silver and gold leaf, Rhoplex and wax on silk
National Gallery of Canada, Ottawa, Ontario

Mary Scott challenged the tradition of painting on practically every front. An instructor at the Alberta College of Art and Design, she was one of Alberta's key artists of the post-1970 period and a surprise to many (elsewhere) because, as one Toronto critic put it, "artistic radicalism isn't exactly what springs to mind when you think about Alberta."[37] Rather than boycott the medium, Scott, with flare and imagination, put a gaping distance between herself and what is popularly expected of a "painter" and painting.

In response to her time spent reading and researching about how the Western art tradition represents women and especially the female body, Scott's comment is: "I rarely care what the image looks like, I think only about what it means."[38] During her career, she has not gone out of her way to make visually indifferent work (far from it), but buoyed by the writings of French feminists and others, Scott, during her most acclaimed period (1983–89) used unorthodox materials like silk and felt to create strikingly physical works. They are intended to metaphorically "speak directly to the representation of the body."

In the *Imago* series, replacing the canvas are long metres of frayed, shredded, and unravelled silk, while specifically in the *VII* work, *<<she is there>>*, the abstracted female anatomy is rendered in thin sheets of silver and gold leaf. In one curator's opinion, "It is a recent body, a body of lived experiences, a body of moments which cannot be represented or figured symbolically."[39] Conceptually cerebral, these pieces and others from the 1980s earned Scott eight solo exhibitions in public institutions, an almost unprecedented number for an Alberta-based artist.

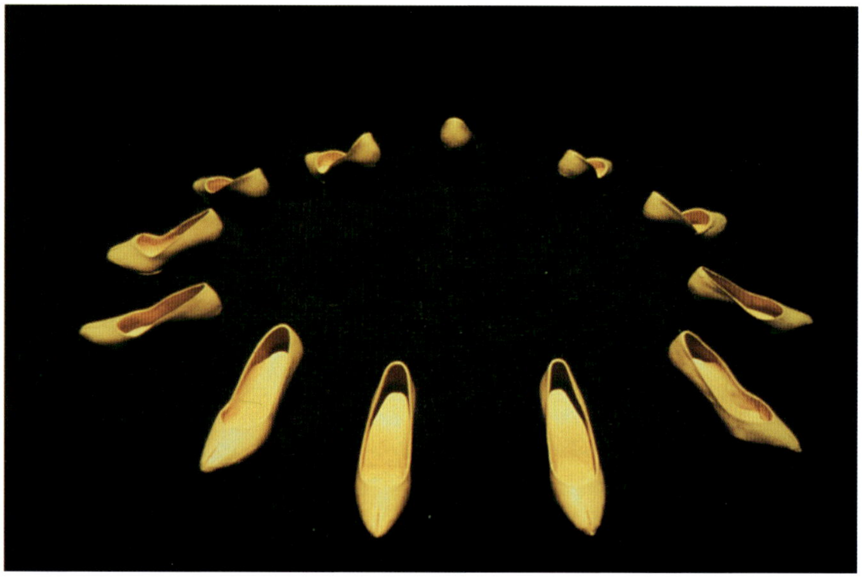

Faye HeavyShield

Sisters, 1993
mixed media
McMichael Canadian Art Collection, Kleinburg, Ontario
Image courtesy of the Luke Lindoe Library, Alberta College of Art and Design, Calgary

At first glance, six pairs of high heels, facing outward in a circle, seem to be all there is to *Sisters*. But a closer inspection shows the toes of the bone-coloured shoes have been altered and transformed, taken from the realm of the familiar to the more earthly. With a small amount of plaster and moulding compound, the toe of each shoe has been made cloven like an animal hoof, making the subtlety of *Sisters* all the more surprising. Representing the artist and her five sisters, this woman-centred work with its poetic allusions to family, personal identity, and place is one of several that made Faye HeavyShield a celebrated name in the Canadian contemporary art world of the 1990s. She is, according to one art reference book, "A sculptor of some distinction … with an enviable reputation for her ability to invest minimalistic structures with inordinate expressive force."[40]

Raised on the Blood (Kainai) Reserve in southwestern Alberta, the Lethbridge-based artist has had no shortage of experiences from which to nurture her art: the daughter of a Blackfoot-speaking family of twelve (her father managed the band ranch); a pupil of a residential school for ten years; a mother of four and later a student at the Alberta College of Art and Design (where she found her vocation as an artist and writer); and, an observant inhabitant of the spare evocative environment of southern Alberta. Whatever the source, though, the introspective HeavyShield believes "[the] personal has to come first. I've never wanted to speak for a race or a gender."[41]

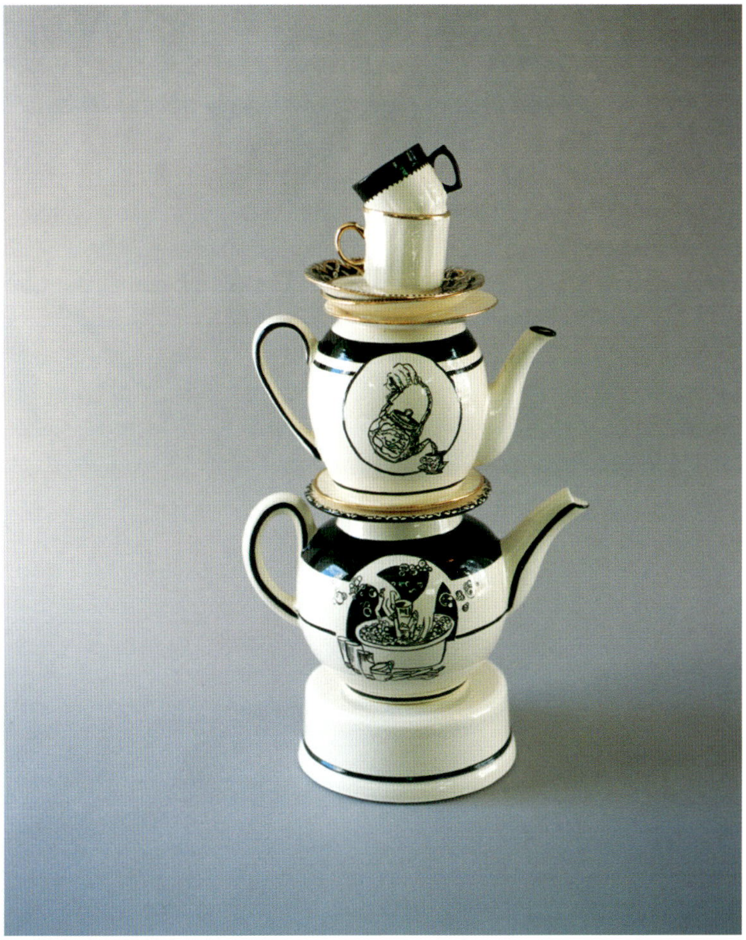

Evelyn Grant
Woman's Work, 1995
cast and assembled earthenware clay with underglaze, china paint, and lustre decoration
Alberta Foundation for the Arts, Edmonton, Alberta

It is a woman's world in *Woman's Work* and rather than be critical, Evelyn Grant is engaged. She is doing, in fact, what many women artists of an older generation avoided in order to be taken seriously. But with a sense of humour and no fear of domesticity, Grant is prepared to raid the kitchen for her playful yet socially reflective art. Out of that contested site—where indeed so much "woman's work" does takes place—Grant particularly favours the teapot as an easily understood format for her autobiographical works. As to why stacking seems to be a familiar response, Grant turns to her psychologist for an explanation. "She says it's because I'm piling things up; trying to do twelve jobs in my own life."[42] Alas, a sentiment not unknown to the modern-day woman.

Working with mostly commercially available moulds or greenware to produce her teapots, tureens, candlesticks, and the like, this well-known potter has long made the kind of art that is irreverent about what constitutes a "serious" work of art. She can't help it, she grew up admiring five-and-dime store china. But with meticulous craftsmanship and a keen appreciation for decoration (the Victorian period is a favourite), Grant has taken all that is scorned as feminine and kitschy, like china painting, and invested it with new meaning.

New Terrains

Prior to the 1970s, art in Alberta was largely defined by its rich legacy of landscape painting. Other kinds of expression, like figurative art or abstraction, did exist, but in the art market and in the public conscience, it is landscape that continued to prevail. In the larger context of international contemporary art, though, it was almost anything but landscape art. This also became the case in Alberta after 1970, when according to one critic "most of the [province's] top contemporary artists do not work in this genre."[43] Or, as was stated in another publication, "Landscape painting has fallen out of vogue in the mainstream of contemporary Canadian art."[44] What then, in the context of post-1970 Alberta art, is an artist to do if he or she has any inclination in this area?

Many artists, of course, have just continued to paint, depict, and interpret the landscape, but on another level, full-blown recognition of landscape art from up-and-coming curators, critics, and the large institutional players has become increasingly scarce. By and large, when it comes to recent developments in art, they have looked to other areas of creative activity. This despite Canadian landscape practice being influenced and altered by new attitudes in art and a widening scope of creative activity that includes art inspired by nature, the history of art, and the current environment, rather than just landscape per se. The following works represent a small selection of landscape artists based (or once resident) in Alberta. They have left some strong impressions about what landscape and art, inspired by nature and the environment, could be in the post-1970 period.

Takao (Tak) Tanabe
The Land 21/75, 1974
acrylic on canvas
Alberta Foundation for the Arts, Edmonton, Alberta

Applied in thin washes of muted colour, Tanabe's 1970s series, *The Land*, is a compelling example of how artists of a younger generation found new ways to artistically dwell on what they saw around them. In Tanabe's case, it was not Banff or the surrounding Rockies where he then lived that inspired him, it was the wide so-called "empty" plains that many artists and visitors had avoided. But not Tanabe. With a background as a nationally recognized abstract painter and a familiarity with Japanese Sumi-e painting, he was able to translate the prairie's very minimalist and spacious presence into works of art that spoke more about its powerful mood than its specific details. Not only that, if being a westerner is also a state of mind then *The Land*, contemplative and subtle, gives voice to that idea.

In 1995, the west coast artist received an honorary degree in fine arts at the University of Lethbridge. Awarded in recognition of his lifetime contribution to art, special note was made of how his Alberta paintings taught many people to see the treeless and flat part of the plains for its own special qualities: "as a special place of wonder, effused with a spiritual sense of light."[45]

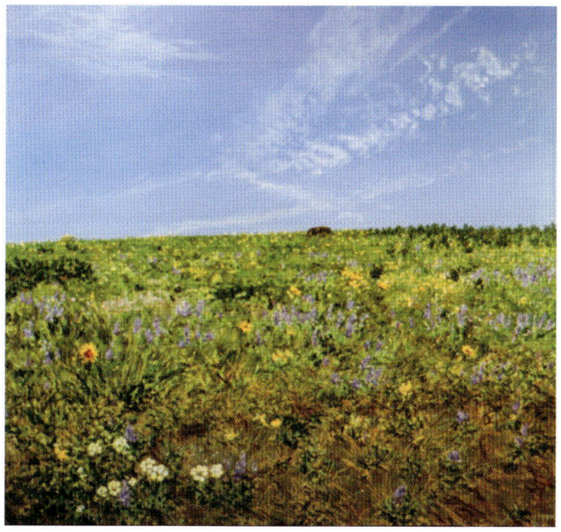

Sylvain Voyer
High Country Flowers, 2003
acrylic on canvas
Private Collection

If Tak Tanabe's landscapes are about what is barely tangible, then Sylvain Voyer's are about what is definitely "there." His vibrant paintings represent what is wondrous in their detail, approximating as closely as possible the colour and clarity of the aspen parkland in and around his hometown of Edmonton. According to one critic, "He creates a world so crystalline, the leaves sparkle in a faint breeze you can almost feel passing by."[46] To which the artist would add, "I go for an intensity of experience," pursuing the most spacious of rural terrains, the bluest of skies, the yellowest of canola, and the freshest of fields.[47]

In this Technicolor ode to the large swath of parkland that cuts across central Alberta, he is aided by a background in abstract art, an understanding of modernist colour theory, and a youthful history of artistic experiment that has embraced not only social-political art but also dedicated itself to "creating art of and from a specific place, not imported from somewhere else."[48] In the lead-up to this adventure, Voyer was only eighteen years old when he started painting plein-aire (outdoors)—a mainstay of his practice to the present day. According to Voyer, painting landscape gives him an art "high," which is fortunate for the viewer considering how his sense of place and belonging is so often exuberantly expressed.

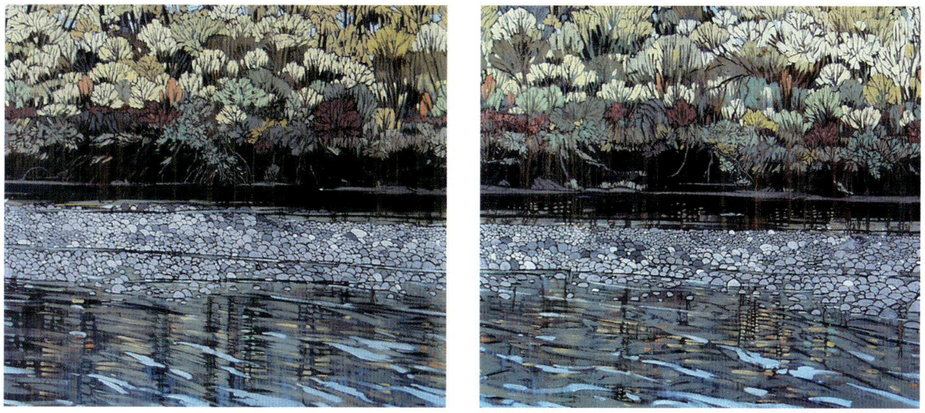

Ted Godwin
Gravel Bar, 1990
oil on canvas from the *Lower Bow* series
Collection of Husky Oil

Ted Godwin had barely completed his lyrical *Tartan* paintings (1967–76) when changes in his life prompted the veteran abstractionist and art instructor to consider the landscape genre as his subject. To many, it was a surprising switch for an artist once associated with the avant-garde Regina Five (1961–64). But more surprises were to come in 1989, when Godwin committed himself to one of the most ambitious landscape projects in Alberta's young art history. Closing his studio to visitors for three-and-a-half years, the artist and ardent fly fisherman with an environmental conscience produced a series of seventy-eight paintings of the lower Bow River between Calgary and Carseland.

Of this enormous task, which included seven diptychs and triptychs measuring up to twelve feet wide, Godwin was quoted as saying the works were not a return to reality from abstraction but instead a step towards *another* reality.[49] And what a special reality it is! The textured patterns and colours of nature have been translated into an almost abstract two-dimensional entity (i.e., a painting), while at the same time presenting an intimate view of the river's tangled shoreline. Remarking that some of the places he depicts exist more in the mind than in reality, much of the impetus for the *Lower Bow* series was, at the time, tied to a proposed new dam and "the political masters we have entrusted our affairs to [who] seem bent on destroying as rapidly as possible what little wilderness there is left."[50]

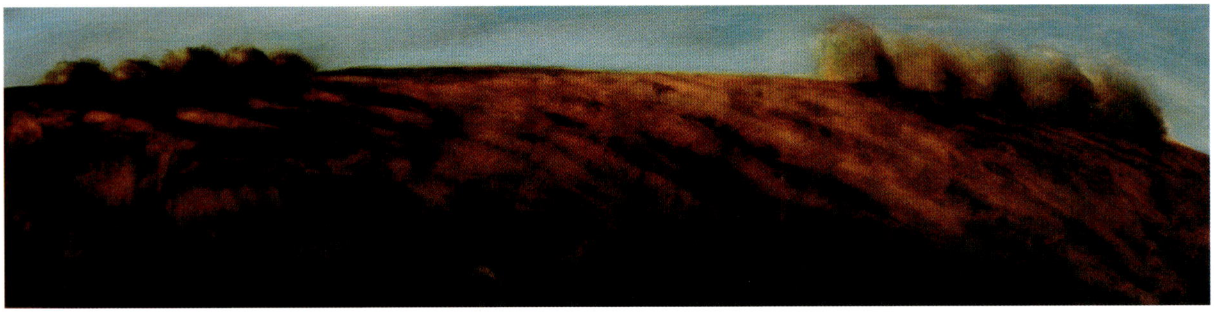

Barbara Milne
Prairie, 1992
oil on panel
Private Collection

Although arriving in Alberta in 1979 with an art degree from Toronto, Barbara Milne is one of several newcomers who have developed a fresh take on the western environment. Overwhelmed at first by what she sees in the West, it is only after some time that her paintings are done from memory instead of from a first-hand sketch. By producing a "mental construct" or a distillation of what she has observed, certain aspects of the land, like its colour and shapes, have been simplified and heightened. In appearance, there is often an ethereal or atmospheric quality to her art, suggestive of the land being not only a physical presence but a spiritual entity as well. A place where, in addition, elemental forces of weather reside.

A moody colourist, Milne has transformed the prairie and its stark sunshine into a deeply introspective place. Not exclusively a painter of the western region, Milne nonetheless, wherever she is, gives a sense that "there is more going on than meets the eye."

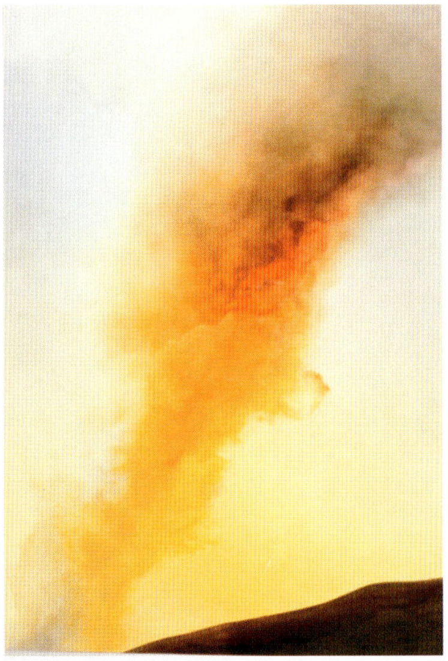

Jeffrey Spalding
Event (Yellow), 1989
oil and wax medium on canvas
Courtesy of the Diane Farris Gallery, Vancouver, BC

Jeffrey Spalding was an art instructor at the University of Lethbridge when *Event (Yellow)* was made. There was nothing in his background as a conceptual painter, or in his lively rapport with contemporary art theory and art history, to suggest that this genre would ever engage him. Not only that, once he did get started—partly inspired by the southern Albertan environment around him—most of Spalding's paintings were about someplace else and some other time in art history! As works of art, they referred to the idealized landscape art of the nineteenth century when it was culturally possible to view nature as untouched and untainted by the presence of a modernizing world.

Instead of depicting panoramic scenery—a device still common in conventional landscape—Spalding has resorted to painting close-ups and details, rich in suggestion and meaning. A favoured subject is Niagara Falls—a warhorse of the landscape genre—where the roaring waters are still wondrous but may be polluted as well. A similar case could be made for *Event (Yellow)*, where even its ambiguous title leaves us wondering if this act of nature is one of beauty or something more noxious. Spalding does not intend to be an environmental artist per se, but his accomplished landscapes touch on many areas, including how the presence of nature "makes us reflect on our own mortality and vanity." [51]

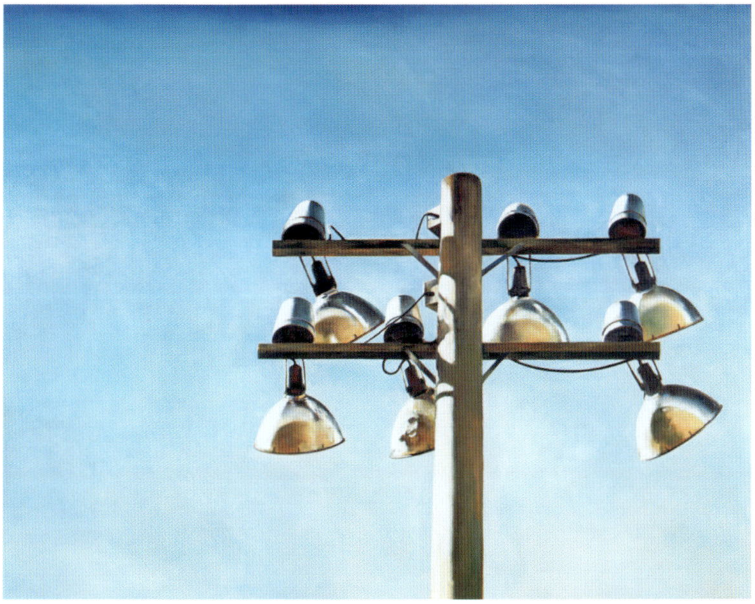

David Janzen
Field Lamp, 1993
oil on canvas
Private Collection

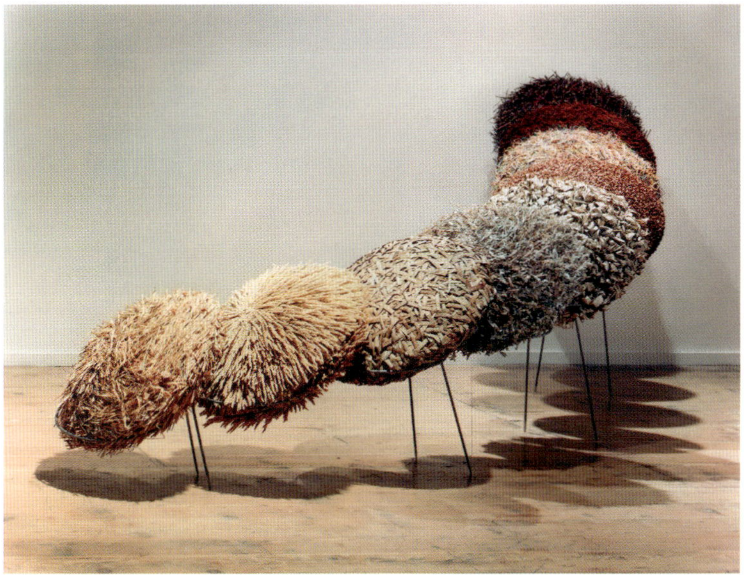

Lyndal Osborne
Spinners, 1997
mixed media installation
Art Gallery of Alberta, Edmonton, Alberta
Photo by Robert Keziere

One of the most fluent painters of his generation, in the 1990s David Janzen looked into the skyscape of the new urban prairie and found a place, he says, bristling with poles, lamps, and antennae. These protrusions and what they signal about his time and place have become his subject matter. Committed, since graduating art school in 1983, to the recording of everyday things in his environment, including interrupted views of the natural world glanced at through a car window, Janzen has transformed the technologically inhabited landscape of Alberta into art. In mood, some of his landscapes are benign, while others are more ambivalent or threatening about what they convey about modern society.

He describes what he does as "low-tech observations," and while it is true that the craft of painting is antediluvian in comparison to much of what he depicts—satellite dishes, transmission towers, refinery stacks, and so on—his crisp compositions and disciplined treatment make these works iconic for Alberta in the twenty-first century. As in *Field Lamp*, the mythic Alberta-blue sky is still there but something new has taken charge.

Made of sage, day lilies, rhubarb seeds, dogwood, lime grass, cattail leaves, yellow willow, spear grass, gaillardia seeds, palm leaves, paper, discarded telephone wire, and steel, there is nothing the least remote or distanced about how *Spinners* relates to the natural world. Osborne collects natural articles, stores them, and when the time is right, creates some of the most distinctive nature-based art in the country, saying that latent in her semi-sculptural installations are issues of collecting and categorizing, vulnerability and power, preservation and endangerment.

But given her art's appearance—comparable to some of the stranger life on Earth or possibly elsewhere—a Lyndal Osborne is always open to different readings. I wonder if *Spinners*, with its four sets of legs, might bear some relation to primordial life forms found in the Burgess Shale at Field, British Columbia. Intrigued for many years with the organic and what is commonplace to rural Alberta where she has lived, the retired University of Alberta art professor says the perishable nature of her materials reflects largely on a desire to make the "life and death process" vivid. [52]

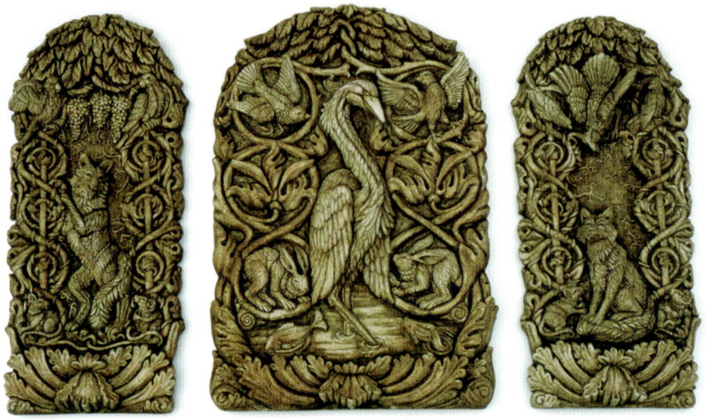

Garry Williams
Aesop's Fable, 2002
ceramic
Collection of the Artist

This contemporary treatment of "The Wolf and the Crane" is both a Garden of Eden and a garden of culture by Canadian clay maverick, Garry Williams. Astonishing for its decorative fervour and careful attention to animal expression, nature and culture meld together as seamlessly in this lively work as they do in the ancient fables, which rely on animals to convey witty social insights.

Produced in high relief and altar-like in its shape, *Aesop's Fable*, as in many of Williams's sculptures, has its origins in storytelling and myth rather than in the aesthetics of clay. Historical art was also of great interest to him and its motifs and designs were often incorporated into what he made. In addition, a concern with personal, cultural, and social content also prevailed. In one case, this focus led to the creation of a series of large male porcelain figures (1998) that address male archetypes and the state of contemporary masculinity. In another work, an installation entitled *Cathedrals* (1993), the environment and its exploitation is the work's central theme. A particularly strong thread in his oeuvre is the interpretation of the natural world, where clay objects and natural and industrial materials are combined to make room-size installations.

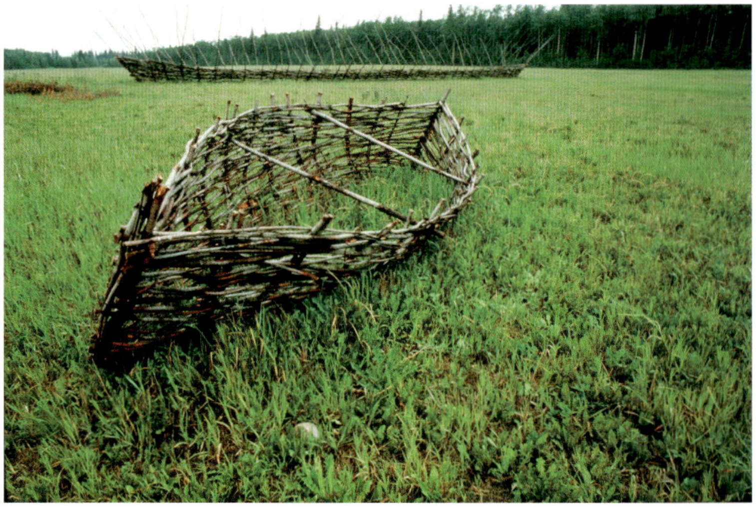

Peter von Tiesenhausen
Small Vessel and *Ship*, 1994
willow
Both boats are located on von Tiesenhausen's property west of Grande Prairie, in Demmitt, Alberta
Photo by Randall Adams

"I have chosen to live in the woods. My art deals with my environment and as a result, my paintings and structures are about nature and interacting with it."[53] The "woods" Peter von Tiesenhausen refers to is a family homestead near Demmitt, Alberta, five hours northwest of Edmonton. Regionally, the homestead is located in the fabled Peace River Country, where forestry and oil and gas extraction are steadily transforming frontier and farmland. But on von Tiesenhausen's land, a different kind of transformation has taken place. Since 1990 the artist, already a promising painter, has built a number of large-scale outdoor sculptures made of woven willow. They include the sturdy but wistful eighteen-foot *Vessel* (1992) and (in the background of this picture) the slender 110-foot *Ship* (1993).

Made to be gradually subsumed by nature, these metaphorically rich objects have been followed by other large woven willow constructions, including, high up in the trees, hanging pods, and, without the aid of a single nail, a narrow, forty-five-foot woven tower. Part nature-boy and part visionary, von Tiesenhausen has also engaged and enthralled audiences in other Canadian and European locales with large site-specific installations, oil paintings on burnt wood, drawings, tactile sculpture, and on occasion, performance. Considered a master of keeping the design and form of his artwork to the bare minimum, as one critic has suggested, his artwork seems "to exceed their materiality, they have an archetypal resonance."[54]

Sculpture from Another Avenue

By the end of the twentieth century, it was almost a cliché to describe Calgary art as "eclectic." But adjectives like "individualistic," "pluralistic," "postmodern," and "eccentric" do get used, and in the case of three of the city's top sculptors—Gordon Ferguson, Walter May, and Blake Senini—they are entirely appropriate. For instance, in the exhibition, *Gang of Three: New Sculpture from Calgary* (Winnipeg, 1987), their expressive and savvy art was said to be representative of "a frontier and self-reliant attitude in Calgary," where "personal vision, rather than social or political content, is the predominant focus of most of the artists."[55]

The 3-D creations of Ferguson, May, and Senini, all instructors at the Alberta College of Art and Design, are indeed idiosyncratic and very different from the abstract welded steel sculpture of Edmonton's modernist community. Rather than being non-representational, their work, over a twenty-year period, has ranged from the suggestive to the pictorial. (There are, for instance, Senini's anecdotal drawings on plaster forms.) The materials they employ have also been diverse. At one point, also in the 1980s, warped tree branches played a starring role in a series of Walter May sculptures, while in a more industrial mode, sections of two-inch plastic pipe were a highlight of Gordon Ferguson's work. For these artists, mixed media is their calling: meaning and material at play with each other. They are masters of allusion and metaphor.

In Calgary, the three artists are by no means the only ones actively exhibiting sculpture, but on the strength and sheer presence of their work, they do give this medium a more visible and energetic profile in a centre where painting has always dominated. In addition, their art can be fun, witty, and irreverent—characteristics not unique to their art alone, but ones which give the city an off-the-wall flavour, much at odds with its conservative politics and national image.

To this mix can be added Katie Ohe and Bart Habermiller. They also have an association with the Alberta College of Art and Design: Ohe as an alumnus and senior instructor, while the much younger Habermiller was a student instructed by all four instructors: Ferguson, May, Senini, and Ohe. Sculpture has been Ohe's calling since the 1960s and she has worked imaginatively in all of the traditional materials associated with the medium, such as metal and stone. Habermiller, on the other hand, is drawn to what can be scavenged from a junkyard and made into assemblages, or what he calls "temporary monuments," that draw attention to the throwaway consumerism of contemporary society.

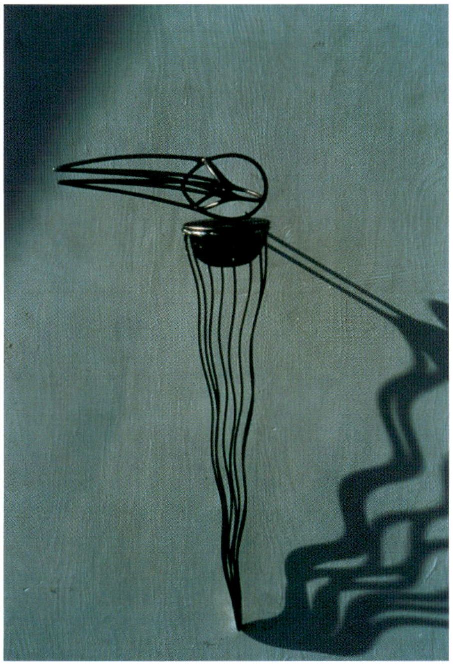

Katie Ohe
Goodbye Magpie II (*Sculpture Prayers*), 1997
steel
Collection of the Artist

By the time Katie Ohe's *Sculpture Prayers* series was underway in 1996, the artist had thirty years of experience working with metal, clay, and sometimes stone. Considered one of the first artists to make modern sculpture in Alberta, Ohe had developed a reputation for what she likes to call "participative" art, or sculpture with moveable elements. Made with the aid of local industry, these kinetic works were realized either as large-scale public art, or, more surprisingly, as hand-held sculpture. Described as "brilliantly engineered," one critic marvelled about whether this art, so polished and precise, had actually been made by a human.[56]

With her *Sculpture Prayers* series, though, there is no doubt about its human origins. Made out of welded steel rod, these delicate small-scale configurations, attached to the wall at eye level, are pure whimsy. Ohe asks us to share in the delight of something so succinctly expressed about the living world around her. Look closely and also be amazed by the use of steel as a material with poetic potential. Inspired by the Festival of Lights on India's Ganges River, each sculpture represents a personal prayer, in which the hand-sized half hemisphere is said to represent the small candlelit offerings released onto the nighttime waters.

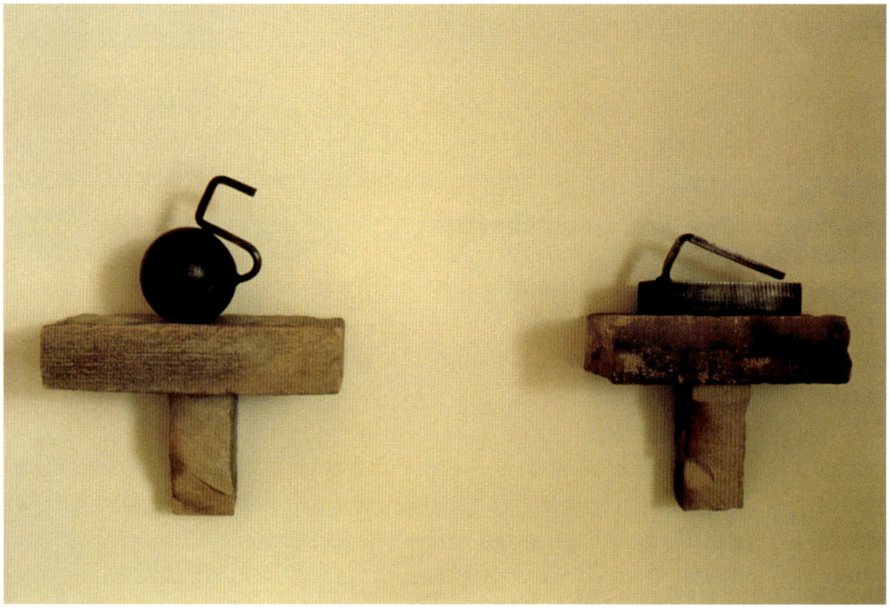

Walter May
Wisdom & Folly, 1989
steel objects on carved sandstone shelves
Alberta Foundation for the Arts, Edmonton, Alberta

Standing only a few feet in length and height, *Wisdom & Folly* is another example of how a non-monumental piece of sculpture can carry itself with great presence and meaning. Walter May does not work exclusively on such a small scale, but this work is indicative of why, among sculptors in Calgary, he is a philosopher and a restoration expert, although what he "restores," he often alters. In the metaphorical *Wisdom & Folly* this has meant adding a metal handle to the vintage steel ball and steel brick and then placing them each on a small sandstone shelf, their function and meaning transformed.

By instinct a scavenger and collector of old and odd things, May describes this period in his oeuvre as partly a fascination with "a local history … the prairies, agricultural based, western Canada, evidence of a certain kind of unique quality."[57] But this work goes further by suggesting a duality to human existence. There is no wisdom without folly, nor, on a more pragmatic level, is there innovation (i.e., the useful steel brick with handle) without failure (i.e., steel ball with odd-shaped handle).

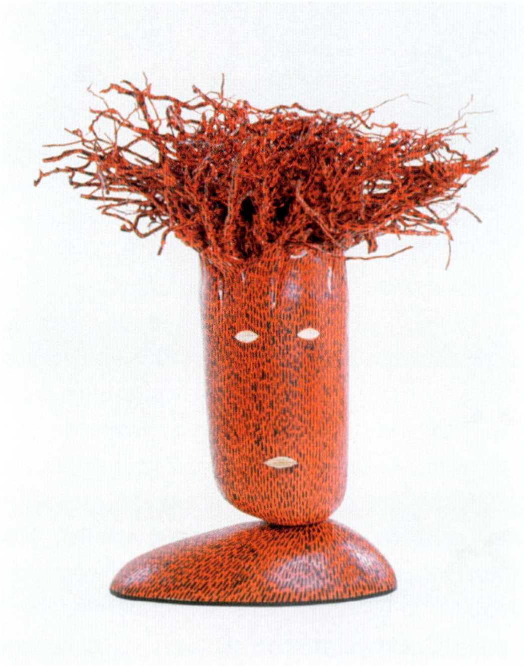

Gordon Ferguson
Red Head, 1986
painted wood
University of Lethbridge Art Collection, Alberta

Carved from a dead up-ended honeysuckle root and painstakingly painted with red and black dashes, *Red Head* is one of a series of androgynous heads and full figures Ferguson made in the mid-1980s. Besides alluding to unfamiliar humanoid life forms, this figurative sculpture stands out for its sheer strangeness during a decade when angst and the human condition were popular in international contemporary art. Whatever these wood, or steel and rubber, creatures may be, they are (thankfully) not angst-ridden. Instead, they exhibit qualities associated with some Calgary art of that period: humour, irreverence, and quirkiness. They are also extraordinarily hands-on creations, in that the effort is tangible and the materials, such as the tangled honeysuckle root of *Red Head*, instinctively led the artist in a certain direction. Rather than being the "divine" creator, Ferguson's fate as an artist is actually in the hands of something more humble: a root. It's not all a one-way street, though; in return for its use, the artist skilfully transforms this Medusa-like entity into perhaps a brainier android version for the digital age.

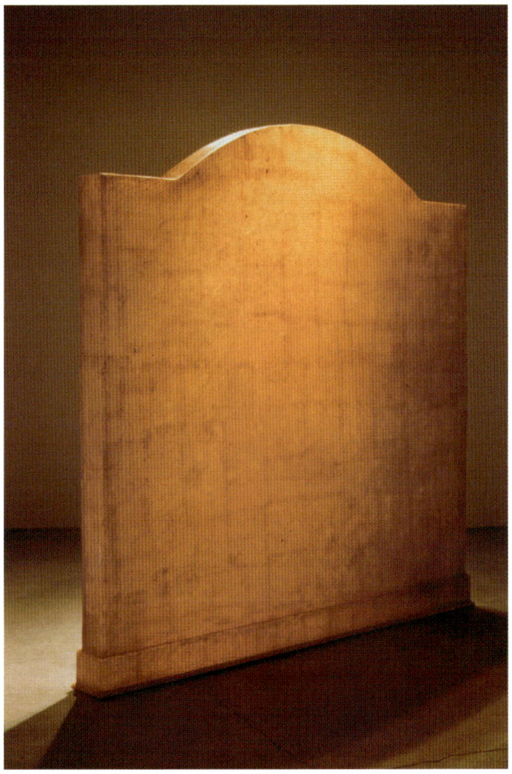

Blake Senini
Shape of The Light, 1996
polyester resin
Alberta Foundation for the Arts, Edmonton, Alberta

Despite its religious and spiritual overtones, the source of this translucent tombstone-like structure is as ordinary as can be. It is based on the shape of a reflection seen by the artist when the sunlight streams through an archway onto his living room wall. This ability to take what is merely interesting or transitory and transform it into something more particular and unexpected is a common trait of Senini and his two colleagues. In Senini's case, *Shape of The Light* is revelatory, full of promise. Not only that, but whoever heard of a sculptor trying to depict or capture something as ephemeral as the reflection of light? Photographers and painters do, but in sculpture, light is a more difficult subject.

Made of a translucent shell of resin, this graceful form is also, as one writer pointed out, paradoxical.[58] A heavy object like a tombstone becomes light enough to lift, while a reflection of light is made into a tangible object. Part of a body of work produced in the 1990s when Senini's art was less narrative and concerned with more simplified forms taken from architecture and the decorative arts, a new kind of content emerges with these stunning metaphysical objects.

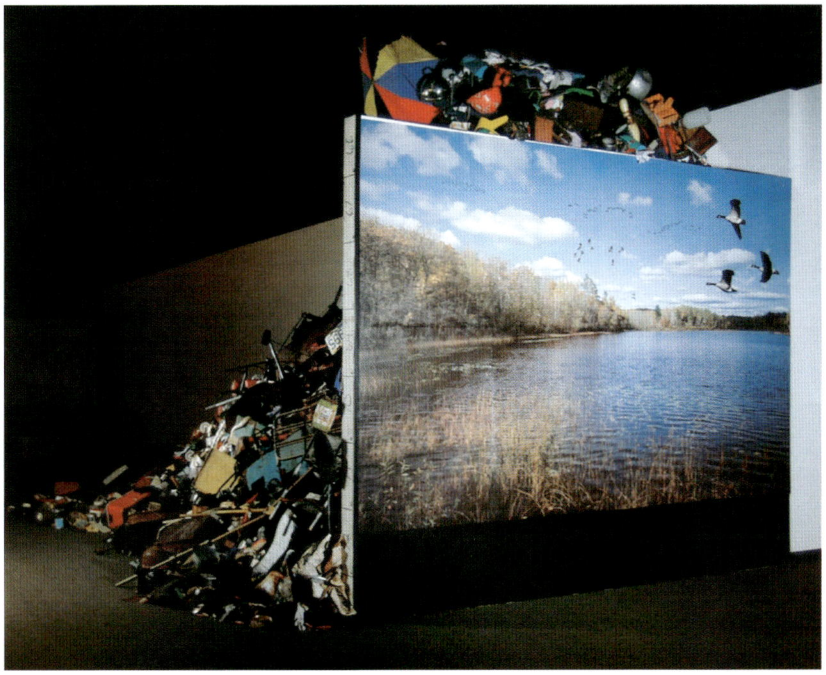

Bart Habermiller
Our Home and Native Land, 1988
sculpture installation: urban discard, billboard
Collection of Artist

Younger than Ferguson, May, Senini, and Ohe by about ten years, Bart Habermiller (like none other) brought a scavenger's aesthetic to his youthful art. The fact that there was a bona fide junkyard (Calgary Demolition Co. and Salvage Ltd.) that he had access to helped, of course, and in *Our Home and Native Land*, a monumental stack of the junkyard's refuse is used to make a social statement. But the making of statements is not all there is to Habermiller's obsession with the "artefacts" of what he sees as a consuming and wasteful society. He is sentimental about what is thrown away and looks for old radios, light fixtures, and other consumed relics that are capable of stirring up memories for people. Placed within the context of other disposed objects, he has not only imbued them with fresh meaning but also incorporated them into elaborate sculptural compositions.

For a decade (1986–97), Habermiller and other artists made use of the seven-acre junkyard, setting up makeshift studios, making temporary on-site artwork, and throwing performance art extravaganzas, such as *Night of the Living Junk Monkeys* and the annual *Graceland Art Rodeo*. Attracting national media attention, the appeal of Graceland was its "underground" character as a place where artists like Habermiller could bust loose from the constraints of the art gallery system.

Interpreting Culture and Identity

This chapter can hardly represent Alberta artistically in all of its cultural and social guises, but suffice it to say, as far as archaeologists can tell, people have migrated to the region for at least twelve thousand years. Attracted by abundant resources, Aboriginal cultures have long been present, while more recently, migrations of non-Aboriginal groups have added to the province's diversity. But in a socially stratified province, with its own linguistic, racial, and ethnic barriers, the story of a diversifying society has been neither entirely festive nor folkloric.

In the post-1970 period, certain artists have paid particular attention to the subject of cultural identity. Thus, in Joane Cardinal-Schubert's *The Lesson* (1989), her schoolroom installation presents, on a large chalkboard, a defiant retelling of Canadian history from her perspective as an individual with Blackfoot (Kainai) heritage. More subtle, but not without wider meaning, are Orest Semchisen's photographs of Byzantine churches in Alberta. They can be seen as signposts of how the cultural distinctiveness of central and eastern European immigrants, with their inability to speak English and the prejudice they struggled against, kept them, as one historian observed, "on the margins of western Canadian society for decades."[59]

Given Canada's widespread condition of multiculturalism, it is not surprising that visual art that directly addresses or is reflective of culture and identity has become a coast-to-coast phenomenon since the beginning of the post-1970 era. More broadly, as visual arts in the Western world developed a more critical eye (or discourse) around such subject matter, terms like "otherness" and "difference" have entered into academic and critical discussion about such art. Like feminism, this thematic art is a pluralizing force that has widened Canada's historical art canon.

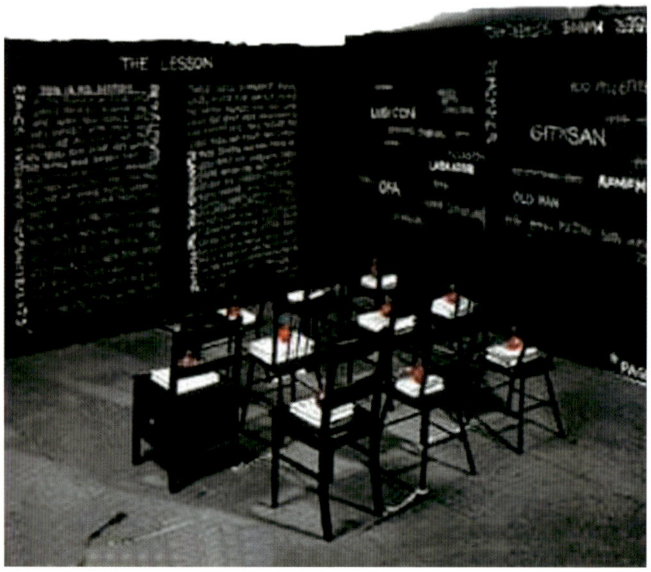

Joane Cardinal-Schubert
The Lesson, 1989
mixed media installation
Courtesy of the Artist

By the time Joane Cardinal-Schubert assembled this installation designed for a small-size room, she was already recognized as one of a new generation of First Nations artists—following in the footsteps of such art elders as Alex Janvier, Daphne Odjig, and Norval Morriseau. Cardinal-Schubert was a participant of a more politically vocal generation. *The Lesson* took the residential school model that was used extensively to assimilate Aboriginals, and turns it on its head.

Physically, *The Lesson* was like any classroom of an earlier era except that on the blackboards the "instruction" was of a completely different kind. On one blackboard was written an Aboriginal narrative entitled "This is My History," while on the other were names of people and events linked to Aboriginal history, such as the Oka blockade in Quebec. In addition, sitting on each seat of the classroom's ten black chairs was a white-coloured book topped with an apple pierced with a screw hook. To complete the installation, the artist sometimes added a performative element involving ten Native people sitting on the chairs and interacting with the viewers.

Created for Articule Gallery in Quebec, *The Lesson* was reconstructed in over twenty venues across Canada, the United States, and Europe. As an installation work, it represents one side of a multi-faceted artist also known for visually rich painting and mixed media works incorporating the figure, Aboriginal symbolism (of her own design), and landscape significant to Aboriginal culture in southern Alberta.

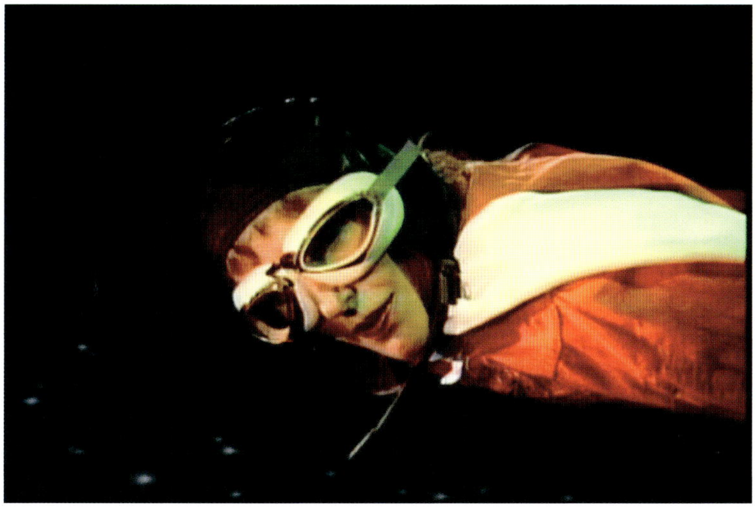

Leila Sujir
The Dreams of the Night Cleaners, 1995
colour video, 46 minutes
Co-produced with the National Film Board and the Banff Centre, Alberta

One of the most ambitious video works to come out of the visual arts community in Alberta, *The Dreams of the Night Cleaners* is no ordinary dramatization about immigration and its impact on individual lives. Presented as a docu-fiction, the video is a visually rich brew of pure fantasy mixed with the presentation style of contemporary television. A TV news talk show is staged and archival footage used for a newscast. Animation is also employed when the script requires an eggplant to fly through a living room. Just as strange too, is the storyteller who speaks to Devika, the airport night cleaner, from the label of a soap bottle.

What is the purpose of this semi-autobiographical story whose art direction also incorporates the decorative patterns of Indian miniatures? Partly inspired by Sujir's own Indian father, who as an airline pilot in Canada experienced racial and cultural discrimination, *The Dreams* draws a suggestive link between the aspirations of the immigrant and the history of Canadian immigration policies. Through the lives of three night-shift employees at a Canadian airport, Sujir's work points out how "anyone's dreams, regardless of their economic class, can be crushed by the clash of cultures."[60]

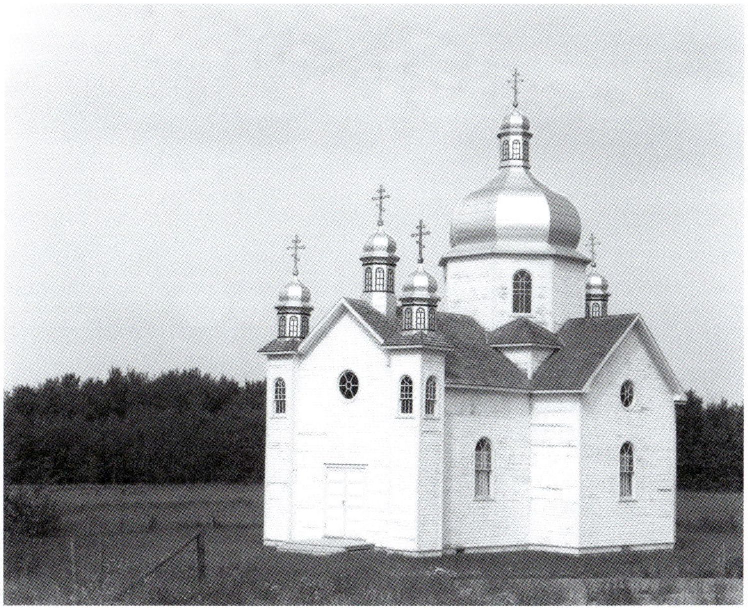

Orest Semchishen
Ukrainian Orthodox Church, Stry, Alberta, 1975
gelatine silver print
Collection of Canadian Museum of Contemporary Photography, Ottawa, Ontario

With their distinctive onion-shaped domes, Eastern Rite churches are one of the most striking landmarks found in central and northeastern Alberta. Constructed in the early decades of the twentieth century by local craftsmen, these structures are as symbolic to the settlement of the West as the prairie grain elevator. (Both structures are now also frequently abandoned and/or torn down as rural populations move to larger urban centres.)

In 1973, Semchishen, a radiologist by training, set out to create a photographic study of more than 250 churches, such as this gem-like place of worship found northeast of Edmonton in the Stry district. Described as offering more than factual documentation, the photographs are an eloquent statement about not only Semchishen's attachment to his heritage but also the connection many can feel to a remote but enduring past. One of the province's most acclaimed photographers in the documentary form, Semchishen has also focused his lens on other, less publicly well-known communities, such as the Japanese-Canadian community living around Raymond, Alberta, with its historic Buddhist temple, and the Métis trappers of the northern boreal forest.

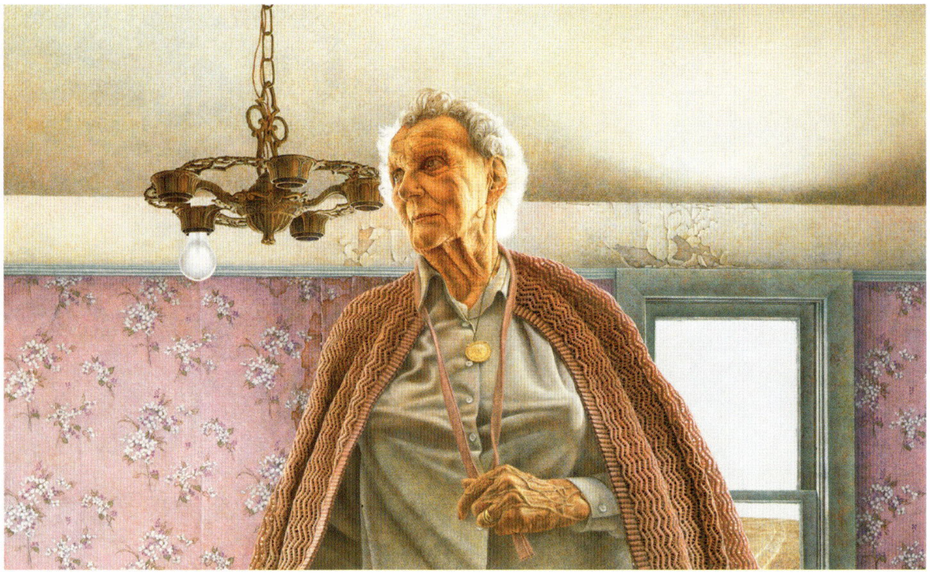

Patrick Douglass Cox
The Pioneer's Daughter, 1986
egg tempera
Alberta Foundation for the Arts, Edmonton, Alberta

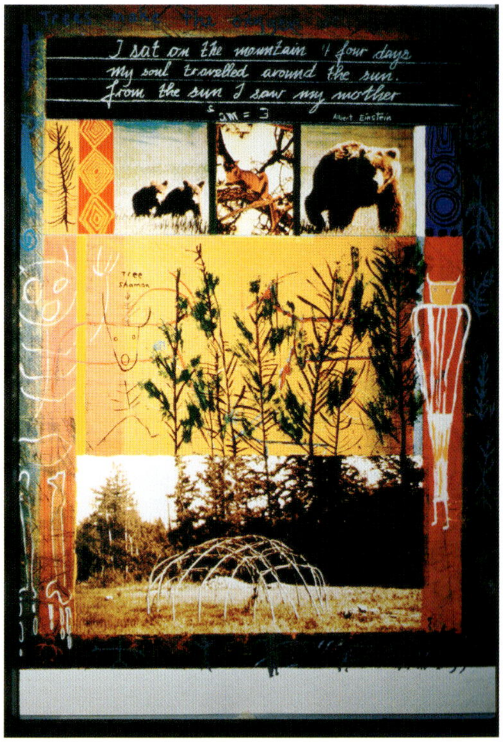

Jane Ash Poitras
2 See Mother = Earth, 1993
silkscreen on paper
Alberta Foundation for the Arts, Edmonton, Alberta

With a title like *The Pioneer's Daughter*, this portrait of the artist's maternal grandmother, Elsie Dorothy Douglass, is intrinsically connected to Alberta's first hundred years of existence. With a face that suggests sacrifice and hard work, and now-deserted surroundings, this poignant work depicts a sense of passage.

The Pioneer's Daughter is also in keeping with the "West" as Patrick Douglass Cox experiences it every day. Living near his family's homestead, where for four generations it has simply been known as "The Ranch," it is not the romantic mythological "West" as represented in popular culture that compels Cox to paint. What moves him about his environment is its people and their day-to-day activities indoors—and out. The frontier is tamed but it is still a hard-scrabble place. In relation to Alberta's increasingly urbanized and cosmopolitan landscape, the rural environment is a place of otherness. It is also a place where a sense of a western identity is strong, subtly echoed by the Alberta seventy-fifth anniversary gold medal around Elsie Douglass's neck.

"I sat on the mountains 4 four days my soul travelled around the sun. from the sun I saw my mother" reads the chalkboard inscription near the top of this silkscreen. Typical of the mixed media techniques used by this Edmonton-based artist in her paintings and prints of the 1990s, *2 See Mother = Earth* is a part of a cycle of visionary work inspired by the time Poitras spent in New Mexico in 1992. With Natives from that area, Poitras experienced her first sun dance and peyote ceremony. More specifically, the title of the tiered work and its imagery addresses Einstein's famous equation about energy, which Poitras reinterprets according to a different understanding of the universe.

Drawing on the personal, the political, and the sacred to create an identity for herself—Poitras was raised in a foster home with no knowledge of her Cree heritage—the artist has turned heads with her socially and politically engaged art. "My art is a social statement," she once asserted.[61] Many of her collaged paintings and prints, too, are edgy, graffitied compositions about environmental, spiritual, and cultural renewal. A participant in many of the major exhibitions about First Nations art in the late twentieth century, Poitras and many of her generation have made large strides into the collections and exhibiting programs of Canada's foremost art institutions.

Blurring the Boundaries

In this exploration of contemporary art in Alberta, a few examples of artworks have already been shown where a room or area is transformed by an ensemble of objects and/or other matter like light, text, video, and audio. Often referred to as "site-specific" art—made for a particular interior or an outdoor location—such work appears for only a limited amount of time with the documentation of it being the only thing left after the work is dismantled. Unlike a painting or photograph on a wall, or a sculpture on display, one motivation behind installation art is to get away from the notion of art being a precious object, in other words, something that is readily collectible and able to be turned "into a tidy profit" when the artwork is resold. That is the theory, although in practice installation art has its collectors, too, most often museums and art institutions.

More important to the critical popularity of installation art is the idea that such work blurs the boundaries between artistic disciplines. It is a multimedia effort with seemingly limitless possibilities. It can engage with any kind of materials (or non-tangibles like audio and light) and employ any approach. Examples of installation art from Alberta include the video-driven yet low-tech installations of David Hoffos; the performance and process pieces of Blair Brennan; the narrative new media works of Janet Cardiff and George Bures Miller; the room-encompassing disturbances of Alan Dunning; and the labour-intensive rose-petal collaborations of Laura Vickerson.

Since around the 1960s, installation art has always managed to be one of the most radical, the most experimental, the most, it seems, "contemporary" of visual art. By the end of the twentieth century, installation art was the paradigm or the dominant mode of art production seen in many art magazines, international art exhibitions, and museums and other venues that concern themselves with the field of contemporary art.

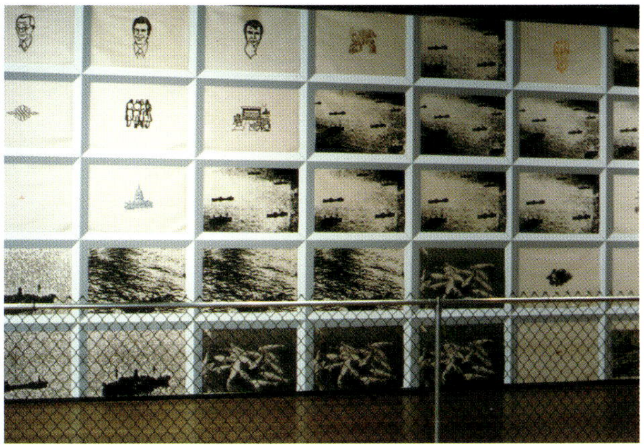

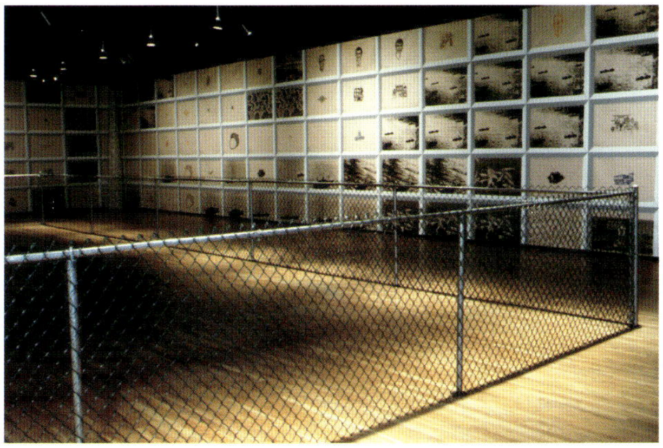

Alan Dunning
Billy Budd's Stammer—The Structure of the New Defence, 1988
silk-screened newsprint, paint, chain-link fencing, book
Installed temporarily at the Walter Phillips Gallery, the Banff Centre, Banff, Alberta

With its stark chain-link fence enclosure affecting how you can move around the gallery, viewing *Billy Budd's Stammer—The Structure of the New Defence* is an unsettling experience. It draws on the Herman Melville story about the sailor Billy Budd, who, when faced with an unjust accusation, can only stutter in his defence. With *Billy Budd's Stammer*, Alan Dunning has created a floor-to-ceiling picture gallery with six hundred images and symbols that repeat—and are perhaps linked—but as a whole are barely decipherable.

Silk-screened on newsprint with each image contained within a *trompe l'oeil* moulding, there is for the viewer (and the artist), no one single meaning or reading to take away from this well-ordered but puzzling display. Instead, it is up to you, the viewer, to make of it what you can. In modern-day society with its plethora of communication and professionalized expertise, Dunning, the well-educated professional artist, is perhaps encouraging a certain amount of stammering as a reaction or defence against an "over-rationalized world."[62] In a society flooded with information and plenty of authoritative opinion, he steps away from the role of the artist as prophet and visionary. He is not a Romantic, only one involved in time-consuming labour of a different and conceptually compelling kind.

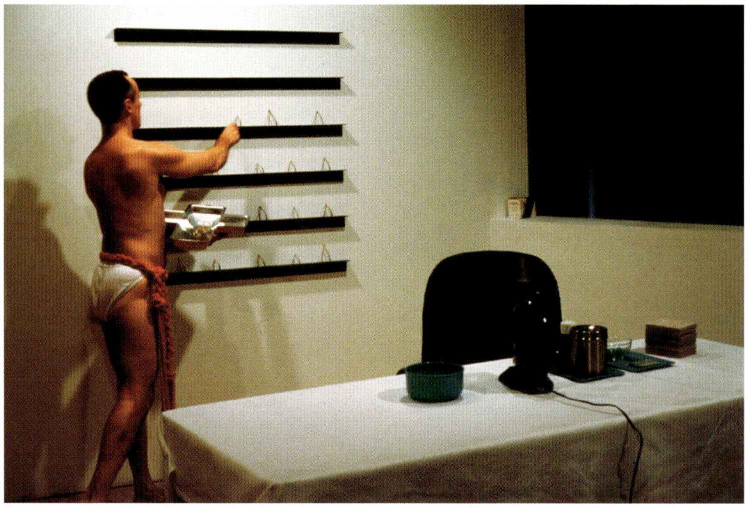

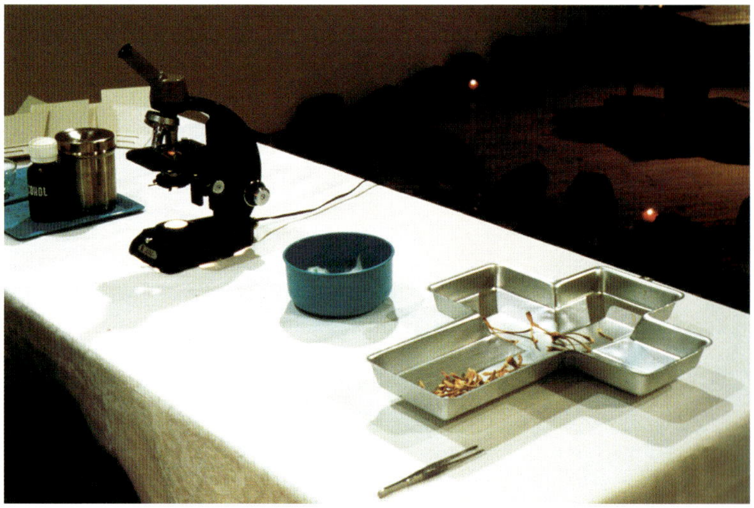

Blair Brennan
Magic/Magick/Miracles, 1993
collaborative installation with performance by Brian Webb
Premiere Presentation at Gallery 101, Ottawa, Ontario

A beacon of contemporary art practice in Edmonton, Blair Brennan and his collaborations with choreographer and dancer Brian Webb (Brian Webb Dance Company) have had a certain resonance in a province with "bible belt" regions or areas. Their collaborations have been concerned with ritual, religion (Christianity), magic, and most pertinent, modern society's faith in science. Together, the two men have extrapolated on what they saw as the connections between all four, including the desire for a scientific "miracle" that might cure AIDS or even cancer.

Magic/Magick/Miracles was a project not without controversy. In Ottawa, where it made its debut, patrons of the nearby Bible House expressed alarm that Christianity was being mocked. A charge the two artists, themselves raised as Christians, denied, explaining their interest was in ritual and the interaction between the artist (Webb) and the site and the audience. With items like crosses and candles obtained from religious supply stores, a registered nurse on hand to take a blood sample from Webb (a health-care ritual), and other artifacts made by Brennan, the emphasis in this installation was on the "process" or the rituals performed by or on Webb, rather than on a finished "product" to be displayed.

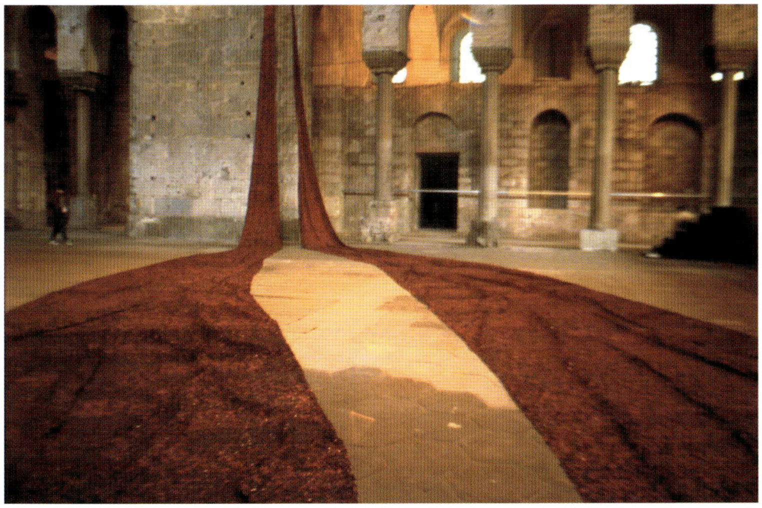

Laura Vickerson
Velvet, 1995
rose petals, dress pins, and bridal tulle
Presented in a fourth-century church, Hagia Eireni, 5th International Istanbul Biennial, 1997
Istanbul, Turkey

Involving nine hundred square feet of bridal tulle pinned with half a million red rose petals, *Velvet* is installation on a grand scale. Made of two long bands, each 130 feet in length, *Velvet* is opulent and regal. Closer-up, its character changes: the rose petals are fragile, each one delicately pinned. Such effort recalls, perhaps, the role of female labour, while more broadly in appearance, embedded in *Velvet,* is the entity of woman whose monthly flow makes life possible.

Taking six months to complete and exhibited in Calgary, Winnipeg, and Istanbul, *Velvet* was one of several artworks Vickerson completed in the 1990s where the flower, and especially the rose, was used as both material and metaphor. Conscious of how the flower has historically served in Western culture as a symbol of caring, beauty, romance, celebration, and loss, Vickerson, along with the collaboration of friends and colleagues, partook in a kind of communal endeavour where the discarded roses of florists were turned into ambitious and awe-inspiring works of art. Made of soft petals and sharp gleaming dressmaker's pins, some observers pointed to the contrast between pleasure and pain in *Velvet*, its sacred and profane associations, and its allusions to fertility and the funereal. It was an abstract work, but like a ceremonial train, it evoked more meaning than its wearer could ever imagine.

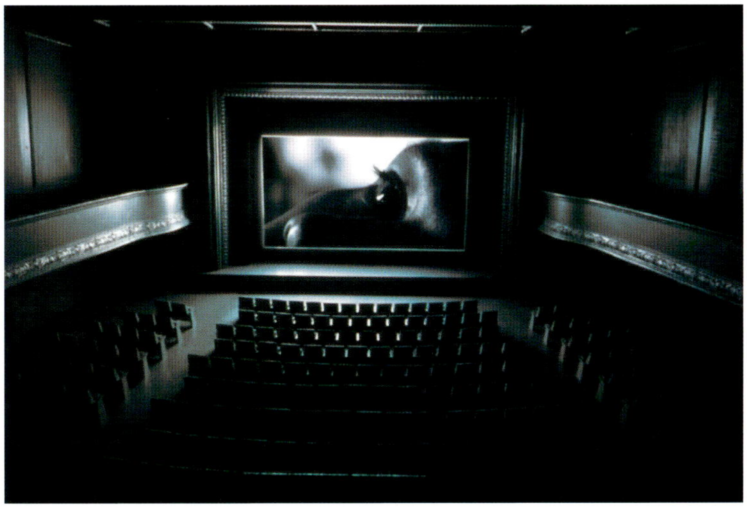

Janet Cardiff and George Bures Miller
The Paradise Institute, 2001 (detail)
mixed media with audio and video
Editions of the work reside in the National Gallery of Canada; Corcoran Gallery of Art, Washington, DC; Castello di Rivoli, Turin, Italy; and Astrup Fearnley Museum of Modern Art, Oslo, Norway
Image courtesy Art Galley of Alberta, Edmonton, Alberta

Created on the cusp of the twenty-first century, *The Paradise Institute* is a premier candidate for showing that the traditional concept of visual art, being a painting on a wall, no longer holds true. The winner of a major prize at the 2001 Venice Biennale, the equivalent, according to the *Ottawa Citizen*, of being awarded the Stanley Cup of contemporary art, *The Paradise Institute* was cited by the jury for "involving the audience in a new cinematic experience."[63]

The idea was simple but its execution more complicated—entailing a beautifully detailed mock theatre where, behind the faux balcony, an audience of at least seventeen people could sit and watch a twenty-minute video simulating a film. In this pretend situation, nothing seemed real. The video was a strange concoction of a thriller-style movie. And the theatre itself—pure *trompe l'oeil* as the audience found itself surrounded by the taped sounds of people whispering in the dark, the shuffling of feet, and the eating of popcorn. Described as an entertaining but mind-scrambling work of art that, in a surreal fashion, mimicked the concept of the home entertainment centre, the purpose of this experiential work, said Cardiff, was to make people think about their perception of reality, what is real and what is fiction.[64] It is an idea she had already experimented with to great critical success in her unique sound-based "audio walks" of the 1990s.

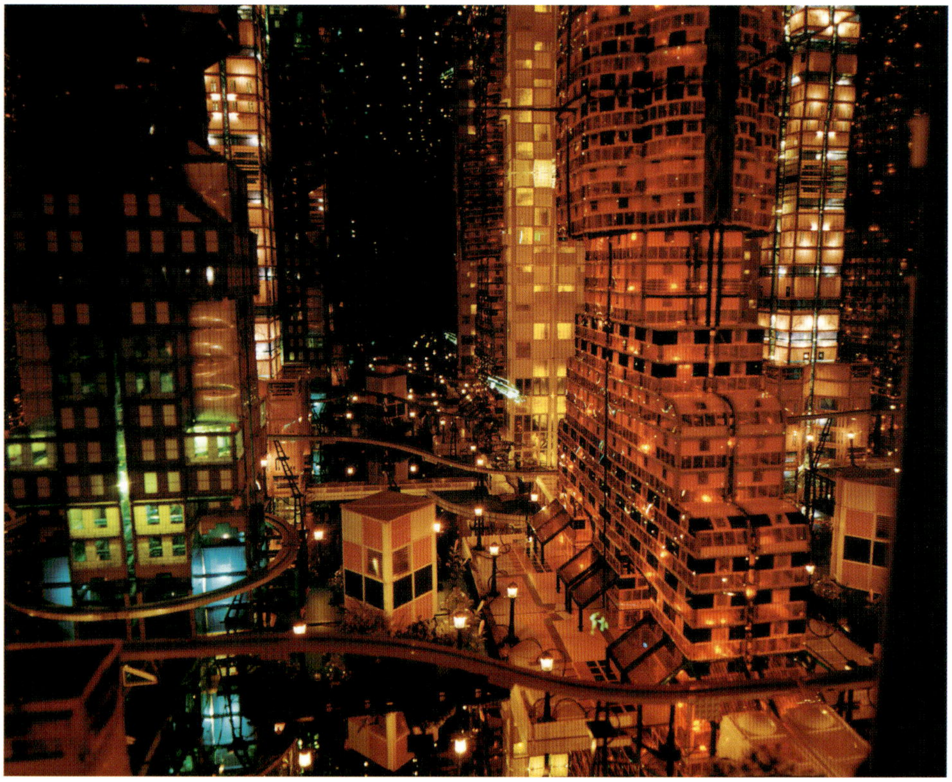

David Hoffos
Another City, 1999 **(detail)**
five channel video and audio installation with miniature model, mirrors, two-way glass, homemade TV projectors, cyclorama screen, ghost video glass, cut-outs, tables; original music composed by Merrilee Wolsey
Edition of two, courtesy of the artist, TrépanierBaer, and a private collector
Photo by Hutch Hutchinson

Like Janet Cardiff and George Bures Miller, David Hoffos pushes the envelope of contemporary illusion, but in a more playful spirit. Captivated by the early days of animation and cinematography, Hoffos takes a low-tech approach to creating the special effects that animate his fantastic miniature worlds. His special effects include casting video projections on cut-outs and miniature models, and using long-ago illusionistic devices (like the cyclorama) to deceive the eye. In *Another City*, a model-size high-rise cityscape encased in a mirrored chamber becomes a futuristic metropolis with flying cars and, amidst all the glitter and light, embracing couples.

Inspired in part by the make-believe of world fairs and old sci-fi movies, Hoffos thinks that what *Another City* depicts is somewhat corny and cliché, although the real hokeyness lies in the spirit of how his work is put together. Most of what goes into his jerry-built installations is obtained second-hand and the fact that the source of the illusion is often obvious doesn't mean the magic is any less effective. Hoffos isn't trying to be the conventional magician, where everything is a neatly tucked-away secret. Instead, his strange mysterious realms—lovingly constructed with a flair for the homemade ingenious—are a much-needed antidote to the slick contrivances of popular culture and such mega-bonanzas as *Star Wars* and *The Lord of the Rings*.

A Contemporary Eyeful

In this chapter, there is no one theme or style or approach to the making of art that links these artists firmly together. At best, their work exhibits some of the concerns, ideas, and trends found in contemporary art of the post-1970 period. Their range of influences or what feeds their art is wide-ranging, drawing not only on art history, especially from the last hundred years, but also gleaning influences from popular culture and contemporary society. Personal and idiosyncratic sources also surface in their art, as with Allen Ball's "portraits" of his French bulldog, Fattie, and his desire to make works connected to his domestic space.

Much of the art represented in this book can be called "contemporary," in that it is art made by a living artist. But the term actually encompasses much more in that it can be defined, in part, as artwork that challenges the status quo, which, in the period covered in this book (1970–2000), means late modern art and its preoccupations with aesthetic concerns over all else. In some contemporary artwork there is a blurring between art and life, between so-called high and low culture, and between abstraction and representation. Once described as modern art's "troublesome stepchild," contemporary art is a many-sided development that emerged from the rebellious and eclectic spirit of the late 1960s and 1970s. The word that often gets used to describe its character is "postmodern," and it involves a mindset where the art is still forming, in play, and as one curator put it, "reflects an artistic development that isn't fixed."[65]

The artists surveyed within the following section have attracted attention for providing an eyeful-and-more of contemporary art. Some, such as the veteran Ron Moppett and Eric Cameron, are two of Alberta's most nationally recognized artists with both receiving, in 1997 and 1994 respectively, the Gershon Iskowitz Prize, one of the largest national awards given annually to a visual artist in Canada. Others, like the younger Shelley Ouellet and Allen Ball, have become better known through the pulse-taking Alberta Biennial of Contemporary Art.

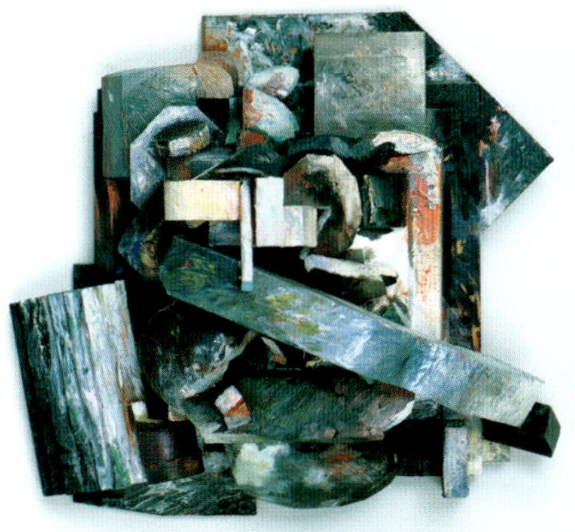

Carroll (Moppett) Taylor-Lindoe
Grey Landscape, 1983
wood, plaster, oil, and enamel paints
Collection of Ron Moppett

This compressed sculptural landscape—intended to be displayed on a wall—asks us to consider what beckons after decades of perceiving the western environment through easel painting. It is a question Carroll Moppett (as she was then known) was ready to consider when her investigation of space, or how we see the world structurally, engendered a series of rich charcoal drawings and polychromed wood sculptures. Inflected with cubism, Moppett's response to the landscape was to deal with it in a volumetric way: a dense configuration of architectonic and vegetal forms, seen from several points of view. Inspired in part by her walks on a ridge high above downtown Calgary and the river valley, *Grey Landscape* is an urban landscape where the paint is intended to function in an atmospheric manner. "I found I was painting the air," she observed.[66]

In *Grey Landscape*, the air is darkened but with a few pinkish tones suggesting, as one critic did, that perhaps it is dusk. Not intended to be illustrative, these semi-abstract, collaged places became instead, for the artist, an equivalent of her experience, expressing what she sensed, intuited, imagined, and objectively observed. Described nearly twenty years later as "maddeningly attractive little polychromed wall sculptures," this memorable body of work was, along with her dynamic charcoal drawings, a breakthrough for the artist. It earned her national stature as she and other Calgary-based artists like Ron Moppett, John Hall, and many others created, through their art, an epicentre for contemporary art-making and more pluralistic art practices in the province. Through to the end of the century and into the next, she has continued to be an eclectic figure, adding a photographic component to her œuvre, as well as painting and installation.

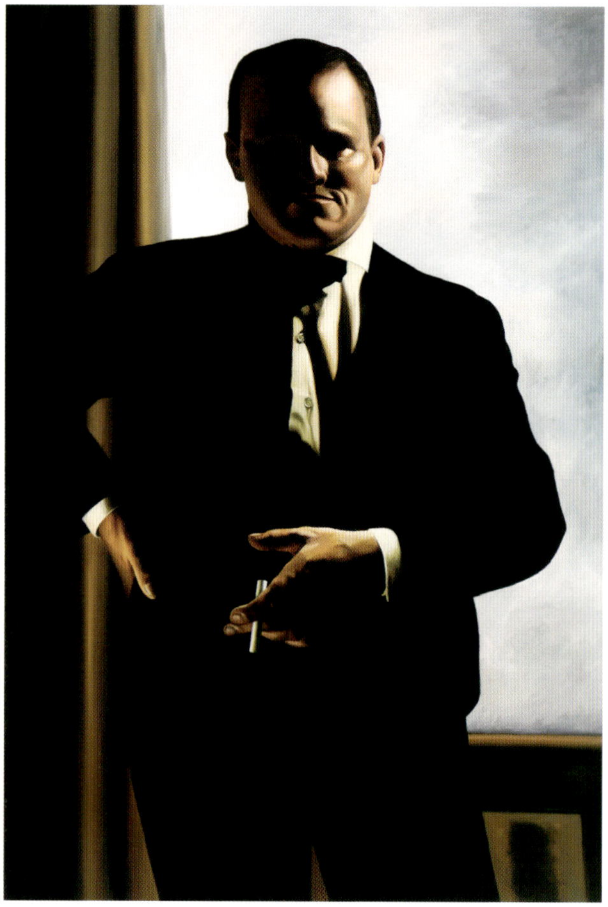

Chris Cran
Self-portrait As Max Beckmann, 1986
oil on canvas
Collection of the Nickle Arts Museum, Calgary, Alberta

It takes nerve to insert your own face into a self-portrait by a famous German modernist (Max Beckmann, 1884–1950). Chris Cran has that nerve and in the mid-1980s, the young artist captured the critical attention of the country with his blatantly absurd, over-the-top images depicted in a deadpan realist style. From the unnamed series of this period, the Beckmann portrait is more serious in posture but still rendered to "appear" as if nothing is amiss—as if it might be totally normal in a postmodern age for individuals to masquerade because it is all about appearances anyway. In this age of media saturation and celebrity it is what's on the surface that counts. In another sense, the hijacked portrait is also an appropriation or borrowing, a strategy popular in contemporary art of the 1980s.

According to Cran, his depiction is the same size as the original and although Cran had to extend his own lower jaw to get that "Teutonic" look, the Beckmann portrait was compelling because it seemed to him that the German was only acting the part of a suave and sophisticated artist. In the final analysis, though, the upstart artist doesn't attach a single meaning to the work because in the end it is all up to the viewer. *Self-portrait As Max Beckmann*, he observes, takes advantage of visual art's "great expertise" namely that of being "a mute apparatus: it sits and waits for thoughts and words to be applied to it."[67]

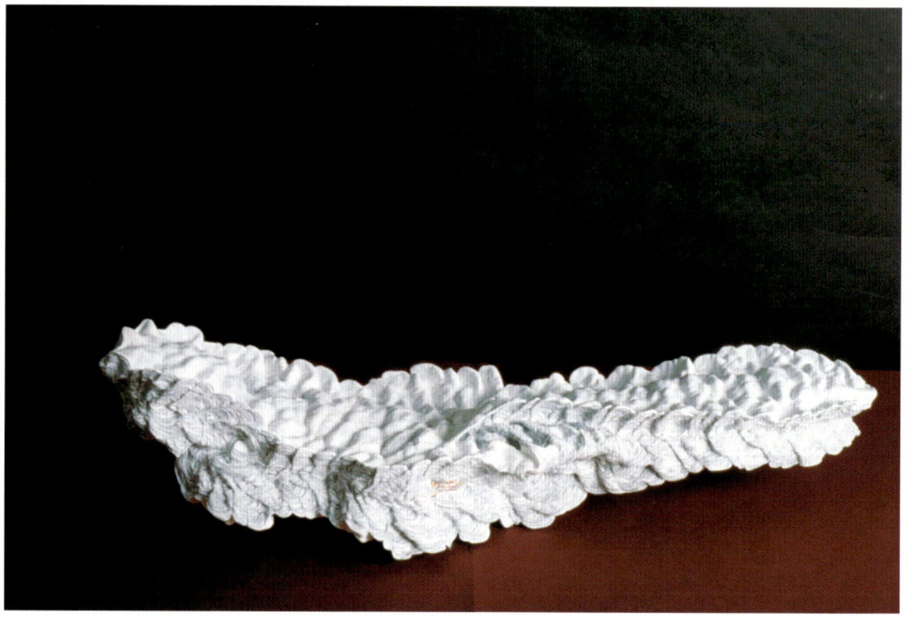

Eric Cameron
Alice's-Rose-is-a-rose-is-a-rose (1000), 1996–2000
rose, gesso, acrylic
Collection of the Nickle Arts Museum, Calgary, Alberta

In *Alice's-Rose*, from 1996 to 2000, one sweet rose has its essential form transformed by the daily application of a half-coat of white gesso and then after drying, a half-coat of grey acrylic. Eric Cameron will call this, without a moment's hesitation, "painting": using paint to transform an object rather than create the illusion of an object in paint. Instead of a still life with rose, after a thousand half-coats of paint *Alice's-Rose* is another example of a work that Cameron once aptly titled *Thick Paintings (to be continued)* (1979–). His procedure was developed in 1979 and since then his art has centred on applying hundreds, and eventually thousands, of coats of paint to banal objects: a chair, a pair of shoes, a matchbox, a head of lettuce, a lobster, a beer bottle, an egg, and so on.

Described as a remarkable undertaking with metaphorical and metaphysical connotations, these "wintry white paintings in-the-round" are considered one of the most distinctive bodies of work produced in Canadian contemporary art.[68] They are also mesmerizing to look at—layered thick-skinned masses that take on a glowing whiteness in a darkened room. Nearly sixty in all, they project an otherworldliness difficult to describe. Cameron is not the first artist to admit that his particular type of art has developed along "an independent track, seemingly more of its choosing than of mine."[69] But his procedural attempt to take the activity of painting beyond the role of imitation and beyond an act of self-expression has earned him plenty of recognition and, significantly, a meditative daily ritual whose results, he says, continue to surprise him.

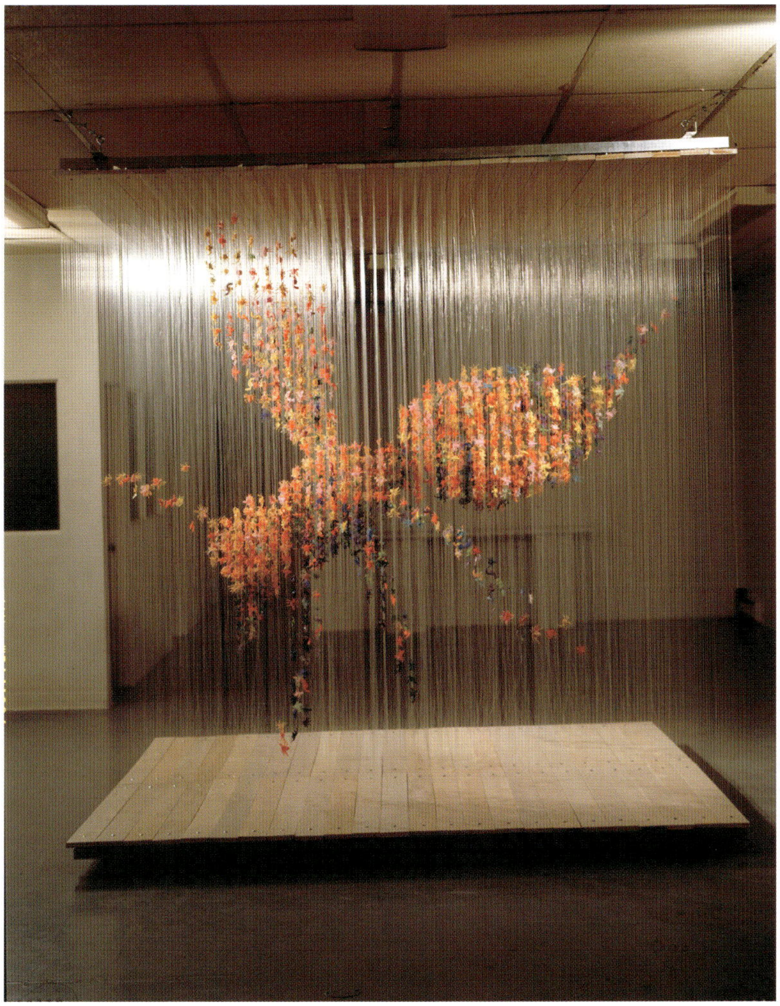

Shelley Ouellet
Entomology (version 3), 1998
wood and aluminum frame, fishing line, approximately nine thousand rubber bugs
Alberta Foundation for the Arts, Edmonton, Alberta
Photo by mn Hutchinson

This bug of bugs, made of thousands of smaller bugs strung by hand is, on one level, a three-dimensional drawing—a pixilated monster whose assemblage required the "whiz" of computer-generated diagrams and the patience of many volunteers. Comparing this collective effort to a quilting bee, Ouellet says her installations and large-scale sculptures of the 1990s were designed to be community-based efforts that demystify the making of art and offer an alternative to the old Romantic model of the "artist-genius" alienated and alone in his garret.

But there is more—working as many contemporary artists do with accessible non-art-related materials, Ouellet struck it rich when it became apparent that bucketfuls of coloured rubber bugs could be obtained from a local novelty store. A superbug was devised, created she says with an empathy for ten-minute attention spans, an awareness of spectacle, and "a complete awe for the power of numbers."[70] Others were in awe, too, as this accessible yet unexpected work—taking its inspiration from science fiction perhaps—was remade for extraterrestrial landings in Edmonton, Victoria, and Halifax.

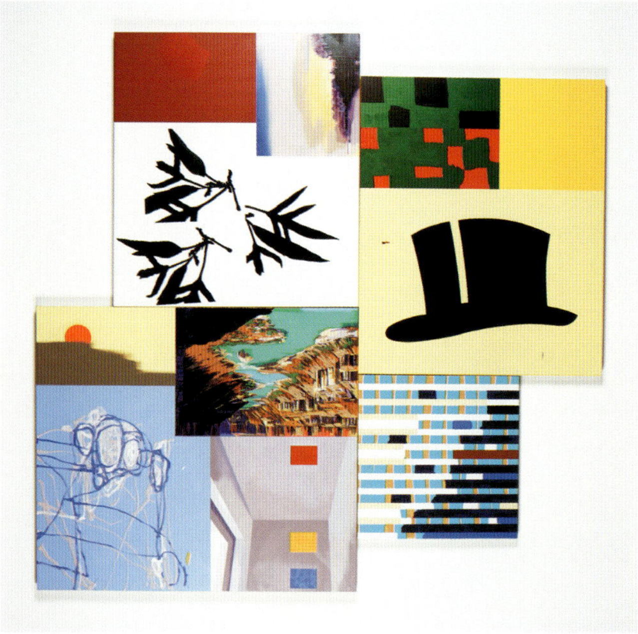

Ron Moppett
Day, 2000–2001
oil and acrylic on canvas
Collection of the Artist

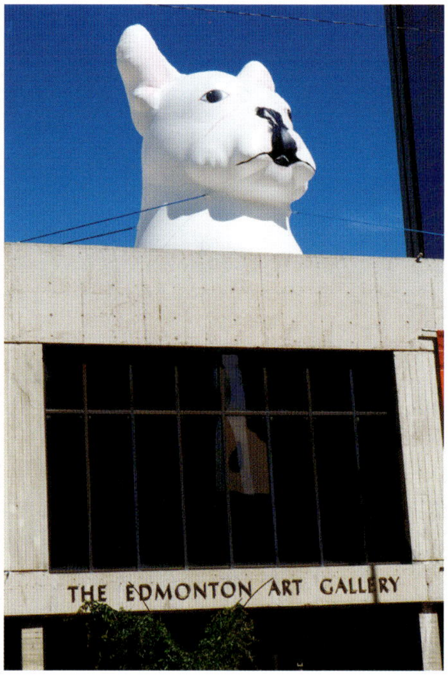

Allen Ball
El Cid, 2000
inflatable balloon doll
No longer extant, inflatable material recycled for another balloon

In contrast to Shelley Ouellet's *Entomology*, Ron Moppett would say his art is a "slow read," not easily interpreted; some areas of his paintings being purely descriptive and others totally imagined. That is one side to this veteran artist; the other is just how visually striking his collection of signs and images can be: a smart top hat rendered in a crisp illustrational style, a landscape rich in the romance of paint, and a geometric abstract mining of the rigour of non-objective art. These are just a few of the "moves" that make up this artist's complex vocabulary, sourced from a knowledge of art history, personal and regional experience, and the purely serendipitous.

As a multi-panelled work, Moppett's *Day* is an example of what has turned people's heads following his thirty years of experience as an artist who never lost faith in painting during an era when it seemed everyone else did. Even a western icon like Illingworth Kerr, for example, inspires him because, according to Moppett, Kerr is a "wonderful example of someone who lived for painting."[71] Thus, his art is made not for theoretical or strategic purposes, but for personal reasons, where the most compelling territory for the artist is the landscape of his mind. In his later work, Moppett's paintings have become clearer and cleaner, more optimistic and even sublime in feeling. He is not entirely wedded to the canvas though—in Moppett's oeuvre there is also his contribution to sculpture made of found objects and playful in spirit.

When Allen Ball was invited to participate in the Alberta Biennial of Contemporary Art, 2000, he wasn't kidding when he decided to literally be on "top" of the exhibition rather than "in" it. Hence his submission of an inflatable dog anchored to the roof of the Edmonton Art Gallery! Made of aircraft nylon, the custom-fabricated sculpture was another example of where showmanship meets serious art, an intended advertisement for the contents inside. Interested in the idea of art as a "product," *El Cid* was Allen Ball's own considered response to the dominance of consumer culture, where the distinctions between high and low or, in this case, purebred and mongrel are levelled for public consumption.

To do this, he reached into his own backyard and into an earlier era of contemporary art, when Pop Art valorized the "everyday" and the banal like a Campbell's soup can. More recently, Ball has been engaged with the idea of giving people what they want: art that is both accessible and entertaining. It is Fattie, Ball's French bulldog, who poses as the dignified subject, fulfilling the artist's wish that his home environment and its inhabitants should serve as his muse. As for the rather grand name of the piece, *El Cid*, or "The Lord," it is open to interpretation, although Fattie does seem to present a sly comment about companion animals in western society and their pampered place in the lives of many.

Straddling the Divide: Craft-based Art

The Alberta arts scene would not be what it is if those who work in ceramics, fibre, glass, jewellery, metalsmithing, and other craft-related forms had not been around to make it a more lively and imaginative place. More often than not, there has been a *joie de vivre* in this area of creative work, which has largely been absent in the contemporary art world as theory, ideology, and academic discourse made its own demands on the latter. That is not to say there hasn't been debate or a shortage of ideas about craft versus art, or the place of craft-related forms in a more pluralist postmodern world. It's just that the craft world has not been so often consumed by these concerns. The crafts have had fun—fun with materials and techniques (both traditional and modern), and fun with content and direction. The crafts could pursue any avenue intellectually, spiritually, or aesthetically, and a beautiful art object was still an okay thing to make.

The artists described below share one thing in common: they are part of the developing story about Alberta craft that took more abundant shape in the post-1970 period. Some, like John Chalke, Martha Henry, and Norman Faulkner, have had notable histories stretching over three decades, while others are more recent but no less engaged. In one form or another, the presence of these artists, who often straddle the world of contemporary art and current craft, has been recognized through major public collections like that of the Alberta Foundation for the Arts; through public art commissions; and through the tireless efforts of the pioneering Alberta Potters Association (est. 1972), the Alberta Craft Council (est. 1980), and the guilds operating at the grassroots.

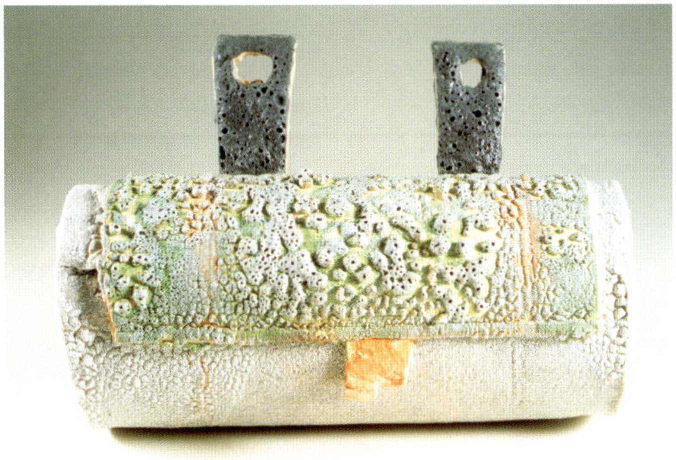

John Chalke
Orange Clasp, 1996
multi-textured glaze ceramic
Private Collection

If *Orange Clasp* had been made out of something more pliable than fired clay, this container would be functional. Instead its functionality has been sidestepped for another purpose, namely, for the sheer love that the potter John Chalke has for the vessel form. Vessels come in myriad shapes, and making them speak with a spirit and a presence is what has earned Chalke worldwide recognition. Chalke's work is included in thirty-eight books on ceramic art, and can be found in major public collections, such as Britain's Victoria and Albert Museum. A John Chalke can be incredibly quirky, too, because of its textured surface, unexpected colour, and hybrid form. For instance, aspects of Japanese Oribe pottery and eighteenth-century North American folk traditions find their way into his art.

John Chalke is the great assimilator but his pottery, which ranges from very humble functional bowls and cups to more challenging sculptural objects, is distinctive. He is a recognized master at creating unorthodox glazes, those cracked, bumpy, and blistered surfaces that, in a piece like *Orange Clasp*, can be surprisingly elegant. A comfortable way of describing his work, he says, is to simply say "it's a diary of kiln experiences."[72]

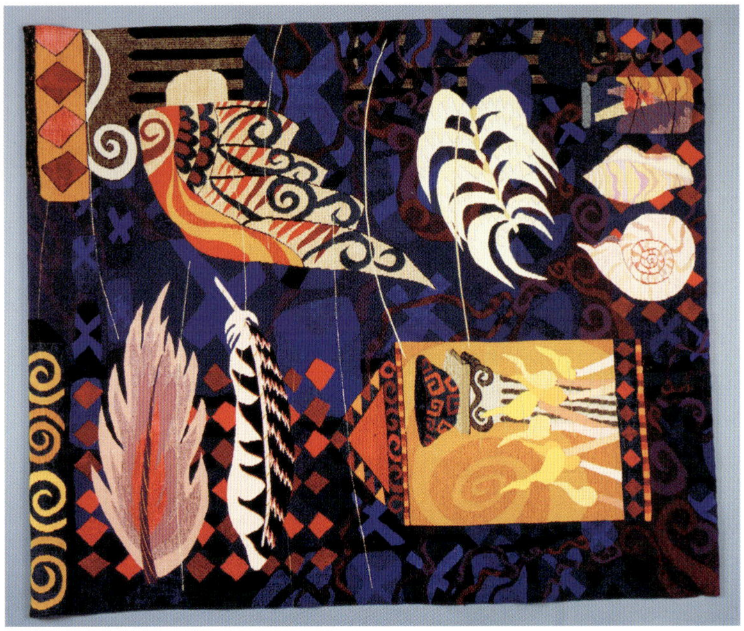

Jane Kidd
The Journey: Tools and Devices, 1993
woven tapestry
Mr. Leslie Nielsen, Los Angeles, California

This 52" by 60" wall work is a fine example of how a craft-based art form can intermingle with the contemporary art trends of the post-1970 era. Jane Kidd's training is in fine art and evident in her works is the influence of the Pattern and Decoration movement and a feminist embrace of the fibre arts. In attitude, though, Kidd does not regard her tapestries as a kind of painting, they are what they are: tactile compositions of different fibres ranging from metallic threads to wool yarns to cotton chenille. Touch is elicited, while their rich saturated colours pack a visual impact far beyond what most paint pigment can do.

Kidd committed herself to tapestry in the mid-1980s and ever since then has made her mark as one of Canada's most outstanding fibre artists. Her creations have been perceptively described as a "symphony" of personal motifs and stylized forms inspired in some instances by the monumental and sacred architecture of other cultures.[73] Travel has been central to this development, including her own study of other textile traditions found in Asia and Latin America. In *The Journey: Tools and Devices*, the wings and feathers allude to travel and the desire, as it has been interpreted, "to step off the established path," which all artists must eventually do.[74]

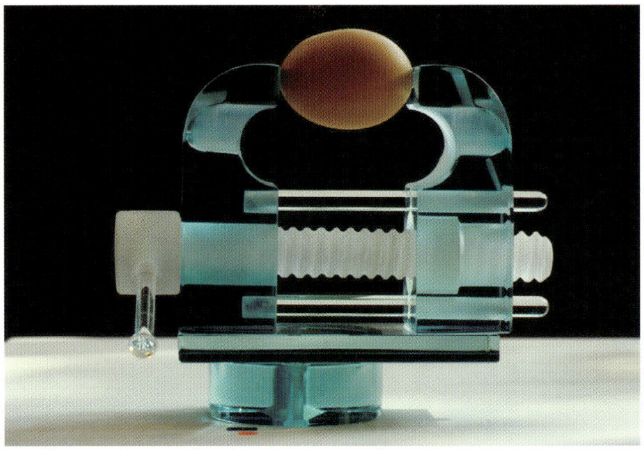

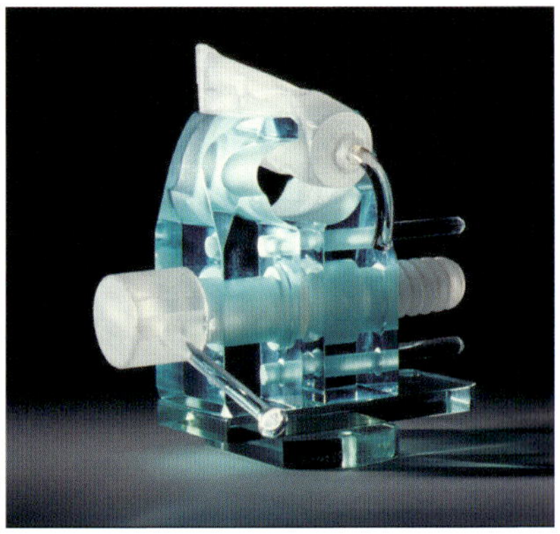

Norman Faulkner
Vice Series, 1986
cast lead glass and egg
Collection of Eduardo Prado, Brazil

Glass—a fragile material? Not according to this seven-inch high work of art that operates as an actual vice! The tables are turned in this perfect universe, typical of Norman Faulkner's less decorative approach to glass. He is an historian and a philosopher who above all appreciates the irony of this vitreous material. "It can be bulletproof or you can break with it with your fingernail."[75] More than that, it is a medium that has sent him around the world (along with his wife, Marie DeRoy), documenting the various low-tech ways glass is made in more ancient cultures. Produced as videos, these documentaries are marketed internationally, just one of the avenues used by this pioneer to speak about the creative potential of glass, especially in the studio.

Faulkner first began spreading the "good news" about this fledgling art form in Canada after setting up his own glass studio in Calgary. A few years later, he convinced his alma mater, the Alberta College of Art, to teach it as a course. That was in 1975 and since then Faulkner and the art college have played an important role in nurturing what has become a full-fledged art scene in Canada, with glass-blowing (hot glass) at the centre of all the excitement. Ready to take that news elsewhere, in 2000, Faulkner built Brazil's first glass art studio in São Paulo.

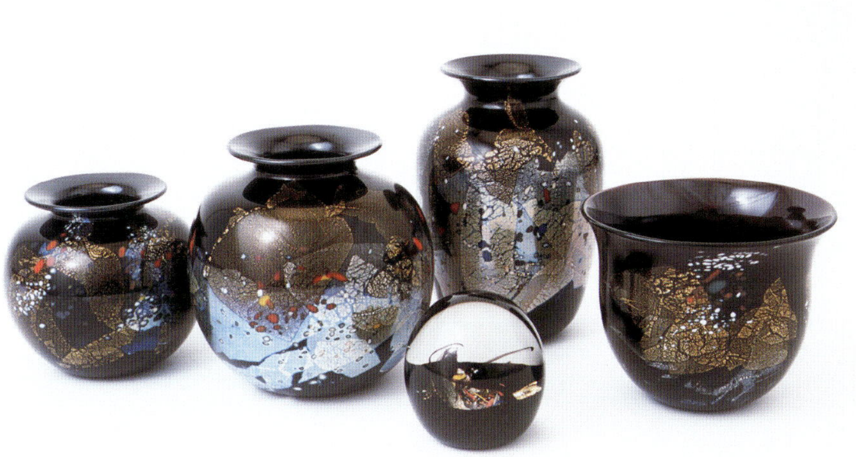

Martha Henry
Gold and Silver-leaf Series, 2004
blown glass with application of 23K gold and silver leaf with coloured glass overlay
Collection of the Artist

This particular series is a planetary allusion encased in a silent-and-still universe, drenched in luminous black. In an otherwise impenetrable place, the gold and silverleaf add depth and colour. Also produced in a series before 2000, these elegant small-scale objects, with their deep lustre and use of metallic leaf, are part of what gives Martha Henry a noted place in the studio glass art scene in Canada. Plus she has been around almost since its inception, opening, with Robert Held, in 1979 the Skookum Art Glass studio in Calgary. That same year, she also helped build the hot glass facilities for Red Deer College's still-busy summer art program, Series.

Described as "the most pictorial" of what is produced in Alberta, some of her glass objects are sandblasted with her own designs of petroglyphs and wildlife that remind the viewer of Henry's sense of place. Her art tends to be not as large, sculptural, or even as sumptuous as some of her younger colleagues. But, she is still an innovator, experimenting with techniques like sandblasting, engraving, and copper electroplating on glass to extend this ancient material's expressive and aesthetic scope. All of this is, of course, in contrast to working with hot molten glass, which she says brings a necessary dose of spontaneity to her creative process. A kind of yin and yang for the spiritual side of glassmaking.

Jackie Anderson
Buffalo Gal, 1993
brooch and stand made of sterling, aquamarine, quartz, moonstone, paint, wood, arborite, linoleum, granite, and pewter
Collection of the Artist

This unusual brooch, with its own stand and use of non-precious and precious stones, is Jackie Anderson to a T. *Buffalo Gal* is jewellery, but it is much more than that. It is wearable art: it is an ornament; it is a miniature piece of free-standing sculpture as self-contained as anything created at a much larger scale. Anderson is also known for her eclectic sense of design that draws inspiration from not only twentieth-century design movements like Art Deco but also the "visual culture" around her: old commercial signage, architectural detail, and regional icons like the bison. Anderson has pushed the metal-smithing and jewellery envelope like almost no one else in the province.

It is her multimedia approach and ability to combine the elegant with the vernacular, and the vain with the quirky that make a Jackie Anderson such a fascinating read. But even without that, there is both its shine and quiet sparkle, an appreciation for materials seen at their very best. As for *Buffalo Gal,* it is an autobiographical piece incorporating her birthstone, aquamarine, with a (silver) pyramid alluding to her childhood nickname "the Blond Egyptian," and a (silver) buffalo symbolizing the beast she nearly bought with a brother in the early 1970s. The title of the work though was inspired by a song … but that is another story.

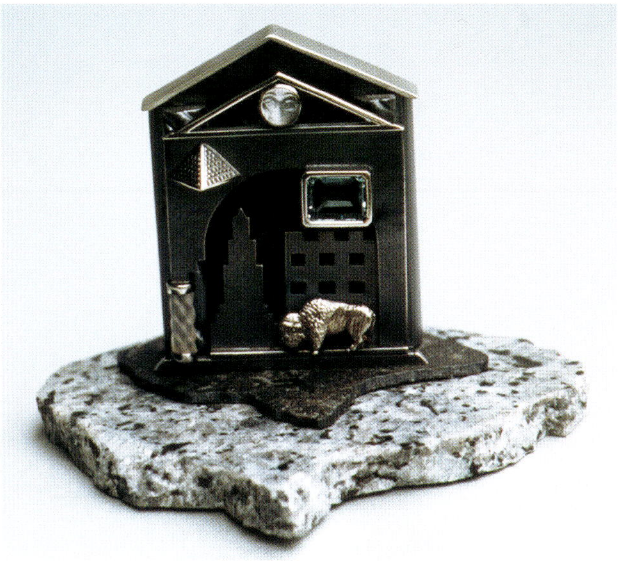

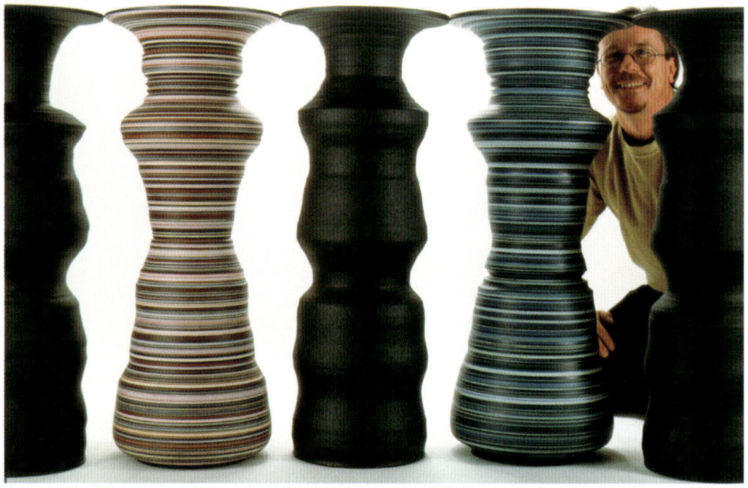

in the photo crouching behind the work, *Apparently* represents life-size children at the age of three.

The vases in *Apparently* are the largest Payce can fire in his own kiln. He'll improvise if something larger is required, as he did when he fashioned two seven-foot-high jars (*Al Barelli*, 2001) which were eventually acquired by a museum in Seoul, Korea. Appealing to many is his sense of invention, prompting one critic to write that Payce's work is "as much about mind games as it is about clay."[76] Payce still earns praise for sticking with many of pottery's traditional forms, like vases, jars, plates, and platters, but he takes them into new terrain. Onto their surfaces he creates textured skins of colour, and paints decorative patterns and designs that relate to art and craft history, and his appreciation for other cultures.

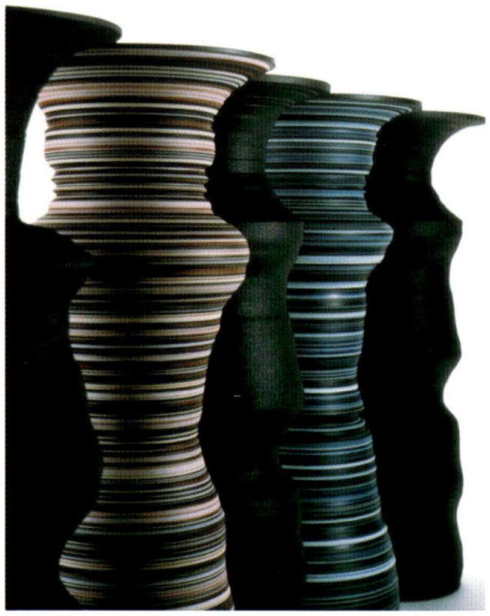

Greg Payce
Apparently, 1999
wheel-thrown red earthenware clay and glaze
The two girls are in the collection of the Glenbow Museum, Calgary. The three boys are in the collection of the George R. Gardiner Museum of Ceramic Art, Toronto.

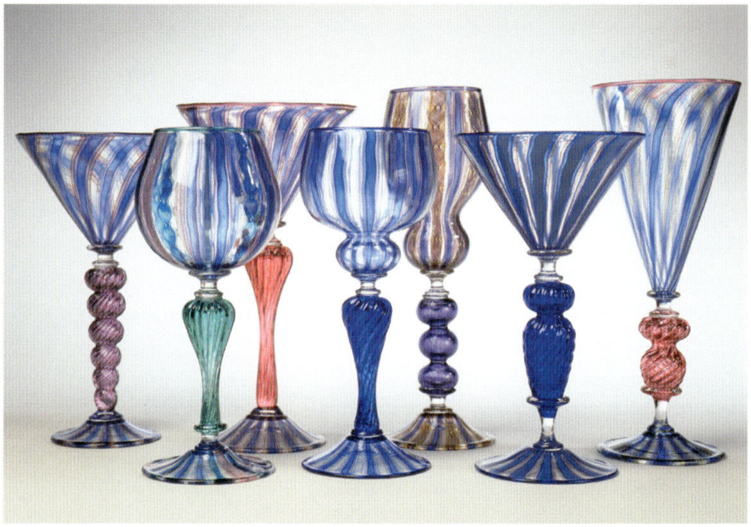

Darren Petersen
Cane Cups, 2000
blown glass (filigree canes)
Private Collections
Photo by John Dean

The boy genius of Canadian contemporary ceramics, it all came together for Greg Payce in the 1990s. There are many facets to his art—not to mention its virtuoso rendering—but beyond all the impressive technique, Payce's work holds the bright spark, the idea that turns on the proverbial light bulb. In the case of *Apparently* and other garniture works of that period, it is negative space and other playful gestures that have an impact on how the viewer perceives the work. Look between the shapely vases in the picture and focus your eye on four of the five individual children who appear in sequence, three males and one of the two females. According to Payce, who is

Darren Petersen is an example of what happens when a particular medium takes off as glass art did in Alberta in the 1990s. And all it took in his case was one elective course in glassmaking. Since then, Petersen and others of his generation have put the province on the map internationally as a centre for highly crafted and seductive glass. Notably too, this activity is not so much a big city pursuit as one that is located in smaller centres like Red Deer, where Petersen, for instance, has established his own glassmaking facility.

Cast glass sculpture made from his own moulds is part of Petersen's oeuvre, but so are the blown glass *Cane Cups*, or goblets inspired by the famous glass factories of sixteenth-century Venice. Sophisticated and beautifully reflective, these functional objects are made from the fusing of coloured glass canes to create a bubble which forms the bowl and foot of the goblet. In making this highly prized Venetian-style glassware with a contemporary sensibility, Petersen regards himself as an apprentice working within a certain tradition that demands a more humble attitude about what he can produce. What he achieves though, with the swirling lines of colour in each goblet and their potent optical effect, is pure artistry.

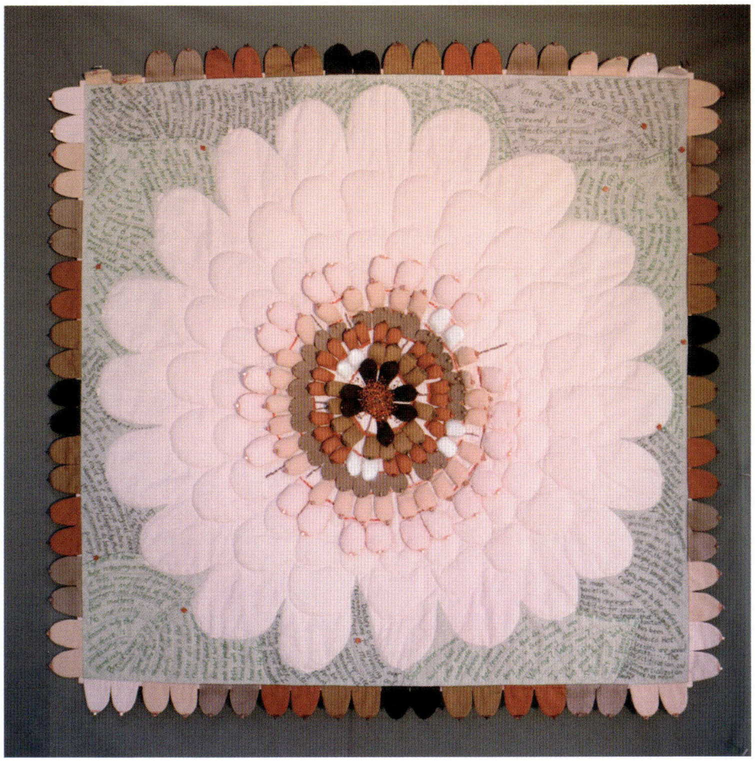

Jayne Willoughby Scott
Respect Me?...Respect Me Not..., 1993
fabric, plastic, net, Ultrasuede, paint, marking pens, beads, thread
Collection of the Artist
Photo by Chris Tapper

This work is a perfect example of why quilts are really one of the most visual of the visual arts. Rich in pattern and, in more contemporary examples, alive with the texture of materials other than fabric, a quilt like *Respect Me?...Respect Me Not...* is a multi-layered bouquet of social meaning and optical illusion. Made by Willoughby Scott in reaction to having friends with breast cancer, the petals of the carnation and those around the edge of the quilt reveal themselves—upon closer inspection—to be breasts of different skin colours. In addition, in the space between the carnation and the quilt's edge, she has used a blue and green marker pen to write about cancer. The incorporation of text as something to be read and digested, as well as something to serve as a visual pattern is quite in keeping with a more postmodern style of quilt art.

When exhibited, *Respect Me?...Respect Me Not...* struck an emotional bell with its audience. Willoughby Scott says some people reacted by "coming up to me, crying and telling their stories."[77] In 1993, this three-foot-square artwork captured the Judges Choice Award in a national juried exhibition hosted by the Canadian Quilters' Association. Since then, this trained nurse and fibre artist has continued to win awards, adding her voice to Alberta's quilt art scene.

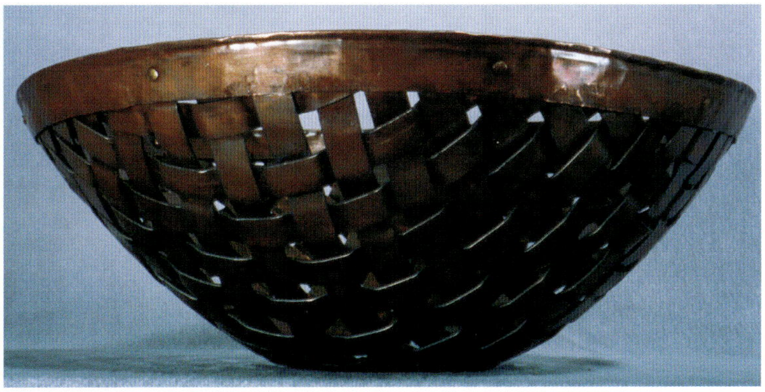

Crys Harse
Conduit, 1996
recycled copper
Collection of the Artist

Before Crys Harse ventured into the world of scrap metals, hammers, stakes, and heat, she wove baskets from reeds and grasses. Weaving attracted her, she says, because of its texture, rhythm, and repetition. Now her art "interlaces one discipline with another, blending textile techniques and the properties of metal to create the unexpected."[78] This blending has led to woven metal baskets, whose hammer marks and rivets hint at their humble origins: scrap metal collected from nearby scrap yards. Harse admits to being drawn to industrial debris the same way another metalsmith might be drawn to precious metals. But she also labours within the age-old discipline of vessel-making, where a receptacle is created that can be as purposeful as a container, or as poetic as an art object. A vessel can also incorporate spiritual and ritual functions, which seems to be true with *Conduit*. There is, of course, the title's reference to the work's origins as a metal (copper) for conduction, but as a "conduit" it could also imply something more transcendental.

Notes: A New Era for Alberta Art: 1970–2000

1. Terrence Heath, *Western Untitled* (Calgary: Glenbow-Alberta Institute, 1976) unpaginated.
2. Interview with artist, Calgary, September 19, 1997.
3. Mary-Beth Laviolette, *An Alberta Art Chronicle: Adventures in Recent and Contemporary Art* (Canmore, Alberta: Altitude Publishing, 2005) 138.
4. Mary-Beth Laviolette, *75 Years of Art: Alberta College of Art and Design*, Christine E. Sammon, ed. (Calgary: Alberta College of Art and Design, 2001) 27.
5. David and Peggy Leighton, *Artists, Builders and Dreamers: 50 years at The Banff School* (Toronto: McClelland and Stewart, 1982) 68.
6. Reprint of *The Edmonton Journal* article, "Lougheed's wife steals thunder," by Kevin Petersen in the Alberta Art Foundation AFF *Newsletter* #4 (Fall 1976) 5.
7. John Bentley Mays, "Rothko buy a good portent of things to come to the NGC," *The Globe and Mail* (July 17, 1993) C4.
8. Karen Wilken, *Douglas Haynes: The Toledo Series* (Edmonton: Edmonton Art Gallery, 1991) 2.
9. Ibid., 1.
10. Elizabeth Beauchamp, "Studio spawns other-worldly works: Abstract artist commissioned for city hall," *The Edmonton Journal* (April 20, 1992) B5.
11. Lelde Muehlenbachs, "Scott's abstract excellence," *Pique* (Edmonton, Sept 30 1993).
12. Elizabeth Kidd, "Edmonton and Modernism," *Recent Work by Robert Scott: 1987–1993* (Edmonton: Edmonton Art Gallery, 1994) 10.
13. Ibid.
14. Terry Fenton, *Robert Scott's Paintings* (New York: Gallery Moos, 1987) unpaginated.
15. Russell Bingham, "Interview with Graham Peacock," *Colour & Dimension: The Recent Paintings of Graham Peacock* (Edmonton: Graham Peacock, 1992) unpaginated.
16. Roger Boulet, *Graham Peacock: Paint, Process and Spirit* (Edmonton: Edmonton Art Gallery, 1988) unpaginated.
17. Lee Bale, "David Cantine," *Galleries West* (Fall–Winter 2004) 19.
18. The term "Edmonton Steel" is used in many instances including as an exhibition title in a 1983 exhibition at Beaver House Art Gallery, Edmonton.
19. Peter Hide, "Artist statement," *Alberta Biennial of Contemporary Art* (The Edmonton Art Gallery and Glenbow Museum, 1996) unpaginated exhibition notes.
20. John Bentley Mays, "Steel magnolias," *The Globe and Mail* (May 7, 1994) C7.
21. Elizabeth Kidd, "Three Dimensions: Betty Godwin, Walter May, Catherine Burgess," *Outlook* (Edmonton: Edmonton Art Gallery, Summer 1990) 4.
22. Catherine Burgess, "Statement about new work" (April 17, 1994).
23. Clay Ellis, "Artist statement," *Sculpture* (Edmonton: The Works, 2001) 22.
24. Robert Atkins, *ArtSpeak: A Guide to Modern Ideas, Movements and Buzzwords* (New York: Abbeville Press, 1993) 183.
25. John Hall, "Artist statement," *Environment* 71 (1971) unpaginated exhibition notes.
26. Nancy Tousley, "Artist keeps faith with realism," *Calgary Herald* (March 30, 1986).
27. John Bentley Mays, "Hall's comfortable as the odd man out," *The Globe and Mail* (May 18, 1985) E5.
28. According to John Hall, his remark is based on a review by Nancy Tousley, "Artist finds space—and peace—to paint in Banff," *Calgary Herald* (January 4, 1987).
29. Christopher Hume, "Calgary artist closes in on the details of a vast land," *Sunday Star* (Toronto: April 11, 1982).
30. Alexandra Haeseker, letter to John Hall in "Subject and other matters," *Alexandra Haeseker: Twenty Years* (Calgary: Illingworth Kerr Gallery, Alberta College of Art, 1992) 18.
31. Nancy Tousley, "Display seems out of place in Glenbow," *Calgary Herald* (November 8, 1983) F6.
32. Nora Abercombie, "Prevue," *Vue Weekly* (Edmonton, November 14–20) 21
33. Margit Brehm and Wolfgang Schoppmann, "Marianna Gartner play dead," *Marianna Gartner* (Essen, Germany: 20.21 Galerie, 2004) unpaginated.
34. Kirsten Evenden, *Women's Work: Art by Women in Glenbow Collection* (Calgary: Glenbow Museum, 1996) unpaginated exhibition notes.
35. Lucy Lippard, "Sweeping exchanges: the contribution of feminism to the art of the seventies," *Art Journal* 4, 1–2 (New York College Art Association, 1980) 362.
36. Sandra Vida, "Statement regarding my work," undated.
37. John Bentley Mays, "Art that truly speaks of the body and beauty," *The Globe and Mail* (March 31, 1989).
38. Sandra Vida, "Mary Scott," *Vanguard* (Vancouver: Vancouver Art Gallery, February–March 1986) 63.
39. Bruce Grenville, *Mary Scott* (Lethbridge: Southern Alberta Art Gallery, 1989) 7.
40. Roger Matuz, editor and Katheryn Handley, project coordinator, "Faye HeavyShield," *Contemporary Canadian Artists* (Toronto: Gale Canada, 1997) 250.
41. Mike Murphy, "Intuition before order: a conversation with Faye HeavyShield," *Artichoke: Writings about the Visual Arts* (Calgary: Fall 1993) 55.
42. Nancy Tousley, "Evelyn Grant," *Calgary Herald* (October 19, 1990).
43. Liz Wylie, "Spaces and places: eight decades of landscape painting in Alberta," *Canadian Art* (Summer 1986) 92.

44. *The Cairn* Vol. XVII, No. 3 (Banff: Whyte Museum of the Canadian Rockies, Summer 1994) 5.
45. This comment made by Jeffrey Spalding is quoted in a University of Lethbridge news release titled "Noted Canadian artist receives honorary degree" (September 15, 1995).
46. Elizabeth Beauchamp, "Sylvain Voyer: master of light and sky," *Legacy* (August–October 1997) 13.
47. Ibid.
48. Ibid, 15.
49. "Ted Godwin," *Contemporary Canadian Artists* (Toronto: Gale Canada, 1997) 218.
50. Paula Gustafson, "A portrait of the artist as a conservationist," *Cityscope* (Calgary: May–June 1992) 31.
51. Patricia Ainslie, "Visions of nature: Barbara Milne, Jeffrey Spalding," *New Alberta Art* (1990) unpaginated exhibition card published by Glenbow Museum.
52. Lyndal Osborne, "Artist's statement" (1993) unpublished.
53. von Tiesenhausen quote is found in "Two internationally known Alberta artists at the Whyte Museum in Banff"(Banff: Whyte Museum of the Canadian Rockies, July 17, 1995) news release.
54. David Garneau, "Peter von Tiesenhausen: Deluge," *Gallery* (Lethbridge: Southern Alberta Art Gallery, Summer 2000) unpaginated.
55. Eleanor Bond, "Gang of three: new sculpture from Calgary" (Winnipeg: Ace Art and Plug/In Inc., 1987) unpaginated.
56. Katherine Ylitalo, "OheZen," *Katie Ohe* (Calgary: Illingworth Kerr Gallery, Alberta College of Art and Design, 1991) 36.
57. Walter May. "Interview with Walter May by John Chalke," *Walter May* (Toronto: Mercer Union, November 15–December 15, 1990) 4.
58. Timothy Long, "Blake Senini: Simone," *Simone* (Regina: MacKenzie Art Gallery, 1996) 6.
59. Howard Palmer with Tamara Palmer, *Alberta: A New History* (Edmonton: Hurtig Publishers, 1990) 93.
60. Nancy Tousley, "Artist gives television new look," *Calgary Herald* (May 26, 1995).
61. Gary Gee, "Artist explores spiritual ecology," *The Edmonton Sun* (May 18, 1989) 39.
62. Helga Pakasaar, "Billy Budd's stammer: the structure of the new defence" (Banff: Walter Phillips Gallery, 1988) unpaginated.
63. Michael Petrou, "Canadian artists win major prize at Venice show," *The Ottawa Citizen* (June 11, 2001).
64. Ibid., Michael Petrou.
65. Ray Cronin, "What is contemporary?" *Art Gallery of Nova Scotia Journal* Vol. 19–1 (2002) 12.
66. From author's notes, comment was made by the artist at an artist talk given in Calgary, 1983.
67. E-mail letter to author, dated November 19, 2005, 9:34 PM.
68. Nancy Tousley, "Divine comedy," *Canadian Art* (Spring 1991) 60.
69. "Statement," unpublished and undated.
70. Artist statement titled "Shelley Ouellet," *Alberta Biennial of Contemporary Art 1996* (Calgary: Glenbow Museum–Edmonton Art Gallery, 1996) exhibition card.
71. Author interview with artist, March 2, 1999.
72. Artist statement from "Moons of Ariosto: a reading of John Chalke," *Contact*, Calgary, Vol. 48 (Winter 1981).
73. "Jane Kidd: The Temple Series," *Muttart Art Gallery* Volume 4, Issue 8 (Calgary: March–April 1992) unpaginated.
74. Nancy Tousley, "Tapestries seduce with warmth, beauty," *Calgary Herald* (February 17, 1995).
75. Valerie Fortney, "Norman Faulkner," *Avenue* (Calgary: December 1996) 9.
76. Paula Gustafson, "Postmodern pots trick the mind," *The Georgia Straight* (July 30, 1998) 64.
77. Berenice Gargus, "Art quilters," *AlbertaViews* Vol. 3, No. 2 (Calgary: March–April 2000) 21.
78. *"Mystery of Mastery & Leading Edges," Artist Statements and Biographical Information* (Edmonton: Alberta Crafts Council, June 17–August 26, 2000) exhibition hand-out, unpaginated.

ARTIST BIOGRAPHIES

JAMES MADISON ALDEN (1834–1922) was born near Boston, and graduated from the Naval Academy at Annapolis, Maryland. From 1851 he was the official artist with the US Coastal Survey headquartered in San Francisco. In 1857 he became the official artist of the Northwest Boundary Survey which was to determine the land and water boundary between Canada and the US. He returned to Washington, DC, with over sixty-six watercolours, some fifteen completed in the southwest corner of Alberta around the Waterton Lakes. Alden was prolific, completing over seven hundred drawings between 1857 and 1861.

JACKIE ANDERSON (1953–) was born and raised in Calgary, Alberta. In 1976, she graduated from the metal and jewellery art program at the Alberta College of Art and Design. She continued with graduate studies at the Calgary-based art college from 1977 to 1978. Over the years, she has given many lectures and workshops at Canadian universities, colleges, museums, and galleries about her art, her hybrid designs, and her incorporation of nonprecious materials with precious gems and metals. Anderson has a steady history of exhibiting her work in Canada and abroad. In 1993, the Illingworth Kerr Gallery showcased her work in a solo exhibition accompanied with a catalogue. Other highlights in her exhibiting history include *Bodywork: A Selection of Contemporary Canadian Jewellery* (Alberta College of Art Gallery, Calgary, 1986); *Architectural Influences* (International Gallery, San Diego, California, 1988); *Contemporary Canadian Jewellers* (Brisbane, Australia, 1989); and *Lois Etherington Betteridge: A Tribute Exhibition* (MacDonald Stewart Art Centre, Guelph, Ontario, 2000).

WILLIAM ARMSTRONG (1822–1914) was born in Dublin, Ireland, where he studied art. He was apprenticed as an engineer on the railways before immigrating to Canada in 1851. He worked for several Canadian railway companies and in 1858 became a partner in the company of Armstrong, Beere & Hime, civil engineers and photographers. In 1870, he travelled west as chief engineer with the Wolseley expedition sent to quell the North-West Rebellion, though it is unlikely he travelled into Alberta on this occasion. In 1877, he visited the Rockies with Sir Sandford Fleming's Canadian Pacific Railway Survey expedition and in 1902 he was in Fort Macleod. He turned to painting more actively in the 1880s, taught drawing in Toronto schools, and in 1882 was elected an associate of the Royal Canadian Academy. He died in Toronto.

GREGORY ARNOLD (1916–68) was born in Meota, Saskatchewan, and moved to Calgary to study at the Provincial Institute of Technology and Art under J. W. G. Macdonald and Illingworth Kerr from 1946 to 1950. He returned to the institute a year later to study ceramics. In 1957, he travelled to Florence, Italy, to study painting. Through the 1950s he worked as a commercial designer and then taught at the institute from 1961 until his death. He was a member of the Alberta Society of Artists and president of the society from 1962 to 1963.

ALLEN BALL (1962–) was born and raised in London, England. He majored in painting and printmaking at the city's Camberwell College of Arts and Crafts, earning a bachelor's degree in fine art in 1984. He next earned a master's degree in visual arts (painting) from the University of Alberta in 1990. Upon graduating, Ball worked as a sessional instructor at the university and at Grant MacEwan Community College. He also worked as an arts administrator for two of Edmonton's artist-run centres, Latitude 53 Gallery and Harcourt House Arts Centre. In 2002, he was appointed assistant professor, painting, at the University of Alberta. His postmodern sensibility, which also extends to the making of installation art, is represented by such exhibitions as *Colour Me Pop* (Latitude 53 Gallery, Edmonton, 1992); *The Metaphysics of Laundry* (Alberta Foundation for the Arts, 1993); *Heliotropic 2* (Mercer Union, Toronto, 1993); *Corsage* (The Edmonton Art Gallery, 1995); *Alberta Biennial of Contemporary Art, 1996 and 2000*; *The Art of Chinese Paper Folding* (Medicine Hat Museum and Art Gallery, 2001).

MAXWELL BATES (1906–80) was born in Calgary and studied at the Provincial Institute of Technology and Art under Lars Haukaness. In 1929, he and William Stevenson went to Chicago to study impressionist and post-impressionist painting at the Art Institute. He moved to England in 1931 and continued to travel while working in an architect's office. During the Second World War, he enlisted and became a prisoner of war in Unterbreizbach, Thuringia, Germany. Despite extreme privation, he kept a notebook recording his experiences. Freed by American soldiers, he was returned to England in 1945. After coming back to Calgary in 1946, he worked as an architect full-time until 1961. In addition to being an architect, he was also a prolific artist, unleashing an exceptional torrent of work. He studied with the renowned German Expressionist artist Max Beckmann in New York in 1949. He moved to Victoria, British Columbia, in 1962.

CHARLES A. BEIL (1894–1976) was raised on a ranch in Nevada and worked as a cowboy. From 1921 to 1926, Beil was a student of American cowboy artist Charles Russell. Beil also studied in California in 1927 with Edward Borein at the Art School in Santa Barbara. In 1930, he settled in Banff, working as a painter and sculptor. For twenty-five years he modelled and cast a dozen trophies each year for the Calgary Stampede rodeo competition. He also painted public murals, including one still on display in the Rimrock Room in the Palliser Hotel in Calgary.

FREDERIC MARLETT BELL-SMITH (1846–1923) was born in London, England. He studied at the South Kensington School of Art and then in Paris at the Académie Colarossi. He worked initially as a photographer when he moved to Montreal in 1866. He moved to Hamilton in 1871, and taught art in public schools in southern Ontario. In 1889, he became the director of the Toronto Art School. He became a member of the Ontario Society of Artists in 1872 and an associate member of the Royal Canadian Academy in 1880. He made ten trips to the Alberta Rockies between 1887 and 1918; four of these trips were in consecutive years from 1887. During this time he was known as the premier painter of the Rockies.

ROLOFF BENY (1924–84) was born in Medicine Hat. His first work was exhibited with the Manitoba Society of Artists in 1939 and resulted in a scholarship to the Banff School of Fine Arts, where he studied with Henry Glyde. From 1941 he was in Toronto, where he obtained a bachelor of fine arts degree from Trinity College, University of Toronto, in 1945. He moved to the University of Iowa to study printmaking with renowned artist Mauricio Lasanky and obtained a master of fine arts in 1947. From there he went to New York to study at Columbia University and the Institute of Fine Art at New York University. From 1948, he travelled and studied widely in Europe and that same year began to exhibit internationally, returning to see his family, who had moved to Lethbridge. By the early 1950s, he maintained residences in Lethbridge, New York, and Rome. Initially a painter and printmaker, by the late 1950s he had developed an international reputation as a photographer, producing his first book of photographs in 1958: *Thrones of Earth and Heaven* (London: Thames and Hudson). Among his many other achievements, he was awarded the Order of Canada in 1972.

SARA MARY BLAKE (1864–1933) was born in Galway, Ireland, and studied art at a convent in St. Leonard's-on-Sea in Sussex. None of her early paintings exist. She moved to Canada to join her brother at the Deer Horn Ranch in Pincher Creek, Alberta, where he had begun to homestead in 1887. Blake ran the household. In 1890, she married Alfred Lynch-Staunton, who had come west with the second detachment of the North-West Mounted Police, and moved to his ranch two miles west of Pincher Creek. With eight children and ranch duties, she had little time to paint.

ALFRED BLYTH (1901–80) was born in Ayrshire, Scotland, and came to Edmonton in 1913. In 1916, he began his photographic career, working initially as a darkroom technician and then as a photographer in 1917 for McDermid Studios in Edmonton. Blyth opened his own studio in 1928, recording many aspects of the changing Edmonton scene. Although commercial subjects were the mainstay of his business, portraiture, weddings, and buildings were also part of it. His speciality was store window displays. He recorded major events and was an official photographer for the Royal visits in 1939, 1951, and 1959.

WILLIAM HANSON BOORNE (active 1885–90) from Bristol, England, became a pioneer photographer in Alberta. He moved to Calgary in 1885 and opened a photography studio, Boorne and May, on 3rd Avenue SW, with his cousin Ernest May who was the darkroom technician. The studio produced stock photographs, souvenir albums, and lantern slides. He produced a wide range of images, which included picturesque mountain scenes, CPR trains, bridges, tunnels and workers, and ranching scenes, as well as portraits and images of First Nations people and their ceremonies. Boorne opened branch studios in Banff in 1889, and Edmonton in 1891. By 1893 the company was in financial trouble and Boorne sold the Edmonton studio to C. W. Mathers. The other studios soon folded, and Boorne returned to England.

BLAIR BRENNAN (1959–) was born in Edmonton, Alberta. He studied art and design at the University of Alberta where he received a bachelor of fine arts in 1981. Brennan is primarily known for his sculpture and installation work. In the early 1980s he emerged as an abstract artist working in welded steel and appeared in key exhibitions about this type of work: *Edmonton Steel* (Beaver House Gallery, Edmonton, 1983) and *Sculpture City* (Edmonton Art Gallery, 1985). In 1988, he and Edmonton dancer and choreographer Brian Webb started their groundbreaking collaboration in installation-performance projects. Six of these pieces have been presented nationally. Selected works with Webb include *Bone White Time* (Brian Webb Dance Company, Edmonton, 1988) and *Victories Over Us/Defeat at our Hands* (performed in Edmonton, Vancouver, and Montreal, 1991).

JOHN BROCKE (1953–) was born in Edmonton. As a painting major, he graduated with honours from the Alberta College of Art in 1981. Since 1994, Brocke has worked as an instructor in the extension program of the art college. Within a few years of exhibiting in such group shows as the travelling *Six Calgary Realists* (Alberta Culture, 1984); *Young Calgary Realists* (Canadian Art Galleries, 1985); and *Three Artists from Calgary* (Wynick/Tuck Gallery, Toronto, 1985), Brocke's art was attracting national attention. His first solo show was in 1984 at Calgary's Gulf Canada Square, with subsequent shows at the Mira Godard Gallery in Toronto (1989–92), a leading exhibitor of Canadian new realism. In 2005, after a ten-year hiatus, Brocke completed a commissioned portrait of the Speaker of the Senate. Afterward, he returned to his studio full-time.

ANNORA BROWN (1899–1987) was born in Fort Macleod. She attended Normal School in Calgary and after teaching for four years, she attended the Ontario College of Art. From 1929 to 1931 she taught art at Mount Royal College and then returned to Fort Macleod and did fieldwork in art and handicraft for the University of Alberta Extension Department. From 1945 to 1950, she taught at the Banff School of Fine Arts. As well as landscape painting, she completed hundreds of plant studies. She was a member of the Alberta Society of Artists.

GEORGE BLAIR BROWN (1878–1965) was born in Scotland and came to Canada in 1910. He was primarily self-taught. He became a member of the Edmonton Art Club in 1923. In the 1930s, he began to show etchings with the Canadian Society of Graphic Art based in Toronto and later became their Alberta representative. One of his prints, *Pyramid Mountain*, ca. 1939, was included in the New York World's Fair in 1939.

BELMORE BROWNE (1880–1954) was born in Staten Island, New York, and studied at the New York School of Art from 1898 to 1900 and at the Académie Julian in Paris in 1908. An explorer and naturalist, he worked from 1907 as an illustrator for magazines that included *Collier's Weekly* and *Scribner's*. In the early 1930s, he was the director of the Santa Barbara School of Art in California. While living in Banff from 1921 to 1943, and then in the Kananaskis until his death, he concentrated on mountain and wildlife painting. He wrote books and completed dioramas for natural history museums. He was a member of the Alberta Society of Artists and an associate of the National Academy of Design in New York. A mountain in the Kananaskis is named after him.

OLIVER B. BUELL (1844–1910) was born in Illinois, the son of a photographer. From 1873 until at least 1905 he made his living primarily through travelling lantern slide and lecture shows, which he called "entertainments." With his entertainments he travelled widely throughout the United States and Canada. In 1884 he travelled to western Canada to photograph views along the Canadian Pacific Railway (CPR). In May 1886, CPR provided him with a special photographer's car to travel to British Columbia. CPR later used some of his photos for advertising purposes. He made two later trips to western Canada in 1904 and 1905. He died in Montreal.

CATHERINE BURGESS (1953–) was born in Ponoka. She received a bachelor of fine arts degree at the University of Alberta in 1975, and later attended a 1977 Emma Lake workshop taught by British sculptor Anthony Caro, a leading figure of late modern abstract sculpture. From 1978 to 1985 she worked as a sessional instructor in Peter Hide's sculpture program at the University of Alberta. She made abstract wood sculptures (1975–81) before moving into the medium of steel. It was at this point that Burgess became associated with the abstract sculpture group Edmonton Steel. Major exhibitions of that period include *Edmonton Steel* (Beaver House Gallery, Edmonton, 1983) and *Sculpture City* (Edmonton Art Gallery, 1985). Later, group shows like *Alberta Sculpture Survey '89* (Triangle Gallery, Calgary); *The Other Alberta Sculpture* (Carleton University, Ottawa, 1995); and the *Alberta Biennial of Contemporary Art, 1996* showcased a more independent stance. Burgess is one of Edmonton's most widely exhibited artists with over twenty-five solo exhibits to her credit.

ISLA BURNS (1952–) was born in Calcutta, India. She received a sculpture diploma from the Alberta College of Art in 1974, where her mentor Katie Ohe introduced her to the technique of welding metal. In 1978, she earned a master of visual arts degree at the University of Alberta, where she also taught as a sessional instructor (1983–85, 1989–90). Some of Burns's group exhibitions include *Canadian Contemporary Art—The Current Generation* (Edmonton Art Gallery, 1983); *The Other Alberta Sculpture* (Carleton University, 1995); and *75th Anniversary Exhibition* (Alberta College of Art and Design, 2001). Burns has had three solo exhibitions at the Edmonton Art Gallery and several at the Paul Kuhn Fine Arts in Calgary and the Vanderleelie Gallery in Edmonton.

ERIC CAMERON (1935–) was born in Leicester, England. His extensive *curriculum vitae* includes studies in painting with a bachelor's degree with first class honours (King's College, Durham University, England, 1957); an academic diploma in history of art (Courtauld Institute, London, England, 1959); and over forty years of teaching in England and Canada. Since 1987, he has been a full professor at the University of Calgary. His art, including his renowned *Thick Paintings (to be continued)* (1979–), has been exhibited widely across Canada with showings in the United States, Europe, and England. Notable solo exhibitions include *to be continued* (organized by A Space, Toronto, 1982); *Bent Axis Approach* (Nickle Arts Museum, Calgary, 1984); *Divine Comedy* (organized by the National Gallery of Canada, 1990); and *English Roots Eric Cameron* (organized by University of Lethbridge Art Gallery, 1999). He was the 1994 recipient of the Gershon Iskowitz Prize and in 2004 received the Governor General's Award in Visual Arts.

ROBERT CAMPBELL (1883–1967) was born in Dumbarton, Scotland, and came to Minden, Alberta, to homestead in 1906. While in service in England during the First World War, he studied watercolour painting. After the war, he moved to Edmonton, worked as a dental technician, and continued to paint. He went on painting trips with A. C. Leighton, Henry Glyde, and Walter Phillips. He was a charter member of the Edmonton Art Club and a member of the Alberta Society of Artists.

DAVID CANTINE (1939–) was born in Jackson, Michigan, USA. He received a bachelor of art degree at the University of Iowa, Iowa City, in 1962, and a master of art degree at the University of Iowa in 1964. From 1965 to 1996, Cantine taught drawing and painting at the University of Alberta, Edmonton. Since 1962 he has exhibited in Canada and the United States, including the following group shows: *Alberta Art Foundation Exhibition* (Expo '86, Vancouver); *The Art Show* (7th Regiment Armory, New York, 1991); and the *Alberta Biennial of Contemporary Art 2000* (Edmonton Art Gallery–Art Gallery of Calgary). His work has also been exhibited at several solo shows at Edmonton's Vanderleelie Gallery and New York's Kraushaar Galleries. His work is included in a small number of private and public collections, including the Edmonton Art Gallery and Alberta Foundation for the Arts.

JANET CARDIFF (1957–) **AND GEORGE BURES MILLER** (1960–) Cardiff was born in Brussels, Ontario, Miller in Vegreville, Alberta. Cardiff's formal education consists of bachelor of fine arts (Queen's University, Ontario, 1980) and a master of visual arts (University of Alberta, 1983). In addition, she has participated in residency programs at the Banff Centre (photography, 1991) and Vancouver's Western Front (Media, 1995). Miller graduated from Toronto's Ontario College of Art (1986) in Photo and Electric Arts and later participated in a residency program at the Banff Centre (1991). Both artists have individual practices and exhibition histories but also collaborate on multimedia works involving site-specific installation and/or audio and video and film projections. An example of an early collaboration is *The Dark Pool* (Walter Phillips Gallery, Banff, 1995), which also appeared in the first *Alberta Biennial of Contemporary Art* (Glenbow Museum and Edmonton Art Gallery, 1996). Later the Lethbridge-based couple attracted national and international attention and prizes with the audio installation, *Forty-Part Motet* (Milllennium Prize, National Gallery of Canada, 2001) and the film and audio installation, *The Paradise Institute* (Special Jury Award and Benesse Prize, Venice Biennial, 2001). A mid-career survey, *Janet Cardiff: A Survey of Works, Including Collaborations with George Bures Miller* was presented by New York's P.S.1 Contemporary Art Center and Montreal's Musée d'art contemporain de Montréal in 2001.

JOANE CARDINAL-SCHUBERT (1942–) was born in Red Deer. Her formal training in art consists of three years at the Alberta College of Art in the late 1960s. Later she earned a bachelor of fine arts in printmaking and painting at the University of Calgary in 1977. Cardinal-Schubert's exhibition record dates back to the late 1960s. Significant early solo efforts include *Canadian Heroes* (Red Deer Museum, 1978); *This is my History* (Thunder Bay Gallery, 1985); and *Preservation of a Species*, which first appeared in Calgary (1987). As an installation artist, printmaker, and painter, she also appeared in many exhibitions featuring contemporary artists of First Nations heritage. These include the groundbreaking *Stardusters* (Thunder Bay Art Gallery, 1986–87); *Re-Visions* (Walter Phillips Gallery, The Banff Centre, 1988); *Beyond History* (Vancouver Art Gallery, 1989); and *INDIGENA* (Canadian Museum of Civilization, Hull, Quebec). Retrospectives of her work include *Passages to Origins I: Joane Cardinal-Schubert* (Fab Gallery, University of Alberta, 1993) and *Joane Cardinal-Schubert: Two Decades* (Muttart Art Gallery, Calgary, 1997). She was elected to the Royal Canadian Academy in 1986.

WALTER CASSELS (unknown) was active as an artist during the late nineteenth century. Nothing is known about Cassels, but it is believed that he travelled in the West as an engineer or surveyor, perhaps between the 1860s and the 1880s.

JOHN CHALKE (1940–) was born in Gloucestershire, England. He received art training and a teacher's certificate in art education at the Bath Academy of Art in 1962. He taught ceramics at many London area art colleges before moving to Canada in 1968, where he taught at the Alberta College of Art, University of Calgary, and University of Alberta. Over a lengthy artistic career, Chalke is described as exploring and developing a variety of styles, ranging from functional ceramics to thought-provoking sculptural ceramic objects using both conventional and vapour-glazing techniques. He has exhibited in 260 individual and group exhibitions around the world. Some of his notable exhibitions include *1992 International Invitational Exhibition of Ceramic Art* (National Museum of History, Taiwan); *5th Biennale Nationale de Ceramique* (awarded Prix d'Excellence, Trois-Rivieres, Quebec, 1992); *Containment: The Space Within* (Canadian Clay & Glass Gallery, Waterloo, Ontario, 1994); *New Zealand Top Potters' Exhibit with the Fletcher Challenge Ceramic Award Judge (John Chalke)* (Auckland, New Zealand, 1996); *Canada-Clay Today* (touring, George R. Gardiner Museum of Ceramic Art, Toronto, 1999). In 1999, he received the Governor General's Award in the fine craft category. An important survey, *Celebrating Chalke: Past & Present*, was organized by the Alberta Craft Council in 2001.

ARTHUR PHILEMON COLEMAN (1852–1939) was born at Lachute, Lower Canada. He studied in Germany where he obtained a doctor of philosophy from the University of Breslau in 1881. He was a professor of geology at various universities, finally retiring from the University of Toronto in 1922. He started exploring the Rockies in 1884, climbing peaks in the vicinity of the Athabasca Pass in 1892, and making two attempts at climbing Mount Robson in 1907 and 1908. He was the author of *The Canadian Rockies* (Toronto: Henry Frowde, 1911) and *Ice Ages, Recent and Ancient* (New York: Macmillan, 1926). Coleman Mountain in Banff National Park is named in his honour.

PATRICK DOUGLASS COX (1953–) was born in Edmonton. He grew up in rural Alberta (Carstairs) and continues to live on a small acreage near Gem, Alberta, close to where his pioneering grandparents ranched. (The Douglass family's B2P brand appears on the back of most of Cox's paintings.) Cox obtained a diploma in visual communications at the Alberta College of Art in 1976. That same year he participated in the Illustrators' Workshop in Tarrytown, New York, where he was able to work under the direction of the influential American illustrator Alan Cober. After becoming established and working with two partners in the design field (Crow Quill Studios Ltd., 1978–82), Cox took up painting full-time. Since then he has exhibited his egg tempera works, watercolours, and drawings in several one-person shows at the Master Gallery Ltd., in Calgary. In 1994, he had a solo exhibition at Calgary's Glenbow Museum and one at the Medicine Hat Museum and Art Gallery in 1999.

CHRIS CRAN (1949–) was born in Ocean Falls, British Columbia, and raised in Salmon Arm. From 1975 to 1976, he attended the Kootenay School of Art in Nelson, BC, and then studied at Calgary's Alberta College of Art from 1976 to 1979. He is an internationally recognized painter, instructor (Alberta College of Art and Design), occasional curator, and set designer (One Yellow Rabbit Performance Theatre, Calgary). His image-making, which absorbs examples from art history, photography, popular culture, and optical illusions, has made Cran one of Alberta's most sought-after artists since 1985. His exhibition history is extensive and his development has been tracked in several exhibition catalogues. A selection of his participation in group shows includes *Aspects of Contemporary Painting in Alberta* (Glenbow Museum, Calgary, 1987); *Transference* (Walter Phillips Gallery, Banff, 1987); *Alberta Biennial of Contemporary Art 1996* (Edmonton Art Gallery & Glenbow Museum); and *Concealing Revealing: Voices From the Canadian Foothills* (Museum of Fine Arts, Tallahassee, Florida, 1997). Notable solo exhibitions in public art galleries include *Inherent Vice* (Southern Alberta Art Gallery, Lethbridge, 1987); *Loved By Millions* (Art Gallery of Windsor, 1989); *Chris Cran* (49th Parallel, New York, 1992); *Chris Cran: Paintings 1993–1996* (Art Gallery of Peel, Ontario, 1996); and *surveying the damage, 1977–1997* (Kelowna Art Gallery, BC, 1998).

FREDERICK GEORGE CROSS (1881–1941) was born in Exeter, Devon, England, and studied engineering in London. He came to Canada in 1906 to work for the Canadian Pacific Railway Irrigation Department, working first around southern Alberta, in Brooks from 1919 and in Lethbridge from 1936. Although self-taught as an artist, he likely received instruction in drawing as part of his studies in engineering. He exhibited internationally in Canadian exhibitions in Edinburgh, Scotland; the Tate Gallery in London; and in Johannesburg, South Africa. He was a member of the Canadian Society of Painters in Watercolour and the Alberta Society of Artists.

ED DRAHANCHUK (1938–) was born in Calgary and studied at the Provincial Institute of Technology and Art under his brother, Walter Drohan, graduating in 1963. He worked in stoneware and experimented with relief decoration and wax emulsion, which provided a fine sensitive line in his work. In 1963, he was the first graduate of the institute to establish a successful commercial ceramic studio. He was widely admired for his technical ability and for his speed in throwing pots.

WALTER DROHAN (1932–) was born in Calgary. He studied at the Provincial Institute of Technology and Art from 1952 to 1956 with Luke Lindoe, at the Cranbrook Academy of Art in Michigan in 1957, and attended the Emma Lake Workshop in Saskatchewan in 1959. For four years, beginning in 1958, he was a designer for Ceramic Arts in Calgary. From 1957 to 1986 he was an instructor in ceramics at the institute. He was instrumental in the formation of the Alberta Potter's Association.

ALAN DUNNING (1950–) was born in Teddington, England. He obtained a diploma in painting at the Bath Academy of Art in the United Kingdom in 1972 and a masters of visual arts at the University of Alberta in Edmonton in 1977. He has taught at the Alberta College of Art and Design since 1980. Dunning is primarily known for his textual installations, artists' books, and digital works. Since 1980 he has had over two dozen solo exhibitions, including *Billy Budd's Stammer* (Walter Phillips Gallery, Banff, 1988); *mother* (Stride Gallery, Calgary, 1990); *Chevaux de Frise* (Alberta College of Art Gallery, 1991); *City of Lights/Ville de lumieres* (National Gallery of Canada, Ottawa, 1994). He has also had a presence in several prominent group shows, such as *Aspects of Contemporary Painting in Alberta* (Glenbow Museum, Calgary, 1987); *Digital Village* (University of Maryland, Baltimore, 1995); and the *Alberta Biennial of Contemporary Art 1998* (with Paul Woodrow, Glenbow Museum and

Edmonton Art Gallery). Since 1996 he has been part of the team developing the art and science work, *Einstein's Brain Project*, featured in Mark Hansen's *New Philosophy for New Media* (MIT, 2004).

HERBERT EARLE (1884–1975) was born in Dulwich, England. He was a master engraver in copperplate and steel die engraving. In 1920, he came to Calgary where he operated the Engraving Company on 8th Avenue, until his retirement in 1959. He taught etching at Coste House in Calgary. He was a member of the Alberta Society of Artists and the Calgary Sketch Club.

CLAY ELLIS (1955–) was born in Medicine Hat. In 1975, he worked in ceramics under Luke Lindoe at Plainsman Clay Ltd., in Medicine Hat. In 1976, he attended a senior ceramics session at the Banff School of Fine Arts. A self-developed artist, Ellis has a long record of attending artist workshops in Canada, the United States, England, Spain, and South Africa. He was also a sessional instructor at the University of Alberta from 1983 to 1999. Besides participating in such landmark group shows as *Edmonton Steel* (Beaver House Gallery, Edmonton, 1983) and *Sculpture City* (Edmonton Art Gallery, 1985), he has had two solo shows at the Edmonton Art Gallery (in 1983 and 1991). In 1994, his debut exhibition in New York City's Black & Greenberg Gallery, *Clay Ellis*, was reviewed in *Art in America*, *Sculpture Magazine*, *Partisan Review,* and the *New York Review of Art*. His work recently appeared in the *2005 Alberta Biennial*.

JOHN K. ESLER (1933–2001) was born in Pilot Mound, Manitoba. He worked initially as an accountant then obtained a bachelor of fine arts degree in 1960 and bachelor of education degree in 1962 from the University of Manitoba. He taught printmaking at the Alberta College of Art from 1964 to 1968 and then at the University of Calgary, where he set up the program and taught intaglio, lithography, and drawing until 1980. He founded Trojan Press in 1978 and (Studio) JKE in 1981. He was a prolific printmaker, producing approximately three hundred prints over the course of his career.

NORMAN FAULKNER (1944–) was born in Edmonton. His education in art consists of a diploma in ceramics (Alberta College of Art, 1973) and a master's degree in glass (Royal College of Art, London, England, 1986). Faulkner turned to glass in the early 1970s after a year-long stint working as a ceramics technician at Ontario's Sheridan College, where he was introduced to the medium. Despite the long history of glass production worldwide, as a studio practice, it was only introduced to North America in the 1960s, with Toronto's Sheridan College offering it as a course in 1968. Faulkner has taught at the Alberta College of Art and Design since 1974. He has exhibited his work as far away as Brazil (*Arte Em Vidro*, Museo de Arte São Paulo, 1986) and Japan (*Cold Fusion*, Aichi Prefectural Museum, Seto, 1998). In 1987, Faulkner represented Canada in *Glass Art of Canada* (Indiana State Museum, Indianapolis, 1987). A selection of other exhibitions include *Vitrix* (Royal Canadian Academy of Arts, Toronto, 1989); *Canadian Glass 1970–1990* (Ontario Craft Council Gallery, Toronto, 1991); *Calgary Glass* (Gallerie Verre d'Art, Montreal, 1997); and *Glass as Sculpture* (Alberta Craft Council Gallery, Edmonton, 1995).

GORDON FERGUSON (1953–) was born in High River. Central to his sculptural inclination towards taking things apart and putting them back together differently is his background working in his father's hardware store in Oyen, Alberta. He received a diploma in applied art (Alberta College of Art, 1976) and pursued further studies at the University of Montana, Missoula, where he earned a bachelor of fine arts degree (1978) and a master of fine arts degree (1981). Since 1981, he has taught in the foundation studies and sculpture department at the Alberta College of Art and Design. Significant to his development as an artist were his presentations at artist-run centres in Calgary and Winnipeg during the 1980s, including *Gang of Three* (Plug-In and Ace Galleries, Winnipeg, 1987), featuring Ferguson, Blake Senini, and Walter May. Other selected exhibitions include *Five Sculptors from Southern Alberta* (Whyte Museum, Banff, 1985); *Gordon Ferguson: Sense Your Place* (Southern Alberta Art Gallery, Lethbridge, 1988); *Squint: Laura Vickerson, Gordon Ferguson, Walter May* (ArtWeek, Calgary, 1996); and the *Alberta Biennial of Contemporary Art, 2002* (Edmonton and Calgary).

DULCIE FOO FAT (1946–) was born in London, England. She obtained a bachelor of arts degree in painting (Reading University, 1969) and a master's degree in fine art (University of Calgary, 1974). Besides practising as a landscape artist, Foo Fat is also a painter of still lifes and quiet domestic interiors. Her close-up representations of the ground have taken her to several locations, including an expedition to the northern Yukon in 1990. Throughout the past thirty years, her paintings have been exhibited nationally and internationally, including *Dance with Minutae: The Paintings of Dulcie Foo Fat* (a travelling exhibition organized by Banff's Whyte Museum, 1987) and the landmark *Spaces and Places: Eight Decades of Landscape Painting in Alberta* (a travelling group exhibition organized by the Alberta Art Foundation, 1986–87). She has also been a visiting artist at the Djeras Foundation in Woodside, California (1985) and University of Waterloo in Ontario (1990).

JOHN ARTHUR FRASER (1838–98) was born in London, England, and studied at the Royal Academy Schools. He painted portraits. He came to Canada in 1856 and soon joined the William Notman company, the largest and most successful photographic studio in Canada, painting in watercolour onto photographic prints. Fraser opened Notman's Toronto studio in 1867 and became a partner in the company at that time. He organized the Ontario Society of Artists and became its first vice-president in 1872. He travelled west to Calgary at the end of the CPR line in 1883, but it is unlikely that he reached the Rockies. He then went to the United States. After completing commissions for CPR in early 1886, he returned to Canada to travel west with a free CPR pass. He moved to London in 1887 and New York in 1889.

ROBERT GAGEN (1847–1926) was born in London, England, and came to Canada in 1862. He settled in Seaforth, Ontario, where he was taught by William Cresswell, a Royal Academician from London. He went to work in Toronto for the Notman-Fraser company for nine years, where he painted miniatures and watercolour portraits over photographic bases. John Fraser was an important mentor in helping to develop Gagen's landscape painting. Gagen was a founding member of the Ontario Society of Artists, and became an associate charter member of the Royal Canadian Academy in 1880. He may have travelled west in 1886, and was there again in 1901.

HELEN BENY GIBSON (1902–93) was born in New York and moved to Medicine Hat in 1904. She obtained both a bachelor of arts degree (1924) and an honorary doctorate (1967) from the University of Alberta. The latter was awarded for her considerable work in the community, including her work as alderman of the Medicine Hat city council from 1957 to 1971. She was a founding member of the Medicine Hat Art Club in 1945 and the aunt of Roloff Beny. She was a member of the Alberta Society of Artists.

ROLAND GISSING (1895–1967) was born in England and came to Canada in 1913, working initially as a ranch hand. Largely self-taught, he received some instruction from A. C. Leighton. Known for his landscape painting, he was a member of the Alberta Society of Artists and the Calgary Sketch Club.

HENRY GEORGE GLYDE (1906–98) was born in Luton, Bedfordshire, England. He studied art at the Brassey Institute in Hastings, Sussex, from 1920 to 1926 and the Royal College of Art from 1926 to 1930. He taught, painted portraits and murals, and exhibited twice at the Royal Academy. In 1935, he came to Canada to teach and in 1936 became head of the Provincial Institute of Technology and Art. He also taught at the Banff School of Fine Arts and the University of Alberta Extension Department. A member of the Alberta Society of Artists, he served as president from 1942 to 1948. In 1943, he travelled to the Yukon with A. Y. Jackson to record the construction of the Alaska Highway for the National Gallery of Canada. In 1946, he moved to Edmonton to establish the division of fine art at the University of Alberta, later retiring from there in 1966. He lived on Pender Island and in Victoria in his later years.

TED GODWIN (1933–) was born in Calgary. From 1951 to 1955, he studied at the Provincial Institute of Technology and Art and then worked for several years as a television art director and, from 1958, as a neon sign designer in Regina. After attending Emma Lake Workshops under the direction of Barnett Newman (1959) and John Ferren (1960), he rose to prominence as a member of the Regina Five. With *Five Painters from Regina* at the National Gallery of Canada (1961), western Canada had an internationally recognized group of abstract painters. In 1964, Godwin began his career as a university art instructor at what became the Department of Visual Arts, University of Regina. He retired as a full professor in 1985. The artist has an extensive history of exhibiting with such highlights as the National Gallery of Canada's travelling *Abstraction West: Emma Lake and After* (1976) and *The Crisis of Abstraction in Canada* (1992). His contribution was also recognized in the travelling *The Flat Side of the Landscape: The Emma Lake Artists' Workshops* (Mendel Art Gallery, Saskatoon, 1989). His encounter with landscape, rendered with a sense of abstraction, began in the early 1970s and has continued to the present with his series and book, *Lower Bow, A Celebration of Wilderness, Art and Fishing* (1991) being his best-known work.

LES GRAFF (1936–) was born in Camrose. He studied at the Banff School of Fine Arts in 1955, the Provincial Institute of Technology and Art from 1955 to 1959, and the Cranbrook Academy of Art in Bloomfield Hills, Michigan, in 1960. He worked as an arts administrator for the Government of Alberta until 1991.

NICHOLAS DE GRANDMAISON (1892–1978) was born in Moscow. He studied at the St. John's Wood School of Art in London, England. He immigrated to Canada in 1923, moving from Winnipeg to Calgary around 1932 and then to Banff in 1939. Painting initially in oils, he subsequently worked almost exclusively in pastel. Noted for his First Nations portraits, he travelled to many First Nations communities throughout his career. In 1959, he was made an honorary chief of the Peigan and given the name "Chief Little Plume." He received the Order of Canada in 1972.

EVELYN GRANT (1953–) was born in St. Catharines, Ontario. Majoring in ceramics, she obtained a diploma at the Alberta College of Art in 1976 and a bachelor of fine arts degree in ceramics at the University of Calgary in 1981. In order to make her playful and narrative art, she has attended a number of workshops over the years on slip casting and mould making. She has gone on to teach these techniques at the Alberta College of Art and Design. She also has a long association with the City of Calgary's Leisure Learning Services, organizing its ceramic and glass programs and several international ceramic conferences. Her exhibition history is extensive with over seventy appearances in juried and invitational group shows across Canada and the United States. Her teapots, in particular, have attracted attention and have appeared in such stellar presentations as *The Artful Teapot* (Sonny and Gloria Kamn Collection, Gardiner Museum of Ceramic Art, Toronto, 2003) and *The Canadian Teapot* (Nancy Margolis Gallery, New York, 1993).

ROBERT GUEST (1938–) was born in Beaverlodge, Alberta. He studied at the Provincial Institute of Technology and Art from 1959 to 1963 and graduated in art education from the University of Alberta in the early 1970s. He taught in Edmonton at the Edmonton Art Gallery and the Northern Institute of Technology and in 1974 returned north to set up the art department at Grande Prairie Regional College, where he taught until 1984. He became a charter member of the Alberta Art Foundation in 1973. He founded the Peace Watercolour Society in 1976, and two conservation societies, Canadian Wolf Defenders in 1968 and Wild Kakwa in 1970.

THOMAS GUSHUL (1889–1962) and **LENA GUSHUL** (1898–1981) Born in Rosniw, Western Ukraine, Thomas immigrated to Canada in 1906. He worked initially for CPR on the railroad, then as a miner in Crowsnest Pass. In 1914, he married Lena Sawiek, who had come to Canada the same year from his Ukrainian village, and they began their photographic work. From 1912 to 1913, Thomas studied photography in Winnipeg and in 1918 they opened a photographic studio in Coleman and another in Blairmore in 1921. They concentrated on family portraits, wedding and funeral photographs, and the daily life of the area. However, Thomas's greatest contribution was his photography of the coal mining industry and labour unrest in the Crowsnest Pass in the 1920s and 1930s. After Thomas's death, Lena continued to work in the studio.

BART HABERMILLER (1962–) was born in Regina. He obtained a sculpture diploma at the Alberta College of Art in 1986 and a master of fine arts degree at the School of the Art Institute of Chicago in 1990. During this same time Habermiller founded Graceland (1986–97), a site for contemporary art-making at an old Calgary junkyard. Later, Graceland's annual Art Rodeo would serve as a prime site for alternative art activity (on-site sculpture, installation, and performance) outside of the gallery system. Besides his contributions as a curator and art impressario, Habermiller has also had an active exhibition history of his own, featuring assemblages and installations made from found materials and objects. Selected exhibits include *Graceland* (2nd Story Gallery, Calgary, 1986); *Frank's Wild Years* (Off Centre Centre, Calgary, 1987); *Elemental Instincts* (Nickle Arts Museum, Calgary, 1988); *Graceland Art Rodeo* (Calgary, 1989); *1040 ½ W. Huron* (Gallery 2, Chicago); *London Life Young Contemporaries* (group touring, London Regional Art and Historical Museum, London, Ontario, 1997); and *Nature Redux* (group, Southern Alberta Art Gallery, Lethbridge, 1996).

ALEXANDRA HAESEKER (1945–) was born in Breda, Holland, and spent almost ten years in Indonesia before moving to Calgary in 1955. She obtained both a bachelor's degree (1966) and master's degree (1972) from the University of Calgary and a fine arts diploma from the Alberta College of Art (1968). She was an instructor at the college in painting, drawing, and printmaking from 1973 to 2003, and was awarded lecturer emeritus in 2004. Her exhibition record stretches back to 1968 and includes the retrospective, *Alexandra Haeseker: Twenty Years* (Illingworth Kerr Gallery, Alberta College of Art, 1992), as well as numerous appearances as a noted lithographer in international print shows in New York; Ibiza and Seville, Spain; Krakow, Poland; Maastricht, Holland; Shanghai, China; and London, England.

JOHN HALL (1943–) was born in Edmonton. A graduate of the Alberta College of Art in 1965, with further study undertaken at the Instituto Allende in Mexico in 1966, Hall's role models include early Calgary abstractionists Ron Spickett and Marion Nicoll. He taught art at Ohio's Wesleyan University, the Alberta College of Art, and the University of Calgary, where he retired from a full professorship in painting and drawing (he is now a professor emeritus). In 1975, he was elected as a member of the Royal Canadian Academy of Arts. Early in his career, Hall came to national attention with a one-person show *John Hall: Paintings and Auxiliary Works 1969–78* hosted by the National Gallery of Canada (1979–80). In 1993, a major retrospective of his work was exhibited at Mexico City's Museo de Arte Moderno. He is one of a small number of contemporary Alberta artists to have art in such public collections as the National Gallery of Canada, the Art Gallery of Ontario, and the Montreal Museum of Fine Arts.

JOHN HAMMOND (1843–1939) was born in Montreal. He participated in the first Geological Survey of Canada Transcontinental Survey in 1870. He joined the William Notman Company, the largest and most successful photographic studio in Canada, the following year and was elected to the Ontario Society of Artists in 1873. In 1885 he went to Europe, where he studied with James McNeill Whistler in Holland and François Millet in France. He was elected an associate of the Royal Canadian Academy in 1890 and became a full member three years later. Hammond began a distinguished educational career in 1892, first in Saint John, New Brunswick, and then Sackville, New Brunswick, where he was the director of the School of Art at Mount Allison College from 1907 to 1919.

BYRON HARMON (1876–1942) was born in Tacoma, Washington, and operated a photographic studio there. In 1903, he moved to Banff, where he opened his own studio. For over thirty years he travelled by foot and packhorse through the Rockies, becoming the premier mountain photographer for that time. He was a charter member of the Alpine Club of Canada, which was established in 1906, and was its official photographer from 1906 to 1913. As well as annual week-long trips into the mountains with the club, he went on more extended special trips, such as the ninety-day journey he took to Rainbow Mountain, in what is now Jasper National Park, in 1911 with A. O. Wheeler, one of Canada's foremost surveyors and cartographers; European guide Conrad Kain; and four scientists from the Smithsonian Institution in Washington. The purpose of the trip was to survey the region and study the geology, flora, and fauna. His movie footage from that trip was used in newsreels internationally. In his later years, he travelled widely and took photographs around the world. He is best remembered for his stunning mountain photographs.

LAWREN STEWART HARRIS (1885–1970) was born in Brantford, Ontario, and studied art in Berlin from 1904 to 1907. He became a charter member of the Arts and Letters Club in Toronto, where he met future members of the Group of Seven. In 1913, with Dr. James MacCallum, he financed and built the Studio Building in Toronto where most of the Group of Seven subsequently worked. He travelled to the more remote regions of Canada to capture the rugged landscape, including Algoma, Ontario, in 1917; the north shore of Lake Superior in 1922; and Greenland and the Arctic in 1930. He painted in the Rockies from 1924 to 1929 and probably again from 1940 to 1957. He left Toronto in 1934 to live in the United States, and moved to Vancouver in 1940.

CRYS HARSE (1939–) was born and educated in London, England. Initially a basketmaker, she turned to metalsmithing in the late 1980s and has worked in a variety of materials, including copper, brass, bronze, and silver. In 1994, she obtained a diploma in visual arts (jewellery and metals, with distinction) and in 1997 a bachelor of fine arts (jewellery and metals, with distinction) from the Alberta College of Art and Design. She has also taught throughout the province, including at the Alberta College of Art and Design, Red Deer College, and the Leighton Art Foundation. Some of her numerous exhibitions include the touring *Champagne Breakfast* (organized at Alberta Craft Council, 1990–92); *The Medium is Metal* (organized by the Canadian Metal Arts Guild, 1991); *Selected Treasures* (Taipei, Taiwan, Hong Kong, Chicago, Tokyo, 1993); *Metalsmithing in the New Millennium* (Portland, Maine, 1998); and *Identity* (organized by the Canadian Metal Arts Guild, 1998–2000).

ELLA HARTT (1865–1943), a nurse from Cook County, Illinois, first went west during the 1890s to visit her brother in Montana, and continued to visit him after 1906, when he moved to Thelma in south-eastern Alberta. In 1910, she married her brother's partner, Al Suiste, and lived in Thelma until 1916, when they were separated. She returned to Illinois, but eventually retired to Thelma. Likely self-taught, she developed photographic expertise and used the professional method of dry-plate photography. She documented the varied life of the West in candid shots of outdoor scenes of cowboys, farming, early dwellings, and family and cowboy gatherings, but she also photographed intimate domestic scenes and children at play.

LARS HAUKANESS (1862–1929) was born in Granvin, Norway, and studied at the Royal Academy in Oslo where he became well-versed in modern art movements. He settled in the United States in 1888, where he was active as an artist and exhibited at the Art Institute of Chicago. He moved to Winnipeg in 1920 to teach at the School of Art and moved to Calgary in 1926 to teach at the Provincial Institute of Technology and Art. Haukaness is acknowledged as the original founder of the Alberta College of Art.

DOUGLAS HAYNES (1936–) was born in Regina. He graduated from Calgary's Provincial Institute of Technology and Art in 1958 and then pursued further studies from 1960 to 1961 at the Royal Academy of Art in The Hague, Holland. Haynes joined the teaching staff of the University of Alberta's Department of Art and Design in 1970 and was later appointed head of the department (1976–80). He retired in 1995. One of Alberta's most recognized artists, his solo exhibitions include *Cubism Revisited: The Paintings of Douglas Haynes* (Edmonton Art Gallery, 1985); *The Toledo Series* (organized by the Edmonton Art Gallery, 1991–93); and *Douglas Haynes: 25 Years* (Edmonton Art Gallery, 2000). Haynes considers *The Toledo Series* his most important body of work and has donated all thirteen paintings in the series to the Edmonton Art Gallery. He is also represented in over two dozen public art collections, including the National Gallery of Canada.

FAYE HEAVYSHIELD (1953–) was born and raised on the Blood (Kainai) reserve located in southern Alberta. HeavyShield graduated in 1985 from the Alberta College of Art with an additional year at the University of Calgary (1986). Since the early 1990s, her sculptural art has generally appeared in exhibitions concerned with First Nations art or women-centred themes. Some of her notable group exhibitions include *Land Spirit Power* (National Gallery of Canada, 1992) and *Artists who are Indians* (Denver Art Museum, Colorado, 1994). Her solo exhibits include *Heart Hoof Horn* (Glenbow Museum, 1994); *Into the garden of angels* (The Power Plant, Toronto, 1994); and *venus as torpedo* (Dunlop Art Gallery, Saskatoon, 1995). Since the late 1990s, HeavyShield has been engaged with writing and more text-based art and installations.

MARTHA HENRY (1953–) was born in Montreal. She studied glass-blowing and graduated with honours from Sheridan College School of Design, Oakville, Ontario, in 1974. In 1976, she moved to Calgary and studied glass and sculpture at the Alberta College of Art and Design. In 1979, she helped set up Skookum Art Glass, a Calgary-based "hot shop" for making glass art objects. Throughout the 1980s she began working with metals and glass, experimenting with gold leaf—one of her signature elements. In 1990, Skookum closed its doors and Henry opened up her own studio, dividing her time between studio work and teaching at the Alberta College of Art and Design. As one of Canada's leading glass artists, she has an extensive history of exhibiting since 1976, presenting her work in some of the country's leading fine craft galleries, such as the Cartwright Gallery (Vancouver); Rubaiyat Gallery (Calgary); Canadian Clay and Glass Gallery (Waterloo, Ontario); and Galerie Elena Lee Verre D'Art (Montreal). Her art has also been selected for such group exhibitions as *Art in the Everyday* (Power Plant, Toronto, 1988); *Tradition of Excellence* (Alberta Craft Council Gallery, Edmonton, 1991); *A Treasury of Canadian Crafts* (Canadian Craft Museum, Vancouver, 1992); and *Selected Treasures* (Toronto, Chicago, Taipei, Hong Kong, 1992–93).

PERCY HENSON (1890–1975) was born in Sussex, England, and came to Canada in 1910. Largely self-taught, he took classes for five years at the Ontario College of Art summer schools with J. W. Beatty in the late 1940s. He was the director of the Edmonton Art Gallery from 1950 to 1964, and taught landscape painting in the University of Alberta Extension Department. He was a member of the Alberta Society of Artists and the Edmonton Art Club.

PETER HIDE (1944–) was born in Carshalton, Surrey, England. He attended the Croydon College of Art (1961–64), completed post-graduate studies at St. Martin's School of Art (1964–67), and then worked one year as a part-time assistant to sculptor Anthony Caro. Hide moved to Canada in 1977 to join the teaching staff at the University of Alberta and continues to lead the apprentice-based sculpture program there, both at the undergraduate and post-graduate level. He has also conducted or attended workshops, such as Triangle (Pine Plains, New York, London, and Barcelona), Hardingham (Norwich, England), and Philip Berman (Allentown, Pennsylvania). Noted for developing an approach to welded abstract steel sculpture different from Caro's more open-collage style, Hide's large-scale, compacted, and generally vertical sculpture has been featured in dozens of group shows in Canada and abroad. Solo exhibitions include two retrospectives (Edmonton Art Gallery, 1986, 1998) and showings at the Kathleen Laverty Gallery (Edmonton); Mira Godard Gallery (Toronto); and Andre Emmerich Gallery (New York).

WILLIAM GEORGE RICHARDSON HIND (1833–88) was born in Nottingham, England, and studied art in London and Europe. He came to Canada in 1852 for two years and again in 1861 to join his brother Henry Youle Hind, a leading intellectual who had undertaken trips to the West in 1857 and 1858. In 1861, William Hind accompanied his brother on a government-sponsored expedition to the Labrador Peninsula and provided illustrations for the subsequent report. In April 1862, he travelled west with a group of young Easterners, the "Overlanders of '62," lured west by the search for gold and adventure. They travelled across the prairies on old fur trails and through the Rockies via the Leather (Yellowhead) Pass to Lillooet, where Hind sketched gold miners. Hind then travelled to Victoria, where he set up a studio from 1863 to 1865. He spent his later years working as a draughtsman for the railways in Nova Scotia and New Brunswick. He died in New Brunswick.

DAVID HOFFOS (1966–) was born in Montreal. He received a bachelor of fine arts, with great distinction, from the University of Lethbridge in 1994. Since his graduation, Hoffos has forged a reputation for multimedia installations that emphasize the creation of dreamy and ghostly illusions projected on miniature models that he builds himself. Based in Lethbridge, his cinematic illusions, which rely on recovered equipment like old TV screens, have attracted much attention. A selection of his exhibitions include *You Will Remember When You Need to Know* (solo, Stride Gallery, Calgary, 1995); *Alberta Biennial of Contemporary Art* (Edmonton Art Gallery and Glenbow Museum, 1996); *Three Small Rooms and a TV* (Muttart Public Art Gallery, Calgary); *Catastophe* (Illingworth Kerr Gallery, Calgary, 1998); *Another City* (Southern Alberta Art Gallery, Lethbridge, 1999); *Galeria João Graça* (Lisbon, Portugal, 2001); and *20:01:2000* (TrépanierBaer Gallery, Calgary). The artist has received awards, including second place in the inaugural 2002 Sobey Art Award, given to outstanding young contemporary Canadian artists, and the 2004 York Wilson Endowment Award.

CHARLES HORETZKY (1838–1900) joined the Hudson's Bay Company in Scotland and arrived in Canada in 1854. In 1864, he was sent to Moose Factory, Rupert's Land (currently northern Ontario), where he became an amateur photographer. In 1871, he was hired as a photographer by Sandford Fleming to record the physical features of the region between Fort Garry, Manitoba, and the Rockies for Canadian Pacific Railway (CPR). In 1872, he made a second trip to the Peace River country and the west coast. He published a book on his travels in 1874. He went west again in 1874 and 1875, and for the last time in 1879. He left CPR in 1880. Horetzky's photographs were the first taken of Alberta and serve as a valuable historical record.

MARTHA HOUSTON (1896–ca. 1983) was born in Newark, New Jersey. She studied for eleven summers at the Banff School of Fine Arts, mostly with Walter Phillips and Henry Glyde, and attended evening classes at the Provincial Institute of Technology and Art. She taught French and art at the high school in High River. She organized the High River Sketch Club and arranged for Walter Phillips and Annora Brown to teach there.

ALEXANDER YOUNG JACKSON (1882–1974) was born in Montreal and studied there at the Art Association and at the Académie Julian in Paris in 1907. He travelled and painted in France and Italy until 1911. He worked initially as a commercial artist. He moved to Toronto in 1913, and lived in the Studio Building for over forty years. A member of the Group of Seven, he travelled on extensive sketching trips for months at a time, all over Quebec and Ontario, the Arctic, Northwest Territories, and western Canada. He came to Alberta in 1914 and again in 1924. In the 1930s, he began making annual visits to his brother Ernest, a judge in Lethbridge. In the 1940s, southern Alberta scenes predominated in his work. From the summer of 1943 until 1949, he taught at the Banff School of Fine Arts.

ALEX JANVIER (1935–), a member of the Dene Nation (Chippewan), was born on the Le Goff Reserve, near Cold Lake, Alberta. He attended the Blue Quills residential school in St. Paul, Alberta, and St. Thomas College in North Battleford, Saskatchewan. He studied at the Provincial Institute of Technology and Art under Illingworth Kerr, Marion Nicoll, and Ron Spickett, graduating in 1960. Full-time work with the Department of Indian Affairs in Ottawa, and teaching at the University of Alberta Extension Department allowed him to paint only part-time. In 1971, he began to paint full-time and returned to live near Cold Lake in the late 1970s.

DAVID JANZEN (1959–) was born in Toronto. In 1983, he completed his studies at the Alberta College of Art and Design specializing in painting. Almost immediately upon graduating, he became known for his still lifes of solitary household appliances and shaped paintings of other subject matter. A solo exhibition, *Paintings/Constructions*, at the artist-run Second Story Gallery (Calgary, 1985) was especially important and was followed by other solo presentations at artist-run centres and commercial galleries in Calgary, such as Paul Kuhn Fine Arts and TrépanierBaer. Since the early 1990s, his focus has been on the urban landscape, especially on the skyline and the technological intrusions into this space. His contemporary treatments have also been recognized in such group shows as *Points North* (Southern Alberta Art Gallery, Lethbridge, 1985–86); *Reflecting Paradise* (Artweek, Calgary, 1994); *Transformations: Imaging Nature* (Mendel Art Gallery, Saskatoon, 1998); and the *Alberta Biennial of Contemporary Art* (Edmonton Art Gallery and Glenbow Museum, Calgary, 1998).

CHARLES WILLIAM JEFFERYS (1869–1951) was born in Rochester, Kent, England, and settled in Toronto around 1880. He studied art with G. A. Reid and at the Toronto Art Students' League. He worked at the Toronto Lithographing Company and in 1892 went to New York City to work at *The New York Herald*. He returned to Toronto in 1901, after which he made his first trip west, and five subsequent trips, the last in 1924. Jefferys produced many illustrations for books and articles on the history of Canada, and was considered an authority as an historical artist. He was a drawing instructor in the department of architecture at the University of Toronto from 1912 to 1939.

HOPE JOHNSON (1916–) was born in Vancouver, BC, and moved to the Medicine Hat area in 1945. Primarily self-taught, she joined the Medicine Hat Art Club, which was visited by instructors from the University of Alberta Extension Department. She became the group's local instructor from 1951 to 1976. She is a noted amateur botanist, geologist, and palaeontologist, and a published author and illustrator. She began a lifelong study of fossils and the natural environment in the late 1940s, and has produced many botanical and fossil drawings. Her work has been widely exhibited. Recognized by the scientific community, she received an honorary doctorate of laws from the University of Lethbridge in 1981.

WILLIAM JOHNSTONE (1868–1927) was trained in Edinburgh, Scotland, and came to Edmonton in 1912. He was the first professional artist in Edmonton and one year later was giving art classes. He was a founding member of the Edmonton Art Club and its first president. He was also a founding member of the Edmonton Museum of Arts and served on the board. He was a noted portrait painter.

PAUL KANE (1818–71) was born in Ireland and immigrated with his family to Toronto in 1819. He studied art with Thomas Drury, the art master at Upper Canada College, and then worked as a furniture decorator and painted portraits in Coburg, Ontario; Detroit, Michigan; and later Mobile, Alabama. It is unknown why he made these moves, but it was likely done to find work. Intent on going to Europe to study art, he saved money earned from his painting. He sailed from New Orleans to Marseilles, France, in 1841. He studied the Old Masters in Rome, Naples, Florence, and Venice and then travelled to London, where he was inspired by George Catlin's paintings of American Indians. He returned to North America and spent two years in the United States, then returned to Canada in 1845, intent on travelling west to depict the life of the First Nations. He made three separate trips, the first from June to September 1845 to Sault Ste Marie; the second to Oregon Territory and Fort Victoria between May 1846 and October 1848; and the third to Fort Garry in 1849.

ILLINGWORTH KERR (1905–89) was born in Lumsden, Saskatchewan, and studied with Group of Seven artists J. E. H. MacDonald, Arthur Lismer, and Fred Varley at the Ontario College of Art in Toronto from 1924 to 1927. Back in Lumsden, he did seasonal work, and painted and wrote until he went to Britain in 1936, where he studied at the Westminster School of Art. He moved to Vancouver in 1940, worked for Boeing aircraft for four years, and then taught at the Vancouver School of Art. From 1947 to 1967, he was the head of the Provincial Institute of Technology and Art in Calgary. He was a member of Alberta Society of Artists and served as president from 1952 to 1954. He studied with Hans Hofmann in Provincetown, Massachusetts, in 1954, and at Emma Lake, Saskatchewan, with Jack Shadbolt in 1955 and Will Barnet in 1957. He was awarded the Order of Canada in 1983.

JANE KIDD (1952–) was born in Victoria, BC. She studied fine arts, art history, and textile design at the Vancouver School of Art and University of Victoria. Upon graduating in 1979, she moved to Calgary to teach textile design, theory, and contemporary tapestry at the Alberta College of Art and Design. Still teaching, Kidd maintains an active studio practice and has travelled extensively to pursue her interest in historic and multicultural textile production. She has completed several commissions, including a large one (1986) for the Red Deer Arts Centre building designed by Arthur Erickson. In 1980, Kidd's work appeared in the ground-breaking *Fibrations: A New Generation of Fibre Art In Alberta* (Student Union Gallery, University of Alberta and Nickle Arts Museum, Calgary). A few of her other notable exhibitions include *Reflection on Three Plains: Contemporary Crafts* (Winnipeg Art Gallery, 1984); *Textile Works by Three Canadian Artists* (Kyoto, Japan, 1991); *The Temple Series* (solo, The Alberta Craft Council Gallery, Edmonton, 1992); *Tapestry Visions* (Convergence 94, Minneapolis, Minnesota, 1994); and *Journey: Jane Kidd* (retrospective, Illingworth Kerr Gallery, Calgary, 1995).

HARRY KIYOOKA (1928–) was born in Calgary. He received his bachelor of education at the University of Alberta in 1952, studying under Henry Glyde, and a bachelor of fine arts at the University of Manitoba in 1954, where he was inspired by the new artistic developments in the United States through his American instructors Roland Wise and Richard Bowman. He went to the United States and obtained a master's of arts at Michigan State University in 1956 and master of fine arts at the University of Colorado, in 1957. He studied and painted in Italy from 1958 to 1961. He has travelled extensively in Europe, Japan, India, and the United States. He taught at the University of Calgary from 1961 to 1988. He is a life member of the Alberta Society of Artists and served as its president in 1967, 1969, and 1970. He is a founding member of the Calgary Contemporary Arts Society (founded in 1982), which established the Triangle Art Gallery in Calgary.

ROY KIYOOKA (1926–99) was born in Moose Jaw, Saskatchewan. In 1941, after Pearl Harbor, his family became "enemy aliens" and moved to Opal, northeast of Edmonton, the only Japanese community in northern Alberta. He came to Calgary to attend the Provincial Institute of Technology and Art and studied under Jock Macdonald and Illingworth Kerr from 1946 to 1949. After graduating, he worked at various jobs in Calgary, Nelson, and Toronto, including commercial art, some seasonal work, and some teaching, all the while developing his painting. In 1955, he won a scholarship to attend the Instituto Allende in San Miguel, Mexico, during the same time that Ron Spickett was there. He taught at the University of Saskatchewan in Regina (1957–59), the Vancouver School of Art (1960–65), Sir George Williams University in Montreal (1965–70), and the University of British Columbia (1973–91). He attended Emma Lake Workshops from 1957 to 1962, and in 1972 was workshop leader. In the 1960s, he turned to sculpture and had his last exhibit as a studio artist in 1971. After this, he took up photography, writing, and music.

SYBIL LAUBENTHAL (1918–61) was born in Halle, Germany. From 1936, she worked as an apprentice in a pottery workshop near Salerno, Italy, and then for a Berlin potter, Jan Bontjes van Beek, from 1938 to 1941. Both of these studios followed Bauhaus principles. She then worked for a Stuttgart tile company from 1950 until she immigrated to Canada. She settled in Edmonton in 1952, where she taught initially at the Edmonton Potters' Guild from 1953, the University of Alberta Extension Department from 1955 to 1960, and the Banff School of Fine Arts from 1954 to 1957. She was the first Canadian potter to win a prize in an international competition at the Syracuse Museum of Fine Arts in 1956. Her work was also chosen by the National Gallery of Canada to be shown at the Brussels World Fair in 1958.

ROY LEADBEATER (1928–) was born in Ashbourne, Derbyshire, England, and immigrated to Canada in 1951. An engineer by profession, he has no formal training in sculpture, except for his studies with Katie Ohe at the Calgary Allied Arts Centre in the 1960s. Along with Ohe, he learned how to weld from the Dominion Bridge Company in Calgary in 1964. He has worked on many corporate and public commissions, including the Four Western Provinces Pavilion at Expo '67 in Montreal and commissions with the Calgary Petroleum Club, the Triangle Art Gallery in Calgary, and the Citadel Theatre in Edmonton.

ALFRED CROCKER LEIGHTON (1900–65) was born in Hastings, Sussex, England, and studied at the Brassey Institute, Hastings. After graduating in about 1920, he taught for a year and then launched out on his own as a freelance commercial artist. Working from his English studio, he became Canadian Pacific Railway's (CPR's) official commercial artist in 1924. He travelled across Canada for CPR in 1925 and 1927 to paint landscapes to be used to promote tourism. He moved to Calgary in 1929 to become the head of the art department at the Provincial Institute of Technology and Art. In 1931, he founded the Alberta Society of Artists and until 1942 was its first president. In 1933, he started a summer art course in Seebe, Alberta, which led to the formation of the Banff School of Fine Arts. He resigned from teaching in 1935 due to ill health. After living for a time in British Columbia, he returned in the 1950s to live southwest of Calgary near Millarville.

LUKE LINDOE (1913–2000) was born in Bashaw, Alberta. From 1935 to 1940, he studied painting and sculpture at the Provincial Institute of Technology and Art with Henry Glyde, and sculpture at the Ontario College of Art the following year with Emmanuel Hahn. For a year, from 1941 to 1942, he worked at Medicine Hat Potteries and then until 1945 he worked on geological surveys for Imperial Oil Limited, making the first comprehensive maps of stoneware clay deposits on the prairies. In 1946, he established the ceramics program at the institute, teaching there for ten years. During the 1970s, he taught at the Banff School of Fine Arts. In 1955, he founded Lindoe Studios, one of the first commercial studio potteries in Canada. From 1957 to 1967 and then 1975 to 1984, he worked for IXL Industries, where he was responsible for locating and mining clay for commercial ceramic manufacture. From 1964 to 1978, he was president of Plainsman Clays Limited in Medicine Hat, providing quality prepared clays for artists across North America. He completed many architectural commissions in concrete, stone, and ceramic.

ARTHUR LISMER (1885–1969) was born in Sheffield, Yorkshire, England, and studied at the Sheffield School of Art from 1898 to 1905 and at the Académie Royale des Beaux-Arts in Antwerp, Belgium, from 1906 to 1907. Following his studies, he apprenticed as an engraver for seven years. He then settled in Toronto in 1911, where he worked at design and printing companies as a commercial artist, first at Grip Limited and then at Rous and Mann. From 1913, he made regular painting trips north with Group of Seven friends to Georgian Bay, Algonquin Park, and Algoma. He made only one trip west in 1928. A noted Canadian educator, he was principal of the Victoria School of Art and Design in Halifax from 1916 to 1919, and vice-principal of the Ontario College of Art from 1919 until 1927. He also taught at the Art Gallery of Toronto, where he introduced his Saturday morning classes for children; the National Gallery of Canada; the Montreal Museum of Fine Arts; as well as internationally.

J. W. G. (JOCK) MACDONALD (1897–1960) was born in Thurso, Scotland, studied at the Edinburgh College of Art, and worked as a textile designer and instructor before coming to Canada in 1926. He taught at the Vancouver School of Decorative and Applied Arts, where he met Frederick Varley. Together they established the new British Columbia College of Art in 1933, but it went bankrupt in 1935. He continued teaching in Vancouver, and at the Banff School of Fine Arts in 1945. In 1946, he became the head of the Provincial Institute of Technology and Art in Calgary for one year. He taught at the Ontario College of Art in Toronto from 1947 until his death in 1960.

JAMES EDWARD HERVEY MACDONALD (1873–1932) was born near Durham, England, and moved to Canada in 1887. He studied at the Central Ontario School of Art. He worked as a commercial artist for various companies in Toronto and London, England, from 1890 to 1911. A member of the Group of Seven, he painted extensively in central and eastern Canada, including Georgian Bay and Algoma, and worked in the Rockies each summer for three weeks from 1924 to 1930. Sometime after 1924, he met Peter Whyte and they sketched together frequently when MacDonald was in the mountains. On his last trip in 1930, Catharine Whyte also accompanied them. He taught at the Ontario College of Art from 1921, becoming principal there in 1928 until his death.

MURRAY W. MACDONALD (1898–1989) was born in Cape Breton. He came west in 1916 to teach in northern Alberta and then in the Edmonton Public School system in 1927. He was the supervisor of art for Edmonton Public Schools from 1947 to 1963. He taught at the University of Alberta and in the 1950s at the Banff School of Fine Arts with A. Y. Jackson. He initiated children's art classes at the Edmonton Art Gallery and served as its president from 1955 to 1957.

THELMA MANAREY (1913–84) was born in Edmonton. She studied at the Provincial Institute of Technology and Art in Calgary under Henry Glyde from 1939 to 1943, the University of Alberta Extension Department in 1948 and 1949, the University of Washington in 1953, and at the Banff School of Fine Arts from 1955 to 1957. She attended the Emma Lake Workshops of 1960, with leader John Ferren, and 1963, with Kenneth Noland. She was a member of the Alberta Society of Artists. As well as painting, she made serigraphs and etchings.

THOMAS MOWER MARTIN (1838–1934) was born in London, England, and studied art there at the South Kensington School of Art. He came to Canada in 1862 and established a studio in Toronto in 1864, advertising himself as a portrait painter, though he mostly did landscapes, animal studies, and still lifes. He was a founding member of the Ontario Society of Artists and the Royal Canadian Academy and in 1877 became the first director of the Ontario Government Art School. He made his first trip west in 1887 and then went ten more times. Because he continued to paint in a nineteenth-century style well into the twentieth century, his later work is considered out of date.

MARMADUKE MATTHEWS (1837–1913) was born in Warwickshire, England, and studied painting in Oxford and London. He came to Canada in 1858 and soon settled in Toronto, although he did live in New York City from 1865 to 1869. In Toronto, in 1869, he set up a studio and in 1875 advertised himself as a portrait painter, though he became well known as a landscape artist for his paintings of the Rocky Mountains. He was a founding member of both the Ontario Society of Artists and the Royal Canadian Academy. He travelled widely and came west in 1887 and 1889. Many of his paintings are undated and the specific locations are unknown. Likely painted long after he had actually seen the scenes, some of Matthews's paintings appear generic.

WALTER MAY (1950–) was born in Edmonton. He received a bachelor of fine arts degree at the University of Alberta in 1971, and a master of fine arts at the University of Regina in 1977. Since 1982, he has been a full-time faculty member at the Alberta College of Art and Design, teaching in the sculpture and foundation program. May's exhibition history began to take shape in the late 1970s with minimalist-style sculpture made from warped and bent wood boards. He exploited these materials, and eventually other scavenged articles, for their expressive qualities. With concerns that were both formal and conceptual, the 1984 *Walter May* (Paul Kuhn Fine Arts, Calgary), and *Walter May: Recent Sculpture* (Southern Alberta Art Gallery, Lethbridge, 1985) cemented his reputation for new and distinctive work that conveys a sense of drawing and the figure. In the 1990s, his solo exhibits at Paul Kuhn Fine Arts tracked new developments in his work, including his move away from drawing-influenced sculpture to more installation-based art, or singular pieces incorporating ordinary objects and tools that have been altered by the artist. As art, they re-examine the traditional definitions of sculpture and metaphorical concerns. Notable showings include *Walter May* (Edmonton Art Gallery, 1990 and Mercer Union, Toronto, 1990); and the *Alberta Biennial of Contemporary Art* (Edmonton Art Gallery and Glenbow Museum, Calgary, 1998).

EVY MCBRYAN (1911–85) was born in Somerset, England, and arrived in Grande Prairie, Alberta, in 1916. She studied with Euphemia McNaught, at the art school in Vancouver and in 1954 studied art at the University of Alberta. With her work, she recorded the historic places of the Peace River country. During the 1960s, she organized art programs for the recreation centre in Grande Prairie. In the 1970s, she was a board member of the Alberta Art Foundation.

EUPHEMIA MCNAUGHT (1901–2002) was born in Ontario and moved to Beaverlodge, Alberta, in 1912. She studied at the Ontario College of Art with J. E. H. MacDonald and Arthur Lismer from 1924 to 1929. Over the years, she taught in Ontario, Calgary, and Grand Prairie, and then returned to Beaverlodge in 1936. Devoted to painting the northern landscape, she fostered art in the Peace River Region through her workshops for the Beaverlodge Art Club.

GEORGE MIHALCHEON (1924–) was born in Boian, Alberta, and studied at the Provincial Institute of Technology and Art from 1946 to 1950. He worked as a graphic artist in an advertising agency in Calgary until 1960 and taught part-time at the institute. He was a full-time instructor in advertising art, drawing, and painting at the institute from 1960 until 1987. He was also a member of the Alberta Society of Artists.

BARBARA MILNE (1956–) was born in Windsor, Ontario. In 1979, she received a bachelor of fine arts with honours at York University in Toronto. That same year she moved to Calgary and found herself drawn to the new and different landscape. The result has been an extensive history of exhibiting her metaphorical landscapes. A selection of her exhibitions includes *Barbara Milne* (Southern Alberta Art Gallery, Lethbridge, 1988) and the touring *Spirited Places* (Whyte Museum of the Canadian Rockies, Banff, 1990). She has also had a steady history of solo shows with the Paul Kuhn Gallery in Calgary and the Atelier Gallery in Vancouver. Among her notable group exhibitions are *Visions of Nature* (Glenbow Museum, Calgary, 1992) and *The Painter's Newfoundland* (Art Gallery of Newfoundland and Labrador, touring, 1998).

JANET MITCHELL (1912–98) was born in Medicine Hat. She worked for the federal Income Tax Department in Calgary from 1940, painting part-time until her retirement in 1962. Primarily self-taught, she attended night classes at the Provincial Institute of Technology and Art with Henry Glyde and Illingworth Kerr, and studied at the Banff School of Fine Arts in 1942, and in 1959 with Gordon Smith. On a visit to New York in 1950, she was impressed by the work of Paul Klee and Marc Chagall. Mitchell joined the Calgary Sketch Club in 1936 and the Alberta Society of Artists in 1946. She received an honorary doctorate from the University of Calgary in 1988.

GERALDINE MOODIE (1854–1945) was born in Toronto. Starting in the 1880s, she was stationed in Calgary, Medicine Hat, and Lethbridge, Alberta; and Battleford and Maple Creek, Saskatchewan, with her husband, an officer with the North-West Mounted Police. She opened her first photographic studio in Battleford in 1895, but had to re-establish her studio repeatedly as her husband was reassigned to different towns. She had a thirty-year career in photography, recording the West. Although she did studio work on an ongoing basis, she also travelled around the district, working outdoors. Her documentary photographs record prairie and range life, the First Nations, the Mounted Police, domestic scenes, and portraits. One of her first projects in 1895 was to photograph a sun dance ceremony near Battleford, Saskatchewan. She was a rarity at the time: a female professional photographer on the western frontier. The best-documented collection of her photographs is held at the British Museum in London, England.

RON MOPPETT (1945–) was born in Eastbourne, Sussex, England. He immigrated to Canada with his family in 1957 and attended the Alberta College of Art (1963–67). In 1968, he attended the Instituto de Allende in San Miguel, Mexico. Moppett has a long association with the art gallery at the Alberta College of Art and Design, serving as its curator from 1969 to 1971 and 1975 to 1978, and its director-curator from 1985 to 2005. (With John Hall, he also organized Marion Nicoll's first retrospective for the Edmonton Art Gallery in 1975.) His exhibiting history stretches from the late 1960s to the present. Notable solo efforts include a one-person show at Banff's Walter Phillips Gallery (1982); a show at New York's 49th Parallel Center for Contemporary Art (1988); several shows at Paul Kuhn Fine Arts (Calgary); *Painting Nature With a Mirror*, 1974–1989 (touring, Glenbow Museum, 1990); and most recently a show at TrépanierBaer, Calgary. Moppett received the Victor Lynch-Staunton Award (1987) and the Gershon Iskowitz Prize (1997) for his contribution to Canadian painting.

NICHOLAS EVERARD MORANT (1910–99) was born in Kamloops, British Columbia. Self-taught, during the Depression he began to work for the *Winnipeg Free Press*, then did public relations for Canadian Pacific Railway (CPR) from 1928 to 1935 and again from 1939 to 1981, with a break during the Second World War when he was assigned to the Canadian Government Wartime Information Board. A cosmopolitan individual, his reputation grew far beyond CPR through the thousands of photographs he produced. He photographed people, hotels, steamships, airlines, oil wells, mines, and logging activities for magazines, including the *National Geographic*. His photographs were used on stamps and on the ten, fifty, and one hundred dollar bank notes used at the time. He settled in Banff in the 1950s. In 1990, he was awarded the Order of Canada.

EDMOND MORRIS (1871–1913) was born in Perth, Ontario. He studied in Toronto, at the Art Students' League in New York, and at the Académie Julian and Ecole des Beaux-Arts in Paris. He returned to Toronto in 1896, becoming an associate of the Royal Canadian Academy and a founding member of the Canadian Art Club. He was commissioned by various Canadian government agencies to paint portraits of First Nations and completed over fifty of these, including chiefs and warriors of the Cree and Blackfoot nations.

FLORENCE MORTIMER (1885–1959) was born in Wakkerstroom, South Africa. She studied at the South Kensington Art School in London, England, and then taught art in Newport, Wales. She came to Canada in 1908, settling initially in Peace River country. In 1926, she moved to Edmonton and became one of the first art teachers in the city, teaching privately. Her students included Dorothy Barnhouse and Thelma Manarey. She joined the Edmonton Art Club about 1923, and in 1937, the Alberta Society of Artists.

CHERIE MOSES (1949–) was born in Cleveland, Ohio. In addition to a bachelor's degree in English literature, she has a bachelor of fine arts in photography and printmaking (1976, Nova Scotia College of Art and Design, Halifax), followed by a master of visual arts degree in printmaking and mixed media (1979, University of Alberta, Edmonton). Since 1980 she has worked as an instructor in fine arts at Grant MacEwan Community College in Edmonton, and also serves as chair of the program. Her exhibition record dates from 1974, with participation in group and solo shows featuring her printmaking, photography, painting, mixed media, video, and performance. Notable solo efforts include *Brides and Opening Ceremonies* (touring mixed media exhibition and performance event that premiered at SUB Art Gallery, Edmonton, 1981); and *Short Stories* (Stride Gallery Calgary, 1986, and Galerie Powerhouse, Montreal, 1987). Her videos, which examine the role of women, have been featured in film and video festivals across the country and also in New York.

DOUGLAS MOTTER (1913–) was born in Chicago and immigrated to Canada in 1919. He received a bachelor of fine arts from the University of Missouri, Columbia, in 1935. From 1960 to 1968 he taught part-time at the Alberta College of Art, and from 1968 to 1979 he taught full-time in weaving, drawing, and design. He was a member of the Alberta Society of Artists and served as its president in both 1954–55 and 1964–67. He helped found the Calgary Allied Art Centre and served on its board for eighteen years. He began weaving in 1945 and established a custom hand-weaving business in 1961.

RICHARD BARRINGTON NEVITT (1850–1928) was born in Savannah, Georgia. He studied in Quebec and Toronto, where he received a bachelor of medicine degree in 1874. He joined the North-West Mounted Police in 1874 and was stationed at Fort Macleod, Alberta, as an assistant surgeon until 1878. With his job, he travelled around the region, providing medical attention to the Mounties, as well as the local First Nations. It is likely that he learned to draw as part of his medical studies and he became a keen recorder of daily life during his stay in Alberta. He has left an important historical record, the most notable event being the only record of the historic signing of Treaty No. 7. In 1881, the *Canadian Illustrated News* published engravings based on his work. He became a prominent Toronto surgeon after he left southern Alberta.

JAMES MCLAREN NICOLL (1892–1986) was born in Fort Macleod. He trained as a civil engineer at the University of Alberta, obtaining a bachelor of science degree in 1924. Trained as a professional draughtsman, he had a keen eye for structure and form and was attentive to detail. He began to paint in 1930. He met Marion MacKay at the Calgary Sketch Club and they married in 1940. He was a member of the Alberta Society of Artists and served as its president from 1950 to 1952. A poet and writer, he was the founding editor of the Alberta Society of Artist's *Highlights* magazine. He attended the Emma Lake workshop in 1957, and studied at the Art Student's League in New York from 1958 to 1959.

MARION NICOLL (1909–85) was born in Calgary. She attended the Ontario College of Art from 1926 to 1928, where she studied with Frank Johnston. On her return to Calgary, she attended the Provincial Institute of Technology and Art, where A. C. Leighton told her she had not learned how to draw or use colour properly! After her graduation from the institute in 1933, she became a full instructor there and had a distinguished teaching career until 1966. In 1937, she spent a year in London, England, studying design. Jock Macdonald introduced her to the surrealist idea of automatic drawing in 1946. In 1957, she attended the Emma Lake workshop under Will Barnet, followed by a year in New York studying with him at the Art Students' League. Barnet guided Nicoll's work towards abstraction. From New York, she travelled widely in Europe with her husband Jim (James Nicoll). In 1970, Nicoll ceased painting due to arthritis.

WILLIAM MCFARLANE NOTMAN (1857–1913) was the son of William Notman (1826–91), who came to Montreal from Scotland in 1856 and established a photographic studio in 1857 or 1858, which became the largest of its kind in Canada. Notman apprenticed in his father's studio, and became a partner of William Notman & Son in 1882. On his father's death in 1891, he took over the business with his brother. Notman made eight trips west from 1884 to 1909 for Canadian Pacific Railway. The photographs he took were used to promote the use of the railway for tourism and settlement. During his first trips, he concentrated on the spectacular scenery of the mountains and the railway. Later, he focused on Native life, farming, and rural communities. The Notman company gained wide distribution for their photographs through publication, as well as sales in trains and train stations, hotels and resorts, and in their various studios.

LUCIUS O'BRIEN (1832–99) was born at Shanty Bay on Lake Simcoe, Ontario. He graduated from the Upper Canada College in Toronto and worked in an architect's office, where he learned surveying and drawing and became a civil engineer. Self-taught as an artist, he painted as a hobby from about 1852 to 1872, working full-time as an artist from 1872, when he joined the Ontario Society of Artists. He became its vice-president in 1874. He became a charter member of the Royal Canadian Academy and was its first president from 1880 until 1890. He travelled to the Rockies in 1886, 1887, and 1888. He died in Toronto.

KATIE OHE (1937–) was born in Peers, Alberta. She studied at the Provincial Institute of Technology and Art with instruction from Luke Lindoe, Illingworth Kerr, Walter Drohan, and her mentor, Marion Nicoll. After receiving a diploma in 1957, she undertook studies in art education with Arthur Lismer at the Montreal School of Art and Design (1958–59), where she was first exposed to sculpture, and graduate studies in sculpture at New York's Sculpture Centre (1961–63), where she cast a number of her sculptures in bronze and aluminum. In 1964, she learned welding at Dominion Bridge in Calgary and then established her own studio with welding equipment. She made her first steel sculptures in 1968. She taught ceramics and sculpture from 1960 to 1967 at the Calgary Allied Art Centre. Her early sculpture was mainly in clay and cement and she did commissions in cement in the 1960s. In 1970, Ohe returned to the Calgary-based art college and has since made an important contribution as a long-time instructor. Her own abstract and figurative work consists of clay and cement assembled sculpture; kinetic art in steel, bronze, and aluminum; and smaller-scale works for the wall in steel. Significant solo exhibitions include *Markers: Katie Ohe* (Glenbow Museum, 1989); the catalogued *Katie Ohe* (Illingworth Kerr Gallery, Alberta College of Art, 1991); and *Sculpture Prayers* (Stride Gallery, Calgary, 2002). In 1991, Ohe received the Alberta College of Art and Design Medal of Excellence and an honourary doctorate from the University of Calgary in 2001. In 2002 she received the Queen's Jubilee Medal R.C.A. (Royal College of Art).

ROBERT OLDRICH (1920–83) was born in Ostrava, Czechoslovakia, where he trained as a craftsman. He came to Canada in 1951, moving to Calgary in 1958. He taught crafts at the Alberta College of Art for four years and began mural commissions in the late 1950s. In 1962, he went into private business producing architectural commissions, applying relief designs to architectural panels. He completed many commissions, including murals for Palliser Square One, the Calgary Public Library, and both painted and sculptural murals for the Glenbow Museum. His sculptural materials were primarily concrete and welded steel.

WILLIAM JOHN OLIVER (1887–1954) was born in Canterbury, Kent, England. In 1910, he immigrated to southern Alberta. He began his photography career working as a camera assistant at the Frederick B. Cooper Photographic Studio in Calgary. In 1911, he began working for the *Morning Albertan* and also joined the *Calgary Herald* as a staff photographer. He opened the W. J. Oliver Photographic Studio in 1912. Throughout the 1920s and 1930s he took many photographs of Calgary streets, events, institutions, personalities, and businesses, as well as photographs of Alberta's ranching and oil industries. He became extremely skilful at catching the action of Stampede events, of wildly plunging horses, twisting steers, and fast-moving cowboys. He travelled nationally, photographing for the National Parks Branch, Fox News, and others. Oliver retired in 1942.

LYNDAL OSBORNE (1940–) was born in Newcastle, New South Wales, Australia. She has a bachelor of arts degree (National Art School, Sydney, 1960) and a master of fine arts degree (University of Wisconsin, Madison, 1971). Shortly after receiving her master's, Osborne obtained a teaching position in the department of art and design at the University of Alberta in Edmonton, and is now a professor emeritus after a teaching career that stretched from 1971 to 2004. Long associated with the department's highly regarded division of printmaking, Osborne is a multimedia artist with a strong reputation as a printmaker. Since the 1990s, she has also become known as an installation artist able to work with nature-based materials on a grand scale. She has exhibited nationally and internationally in over three hundred exhibitions, including *Edmonton Contemporary Prints* (Edmonton Art Gallery, 1988) and *Lines of Site: Ideas, Forms and Materialities* (London and Toyko, 1999). Her solo exhibitions include *Songs of Stone* (Edmonton, Buenos Aires, and Montevideo, 1990) and *The Poetic Structure of the World* (Edmonton and Lethbridge, 1999). In 2004, Osborne was awarded the City of Edmonton's Salute to Excellence.

SHELLEY OUELLET (1964–) was born in Edmonton. She obtained a bachelor of fine arts degree in printmaking and painting at the University of Calgary in 1991. She then fully immersed herself in the artist-run art scene in Calgary by serving as the director of the Stride Gallery from 1991 to 1995. Subsequently, she trained as a Web-designer and used this experience to teach classes in the new media arts and digital technology program at the Alberta College of Art and Design. Dedicated to creating site-specific projects with collaboration and input from others in the making of the specific work, Ouellet first attracted widespread attention with her multiple versions of *Entomology*, an installation first displayed at Calgary's Truck gallery (1994). This was followed by other installations incorporating a variety of media, including sequins, beads, and video and digital technology. Ouellet's installations have been showcased in solo and group exhibitions throughout the country, including the inaugural *Alberta Biennial of Contemporary Art* (Edmonton Art Gallery and Glenbow Museum, 1996); *Shiny* (Latitude 53, Edmonton, and Gallery 101, Ottawa, 1999–2000); *Marilyn* (solo, Vancouver, 1999); *Bonjour. Je m'appelle Shelley Ouellet* (Quebec City, 2000); *Obsession* (group, The Works, Edmonton, 2001); *Wish you were here ...* (Saskatoon, Fredericton, St. Catharines, and Calgary, 2001–2002).

WILLIAM PANKO (1892–1948) was born in Tulukow, Austria, and came to Canada in 1911. He worked on farms, likely in southern Alberta, in the summer and in Drumheller coal mines in the winter. He contracted tuberculosis in 1937 and spent ten years in the Baker Memorial Sanatorium. He took up painting as a therapy guided by Marion Nicoll. Under her encouragement he began painting. She was insistent that he not receive any formal instruction but follow his innate talent.

GREG PAYCE (1956–) was born in Edmonton, Alberta. He earned a bachelor of fine arts (University of Alberta, 1977) and later, after further study in ceramics at The Banff Centre and art history at the University of Victoria, he obtained a master's degree at the Nova Scotia College of Art & Design (1987). Since 1989 he has been on the faculty of the ceramics department at the Alberta College of Art & Design. In 1991 he received a Canada Council project/travel grant to study in Italy and Crete. Known for his virtuoso craftsmanship, decorative flair, and ability to blend the ceramic traditions of other cultures into a contemporary practice, Payce's vessels have been critically praised and exhibited in a wide range of group and solo exhibitions nationally and internationally. Notable exhibitions include a 1995 catalogued survey of Payce's art at the Southern Alberta Art Gallery (Lethbridge), participation in the 1995 *Clay in Canada-North by Northwest* (Minneapolis, Calgary & Edmonton), and the 1996 internationally touring *White on White* organized by the Canadian Clay and Glass Gallery (Waterloo). He has also exhibited to much critical attention in New York at the Nancy Margolis Gallery.

GRAHAM PEACOCK (1945–) was born in London, England. In 1966, he graduated from the School of Art, Goldsmith's College, London, England, and pursued post-graduate painting and sculpture at Leeds College of Art, England (1966–67). In 1969, he joined the teaching staff at the University of Alberta and served as professor of painting until 2004. As an artist, he participated in such notable workshops as those of New York sculptor Michael Steiner at the Edmonton Art Gallery (1973) and the inaugural year of Triangle and Pine Plains, New York (1982). At these workshops, often a week or more in length, painters and sculptors gathered to experiment and develop new artwork in a collegial environment. Later Peacock was himself a workshop leader at Thupelo, Johannesburg, South Africa (1997). Early in his career, Peacock's work was curated in such national group exhibitions as *Canada x Ten* (touring show organized by the Winnipeg Art Gallery, 1974) and *Abstraction West* (National Gallery of Canada, Ottawa, 1976). More recently, his art was recognized in *Alberta Biennial of Contemporary Art, 2000* (Edmonton Art Gallery and Alberta College of Art and Design) and in American, European, and Canadian exhibits of NEW NEW PAINTING since 1990. He has over thirty solo presentations, including *Paint, Process and Spirit* (Edmonton Art Gallery, 1987) and *Circularity* (Vanderleelie Gallery, Edmonton, and the Art Gallery of Greater Victoria, 1994–95).

STANFORD PERROTT (1917–2001) was born in Claresholm. He studied at the Provincial Institute of Technology and Art in Calgary (with Henry Glyde), the Banff School of Fine Arts, Emma Lake (1957, with Will Barnet), and at the Pennsylvania Academy of Fine Arts in Philadelphia. In 1954, he studied with Hans Hofmann in Provincetown, Massachusetts, and in 1956, he studied with Will Barnet at the Art Student's League in New York. He began to teach at the institute in 1946, and was head of the school from 1967 to 1974, then retired to live in Bragg Creek. He was a member of the Alberta Society of Artists and served as its president from 1956 to 1958. Primarily a landscape artist, he worked mainly in watercolour.

DARREN JAMES PETERSEN (1966–) was born in Edmonton and grew up in Edson, Alberta. He received a bachelor of fine arts in glass with distinction from the Alberta College of Art and Design (1992). That same year, he studied Venetian glass-making techniques at the Pilchuck Glass School in Seattle, Washington. Part of a new generation of glass artists to emerge in the 1990s, Petersen creates glass sculpture and Venetian-inspired vessels at his studio in Red Deer. He also instructs regularly at the summer Series program at Red Deer College, whose facilities are important to the teaching of the glass medium in Alberta. Since graduating, his work has been featured in exhibitions about glass art and in the broader field of contemporary art. Examples of the latter include *New Economy* (Nickle Arts Museum, Calgary, 1994); *The Art of the Telephone* (Edmonton Art Gallery, 1995); and *Return to the Ideal* (Prairie Art Gallery, Grande Prairie, 2000). He has participated in exhibitions, including *A Treasury of Canadian Craft* (Canadian Craft Museum, Vancouver, 1992); *Containment: The Space Within* (Canadian Clay and Glass Gallery, Waterloo, Ontario, 1994); *ACAD Faculty and Alumni Exhibition* (Galerie Elena Lee, Montreal, 1997); and *Contemporary Glass International* (Goldesberry Gallery, Houston, Texas, 2000).

WALTER J. PHILLIPS (1884–1963) was born at Barton-on-Humber, Lincolnshire, England. He studied art part-time at the Birmingham School of Art, England, in 1899, and at Yarmouth School of Art, England, in 1901. From 1903, he spent four years in South Africa working at various jobs. After his return to England in 1907, he worked as a commercial artist in Manchester and London and then taught art at Bishop's School, Salisbury, from 1908 to 1913. After arriving in Winnipeg in 1913, he made etchings under the guidance of Cyril Barraud, but in 1916 turned to the woodcut. He had an international reputation, exhibited widely in Canada, the United States, and Britain, and was included in the British *Studio* magazine publications on the blockprint in 1919, 1927, and 1930. He was a prolific master printmaker, producing thirty etchings, 146 colour woodcuts, and over seventy wood engravings in his lifetime. From 1940 to 1959, he taught at the Banff Summer School, and at the Provincial Institute of Technology and Art from 1941 to 1949. He settled in Banff in 1943 and retired to Victoria, British Columbia, in 1959.

JANE ASH POITRAS (1951–) was born in historic Fort Chipewyan, located on Alberta's northern Lake Athabasca. Raised by a foster parent in Edmonton, it was not until the age of twenty that she returned to "Fort Chip" and rediscovered her Cree heritage. After obtaining a bachelor of science in microbiology at the University of Alberta in 1977, she became interested in art and pursued a bachelor of fine arts degree in printmaking at the same university (1983) and a master in fine arts in printmaking at Columbia University in New York (1985). While at Columbia she completed the *Sweatlodge Etchings* (1985) based on her own experiences in the sweatlodge ceremony, a spiritual cleansing ritual traditional to the Cree and other Plains people. Later, taking a mixed media approach, she incorporated photographs, text, and found objects into paintings that address the experience and history of First Nations peoples. She has participated in important group shows, including *Stardusters* (touring, Thunder Bay Art Gallery, 1986); *Beyond History* (Vancouver Art Gallery, 1989); *4th Biennial Native American Fine Arts Invitational* (The Heard Museum, Pheonix, 1990); *INDIGENA* (Canadian Museum of Civilization, Hull, Quebec, 1999). Her solo efforts include *Sweatlodge Etchings* (Museum of Anthropology, University of British Columbia, 1987); *Indigenous Blackboards* (Woltjen/Udell Gallery, Vancouver, 1990); and *Who Discovered The Americas?* (Thunder Bay Art Gallery, 1992–93).

HARRY POLLARD (1880–1968) was born in Ontario, the son of a photographer, from whom he learned his trade. Arriving in Calgary in 1899, he opened a photographic studio on Stephen Avenue. He photographed prominent citizens, agriculture, ranching and industry, the evolution of the resource industries, the Calgary Stampede, and the Klondike gold rush of 1888–89. He regularly visited Blackfoot, Blood, Sarcee, and Stoney reserves, winning the people's confidence and taking hundreds of photographs. He was appointed press photographer for the Associated Screen News in 1924. He worked as a cinematographer, and began extensive travels photographing famous sites around the world. Closer to home, he spent summers in Banff, photographing famous visitors and promotional views. He retired in 1954.

MELTON PRIOR (1845–1910) was born in England. He worked for *The Illustrated London News* as a reporter-artist. He visited Canada in 1878, travelled across the country in 1888 on the Canadian Pacific Railway, and in 1901 accompanied the tour of the Duke and Duchess of Cornwall.

RAW EATER (active 1880s), a Siksika from southeast Alberta, was a respected leader and warrior among the Siksika during the late nineteenth century.

LAURA EVANS REID (1883–1951) was born in Guelph, Ontario, and moved to Vegreville, Alberta, in 1912. She began to paint in 1935, and organized the Vegreville Art Club and Community Art program in 1936. She studied at the Banff School of Fine Arts in 1937 with Henry Glyde. In 1937, she was instrumental in initiating the first University of Alberta extension art courses in the province, taught by Glyde, which she herself then taught from 1947. She was admired for her originality and was conversant with the avant garde, including American abstract expressionism.

D. B. ROBINSON (active 1875–76) from Cumberland, England, came to Canada to visit his friend Colonel James Macleod and to hunt and paint. While at Fort Macleod, he often sketched with Richard Nevitt. He painted primarily portraits which he identified by inscribing the sitters' names, thus providing key historical information. His sketches have remarkable detail and are the only known depictions of certain Blackfoot individuals.

CLEVELAND ROCKWELL (1837–1907) was born in Youngstown, Ohio, and trained as an engineer. He joined the United States Coastal Survey in 1856. From 1868 until 1891, he spent most summers surveying large areas of Oregon. Rockwell painted as a hobby throughout his life, having studied painting for a year in England and Europe.

EDWARD ROPER (1857–1909) was born in Kent, England. In 1887 he made a tour of Canada, and four years later, he wrote *By Track and Trail: A Journey through Canada with Numerous Sketches by the Author*, which recorded his travels. He died in Hastings, East Sussex, in 1909.

ALEXANDER J. ROSS (1851–94) operated a photographic studio in Winnipeg from 1884 to 1886, when he moved to Calgary to open a branch office. He became known for his mountain views, Native subjects, and studio portraits. He owned a ranch west of Calgary, where he died in 1894.

CARL RUNGIUS (1869–1959) was born in Rixdorf, Germany, and studied at the Royal Academy of Arts in Berlin. In 1894, he made his first visit to the United States and in 1897 he returned to New York to set up a studio. He developed a love of wildlife and hunted in Wyoming and New Brunswick. He began to produce illustrations for outdoor magazines, such as *Forest and Stream*. In 1910, Alberta guide Jimmy Simpson invited Rungius to visit the Canadian Rockies to hunt. This began the pattern for the rest of his life: summers in Banff travelling, studying wildlife, and producing hundreds of sketches in pencil and oil paint; and winters in New York, painting in his studio. From 1913 to 1933, he worked on commissions to document North American big game for the New York Zoological Society. In 1924, he began to make etchings with drypoint, producing forty-six etchings by 1938—this became his "bread and butter."

ROBERT W. RUTHERFORD (1857–1933) was born in Northumberland, England. He was educated in Halifax and at King's College in Windsor, Nova Scotia. He studied art at the Ottawa Art School in 1885. He then joined the Royal Canadian Artillery and in 1885 served in Battleford, Saskatchewan, and in the campaign against Big Bear during the Riel Rebellion. During the military campaign in the West, he contributed illustrations to journals in the East.

DELI SACILOTTO (1936–) was born in Kimberley, British Columbia. He studied at the Provincial Institute of Technology and Art, graduating in 1958. He also studied at the Art Student's League in New York in 1960; at the Pratt Graphics Centre in New York in 1961; and at the Instituto Statale di Belle Arte in Urbino, Italy, in 1965. He was an instructor at the Alberta College of Art from 1961 to 1964, where he set up the print department, teaching part-time. He then moved to the United States, where he taught and wrote an important book on printmaking with Donald Saff, *Printmaking; History and Process* (New York: Holt, Rinehart and Winston, 1978).

MARY SCHÄFFER (1861–1939) was born in Westchester, Pennsylvania. Author, photographer, and botanist, she first visited the Rockies with her friend Mary Vaux in 1889 where she met her future husband, Dr. Charles Schäffer. She returned the following year with him, and after that they travelled annually to the mountains to study botany. Mary continued with her visits after Charles's death in 1903, often travelling in remote regions. She made detailed drawings and photographs of alpine flora. She settled in Banff in 1912 and married her guide, Billy Warren, in 1915.

MARY SCOTT (1948–) was born in Calgary. She was awarded a bachelor of fine arts with distinction at the University of Calgary in 1978. Two years later, she obtained a master of fine arts from the Nova Scotia College of Art and Design in Halifax. In addition to her art practice, Scott has a long history of teaching, administering studio programs (at the Banff Centre, Nova Scotia College of Art and Design, and Alberta College of Art and Design), and creating exhibiting opportunities for other artists. In 1985, Scott, along with Don Corman and Colleen O'Neill, established the artist-run Stride Gallery in Calgary. From 1988 to 1989, she established and directed << >> dl Gallery, and then in 1993 created OWW! (One White Wall!) at her Calgary home. Since 1984, Scott has taught at the Alberta College of Art and Design in painting and drawing and more recently in media arts and digital technologies. During a twenty-year period from 1980 to 2000 she participated in nearly fifty group exhibitions across the country, including the National Gallery of Canada's *Songs of Experience* (1986) and the *Canadian Biennial of Contemporary Art* (1989). Her key solo shows include two travelling exhibitions: *Paintings 1978–1985*, organized by Regina's Dunlop Art Gallery (1986) and *Mary Scott* (Southern Alberta Art Gallery, Lethbridge, 1989).

ROBERT AUSTIN SCOTT (1941–) was born in Melfort, Saskatchewan. He received a diploma of applied arts at the Alberta College of Art in 1969, and a master's in visual arts at the University of Alberta in 1976. He attended New York sculptor Michael Steiner's workshop for painters and sculptors at the Edmonton Art Gallery in 1973, and participated in the inaugural Triangle workshop for painters and sculptors in Plain Pines, New York, in 1982. From 1976 to 1982, he worked as a sessional art instructor at the University of Alberta. His work has been selected to appear in such key survey exhibitions as *Alberta Now* (Edmonton Art Gallery, 1980) and *Survey Alberta '88* (Olympic Arts Festival, Calgary). His notable solo exhibitions include *Robert Scott: Paintings of the 1980s* (Edmonton Art Gallery, 1986); *Robert Scott's Paintings* (Gallery Moos, Toronto and New York, 1987) and *Recent Work by Robert Scott: 1987–1993* (Edmonton Art Gallery, travelling exhibition, 1994–95).

OREST SEMCHISHEN (1932–) was born in Mundare, Alberta, in what is known as "Kalyna Country": a twenty-thousand-square-kilometre area east of Edmonton that served as the largest "bloc" settlement of Ukrainian pioneers in Canada. (Semchishen's paternal grandparents settled in the Mundare area in the late 1890s.) A radiologist by training, Semchishen is primarily self-taught as a photographer, but did study with the American photographer Hubert Hohn, in a University of Alberta extension course Hohn taught in 1972. It was through Hohn that Semchishen became aware of the history of fine art photography, including the documentary style that he himself adopted. His documentation of pioneer Eastern Rite Churches was first publicly seen in *Ten Albums* (National Film Board of Canada, Ottawa, 1975) and then followed by his first solo exhibition, *Byzantine Churches of Alberta* (Edmonton Art Gallery, 1976). Other selected exhibitions include *Bunka* (Southern Alberta Art

Gallery, Lethbridge, 1983); *Orest Semchishen. A Survey of Photographs 1973–1983* (Edmonton Art Gallery, 1983); *Trappers* (Whyte Museum, Banff, 1989); and *In Plain View/Voix Clair* (Canadian Museum of Contemporary Photography, Ottawa, 1994).

BLAKE SENINI (1954–) was born in Nanaimo, British Columbia. From 1971 to 1973 he studied ceramics and sculpture at Malaspina College in Nanaimo and then moved to study sculpture under Mowry Baden and Roland Brener at the University of Victoria in 1975, where he earned a bachelor of fine arts in sculpture. He later received a master of fine arts degree at the University of Calgary in 1981. Since 1982, Senini has taught sculpture at the Alberta College of Art and Design. His exhibiting history gathered momentum in the mid-1980s with a unique body of two-sided narrative sculpture made with plaster. Selected exhibitions of his work include *Five Sculptors from Southern Alberta* (Whyte Museum, Banff, 1985); *In Sweet and Vicious Memory* (Off Centre Centre, Calgary, 1986); *Blake Senini* (Southern Alberta Art Gallery, Lethbridge, 1987); *Gang of Three* (Plug-in Inc. and Ace Art, Winnipeg, Manitoba, 1987); and *Wall/Space (New Sculpture by Six Calgary Artists)* (Glenbow Museum, Calgary, 1987). At the end of the 1990s, solo and group exhibitions in Calgary (especially at Paul Kuhn Fine Arts), Montreal, and Regina showcased major changes in his sculpture, including new methods of fabrication and a less narrative approach.

MARGARET SHELTON (1915–84) was born in Bruce, Alberta, and was raised in Rosedale, near Drumheller. She studied art education at the Normal School in Calgary and art part-time at the Provincial Institute of Technology and Art from 1933 to 1943. She attended the Banff Summer School in 1935, 1937, and 1941. She taught intermittently early on in her career. She painted in watercolour and oils, but her lasting contribution is as a printmaker. She made her first linocut in 1936, as a result of Henry Glyde's teaching, and by 1984 had completed 174 prints.

J. GORDON SINCLAIR (1889–1980) was born in Komoka, Ontario, and moved to Edmonton in 1912. He took private classes from William Johnstone from 1913 to 1918 and then studied in Toronto in 1914, at the Chicago Art Institute in 1916 and 1925, and at the University of Washington in Seattle in 1929, 1930, 1932, and 1933. He was a charter member of the Edmonton Art Club, serving as president in 1927, 1934, and 1941, and was a member of the Alberta Society of Artists. He was the head of the art department at the Edmonton Technical School from 1919 to 1941.

JAMES AGRELL SMITH (1913–88) was born in Stettler, Alberta. Self-taught, he worked primarily as a wood engraver starting in 1948, producing prints and book illustrations. He received the G. A. Reid Award from the Society of Canadian Painter-Etchers and Engravers in 1953 for *Cariboo Cowboy,* 1952. He worked for the post office in Red Deer from 1954 to 1964.

JOHN SNOW (1911–2004) was born in Vancouver and worked for the Royal Bank from 1928 until 1971. After service in the Second World War, he began to paint seriously and from 1947 to 1949 studied at the Provincial Institute of Technology and Art in Calgary. In 1953, he salvaged two old lithographic presses and stones and taught himself lithography, experimenting and collaborating with his close friend Maxwell Bates to produce the first artists' colour lithographs in Alberta. He was also a painter and sculptor. He was a member of the Alberta Society of Artists.

JEFFREY SPALDING (1951–) was born in Edinburgh, Scotland. He obtained a bachelor's degree in fine art at the University of Guelph, Ontario in 1972, a master's degree in art education at Ohio State University in 1975, and a master of fine arts degree at the Nova Scotia College of Art and Design in 1976. Spalding is a recognized artist, educator, writer, and art museum professional. For seventeen years Spalding was a professor of art, the director of the art gallery, and later assistant dean at the school of fine arts at the University of Lethbridge. Among his many accomplishments, he oversaw the building of a permanent collection at the University of Lethbridge from 212 art objects in 1982 to an acclaimed collection of 15,000 art works by 1999. As an artist, he first achieved notoriety with a unique approach to abstract painting based on colour theory. This artwork was highlighted in *Jeffrey Spalding: The Black Paintings* (Southern Alberta Art Gallery, Lethbridge, 1982). Later in the 1980s, Spalding's contemporary treatment of the landscape appeared in both solo and notable group exhibitions about new landscape-based art (*Culture's Nature*, Dunlop Art Gallery, Regina, 1986; *Eye of Nature II*, Walter Phillips Gallery, Banff, 1989). His paintings have also been highlighted in diverse presentations about art from Alberta, including the touring *Seven Artists from Alberta: Art in this Region* (1987) and more recently *Concealing/Revealing: Voices from the Canadian Foothills* (1997). In 1992, Spalding received the Alberta College of Art Board of Governors Award of Excellence.

RONALD SPICKETT (1926–) was born in Regina. He studied at the Provincial Institute of Technology and Art from 1946 to 1949 and at the Instituto Allende in San Miguel, Mexico, in 1955 and 1956, after which he spent a year living in Mexico. His study of Mexican murals had a profound influence on his work. He was an editorial cartoonist in Regina, and a display artist in Toronto and Calgary. He taught at the institute from 1957 to 1967 and then at the University of Calgary (1967–80). He retired from painting in the early 1980s when he converted to Zen Buddhism.

ED SPITERI (1939–) was born in Calgary and studied photography at the Southern Institute of Technology and Art in Calgary. He worked part-time in audio-visual electronics while he was developing his photography career. He was influenced by American photographers W. Eugene Smith and Walker Evans. He began producing photo essays in the 1960s, producing sets of twenty to thirty-five photographs: *Street People of Britain,* mid-1960s; *Malta*, mid-1960s; and a series focusing on a Hutterite colony at Standoff, Alberta, late 1960s. His photo series in 1971 on life behind bars in Alberta jails was published in Germany and helped to launch his international career. An important collaborative project was *Between Friends*, 1975–76, a cross-border project with Canadian and American photographers. He has exhibited widely and has photographs included in major collections throughout Canada.

HELEN STADELBAUER (1910–2006) was born in Calgary. She studied at the Provincial Institute of Technology and Art and the Banff School of Fine Arts. After this she studied at the University of Iowa, where she obtained a bachelor of science and a master of arts from Columbia University in New York. She established the art division at the University of Alberta at Calgary in 1960, modelled on the program at Columbia University. Active with the university for thirty-one years, she was a member of the Alberta Society of Artists. She taught in both the art education faculty and in the bachelor-of-arts program in the faculty of fine arts.

WILLIAM LEROY STEVENSON (1905–66) was born in Guelph, Ontario, and moved to Calgary in 1910. He studied with Lars Haukaness at the Provincial Institute of Technology and Art. There he met Maxwell Bates with whom he travelled to Chicago in 1929, where his experience of modern painting laid the foundation for his mature art. From 1930 to 1945 he lived in Vancouver, returning to Calgary in 1954.

KENNETH G. STURDY (1920–) was born in Pen-y-lan, Wales. He graduated from the Loughborough College of Art, Loughborough, Leicestershire, England, and from the Chelsea School of Art in London in 1953. He came to Canada in 1954. Committed to teaching, he taught at the Provincial Institute of Technology and Art in Calgary from 1954 to 1962, as well as at the Dunton School in Montreal from 1963 to 1966, and the Glasgow School of Art from 1966 to 1967. In 1967, he returned to the Alberta College of Art, becoming the head of the college from 1974 to 1982. He served as president of the Alberta Society of Artists from 1971 to 1973.

LEILA SUJIR (1951–) was born in Hyderabad, India, and speaks of herself as being from two cultures, the Albertan culture of her mother's family and the Indian culture of her father's. Living in Calgary from the age of eight onward, she obtained a bachelor's degree in literature from the University of Alberta (1972), studied experimental film at the Nova Scotia College of Art and Design (1974), and then undertook graduate work at the University of Calgary (1979, 1985). In 1972, she directed her first documentary work, *Spectra*. As a writer, video artist, and instructor, Sujir has addressed a broad range of artistic and social issues through her videotapes and video installations, as well as her own personal story. Selected video work includes *India Hearts Beat* (1988, later shown at New York's Museum of Modern Art, 1994); *My Two Grandmothers, Her Great Grandfather, and Me* (1991); *Working Portraits* (1992); and *The Dreams of the Night Cleaners* (1994, also Special Jury Prize winner at the Alberta Motion Picture Industry Awards, 1995). Her work has been exhibited nationally and internationally, and has also been aired on the ACCESS Network and Women's Television Network. In 2000, a survey of her work was presented at Lethbridge's Southern Alberta Art Gallery.

GERALD TAILFEATHERS (1925–75) was born on the Blood Reserve near Cardston. He was educated at a residential school. For three summers, starting in 1935, he studied with American artist Winold Reiss, who was primarily a portrait painter, in Montana. He studied watercolour with Walter Phillips at the Banff School of Fine Arts in 1941, and completed the three-year art program at the Provincial Institute of Technology and Art in Calgary in 1944. He worked as a draughtsman. In 1959, he returned to the reserve to devote himself full-time to painting.

TAKAO (TAK) TANABE (1926–) was born in Seal Cove, British Columbia. As a young man, he was detained along with his family and twenty-one thousand other Japanese-Canadians and sent inland during the Second World War. Eventually, after several years working as an indentured labourer, he ended up in Winnipeg where he entered the Winnipeg School of Art (1946). After leaving school in 1949, Tanabe continued to practise and study his craft at home and abroad, working at one point with teachers like Hans Hofmann and Reuben Tam in New York. He eventually settled in Vancouver, where he became a member of that city's painting vanguard. From 1973 to 1980, after a stint as a hard-edge abstract artist in Philadelphia and New York, Tanabe became the head of the Banff Centre's art department where he overhauled its programs and set the school on its professional course. It was during this period that he embarked on his groundbreaking landscape series, *The Land* (1973–80). After Banff, Tanabe returned to the west coast, where he continued to focus on painting landscapes in western Canada, the North, and abroad. Solo exhibitions of Tanabe's work have been presented in most of Canada's major cities, as well as Rome, Tokyo, and London. His work can be found in the collections of all of Canada's major galleries, and he has a number of major mural commissions to his credit. In 2003, Tanabe was awarded the prestigious Governor General's Award in Visual and Media Arts.

JACK TAYLOR (1917–70) was born in Charlottetown, Prince Edward Island. In 1936, he spent two years studying at the Art Student's League in New York. He taught art in Charlottetown, and after the Second World War studied at the Ontario College of Art. In 1947, he started teaching at the University of Alberta and the Banff School of Fine Arts. In 1955, he took a sabbatical leave to study at the Slade School of Art in London.

CARROLL (MOPPETT) TAYLOR-LINDOE (1948–) was born in Calgary, the daughter of artists Luke and Vivian Lindoe. She was educated at the Alberta College of Art in Calgary (1966–67, 1974–75), and at the Instituto de Allende in San Miguel, Mexico (1968). She spent several years making sculpture from clay; examples of this work appear in the *History of Ceramics in Alberta* (Edmonton Art Gallery and Alberta College of Art Gallery, 1975). In 1977, she abandoned clay in favour of rudimentary sculpture made from twigs and cloth, and then in 1978 took up milled lumber, which eschews a crafted finish. This development is tracked in *Alberta Works in Wood* (Alberta College of Art Gallery, 1979) and more fully in the touring *Carroll Moppett Sculpture and Drawings* (Glenbow Museum, 1981). The 1980s was a period of national recognition for Taylor-Lindoe, who also began to produce paintings with multiple images. Her selected group shows include *The Winnipeg Perspective-Ritual* (Winnipeg Art Gallery, 1981); *Drawing—A Canadian Survey 1977–82* (Centre Saidye Bronfman, Montreal, 1983); *Art in This Region: Seven Alberta Artists* (touring, London and Bury, United Kingdom; Paris, 1984); *Alberta Biennial of Contemporary Art* (Edmonton Art Gallery and Glenbow Museum, 1996); and *Transformations: Imaging Nature* (Mendel Art Gallery, Saskatoon, 1998). In addition, her contributions have been recognized in *Carroll Moppett, Survey 1985–1992* (Illingworth Kerr Gallery, Calgary, 1992); and *Carroll Taylor-Lindoe: 1980–2000* (TrépanierBaer Gallery, Calgary, 2000).

TWO GUN (PERCY PLAINSWOMAN) (ca. 1885–1961) was born on the Blood Reserve in Alberta and educated at St. Mary's Residential School. He worked as a cowboy. Self-taught, he began to paint in the mid-1930s. He painted murals in the Prince of Wales Hotel in Waterton National Park. He was Gerald Tailfeather's uncle.

ROLF UNGSTAD (1929–82) was born in Ponoka, Alberta. He studied at the Banff School of Fine Arts in 1951 and at the Provincial Institute of Technology and Art in Calgary from 1952 to 1955, specializing in ceramics. He worked for Ceramic Arts, a commercial pottery studio established by Luke Lindoe. He was the first instructor in arts and crafts for the Alberta Cultural Activities branch. From 1959 to 1974 he was an instructor at the Alberta College of Art and was appointed the head of the craft division in 1966.

JESSIE URSENBACH (1895–1987) was born in New Harmony, Utah. She trained as an art teacher. She studied art in Lethbridge with Edith Fanny Kirk; at the University of Alberta Extension Department; at the Banff summer school with A. C. Leighton in 1937 and Walter Phillips in 1943; and at the Ontario College of Art. She was a charter member of the Lethbridge Sketch Club and a member of the Alberta Society of Artists. She was instrumental in helping to establish the University of Alberta summer art classes in Lethbridge under Henry Glyde in 1938. She taught art in schools in southern Alberta, and tutored pupils in Lethbridge.

MARY VAUX (1860–1940), **GEORGE VAUX** (1863–1927), and **WILLIAM VAUX** (1872–1908). The Vaux family were well-educated and widely travelled Victorians from Philadelphia, a major centre for photography. They first saw the Rockies in 1887 when they stayed at Glacier House in Roger's Pass and took the first photographs of Illecillewaet Glacier. In 1898 they began their first formal studies of glaciers and the mountain environment. They gave lectures at the Academy of Natural Sciences in Philadelphia and wrote scientific articles. The three siblings shared credit on publications and photographs. Most of the articles were by William, the brothers took most of the photographs, and Mary was responsible for the technical work on the photographs and did all of the printing. William died in 1908, and after 1911, George did not return to the Rockies. Mary took over the work completely and travelled to the Rockies each year until 1939.

LAURA-KIER VICKERSON (1959–) was born in Edmonton. After participating in two Summer Studio programs at the Banff School of Fine Arts (1975, 1977), she earned a bachelor of fine arts degree at the University of Alberta in 1981 and a master of fine arts degree at the University of Victoria in 1986. She has taught at both the University of Calgary (1989–94) and the Alberta College of Art and Design (1989–2001). In the 1990s, she was a major figure in installation art in the province and brought a lyrical feminist sensibility to her practice. Selected exhibitions of her work include *Hive* (solo, Muttart Art Gallery, Calgary, and Neutral Ground, Regina, 1991); *Velvet* (solo, Illingworth Kerr Gallery, Calgary, 1995, also Winnipeg, 1997, and Istanbul, Turkey, 1997); *Trace* (solo, Southern Alberta Art Gallery, Lethbridge, 1997, also Montreal, 2001); *Beauty and the Banal* (group, Edmonton Art Gallery, 1998); and *Alberta Biennial of Contemporary Art* (Edmonton Art Gallery and Nickle Arts Museum, 2002).

SANDRA VIDA (1947–) (formerly Sandra Tivy) was born in Calgary and is a visual artist of Scottish-Celtic descent. She has a background in psychology and English literature, as well as art, and has exhibited and presented her interdisciplinary work locally and internationally (Berlin, Dublin, Zurich, Glasgow). She has been a speaker, panellist, performer, and organizer at many arts conferences, and her critical writing has been published in national magazines and artist catalogues. As the administrative coordinator at the New Gallery in Calgary for over a decade (1980–95), she facilitated a wide variety of community-based cultural projects. She served as the national administrator of the Artist-Run Network in Toronto from 1993–95. In addition to writing and pursuing her art work, she is currently working as a freelance arts consultant and administrator.

PETER VON TIESENHAUSEN (1959–) was born in New Westminister, British Columbia, and raised in Alberta's northern Peace River country near Demmitt. His formal education in art consists of two years of painting at the Alberta College of Art (1979–81), several workshops, and more self-development through studio residencies at the Banff Centre and in Paris. Since 1990, he has worked full-time as an artist, first showing as a landscape painter but soon expanding his practice to include large-scale outdoor sculpture at his rural property near Demmitt and at other locations in Canada and abroad. His work also includes installations, works in bronze, videoed events, and on occasion, performance art. Highlights of his exhibition history include the travelling *Turbulent Terrrain* (Prairie Art Gallery, Grande Prairie, Alberta, 1989) and *Reframing the Landscape* (Whyte Museum, Banff, 1994). Solo exhibitions of his work include *Projects* (Prairie Art Gallery, 1994); *Forest Figures* (Stride Gallery, Calgary, 1997); and *Lebensläufe* (Kelowna Art Gallery, 1998).

SYLVAIN VOYER (1939–) was born in Edmonton. He attended the Provincial Institute of Technology and Art in Calgary from 1959 to 1961, studying with printmaker Deli Sacilotto and later collaborating with him at Sacilotto's New York studio in 1970. Voyer is a versatile artist who has worked in many media, including hard-edge painting in the 1960s. At a certain point in his career, he was also a noted printmaker with a long involvement in its varied repertoire (lithography, serigraphy, etchings, and woodcuts). In the print medium, his subject matter ranged from landscape to news-related issues and protest art of the 1960s and 1970s. It was through his printmaking activity that he teamed up with Harry Savage, later co-founding with Savage Latitude 53 Society of Artists in 1973, Alberta's first artist-run alternative gallery and resource centre of the post-1970 period. After producing a series of offset lithographs for the 1978 Commonwealth Games in Edmonton, Voyer stopped printing and committed himself to plein-aire (on-site) landscape painting. Exhibitions of his work include the commemorative *Founders Show* (Alberta College of Art Gallery, Calgary, 1986) and the important *Spaces and Places: Eight Decades of Landscape Painting in Alberta* (touring exhibition organized by the Alberta Art Foundation, Edmonton, 1986).

ELLA MAY WALKER (1892–1960) was born in Windon, Minnesota, and moved to Saskatchewan in 1902. Trained as a concert pianist, she taught music in Saskatoon and in Edmonton from 1920 to 1935. After meeting Arthur Lismer in 1932, she began to make art. She studied painting in the University of Alberta Extension Department in 1933 and later taught evening classes there. She joined the Edmonton Art Club and the Alberta Society of Artists in 1935. She attended the Emma Lake workshop in 1957, led by New York artist Will Barnet, and organized an Alberta Society of Artists workshop in Jasper in 1959 conducted by Gordon Smith.

HENRY JAMES WARRE (1819–98) was born in England and educated at Sandhurst Royal Military College. He joined the British army in 1837 and came to Canada in 1839 as aide-de-camp to his uncle, Sir Richard Downes Jackson, commander of forces in British North America. He was sent to the Oregon Territory from 1845 to 1846 on a secret military mission regarding the Canadian-American border question. He travelled via Fort Garry, across the prairies to Fort Edmonton, and then south through the Rockies, along the Columbia River into Oregon territory to Vancouver Island, and returned home by the same route. His sketches from this journey were subsequently published as lithographs in *Sketches in North America and the Oregon Territory* (London, 1848). He left Canada in 1846 and died in London.

GEORGE WEBER (1907–2002) was born in Munich, Germany, where he trained as a draughtsman. He studied at the Ontario College of Art. Moving to Edmonton in 1931, he formed his own company, Art Signs. He introduced silkscreen printing to Alberta and taught workshops at the University of Alberta Extension Department from 1949 to 1952 and at the Edmonton Art Gallery during the same years. He established the western chapter of the Society of Canadian Painter-Etchers and Engravers in 1954. In 1985, his serigraph of Moraine Lake was reproduced by Canada Post to commemorate the centennial of Banff National Park.

WHITE WOLF (active 1920s) Kainai. In the 1920s, he did a series of mural paintings for the Prince of Wales Hotel in Waterton Lakes National Park. Initially a warrior, in his later life he became a ceremonial leader.

CATHARINE ROBB WHYTE (1906–79) was born in Concord, Massachusetts, and studied at the School of the Museum of Fine Arts in Boston from 1925 to 1930, where she met her future husband, Peter Whyte. They were married in 1930, moved to Banff, and built a studio-home. With Peter, she painted extensively out of doors. As she was the one who took care of the household and family business, Catharine made less art than Peter. She began collecting historical Banff material and in 1968, opened the Whyte Museum of the Canadian Rockies, dedicated to Banff pioneers and the Rocky Mountain region.

PETER WHYTE (1905–66) was born in Banff. In his teens, he took classes with Belmore Browne in Banff and then studied art at the Otis Art Institute in Los Angeles from 1923 to 1924, and at the School of the Museum of Fine Arts in Boston from 1925 to 1929. He learned his landscape techniques from J. E. H. MacDonald, with whom he travelled to Lake O'Hara in the Rockies each summer from 1924 to 1930. In Banff, he worked extensively out of doors, producing many small oil sketches. After he developed cataracts in 1952, his painting decreased.

GARRY WILLIAMS (1956–2005) was born in Calgary. A major figure in Alberta's ceramic practice, Williams was one of a small number to cross over into the contemporary art field with his installations incorporating ceramic elements and public sculpture made from clay. He earned a ceramics diploma from the Alberta College of Art in 1978 and a master of fine arts degree from the Nova Scotia College of Art and Design in 1990. He also instructed at both the Alberta College of Art and Design and the University of Calgary, and was twice artist-in-residence at The Banff Centre. Major exhibitions of Williams's work include *Alberta Clay comes of age: Studio Ceramics in Alberta III, 1964–1984* (touring exhibition organized by the Alberta Art Foundation, 1986); *Same Song, Different Chorus* (Illingworth Kerr Gallery, Calgary, 1991); *clay between my fingers* (Walter Phillips Gallery, Banff, 1993); *Cathedrals* (Southern Alberta Art Gallery, Lethbridge, 1993); and *inside out: Four Canadian Ceramic Installations* (The George R. Gardiner Museum of Ceramic Art, Toronto, 1998). He undertook a number of public art commissions, including *Aesop's Fables* (2002), *Rabbit Rise* (1999), and *Chinook* (the latter being a series of manhole covers installed by the City of Calgary).

JAYNE WILLOUGHBY SCOTT (1955–) was born in Medicine Hat. After working as a registered nurse, Willoughby Scott began exhibiting fibre art both nationally and internationally in 1990. Working in the quilt medium, she describes her mixed media work as being experimental with images developed through layering and collage. She has won several awards for colour, design, and workmanship from the Canadian Quilters' Association and other juried shows, such as the Canadian Contemporary Quilt Exhibition and Pacific Northwest Quilt Show. Willoughby Scott has also exhibited across the country and in the United States. In 2001, she completed a bachelor of fine arts degree in art and design at the University of Alberta.

GEORGE WOOD (1932–) was born in Regina. He studied at the Provincial Institute of Technology and Art in Calgary from 1952 to 1956, where his most important teacher was Stan Perrott, and at the University of Manitoba in Winnipeg from 1957 to 1958. He was an instructor at the Alberta College of Art from 1962 to 1986 and the curator of the college's gallery from 1959 to 1967. He worked as an abstract artist throughout the 1960s, but by the 1970s his work became figurative in order to express his political and social concerns. He is also a sculptor and poet.

NORMAN YATES (1923–) was born in Calgary, Alberta, and raised in Regina. His career as an artist, teacher, designer, and mentor spans over five decades. A graduate of the Ontario College of Art in 1950 with first class honours, in 1954 Yates moved to Edmonton to take a teaching position at the University of Alberta. Yates taught a wide range of courses from art history to design, and participated in the Edmonton theatrical community as a stage designer. He retired as professor emeritus in 1989. While in Edmonton, he and Whynona, a recognized weaver who instructed in arts and crafts, played an important role as advocates for visual art. For this volunteer effort, he was awarded the City of Edmonton's Creative and Performing Art award in the Visual Arts (1972). His other major awards include Senior Arts Awards, Canada Council (1975); the McCalla Professorship (1985–86); and the A. C. Rutherford Award from the University of Alberta (1986). He has experimented with various media, including synthetic colours, light-sensitive emulsion on canvas, and mixed media constructions, and has worked with photography and film and produced murals. Solo exhibitions of his art date from 1952 to the present, including at the Brighton Art Gallery and Museum, Great Britain; the Edmonton Art Gallery; the Glenbow-Alberta Institute; the Art Gallery of Nova Scotia; the Art Gallery of Greater Victoria; and most recently, the Fran Willis Gallery, Victoria. Permanent installations of his murals and/or large-scale paintings can be found in Edmonton, Calgary, Whitehorse, and Victoria. Yates was elected to the Royal Canadian Academy of the Arts in 2000.

BIBLIOGRAPHY

The Historical Period to 1920 and A Sense of Place: Modern Art 1920–1970

Artist's files at Glenbow Museum and Alberta Foundation for the Arts.

Ainslie, Patricia. *A Lifelong Journey: The Art and Teaching of H. G. Glyde.* Calgary: Glenbow, 1987.

Ainslie, Patricia. *Margaret Shelton: Block Prints 1936–1984.* Calgary: Glenbow, 1985.

Alberta Clay comes of Age: Studio Ceramics in Alberta III, 1964–1984. Edmonton: Alberta Art Foundation, 1986.

Alberta Society of Artists: The First Seventy Years. Calgary: University of Calgary Press, 2000.

Bell, Michael. *Image of Canada.* Ottawa: Public Archives of Canada, 1972.

Birrell, Andrew. "Fortunes of a misfit, Charles Horetzky." *Alberta Historical Review* 19:1 (Winter 1971): 9–25.

Boulet, Roger. *Frederic Marlett Bell-Smith.* Victoria: Art Gallery of Greater Victoria, 1977.

Brownstone, Arni. *War Paint: Blackfoot and Sarcee Painted Buffalo Robes in the Royal Ontario Museum.* Toronto: Royal Ontario Museum, 1993.

Cavell, Edward. *Legacy in Ice, The Vaux Family and the Canadian Alps.* Banff: The Whyte Foundation, 1983.

Cavell, Edward and Jon Whyte. *Mountain Glory: The Art of Peter and Catharine Whyte.* Banff: Whyte Museum of the Canadian Rockies, 1988.

Chown, Diana. *Laura Evans Reid 1883–1951.* Edmonton: Ring House Gallery, University of Alberta, 1983.

Christensen, Lisa. *A Hiker's Guide to Art of the Canadian Rockies.* Calgary: Glenbow, 1996.

Cochran, Bente Roed. *Printmaking in Alberta 1945–1985.* Edmonton: The University of Alberta Press, 1989.

Collinson, Helen. "Ella May Walker." *Artichoke* 5:3 (Fall 1993): 14–19.

Dempsey, Hugh. *Treasures of the Glenbow Museum.* Calgary: Glenbow, 1991.

Dodd, Eric. *Initiatives: 1966–1976.* Calgary: Nickle Arts Museum, 1991.

Five Painters from Regina. Ottawa: National Gallery of Canada, 1961.

Ford, Susan. *35 Years and 15 Minutes: Prints by John Kenneth Esler.* Calgary: The Nickle Arts Museum, 1994.

Glenbow-Alberta Institute. *Jim Nicoll: Paintings and Poetry.* Calgary, 1977.

Glenbow. *Carl Rungius: Artist and Sportsman.* Toronto: Warwick Publishing, 2001.

Gribbon, Michael. *Walter J. Phillips.* Ottawa: National Gallery of Canada, 1978.

Harmon, Carole and Bart Robinson. *Byron Harmon, Mountain Photographer.* Banff: Altitude Publishing, 1992.

Harvest of the Spirit: Illingworth Kerr Retrospective. Edmonton: Edmonton Art Gallery, 1985.

Ironside, Jetske. *Spaces and Places: Eight Decades of Landscape Painting in Alberta.* Edmonton: Alberta Art Foundation, 1986.

Jackson, Christopher. *Historical Watercolours from the Glenbow Collection.* Calgary: Glenbow, 1985.

Jackson, Christopher. *Lawren Harris.* Calgary: Glenbow, 1991.

Jackson, Christopher. *With Lens and Brush, Images of the Western Canadian Landscape 1845–1890.* Calgary: Glenbow, 1989.

Jameson, Sheila. *W. L. Oliver, Life Through a Master's Lens.* Calgary: Glenbow, 1984.

John Arthur Fraser (1838–1898), Watercolours, Montreal: Concordia Art Gallery, 1984.

Kane, Paul. *Wanderings of an Artist Among the Indians of North America.* London: Longman, Brown, Green, Longmans, and Roberts, 1859.

Keyser, James and Michael Klassen. *Plains Indian Rock Art.* Seattle: University of Washington Press, 2001.

Leclerc, Denise. *The Crisis of Abstraction in Canada: The 1950s.* Ottawa, National Gallery of Canada, 1992.

Leighton, David. *Artists, Builders and Dreamers: 50 Years at the Banff School.* Toronto: McClelland and Stewart Limited, 1982.

MacDonald, Colin. *A Dictionary of Canadian Artists.* Ottawa: Canadian Paperbacks, 1967.

McKaskell, Robert, Sandra Paikowsky, Virginia Wright, and Allan Collier. *Achieving the Modern: Canadian Abstract Painting and Design in the 1950s.* Winnipeg: Winnipeg Art Gallery, 1993.

Mastin, Catharine, Robert Stacey, Marcia Crosby, Anna Hudson, Liz Wylie, and Ann Davis. *The Group of Seven in Western Canada.* Toronto: Key Porter, 2002.

Medland, Wendy. "Harry Pollard, photographer." *Alberta History* 29:2 (Spring 1981): 20–28.

Novak, Barbara. *Nature and Culture: American Landscape Painting 1825–1875.* New York: Oxford University Press, 1980.

O'Brian, John. *The Flat Side of the Landscape: The Emma Lake Artists' Workshops.* Saskatoon: Mendel Art Gallery, 1989.

Oko, Andrew J. *The Frontier Art of R. B. Nevitt.* Calgary: Glenbow, 1974.

Oliver Buell (1844–1910), Photographer. Montreal: Concordia Art Gallery, 1984.

Parke-Taylor, Michael and Geoffrey Simmins. *Edmund Morris "Kyaiyii", 1871–1913.* Regina; Norman Mackenzie Art Gallery, 1984.

Perry, Isabel. *Euphemia McNaught: Pioneer Artist of the Peace.* Beaverlodge, Edmonton: Reidmore Books, 1982.

Reid, Dennis. *Alberta Rhythm: The Later Work of A. Y. Jackson.* Toronto: Art Gallery of Ontario, 1982.

Reid, Dennis. *A Concise History of Canadian Painting.* Toronto: Oxford University Press, 1973.

Reid, Dennis. *Our Own Country Canada.* Ottawa: National Gallery of Canada, 1979.

Render, Lorne. *The Mountains and the Sky.* Calgary: Glenbow, 1974.

Ring, Dan, Guy Vanderhaeghe, and George Melnyk. *The Urban Prairie.* Saskatoon: Mendel Art Gallery and Fifth House Limited, 1993.

Ring House Gallery. *Norman Yates: Toward Landscape.* Edmonton: University of Alberta, 1983.

Silversides, Brock. *Waiting for the Light: Early Mountain Photography in British Columbia and Alberta, 1865–1939*. Saskatoon: Fifth House, 1995.
Stacey, Robert. *Western Sunlight: C. W. Jefferys on the Canadian Prairies.* Saskatoon: Mendel Art Gallery, 1986.
Stenzel, Franz. *James Madison Alden.* Fort Worth: Amon Carter Museum, 1975.
Studio Ceramics in Alberta 1947–1952. Edmonton: Alberta Art Foundation, 1981.
Studio Ceramics in Alberta II 1953–1963. Edmonton: Alberta Art Foundation, 1982.
Thom, Ian. *Maxwell Bates.* Victoria: Art Gallery of Greater Victoria, 1982.
Townshend, Nancy. *Maxwell Bates: Landscapes 1948–1978.* Medicine Hat: Medicine Hat Museum and Art Gallery, 1982.
Triggs, Stanley. *William Notman, The Stamp of a Studio.* Toronto: Art Gallery of Ontario and The Coach House Press, 1985.
University of Alberta, Department of Art. *Staff Exhibition*. Edmonton: Edmonton Art Gallery, 1985.
White, Donny. *In Search of Geraldine Moodie*. Regina: Canadian Plains Research Centre, University of Regina, 1998.
Zemans, Joyce. *Jock Macdonald: The Inner Landscape.* Toronto: The Art Gallery of Ontario, 1981.
Zimon, Kathy. *Founders of the Alberta College of Art*. Calgary: Alberta College of Art Gallery, 1986.

A New Era for Alberta Art: 1970–2000

Atkins, Robert. *ArtSpeak: A Guide to Modern Ideas, Movements and Buzzwords*. New York: Abbeville Press, 1993.
Bingham, Russell, Lelde Muehlenbachs, and Roger Boulet. *Colour & Dimension: The Recent Paintings of Graham Peacock*. Edmonton: Graham Peacock, 1992.
Bond, Eleanor. *Gang of Three: New Sculpture from Calgary*. Winnipeg: Ace Art and Plug/In Inc., 1987.
Boulet, Roger. *Graham Peacock: Paint, Process and Spirit.* Edmonton: Edmonton Art Gallery, 1988.
Brehm, Margit and Wolf Schoppmann. *Marianna Gartner*. Essen, Germany: 20.21 Galerie, 2004.
Collinson, Helen, George Melnyk, Wilfred Watson, and Elizabeth Beauchamp. *Norman Yates: Toward Landscape.* Edmonton: Ring House Gallery, University of Alberta, 1983.
Dawn, Leslie. *Gordon Ferguson: Sense Your Place.* Lethbridge: Southern Alberta Art Gallery, 1988.
Fenton, Terry. *Robert Scott's Paintings*. New York: Gallery Moos, 1987.
Garneau, David. *Lyndal Osborne: The Poetic Structure of the World.* Lethbridge: Southern Alberta Art Gallery, 1999.
Garneau, David, Carroll Moppett. *Carroll Moppett.* Calgary: Illingworth Kerr Gallery, Alberta College of Art and Design, 1992.
Grenville, Bruce. *Mary Scott.* Lethbridge: Southern Alberta Art Gallery, 1989.
Haeseker, Alexandra, John Hall, Henry Lehmann, and Lynn Smith. *Alexandra Haeseker: Twenty Years.* Calgary: Illingworth Kerr Gallery, Alberta College of Art, 1992.
Hanna, Martha. *Orest Semchishen: In Plain View/Voir Clair*. Ottawa: Canadian Museum of Contemporary Photography, 1994.
Heath, Terrence. *Western Untitled.* Calgary: Glenbow-Alberta Institute, 1976.
Kidd, Elizabeth. *Recent Work by Robert Scott: 1987–1993.* Edmonton: Edmonton Art Gallery, 1994.
Kidd, Elizabeth. "Three dimensions: Betty Goodwin, Walter May, Catherine Burgess," *Outlook*. Edmonton: Edmonton Art Gallery, Summer 1990.
Laviolette, Mary-Beth. *An Alberta Art Chronicle: Adventures in Recent and Contemporary Art.* Canmore, Alberta: Altitude Publishing, 2005.
Laviolette, Mary-Beth and Christine E. Sammon. *75 years of Art: Alberta College of Art and Design*. Calgary: Alberta College of Art and Design, 2001.
Leighton, David and Peggy Leighton. *Artists, Builders and Dreamers: 50 Years at the Banff School.* Toronto: McClelland and Stewart, 1982.
Lippard, Lucy. "Sweeping exchanges: the contribution of feminism to the art of the seventies," *Art Journal*. New York: College Art Association, Vol. 4, No. 1–2, 1980.
Long, Timothy. *Simone*. Regina: MacKenzie Art Gallery, 1996.
Matuz, Roger, editor and Kathryn O'Handley, project coordinator. *Contemporary Canadian Artists.* Toronto: Gale Canada.
Nasgaard, Roald and Jeffrey Spalding. *Concealing/Revealing: Voices from the Canadian Foothills.* Tallahassee, FL: Museum of Fine Arts, Florida State University, 1997.
Palmer, Howard and Tamara Palmer. *Alberta: A New History.* Edmonton: Hurtig Publishers, 1990.
Pizanias, Caterina. "Of earth and steel: taming the prairie in Canada," *Canadian Issues*. Montreal: Association for Canadian Studies, Volume XI, 1989.
Pizanias, Caterina. *Three Alberta Sculptors: Ken Macklin, Isla Burns, Clay Ellis.* Edmonton: Edmonton Art Gallery, 1993.
Varga, Vincent. *Aspects of Contemporary Painting in Alberta*. Calgary: Glenbow Museum, 1987.
Wilken, Karen. *Douglas Haynes: The Toledo Series*. Edmonton: Edmonton Art Gallery, 1991.
Ylitalo, Katherine. *Leila Sujir: Luminous Stories.* Peterborough, Ontario: The Art Gallery of Peterborough, 1999.
Ylitalo, Katherine and Nancy Townshend. *Katie Ohe*. Calgary: Illingworth Kerr Gallery, Alberta College of Art and Design, 1991.

ACKNOWLEDGEMENTS

From Patricia:

I was delighted that Mary-Beth Laviolette was enthusiastic about this project and willing to join me in this endeavour. Mary-Beth has been a thoughtful collaborator, and I have valued her insights and appreciated her skilful writing and broad perspective on the art of this region.

I would like to extend my sincere thanks to all of the individuals across Alberta who provided advice and assistance in my research, facilitated access to collections, located and sent me information, and were very supportive of the project. I wish to thank: in Banff, Lisa Christensen, Joanne Gunnenberg, and Don Bourden; in Edmonton, Pam Clark, Jim Corrigan, Christopher Taylor, and Kirk Marlow; in Lethbridge, Josephine Mills, Victoria Baster, Adrian Cooke, Lucy Linhart, Kathy Lea, and Darren Gilbertson; in Medicine Hat, Joanne Marion; in Red Deer, Diana Anderson; and in Peace River, John Kerl and Marie Leduc. Others who assisted include Sue Harris from the Stark Museum in Orange, Texas, Michael Klassen, Robert McKaskell, and Vera Gartley.

I would like to pay special tribute to Betty Rothwell and Gail Lint at the Alberta Foundation for the Arts. They gave both Mary-Beth and me full and prompt access to all of their information, facilitated my research when I was in Edmonton, and provided publication-quality slides free of charge. Almost half of the images in this book come from them. I would also like to thank the foundation for its generous financial contribution to this publication.

I am pleased that I was able to use art from the Glenbow Museum collection, some of which I acquired for the collection during my years as curator of art. I sincerely thank many people at the Glenbow for their support of this project, including Michael Robinson, Quyen Hoang, Barbara Greendale, and Jackie Eliasson. I would especially like to thank Ron Marsh for advising me on the photography for the book and for repeatedly checking the quality of images that were selected. Dr. Gerald Conaty provided knowledgeable comments on the First Nations imagery.

Thank you to the artists I interviewed for this book. I thank you for your candour and the insights you provided on your work, and for providing photographs. Artists include Ted Godwin, Harry Kiyooka, Roy Leadbeater, George Mihalcheon, Katie Ohe, Ed Spiteri, Kenneth Sturdy, George Wood, and Norman Yates. Special thanks go to Jean Mihalcheon and Bonnie Murdoch who advised me on the ceramics. I also thank all of the copyright holders who have given permission to reproduce works in this book.

Finally, both Mary-Beth and I are indebted to Charlene Dobmeier at Fifth House for her support and enthusiasm for this project. We thank her for seeing this through. We also thank Meaghan Craven for her intelligent and sensitive management of the editorial process.

From Mary-Beth:

I wish to acknowledge the amount of time and effort Patricia spent in the writing and submitting of proposals to publishers and in scrutinizing the writers' contract. I am also indebted to Patricia's curatorial work for the Glenbow Museum's New Alberta Art series. The collaborative effort involved in putting this book together was truly a fortuitous meeting of the minds!

I would like to shine a spotlight on the time and effort spent by Bart Habermiller who assisted with the reproductions of the artworks featured in the book. Other hearty thanks must also be given to the artists featured in this book who contributed their artwork free of copyright charge. The last section in the book covering contemporary art could not have been done without their generosity. In addition, thanks must be given to the following individuals who recently or in years past provided information and/or contributed their own observations about recent and contemporary art in Alberta. They include: in Medicine Hat, James Marshall, Allan Jenson, Les Manning, and Gail Carney; in Edmonton, Gail Lint and Peter Hide, Blair Brennan, Allen Ball, Cherie Moses, Alf Bogusky, Les Graff, Elizabeth Kidd, Isla Burns, Russell Bingham, Tin Ng, Ross Bradley, Tom McFall, (the late) Helen Collinson, and Mark Joslin; in Calgary, Ron Moppett, Eric Cameron, Sandra Vida, Peter Duthie, and John Hall; in Lethbridge, Jeffrey Spalding, Adrian Cooke, Joan Stebbins, and Victoria Baster; in Grande Prairie, Elizabeth Ginn, Peter von Tiesenhausen, and Bob Guest; in Red Deer, David More, and Yvette Brideau; and in Toronto, Evan Penny, Bill Kirby, and (the late) Douglas Clark.

Patricia Ainslie, Kelowna, BC
Mary-Beth Laviolette, Canmore, AB
January 2007

INDEX

ABOUT THE AUTHORS

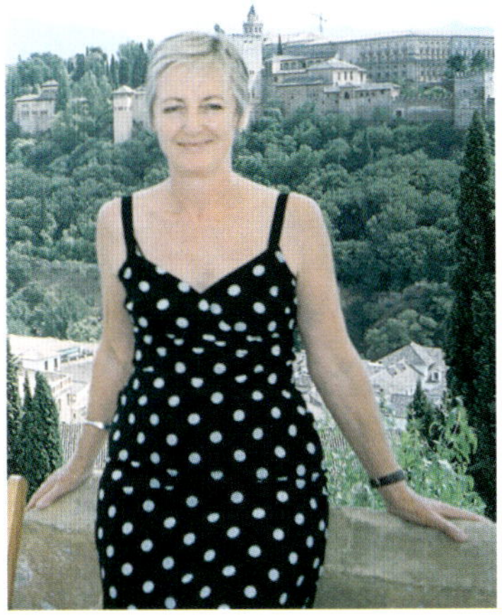

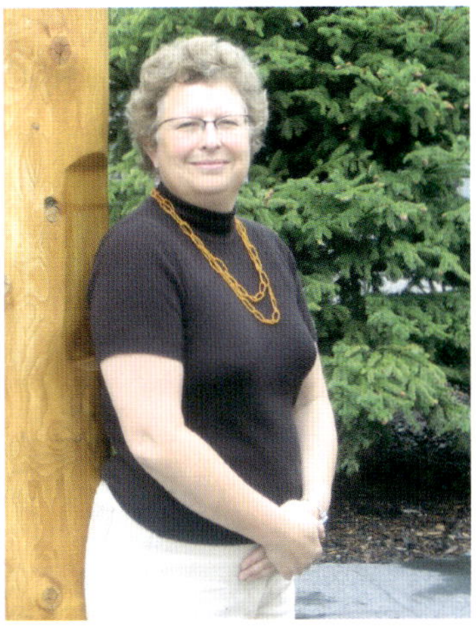

Patricia Ainslie

Patricia was born in England and raised in South Africa. In 1969, she moved to Rhodesia (Zimbabwe) to work at the Rhodes National Gallery with Frank McEwen, organizing and promoting the renowned Workshop School, where artists produced monumental stone sculpture, featured in exhibits at the Rodin Museum, Paris; Commonwealth Institute, London; and MOMA, New York. After her sons Angus and Gareth were born in the early 1970s, she worked as a textile designer in Salisbury, Rhodesia, and Johannesburg, South Africa. She lived in Iran and Mauritius before settling in Calgary, Alberta, in 1977. Eager to work in the arts again, she joined the Glenbow Museum in Calgary in 1979. For more than a decade, working as a curator, she produced art exhibits, built the art collection at the Glenbow, and made regular studio visits to artists.

Her work as a curator includes the groundbreaking exhibit and publication *Images of the Land: Canadian Block Prints, 1919–1945*, which toured Canada, England, and Europe. More in-depth print projects in the 1980s featured artists Margaret Shelton, Laurence Hyde, and Cecil Buller. For her important work in printmaking, she was elected to the Print Council of America in 1990. In 1987, she organized the retrospective exhibition, publication, and tour for *A Lifelong Journey: The Art and Teaching of H. G. Glyde*; in 1991, *Jack Shadbolt: Correspondences*; and in 1998, *Frontiers, Frontières, Fronteras: René Derouin*. As vice-president of collections at the Glenbow from 1993 to 2006, when she retired, Patricia worked on innovative museological projects, including deaccessioning and grading of collections, and repatriation. She has published articles in scholarly journals and presented lectures on these topics in North America, England, and Europe.

Patricia loves the Canadian outdoors, and she canoes, kayaks, skis, walks, and cycles. She is also an avid gardener. She loves music and dance and is a keen dancer herself of mainly Latin dance, including the Argentine tango. She has travelled widely in North America, Mexico, Britain, Europe, and Africa.

Mary-Beth Laviolette

Mary-Beth Laviolette was born in 1955 and raised in Edmonton. She remembers always being interested in the past, including the history of the Earth and earlier forms of life. At one point, she even considered a career in geology and palaeontology.

In 1973, Mary-Beth transferred from University of Alberta to Ottawa's Carleton University, where she enrolled in the bachelor of journalism program with a major in Canadian history. She volunteered at Radio Carleton (CKCU) and there met another student, Nancy Bourgoyne, who worked part-time at the National Gallery of Canada. Through Nancy another door into the world of art was opened, this time Canadian art. From then on, Mary-Beth was hooked and as a way of familiarizing herself with this spectacularly diverse world, she took art history courses in European, Canadian, and modern art in Ottawa and later in Toronto.

After completing her bachelor of journalism, Mary-Beth was fortunate to land a job with a national weekday CBC Radio program on the stereo network called *Arts National*. Because of her knowledge of the visual arts, Mary-Beth eventually specialized in this area for the program and covering artists and art exhibitions across the country.

In 1982, after spending nearly ten fruitful years in Ontario, Mary-Beth returned to Alberta after *Arts National* was downsized. Based on her knowledge of what was going on in the country and especially in Toronto, where she last resided, she sensed that Alberta, in a national context, was overlooked and under-rated. Since then, Mary-Beth has enjoyed herself immensely, covering the visual arts in Alberta and in particular Calgary. While in Calgary for nearly twenty years, she wrote reviews, articles, and essays for various local and regional periodicals and gallery publications, including four years regularly with the *Calgary Herald*, worked part-time for CBC Radio in Calgary as the researcher and programmer of *Sunday Arts* for a decade. With Paula Gustafson and David Garneau, Mary-Beth also co-founded and co-edited *Artichoke: Writings about the Visual Arts* (1989–2005).

In 1999, Mary-Beth relocated to Canmore with her husband Douglas and son Duncan, where she completed the research and writing of *An Alberta Art Chronicle: Adventures in Recent and Contemporary Art* (Altitude Publishing, 2005). This book—which is accompanied with visuals on a CD—takes an in-depth look at the arts scene in Alberta from 1970 to 2000. She continues to research and write and look for other opportunities to create, record, and make Albertans and others aware of this art-rich province.